Alma Mater

Helen Lefkowitz Horowitz

ALMA
MATER

*Design and Experience
in the Women's Colleges
from Their Nineteenth-
Century Beginnings
to the 1930s*

SECOND EDITION

University of Massachusetts Press

AMHERST

Copyright © 1984 by The Sarah Esther Horowitz and
Benjamin Horowitz Ten Year Trust
Second edition copyright © 1993 by Helen Lefkowitz Horowitz

First published by Alfred A. Knopf, 1985
University of Massachusetts Press paperback edition, 1993
All rights reserved
Printed in the United States of America

Library of Congress Cataloging-in-Publication Data
Horowitz, Helen Lefkowitz.
Alma mater : design and experience in the women's colleges from
their nineteenth-century beginnings to the 1930s / Helen Lefkowitz
Horowitz. — 2nd ed.
p.   cm.
Includes bibliographical references and index.
ISBN 0-87023-869-8
1. Women's colleges—United States—History.   I. Title.
LC1756.H67   1993
376'.8'0973—dc20   93-4393
CIP
British Library Cataloguing in Publication data are available.

Contents

Introduction to the Second Edition   xv

Preface   xxi

Acknowledgments   xxvii

PART ONE   *Foundings*   1

1   *Plain, Though Very Neat*   MOUNT HOLYOKE   9

2   *More Lasting Than the Pyramids*   VASSAR   28

3   *That Beauty Which Is Truth*   WELLESLEY   42

4   *Acting a* Manly *Part*   THE BEGINNINGS OF COLLEGE LIFE   56

5   *To Preserve Her Womanliness*   SMITH   69

6   *The Advantages of the So-called "Cottage System"*   82
WELLESLEY, VASSAR

7   *As Unnoticed as the Daughters of Any Cambridge Residents*   95
RADCLIFFE

8   *A Certain Style of "Quaker Lady" Dress*   BRYN MAWR   105

9   *Behold They Are Women!*   BRYN MAWR   117

10 *The Stately Columned Way*   BARNARD   134

PART TWO   *Experience*   143

11 *The Life*   STUDENT LIFE   147

12 *Households of Women*   FACULTY LIFE   179

PART THREE   *The Classic Design*   199

13 *The Necessities Peculiar to Women of Today*   203
    WELLESLEY, SMITH, VASSAR

14 *A Larger School Room*   MOUNT HOLYOKE   223

15 *The Day of Small Things Is Over*   RADCLIFFE, BARNARD   237

16 *A Great Design*   WELLESLEY   262

PART FOUR   *The Post-war Women's College*   275

17 *In Obedience to a Social Convention*   279
    COLLEGE LIFE AFTER 1920

18 *In the Spirit of Our Times*   VASSAR, MOUNT HOLYOKE   295

19 *The Training Which a College Can Give in Character and*   307
    in the Art of Living   1920S DORMITORIES

20 *Without Reference to the Analogy of Colleges for Men*   319
    SARAH LAWRENCE, BENNINGTON, SCRIPPS

    Epilogue   351

    Notes   357

    Index   399

Illustrations

PAGE

20 The seminary in 1838; engraving by John W. Barber; *Mount Holyoke College Library/Archives*

23 A corner of the dining room in the Seminary Building (ca. 1892); *Mount Holyoke College Library/Archives*

23 Domestic work in the Seminary Building dining hall (ca. 1893); *Mount Holyoke College Library/Archives*

26 Bird's-eye view, between 1889 and 1896; *Mount Holyoke College Library/Archives*

34 Vassar College, ca. 1865; *Vassar College Library*

36 Calisthenium; *Vassar College Library*

45 Library, Mount Holyoke Seminary; *Mount Holyoke College Library/Archives*

47 College Hall; *Wellesley College Archives*

47 1894 class crew, College Hall in background; *Wellesley College Archives*

49 Plan of first story, College Hall; *Wellesley College Archives*

50 The Centre, College Hall; *Wellesley College Archives*

52 Browning Room, College Hall; *Wellesley College Archives*

61 Maria Mitchell with students on the stairs of the Observatory parlor; *Vassar College Library*

65 Vassar students in their room, ca. 1890; *Vassar College Library*

67 Trig ceremony; Vassar; *Vassar College Library*

76 College Hall; *Smith College Archives, Smith College, Northampton Massachusetts 01063*

79 The cottages of Smith, taken from College Hall; *Smith College Archives*

79 Hatfield House, 1888; Mary Augusta Jordan at far right; *Smith College Archives*

86 Junior Tree Day, 1887, with honorary class member Lyman Abbott and his wife; Alice Freeman and Eben Horsford in window; *Wellesley College Archives*

87   Freshman Tree Day, 1885, class of 1888; Lyman Abbott, second row, fourth from left; Sophonisba Breckinridge, second row, fifth from left; *Wellesley College Archives*

88   Eliot House group, ca. 1895; *Wellesley College Archives*

89   Norumbega, ca. 1891; n.b. threesome in window; *Wellesley College Archives*

99   Circular, 1879; *Radcliffe College Archives*

101 Carret House, Appian Way (first building used by the Annex); *Radcliffe College Archives*

101 Tutorial session; *Radcliffe College Archives*

103 Fay House (before reconstruction); *Radcliffe College Archives*

103 Fay House library; *Radcliffe College Archives*

108–09 The early Bryn Mawr campus: from left to right, Merion Hall, Taylor Hall, the Deanery; *Bryn Mawr College*

120 The economics and history library in Taylor Library; n.b. students in academic dress; *Bryn Mawr College*

123 May Day, 1900: Maypole dancing; Taylor Hall in background; *Bryn Mawr College*

123 May Day, 1900: The St. George Play; *Bryn Mawr College*

124 Denbigh Hall; *Bryn Mawr College*

125 Pembroke Arch with Taylor Hall on left; n.b. 1901 banner on Pembroke; *Bryn Mawr College*

126 Rockefeller Hall dining room, 1910; *Bryn Mawr College*

128 Reading room, Thomas Library; *Bryn Mawr College*

129 Cloister archway, Thomas Library; *Bryn Mawr College*

131 M. Carey Thomas greeting students from the porch of the Deanery; Mary Garrett under the umbrella; *Bryn Mawr College*

132 The Deanery's Dorothy Vernon Room; *Bryn Mawr College*

133 The Deanery Garden; *Bryn Mawr College*

138–39 Barnard in 1906, Grant's tomb on left; n.b. rubble in foreground; *Barnard College Archives*

140 Entrance Hall, Milbank; *Barnard College Archives*

140 Aerial view of Barnard, with Columbia in muted background, upper half; *Barnard College Archives*

149 Page from a student's scrapbook, Bryn Mawr; *Bryn Mawr College*

151 A senior birthday, Vassar, 1896; *Vassar College Library*

154 Haven House dining room, Smith, 1904; *Smith College Archives*

157 Office of Monthly and Weekly, Students' Building, Smith, 1915; *Smith College Archives*

158 1906 Bryn Mawr Class President, Mary Richardson; snapshot from student album; *Bryn Mawr College*

158 Student government, Barnard, 1916; *Barnard College Archives*

160–161 Basketball game in Alumnae Gymnasium, Smith, 1904; *Smith College Archives*

160 Bryn Mawr playing fields; Constance Applebee on left; *Bryn Mawr College*

161 Athletic spectators, Vassar; *Vassar College Library*

163 Dance Program of a Smith student, sophomore reception, October 15, 1902; *Smith College Archives*

164 House of Commons, Wellesley, 1888; upper floor, Centre College Hall; Professor Katharine Coman in white wig; *Wellesley College Archives*

165 Dramatic production, the Idler, Radcliffe's dramatic club, ca. 1896; *Radcliffe College Archives*

165 Vassar dramatic production, before 1900; n.b. hidden skirts on "male" characters; *Vassar College Library*

168 Suffrage parade; *Radcliffe College Archives*

168 Election night, Mount Holyoke, ca. 1908; *Mount Holyoke College Library/Archives*

170 Fanny Sinclair's room with floral tributes, Bryn Mawr, 1901; *Bryn Mawr College*

171 Porch of Students' Building, Smith, dressed for a prom; *Smith College Archives*

173 Commencement, Mount Holyoke, 1916; *Mount Holyoke College Library/Archives*

173 Ivy exercises, Mount Holyoke, 1902; Frances Perkins leading on left; *Mount Holyoke College Library/Archives*

174–75 Ivy Day, Smith, 1902; *Smith College Archives*

176 Shakespeare Society's *Midsummer Night's Dream*, Wellesley, 1893; Florence Converse on left; *Wellesley College Archives*

176 Vassar Daisy Chain, led by the Wood twins, 1903; *Vassar College Library*

176–77 Tree Day, Wellesley, 1896; *Wellesley College Archives*

177 May Day, Wellesley, 1909; College Hall wing in background; *Wellesley College Archives*

183 Katharine Coman's table, Wellesley, 1887, in front of College Hall; Professor Coman seated to the left of column; *Wellesley College Archives*

186 Low Buildings, Bryn Mawr; *Bryn Mawr College*

189 Dewey House room, Smith, occupied by Vida Scudder and Helen Chadwick, 1880s; *Smith College Archives*

192 Lucy Salmon's study in the Main building, Vassar; third floor, southwest corner; *Vassar College Library*

192 Lucy Salmon's kitchen, Poughkeepsie; *Vassar College Library*

195 Smith teacher Mary Augusta Jordan and five students pause on walking trip to pose in a photographer's studio, ca. 1890; *Smith College Archives*

195 Mary Augusta Jordan in class, Smith, 1915; *Smith College Archives*

204 Alice Freeman Palmer Memorial; *Wellesley College Archives*

207   Houghton Memorial Chapel; *Wellesley College Archives*

211   Wellesley College, aerial view, 1931; the Hazard Quadrangle in the foreground; *Wellesley College Archives*

215   Waiting for admission to basketball game, Smith, 1904; Seelye Hall in far right; *Smith College Archives*

215   Basketball, 1904; Senda Berenson holding ball; *Smith College Archives*

220   Chapel; *Vassar College Library*

220   Taylor Hall dedication; from left to right, Charles Collens, Charles Pratt, H. N. MacCracken, James Taylor; *Vassar College Library*

229   Mary Lyon Hall; *Mount Holyoke College Library/Archives*

230   Brigham Hall; *Mount Holyoke College Library/Archives*

235   Library interior before 1936 renovation; *Mount Holyoke College Library/Archives*

235   Bird's-eye view, 1907; *Mount Holyoke College Library/Archives*

241   Students in study room, Agassiz House; *Radcliffe College Archives*

243   Living room, Agassiz House; *Radcliffe College Archives*

243   Radcliffe student, ca. 1900; *Radcliffe College Archives*

246   Bertram Hall; *Radcliffe College Archives*

249   Undergraduate study, Milbank; *Barnard College Archives*

250   Brooks Hall; *Barnard College Archives*

253   Greek Games, 1920, Barnard College; the first with bobbed hair "horses"; *Barnard College Archives*

254   Tennis courts, the Jungle, and Barnard Hall; *Barnard College Archives*

257   Barnard students in front of Milbank; Virginia Gildersleeve on bottom; *Barnard College Archives*

257   Alpha Phi, ca. 1912; *Barnard College Archives*

270–71   Wellesley College, aerial view, between 1936 and 1958; *Wellesley College Archives*

283   Two Bennington students in open automobile, 1932–33; *Bennington College*

285   Students awaiting transportation, Bennington, 1932–33; *Bennington College*

286   Mount Holyoke Hoover Club, 1928; *Mount Holyoke College Library/Archives*

290–91   1905 Junior Prom in Students' Building, Smith; *Smith College Archives*

299   Blodgett Hall of Euthenics; *Vassar College Library*

301   Cushing Hall; *Vassar College Library*

305   Torrey Hall, originally Lakeside; *Mount Holyoke College Library/Archives*

305   Amphitheater/Eliot; *Mount Holyoke College Library/Archives*

311   Paradise Pond; *Smith College Archives*

312–13   Aerial view, the Quadrangles; inset, a view into the Quadrangles—Wilder House from Comstock; *Smith College Archives*

317 Severance Hall; *Wellesley College Archives*

323 Dudley Lawrence, a Sarah Lawrence dormitory; *Archives of Sarah Lawrence College*

323 Westlands; *Archives of Sarah Lawrence College*

326 Maxwell Geismer, a Sarah Lawrence "don," with student; *Archives of Sarah Lawrence College*

326 Art class, ca. 1934; *Archives of Sarah Lawrence College*

327 Paul Garrett, a member of the Mathematics and Physics faculty, with dance students; *Archives of Sarah Lawrence College*

327 Student Council, Sarah Lawrence, ca. 1936; *Archives of Sarah Lawrence College*

333 Bennington dormitory: Kilpatrick; *Bennington College*

333 The Commons and a row of dormitories; *Bennington College*

335 Two students in front of dormitories, 1932–33; *Bennington College*

335 Faculty-student group, 1932–33; *Bennington College*

335 Professor Kurt Schindler and student; college buildings in background; *Bennington College*

336–37 Aerial view, 1933; *Bennington College*

340 Organization meeting of board of trustees, June 18, 1926; William Bennett Munro on left; Ethel Richardson Allen second from right; *Scripps College Archives*

342 First faculty-student dinner, fall 1928; President Ernest Jaqua seated at far left; standing at right, Professor Hartley Burr Alexander; *Scripps College Archives*

344 Toll Hall; *Scripps College Archives*

344 Scripps campus, mid-1930s; *Scripps College Archives*

345 Two seniors from the first graduating class, at Commencement party, 1931; *Scripps College Archives*

345 Dinner party, Star Court, Toll Hall, 1931; *Scripps College Archives*

346 Gordon Kaufmann's plan, ca. 1926; *Scripps College Archives*

347 Mt. Baldy between Toll and Browning halls, ca. 1930; *Scripps College Archives*

349 Freshmen in the first class, fall 1927, on balcony of Toll Hall; *Scripps College Archives*

352 Smith class of 1882 in 1917; official Smith photographer Katherine McClellan at far right; *Smith College Archives*

Introduction to the Second Edition

How do we read books? Do authors fill readers with texts, etching impressions on their blank minds? Or, as reader-response theorists have suggested, do readers shape texts, imbuing them with meanings to suit their concerns? I have come to see reading as dynamic. Readers bring questions and ideas. Texts pose challenges and riddles. I like to imagine readers and writers as engaged in a conversation in which both can be changed.

My own experience with *Alma Mater* can best be understood in this light. I wrote it at a moment in my life when I was engaged by certain questions. How do buildings and landscapes reflect the culture that creates them? What kind of impact do they have on those who live within and outside them? How does change happen and what are its visible signs? How have the ways that men have thought about women and women about themselves been expressed in buildings? In what ways did the higher education of women seem to threaten patriarchal culture? How have buildings been designed to protect young women from risks, and how have they exposed them to new ones? What has been the dynamic of college life as lived in women's colleges? How have relationships and ritual reshaped the land and its meanings? What happened when new definitions of women and their sexuality entered the college scene?

After writing the book, I began to imagine three different ideal readers. The first and most elusive was the practitioner. I wanted to encourage architects to think more fully about the social and cultural contexts of buildings. I joined a chorus of voices determined to remind designers that structures arise from decisions made by women and men who think and work in a culture that shapes their choices and architectural language. I hoped to prod the study of places and spaces to consider issues of power, gender, and intention.

The second reader was the lover of history. By exploring the design of women's colleges I wanted my colleagues and students in history, especially in women's history, to think about buildings and landscapes as historical texts. I hoped to nudge them to break through their reticence to discuss buildings by demonstrating that it does not require a special license or any sprinkling of magic dust. Learning to do architectural history requires only reading, listening, and a lot of looking.

The third reader was an alumna of a women's college or someone with an interest in higher education. It turned out that this reader forced me to think about the implications of the book and to face a whole new set of questions. As a historian I wrote about the past. Many of these readers took up *Alma Mater* to learn about the present. As I began to travel and speak about the book to alumnae groups and to students and teachers interested in higher education, those in my audience asked questions that at first threw me: Should women's colleges exist? What is or ought to be the role that women's colleges play in today's world? Should my daughter go to Mount Holyoke? Should I?

I was stumped, but from the outset I knew that these questions were thoroughly appropriate. *Alma Mater* makes the implicit argument that education is more than books and courses. In addition to the curriculum, higher education is the interaction of a person with a place and a tradition, with other students in the complex societies that undergraduates make, with professors under the codes—official and actual—that govern faculty and student contact.

Are there reasons why women should choose to go to a college that limits its students, though not its faculty or administrators, to women? If one turns to history, a case can be made. Studies have shown that success as Americans have defined it, the kind of success that has led to inclusion in *Who's Who in America* or *Who's Who of American Women*, has been two times more likely for graduates of women's colleges than for those of coeducational institutions, private or public.[1] To argue from history is one thing. To think about the present is another. Until recently only 3 per cent of female high school seniors have been willing to consider a women's college. One might ask, why have even so many? All but a few previously all-male private colleges are now coeducational, as are almost all state institutions. As a result of women's liberation, women receive at least rhetorical attention in catalogs and are included in college look books. Girls anticipating college have wanted to believe that they could "have it all." Careers

[1]The most important studies are the many articles by M. Elizabeth Tidball, beginning with "Perspective on Academic Women and Affirmative Action," *Educational Record* 54 (1973): 120–35. Mary J. Oates and Susan Williamson argued that it is both the selectivity of the college and the higher class origins of students that are the significant variables ("Women's Colleges and Women Achievers," *Signs* 3 [1978]: 795–806). Tidball refined her research, eliminating the selectivity factor; however, research on social class and students has not been forthcoming that would substantiate or challenge the class argument ("Women's Colleges and Women Achievers Revisited," *Signs* 5 [1980]: 504–17).

were awaiting them, and they had to work hard, but in the meantime college was the place to have fun, to learn the ways of the world and certainly the ways of sex. A women's college? When they could go to Dartmouth or the University of Michigan? You're kidding.

But as I write in 1993, the ground is shifting. At Smith College, applications are up markedly for the second year in a row. And this year Wellesley College is seeing a significant rise in applications, as is Mount Holyoke College. Something is beginning to percolate out there in the high schools. The press is calling it the "Hillary factor." The highly visible professional first lady Hillary Rodham Clinton is a proud graduate of Wellesley. In the front rank of the Clinton administration is Laura D'Andrea Tyson, a Smith alumna, and Madeleine Korbel Albright, Wellesley '59. As they imagine their futures, girls in high school have new models for achievement. They read profiles in news accounts that point to certain women's colleges as instrumental to success.

This rise in applications has not happened in a vacuum. On February 22, 1992, the *New York Times* reported on its front page that researchers at the Wellesley College Center for Research on Women, after a thorough examination of publications and studies about girls and education, primary and secondary, found that American schools discriminate against girls. Female students get less attention from teachers, are dissuaded from careers in mathematics and science, are ignored or stereotyped in textbooks, and face sexual harassment by male schoolmates.

A well-publicized recent study by Lyn Mikel Brown and Carol Gilligan has pointed to threats to girls' integrity as they move into adolescence. The culture requires them, as they negotiate the transit to womanhood, to dissociate from their best selves, to disconnect from the experience and confidence of their childhood. It is "a kind of psychological foot-binding" that girls undergo to keep them from feeling and from using their strengths. What they need at this critical moment is women to listen, respond, and encourage them to resist the effort to silence their authentic voices.[2]

Neither study is about college. Both look at the girl anticipating college. But both dramatically focus attention on the female experience and demonstrate that girls normally do not get their fair share in education. As girls begin to think about their college futures, the women's college takes on a different meaning. Perhaps there is something to be said for a place in which women are the focus of all attention. There might be advantages in a school in which they compose the class, they come to office hours, they run on the track, they hold college offices. What might it mean not to be distracted by the male gaze in class, the library, or the laboratory and not to confront the prejudices of teachers

---

[2]Lyn Mikel Brown and Carol Gilligan, *Meeting at the Crossroads: Women's Psychology and Girls' Development* (Cambridge, Mass.: Harvard University Press, 1992), quote from p. 218.

and staff who see them as less capable, less interesting, less beneficial to know than their male peers? Could there be intangible benefits to living and working in buildings and landscapes designed with women in mind? Do women's college graduates gain inspiration, even an edge, from college traditions that arise from women's culture?

My own experience has been intimately connected with three of the colleges about which I write: Wellesley, my alma mater; Scripps, where I taught over a period of thirteen years; and Smith, where I am currently on the faculty. I teach and advise college students every day. I know that real life for undergraduates, male and female, is complicated. Students who go to college have overwhelming tasks laid upon them. They must not only read and study steadily, they must also attempt to break through to creativity. They must learn to live with others away from their families under new and bewildering codes, no longer simplified by rules. They must imagine a future career and begin to take steps toward it. They must keep, lose, make, or not make a sustaining relationship with another. All of this takes place within eight terms of unremitting work, each ending with papers and examinations that test their abilities and endurance to the breaking point.

Nor are women's colleges utopias for women. There are issues other than gender to face, for each student belongs to a religious or ethnic group and race, each student springs from an economic class. Students are divided by sexual orientation. Some seek partners among other women. Others miss the dailiness of male companionship or heterosexual fun. Real societies of women are not *Herlands*: they have pecking orders, exclusions as well as inclusions. Power still corrupts. Passion still roils.

Yet to state this is only to remind us of what we already know: that women's colleges exist within a society of real human beings. It is not to deny that women's colleges have value.

At one level I am a pragmatist on women's colleges. By my lights women's colleges need to exist as long as they are useful to women. If there were perfect coeducation, perhaps women's colleges would not be as necessary: young women could get the education that they need alongside men. But in most cases coeducation remains an elusive ideal. In addition, as they prepare to confront a society marked by inequities, women can gain a great deal of what they need for their futures by the special opportunities that women's colleges afford.

Yet more than education is at stake. In the late nineteenth and early twentieth centuries, women gathered in separate organizations that gave them a power base for social, economic, and political action. Women's clubs, women's professional organizations, reform groups, settlement houses, and women's colleges coexisted. These were not inward-looking bodies designed to satisfy individual women's private needs. These were groups that looked out to the society of women and men. To some degree they created and sustained a dynamic agenda that linked women's enfranchisement to social justice and peace. This all-female world began to erode in the twenties and, although fragments remained, lost political power by World War II.[3]

Women's colleges were never a full partner in the coalition because they had other tasks and conflicting voices. But, for a range of reasons, they were the institution that survived and thrived. Because they remained from an earlier era, they were there to absorb the second wave of feminism that began in the late 1960s. Although women's colleges remain complex institutions, to an important degree they have been reinfused by feminism. Feminist scholars have created a solid academic base in women's studies. Faculty and administrators have reshaped programs to become workshops for empowering women. Women's college presidents and speakers have used commencements to address broad issues of women's concern. Perhaps most important, women's colleges have large, loyal, and often generous alumnae whose very existence as a group is a testament to women's collective strength. As composite institutions, women's colleges contain multiple voices—academic freedom has ensured that— but they are also critical survivors of an earlier era of powerful women's organizations.

Not all the institutions that I consider in *Alma Mater* continue as women's colleges. Survival has been more likely for women's colleges that coexist in a regional context of private colleges and public universities. This fact itself is suggestive. The women's movement has many voices. Some call for engagement, others withdrawal. Some insist on separation from men, others seek alliances with supportive male allies. Many women's colleges are evidence for the value of partnership. They have benefited by the greater resources and the gender mix of cooperating institutions in ways that have kept them vital and linked to the common enterprise of higher education.

The women's movement in the last decade has been relentlessly self-critical. Its earlier failure to include racial and ethnic minorities goads present efforts to bridge the chasms that divide women today. It is in this spirit that many women's colleges have struggled to diversify their student bodies and to reshape curriculum and programs in the light of new knowledge and sensitivities. The success of these efforts has brought the conflicts of the broader society onto campus. In women's colleges discord may feel more intense than in coeducational ones because of the expectation that women are more cooperative and peaceable than men and because of inflated rhetoric about women's community.

Alma Mater is offered again as a splash of realism. It illumines the mixed motives that attended the foundings of ten women's colleges. It makes an effort to recapture the controversies of earlier eras and to see how they were played

---

[3]Estelle B. Freedman, "Separatism as Strategy: Female Institution Building and American Feminism, 1870–1930," *Feminist Studies* 5 (Fall 1979): 512–29.

out on the ground. It is fundamentally about power, the power to create, to name, to shape places and spaces. It explores the contested power of faculty who seek to become players on presidents' and trustees' turf. It suggests the subversive power of students to re-create, rename, reshape.

It is also about change. We see how power shifts to other actors. We watch as new definitions of women and of their relation to higher education, their futures, men, and each other reshape the college campus. In all this there is perhaps a message for the present as well as for the future. Architecture is not just artifact, it is emblem. We live today not in an era of building but in one of restoration and adaptive reuse. Today on women's college campuses old buildings serve new purposes: a music building is transformed to a students' center; a dormitory becomes offices for the philosophy department; a society house supports an organization of African-American students. As the college is filled with the new wine of today's students, teachers, and knowledge, it must be creatively adapted as well.

A scholar's autobiography is found in her books. *Alma Mater* emerged from my life and has circled back on it many times. It was written in fascination and delight; its publication was a source of abiding joy. As it returns in this new edition, I can only feel immense gratitude to the women's college that educated me, to the one that gave me years of apprenticeship and support, and to the one in which I happily teach. None of them was or is a cloister. Each is very much of this world. It is above all else the vitality and the worldliness of women's colleges that I have sought to recapture in these pages.

Preface

I entered Wellesley College in 1959, without ever having seen the campus or New England. In my home in Shreveport, Louisiana, I had pored over pictures of the college, but these did not prepare me for the immense rolling park with tall trees and a lake. I had lived in a white frame, single-family house; college put me in a brick dormitory with a hundred other females. Three other dormitories joined with mine in a group called the Quad. Students trailed down a steep path to classes in buildings shaped like cathedrals, to the library in a classical temple, and to chapel in a medieval church. Vast spaces separated these buildings. The college had no connection to the town at the edge of the campus. Boston and Cambridge beckoned. The bus that stopped outside the Quad entrance to campus and started us on the long journey became our lifeline to an urban world and to college men.

However appealing to leave the college, life remained centered on the campus. I never got over the sense that when I entered Wellesley I stepped on special ground. Wellesley made new demands on me that opened up the unknown worlds of knowledge and adulthood. In some sense this book is a personal exploration. I want to understand the world that I first entered at seventeen.

I did not begin directly. As an American cultural historian, I have tried to understand the relation between material objects and their contexts. I have been especially interested in areas regarded as the province of geographers and architectural historians, the landscape and the built environment. As a women's historian, I have also explored the cultural implications of gender. Several years ago, I started examining the places and spaces designed for women's exclusive use in the late nineteenth century. A photograph of a "women-only" subway car in New York City from *The American Album* was my point of departure. I outlined a project that surveyed women's clubs, women's buildings at world's fairs, luncheon rooms and parlors in department stores, settlement houses, and women's colleges. To start somewhere I began with the books and magazine articles available in California on the colleges. I soon realized that what I intended as a chapter ought to be a book.

My comfort in limiting the field of inquiry to one type of institution lasted only a short time, for I quickly confronted the vast number of what once were women's colleges in the United States. I began to pay closest attention to those that I knew best, the Eastern colleges originally intended for women and formerly known as the Seven Sisters. As I probed, it became clear that while the Seven College Conference began only in 1926, giving its members the collective nickname Seven Sisters, the colleges' relationships with each other and in the public mind went back longer, in fact to their beginnings.

Sometimes direct connections joined the colleges. At its founding, Smith drew from the same small Amherst College world that supported Mount Holyoke: trustees felt no conflict of interest in serving on both boards. Wellesley had as creator an active Mount Holyoke trustee and donor. Radcliffe founders and supporters knew Wellesley at close hand; both relied on the small number who in late-nineteenth-century Boston actively promoted women's higher education. To this Massachusetts core, Vassar, Bryn Mawr, and Barnard initially seemed far away. Vassar began so stunningly that it forced recognition from the outset. Bryn Mawr copied Smith directly; but, more importantly, M. Carey Thomas' insistence upon high standards at Bryn Mawr commanded instant attention. Barnard's beginnings initially made its acceptance problematic, but firm leadership under talented women made Columbia's annex a prime mover in drawing the others into formal cooperation.

What the connections mean will become clearer as the story unfolds. The most important element is that the colleges were conscious of each other. As the institutions evolved, each knew what the other was doing and sought to imitate, adapt, or move in a new direction. They drew on each other's alumnae for faculty and administrators. When a question of policy arose, presidents and deans consulted each other. The relationship between the seven, although more competitive than cordial in the years before the Seven College Conference, was nonetheless genuine. Other women's colleges, such as Pembroke, Wheaton, and Goucher—equally worthy of study by the historian—appeared occasionally in correspondence or in a periodical's list of the important women's colleges. Yet these colleges remained tangential to the seven and sustained no on-going connection. To use language borrowed from sociology, the Seven Sister colleges formed each other's reference group. At the point at which I recognized this, I realized that I had a subject.

In addition, as I have studied other colleges for women, I have been struck by an important distinction. From the outset, each of the seven women's colleges began with a vision. None of these schools developed in a pragmatic, ad hoc way. In each case, founders shaped their creations with a critical level of conscious intention and design. Daughter seminaries of Mount Holyoke which developed into colleges—Wheaton, Mills, Elmira, and Rockford, for example—share this quality. Except for the problem of diffusion and repetition, they might have been included in this study. But other women's colleges, as, for example, Hollins and Mary Baldwin, do not. They spring out of particular local needs and opportunities and develop as resources permit. Their foundings lack that intense, self-conscious quality that permeates the initial discussions surrounding Wellesley or Smith. This disparity evaporated in the twentieth century, as capable administrators and faculty of many women's colleges reshaped them to fit the standards that the Seven Sisters had set. Given my interest in foundings, it has seemed wise to limit this book to a small network of colleges which shared early commitments. In order to capture more fully the nature of the changes after the First World War, I have broadened my study to include three colleges created in reaction to the Seven Sisters: Sarah Lawrence, Bennington, and Scripps.

The self-conscious intention of these women's colleges is happily reflected in the quality of their archives. To my surprise, with the exception of Mount Holyoke and Barnard, no professional historian has written a comprehensive history of any of the seven colleges. This is hardly for lack of sources. Mount Holyoke, Smith, Vassar, and Wellesley have splendid collections, which have been professionally organized and maintained for decades. Bryn Mawr's archive, while relatively new, is nonetheless excellent. Although the physical accommodations differ in each place, one senses in the five institutions a strong commitment to preserving the historical record and making it available to scholars. This resolve has survived coeducation at Vassar and cooperative arrangements with men's colleges and coeducational universities at the other four. The coordinate institutions, Radcliffe and Barnard, suffer by contrast. In Radcliffe's case, this is partially mitigated by an excellent archivist and the presence of the Schlesinger Library. Barnard, though fortunate in its able archivist, lacks both staff time and physical space for its holdings. As a result, my account of the two former annexes is not built from quite the same materials as that of the five independent colleges. Bennington's beginnings have been meticulously documented. The richness of sources at Sarah Lawrence, Bennington, and Scripps make up for the lack of formal archives.

An alumna (or alumnus, in the case of Vassar, Bennington, and Sarah Lawrence) of one of these women's colleges needs no explanation of why an historian might choose to study her (or his) alma mater and its connections to the others. The hold of one's college on the imagination gives an intrinsic interest to its distinctive qualities. Yet I intend this account for a broad audience, which includes those who share an interest in history, women's studies, education, architecture, landscape, and planning. To them I owe a more general rendering of accounts. The design of these women's colleges, especially their systems of governance and their buildings and landscapes, provides a rich field of data about the way American women were perceived by men and the way they came to perceive themselves.

How did the creators of these colleges conceive of the communities of women that they called into being? These educational pioneers boldly offered women the liberal arts, previously denied to the sex. They courageously claimed a male preserve for women; but having broken with conservative beliefs about women's minds, they frequently gave in to their fears about the effects of the higher learning on women's character and future prospects. While founders could not alter the curriculum, which was, by definition, that of the male liberal arts college, they attempted to shape the communal life of the women's colleges and created distinctive buildings and landscapes to give that life form.

Students who came to the colleges developed, however, quite different notions about what they should and could be. In college life, they developed a powerful peer culture in conflict with the goals of founders and administrators. Living by their own rules of behavior, their own standards of success and failure, students of the women's colleges broke with the common notions of femininity of their era. Through college organizations, athletics, and dramatics, they learned the masculine routes of power: how to cooperate, how to compete openly, how to lead. In the process, they transformed their college landscapes into the settings of their own dramas of college life.

The intentions of founders also faced conflict from what was to have been their most powerful ally, the female faculty. While the seminary had sheltered an earlier generation of women teachers, the women who became professors in the late nineteenth century began to claim for themselves the professional position and autonomy of their male colleagues. They fought for the right to their own religious consciences and political beliefs and demanded privacy for personal lives, apart from college grounds. In their own communities of women outside college gates, they loosened the ties that had linked them with students.

No meanings intrinsically inhere in associational schemes or in buildings. A culture invests both with significance. Nor do institutions and their settings necessarily effect creators' intentions. A form meant to give protection may create new, unanticipated dangers. What is to one generation a gesture of hope may become to another an expression of fear. As one looks at the women's colleges, it is clear that the meanings of their designs have been reinterpreted in successive eras by different constituents. This study attempts to understand not only original purposes but how these were realized or subverted.

It also aims to discover how meanings changed as the colleges experienced new opportunities and threats from within and without. By the turn of the century, the Seven Sister colleges had moved from idiosyncratic beginnings to a common design. They passed from founders' hands to their chosen trustees and administrators. New agents emerged, some of them women, to confront fresh challenges. Each of the colleges went through a process of inner transformation—raising standards, shifting imagery, reorganizing its forms of governance, and erecting new buildings.

In the years following World War I, critics questioned separate colleges for women. Two colleges addressed these criticisms directly. The others responded covertly, planning the inner spaces of residence halls to conform to changing conceptions of womanhood. Several new women's colleges emerged, planned with the same intensity that had characterized the foundings of the Seven Sisters. Bennington, Sarah Lawrence, and Scripps were originally designed to be new colleges for twentieth-century women. Not only their organizational forms and buildings but also their curricula responded to the hostile evaluations of women's higher educational institutions in the 1920s.

While graduates of these colleges may find that familiarity makes the story resonate, those who have attended other colleges will find much that applies to their alma mater. Older graduates will remember the regulations that attempted to protect the reputations of women students. Some may recall special requirements or academic programs for women. All will recognize on their campuses certain building types. Mills, for example, has an 1870s' replica of Mount Holyoke's seminary building, a library whose placement and form were influenced by Beaux Arts principles, and splendid examples of dormitories from the 1920s. Coeducational colleges, such as Pomona, Grinnell, and Carleton, retain elements of an early twentieth-century effort to divide each campus into male and female areas and to give to women students proper dormitories. Even some of the large universities—for example, the University of Michigan and the University of Chicago—have women's buildings that conform to notions of women's special needs, as well as residence halls and sorority houses shaped differently from those of men. My hope is that, in its intense look at a handful of women's colleges, this study will provide a way of reading institutions and their landscapes that will open readers' eyes, enabling them to see in the particular the broader cultural frame. My favorite moment in a course is when an undergraduate suddenly begins to jump in her chair and wave her hand for recognition. She has just had that first unanticipated insight that connects the world she has known to the abstract realm of reading and lecture that had hitherto seemed disassociated from experience. If this book helps to make such a connection between the familiar and the historical past for you, the reader, then it will have served its purpose.

Acknowledgments

I developed preliminary conceptions of this book in 1977–78, a year in which the American Council of Learned Societies granted me a study fellowship. The School of Architecture and Urban Planning at UCLA proved to be an excellent base, and I am indebted to the late Harvey Perloff, Thomas S. Hines, Dolores Hayden, J. B. Jackson, Pauly Stein, and Margaret Whitehead for intellectual stimulation, encouragement, and good conversation. It was in talking with Pauly Stein about topics for her Ph.D. thesis that I sketched an outline for this book. I am thankful to her for preferring the WPA in California to women's colleges.

College archives proved to have not only excellent collections but also splendid archivists. I gratefully acknowledge the rich repositories at Mount Holyoke, Vassar, Wellesley, Smith, Radcliffe, Bryn Mawr, Barnard, Sarah Lawrence, Bennington, and Scripps. In particular, Wilma R. Slaight of the Wellesley College Archives, Mary B. Trotter of the Smith College Archives, Lucy Fisher West of the Bryn Mawr College Archives, and Judith Harvey-Sahak of the Scripps College Archives went beyond archival caretaking to engage in the search for materials with me. Research under these conditions is a great joy. I appreciate the care and generosity with which each archive aided me in locating and reproducing college photographs. Faculty and staff members extended to me many courtesies and gave me excellent advice and information. I am grateful for the extra efforts of Mary Lefkowitz of Wellesley in opening doors. Residents of the houses built by women faculty at the turn of the century allowed a stranger access to their dwellings and told me about the houses and their original occupants. I enjoyed interviewing old hands who enriched written sources with personal recollections: Thomas P. Brockway, Evalyn A. Clark, Frederica de Laguna, Mary Routt, Isabel Fothergill Smith,

Rebecca B. Stickney, and Elinor Amram and Milton C. Nahm. Friends extended generous hospitality which helped me blend research with good times: Marcia Burick, Eileen Gillooly, Lance and Carol Liebman, and Kennedy Smith.

Readers who engage in another's questions relieve the isolation of research and writing. At an early stage I benefited from the advice of Daniel Horowitz, who remains a constant source of good judgment. J. B. Jackson, whose intellectual influence has been profound, sensitized me to elements of good writing. At a later stage, I learned from the criticism of Marcia Burick, Patricia Cline Cohen, Roger Conover, Robert Dawidoff, Richard Dober, Neil Harris, Daniel Horowitz, Linda Kerber, and Carolyn Lyon. I was not always able to satisfy the exacting standards that these readers held for me. Nor could I accommodate their differing perspectives and judgments. But I thank them for the care that they brought to my arguments and my prose. I also had the opportunity to present elements of my research to demanding audiences at the American Historical Association meetings in 1981, the University of Hawaii, the University of California at Riverside, and the Huntington Library–Haynes Foundation gathering of historians of Greater Los Angeles. The comments of Estelle Freedman and of the audiences forced me to clarify my thinking. The informal teaching workshop of historians of United States women's history, which meets each spring, has helped me sharpen my understanding of women's experience.

Scripps College supported my research with grants for travel to archives, research aid, and photocopying, as well as a timely sabbatical. I am obliged to the college for its provision of the material means for research. In the past few years, I have also been blessed by student research assistants whose intelligence and stamina convince me of the value of a liberal arts education: Sarah Shields, Monica Arriola, and Franca Barricelli. Interlibrary loan at the Honnold Library of the Claremont Colleges brought many treasures of the Seven Sisters close to home. Denison Library at Scripps and the Huntington Library in San Marino proved to have surprisingly good collections on women's colleges.

I have had the great pleasure of an editor who has understood my book better than I. Jane Garrett at Knopf helped me to rethink and reshape the book. Her care and tact encouraged my best efforts.

My deepest debt goes to my husband and children. Ben and Sarah Esther tolerate well their mother's eccentricities, including her writing behavior. Dan's sustaining power makes life possible.

PART ONE

Foundings

Despite the illusion fostered by stone walls covered in ivy, the women's colleges did not always exist. Each college came into being as a deliberate act, created by individuals for a specific purpose. Those women's colleges that we know as the Seven Sisters sprang from idiosyncratic, yet related, beginnings. As each courageously offered to women the highest standard of education available to men, it knew of its predecessors' successes and failures, and these informed its initial design. To move chronologically along the continuum of foundings—from Mount Holyoke's origins as a seminary in 1837 to Barnard's incorporation as Columbia University's annex in 1889—is to survey the changing notions about the higher education of women during a critical half-century. In each case, the plan of the campus serves as a text that illustrates the hopes and fears that accompanied the bold act of offering the higher learning to women.

In 1865, when the first women came to Vassar College, they entered a community that differed from that of any college for men. As a true college, Vassar offered to women the full liberal arts curriculum, including the study of the ancient languages, taught by a faculty of professorial grade. In this aspect, Vassar was identical to the conservative men's colleges, such as Yale, which defined for the age the collegiate standard and course of study. Vassar students and faculty, however, lived and studied in a distinctive setting. The buildings of a men's college created an "academical village." Whether planned by Jefferson as a single harmonious composition for the University of Virginia, or added to piecemeal, as at Harvard or Amherst, colleges for men consisted of a growing number of separate buildings for different purposes grouped together on a common. In contrast, patterned after Mount Holyoke Female Seminary, Vassar (1865) and Wellesley (1875) rose as single gigantic buildings that not only housed and fed all faculty and students but gave them spaces for classrooms, laboratories, chapel, library, and museums.

Life within these buildings differed as markedly from life within the men's colleges as did their respective structures. Constant supervision by teachers, rules governing the actions of every hour, and twice-daily periods of silent devotion characterized the disciplinary regime required of the first female collegians. Their seclusion and their enclosure within a single structure made such rigor possible. By contrast, while college men lived with long formal lists of rules, they did so with little oversight and in the relative freedom of dispersed surroundings.

What explains the difference between the initial colleges for women and those for men? At the time, critics called the women's colleges Protestant nunneries. Evangelical origins, however, prevented any direct application of the monastic system of discipline or building type. Colleges for women did not model themselves after convents. They drew on the female seminary. Vassar and Wellesley applied the system of discipline and building form which Mary Lyon had developed at Mount Holyoke.[1]

Mary Lyon aimed not only to offer her students the highest education then available to women, the curriculum of the seminary, but also to alter their consciousness. To do this, she linked to a large congregate building the mother-daughter bond, re-created in the relationship between teacher and student. As students imitated their revered teachers, under a strict disciplinary regimen monitored in a single building, they became rational, disciplined women oriented to the external world.

Mary Lyon was a woman acting in the 1830s. Matthew Vassar was a man, following several decades later. Wishing to create a monument for his immortality, he found an advisor who urged him to establish a liberal arts college of the highest quality for women. The college he created made no compromise with notions about women's minds, gathering a largely male faculty to teach the liberal arts disciplines. But fear of the effects of this bold act on women's character led Vassar and the men who counseled him to adopt Mary Lyon's system. They hardly understood Mount Holyoke's profound psychological effects, but they did know that women students needed protection from the risks of the outside world. Male promoters of women's colleges feared unladylike behavior and scandal above all. Mount Holyoke's seminary system promised them control. This proved illusory, but not until Vassar College erected a single main building for Henry Fowle Durant to copy for Wellesley College.

Durant had known Mount Holyoke at first hand and admired it without reservation. On his estate outside Boston, he founded Wellesley to re-create Mount Holyoke Female Seminary in grand form. Aware of Vassar College, Durant insisted on a curriculum of collegiate grade and imitated in the College

Beautiful Vassar's building. Loyal to Mount Holyoke, however, Durant made one important departure from Vassar: as president and as faculty of his college he hired only women. Wellesley felt the effects of Durant's act well into the twentieth century.

The large seminary structure kept its inmates physically in place and thus secure in a limited sense, but proved to have unintended consequences. In the suites in Vassar's Main building, students began to develop the autonomous culture—characterized by independence and intense friendships—that they called college life. The Amherst men responsible for turning Sophia Smith's bequest into Smith College had seen young women emerge from Mount Holyoke with "affected, unsocial, visionary notions," which may have suited them to become missionaries, but hardly enabled them to become wives and mothers. In addition, while the seminary protected women from men, it did not protect them from other women or from their own imaginations. The close supervision of women in a single building clearly guarded the virtue of young women; but what did this all-female world do to female character?

The educators who shaped Smith College confronted these questions directly. To avoid the effects of an all-female community, they designed Smith, which opened in 1875, to simulate family life within a New England town. Built in a town, rather than as Wellesley or Vassar on a country estate, Smith did not have a single seminary building, but rather a variety of buildings for different uses. Students lived in "cottages," structures designed inside and out to look like family dwellings. Smith broke the seminary's disciplinary code and disposed of the structure of rules monitored by female faculty; as in a family, students lived by informal and unwritten rules. The hope was that, protected by the patriarchal order of the New England town, Smith students would keep their femininity.

Smith made Vassar and Wellesley look hopelessly out-of-date. In response, they tried to imitate Smith as best they could. While stuck with grandiose seminary buildings, both colleges understood the appeal of the cottage, although for divergent reasons. Blessed with expansion, Wellesley built cottages immediately; Vassar, with little student demand, had to wait until the 1890s.

Radcliffe's founders went even further than Smith's in their rejection of the seminary system. Working to open the resources of Harvard College to young women, the creators of the Annex conceived of a plan to gather women in Cambridge where Harvard professors could offer them instruction. Boston's Unitarian world perceived colleges other than Harvard as hopelessly provincial. Radcliffe's promoters wanted nothing that suggested the women's colleges, with their evangelistic overtones. In addition, because of Harvard's reluctance to recognize its annex in any official way, the women's institution sought to appear as inconspicuous as possible. Thus the Annex, opening in

1879, built no structures: students either lived at home or boarded in Cambridge residences. In the early years, the Annex rented rooms for instruction in a private house; as it grew, it purchased a house, thus disguising its nature to the outside. Because the founders of Radcliffe saw no positive building possibilities in the 1880s, they simply pretended that the college as a physical entity did not exist.

Bryn Mawr's founder and trustees wanted to create a female Haverford, to offer higher education to young, orthodox Quaker women in a setting that met both their religious standards and their sense of propriety. Smith College's design suited their intentions perfectly, and they commissioned their architect to repeat its buildings in "Quaker lady" dress. When the first students arrived in 1885, they entered a campus which copied Smith's buildings closely.

Bryn Mawr began in imitation. It became the leader. Under M. Carey Thomas, the first feminist to gain control over a women's college, Bryn Mawr became the innovator in curriculum and campus design. Thomas took as her model Johns Hopkins and brought to Bryn Mawr a German-trained faculty. She protected Bryn Mawr professors from college interference and created a graduate school to keep them current in their fields. She hoped that the presence of graduate students might encourage scholarship and independence among Bryn Mawr collegians. Thomas welcomed the formation of Student Government as a way to recognize undergraduate maturity. To express her sense of the dignity of the academic tradition, Thomas rejected the cottage system that the male founder had ordained, to create the first women's college that boldly proclaimed descent from the male collegiate tradition. As Bryn Mawr added buildings, they drew on the association of scholarship with the quadrangles of Oxford and Cambridge. Collegiate Gothic entered the lexicon of design for women's colleges. Bryn Mawr's landscape carried associations of ceremony and the dignity of scholarship.

Barnard's origins as an annex to Columbia are much like those of Radcliffe. However, created a decade later, in 1889, Barnard needed to establish a clear presence in New York. Under its Bryn Mawr–trained dean, Barnard built monumental academic buildings compatible with the new Morningside Heights campus of Columbia. Off to the side on its own axis, Barnard assumed a dignified form that asserted its separate, yet related, relationship to Columbia University. Barnard never considered regulating its day students, who rode the streetcar to the college's urban, cosmopolitan campus.

By the end of the nineteenth century a new confidence infused these women's colleges. Bryn Mawr's successful example became the salient model. The colleges ceased perceiving their students as needing protection through special systems of discipline encased in distinct building forms. Once they could look like those of men, women's colleges hired architects identified with important buildings at prominent men's colleges. In addition, college life seized hold of undergraduates. Student culture reinterpreted the college landscape as a setting for college life. Women faculty threw off seminary restraints to enjoy professional autonomy on campus and private lives outside. With the turn to the twentieth century, the women's colleges came of age.

I

Plain, Though Very Neat

MOUNT HOLYOKE

I

In 1837, Mary Lyon founded Mount Holyoke Seminary in South Hadley, Massachusetts. Her arduous labors created new possibilities for American women. The transformation that Mount Holyoke wrought in higher education profoundly influenced the women's colleges that followed in its wake. In a real sense, Mount Holyoke is the beginning. Yet to comprehend its origins, one must go back, for in the two hundred years that preceded its founding, American women claimed a significant portion of their intellectual heritage.

The Puritan women who arrived on the shores of Massachusetts in 1630 had come with a unique advantage. While England's patriarchal system survived the Atlantic crossing intact, religious enthusiasm had already breached a critical barrier that traditionally had divided the sexes. Puritan women may have been ruled by husbands and barred from political participation, but they were potentially saints. As such, they listened to Puritan sermons and read the Bible. As Goodwives, they participated in the intellectual life of their time. While no women became ministers, several of them published their religious meditations and Anne Bradstreet presumed to write poetry.[1]

The education that enabled women to read and write remained rudimentary, more suitable for subordinate participants in the culture than for dominant ones. Many New England girls were taught by their mothers or went to dame schools to learn how to read and cipher. They did not attend the grammar schools which taught the classical curriculum, based on the study of the Greek and Latin languages, to boys in preparation for college. Outside New England, provision for schooling for boys as well as girls varied greatly, depending upon the locale.

9

In general, while significant numbers of women knew how to read and write in the American colonies, only unusual women learned more than the rudiments. The grammar schools and colleges which trained the small number of boys and young men designated for the learned professions were male preserves. In the eighteenth century, privileged daughters in the seacoast cities went to private-venture schools where they studied literature, perfected their penmanship, mastered the useful and decorative needle arts, and learned French. These aristocratic accomplishments "finished" young ladies for polite society. Despite these new advantages, because they could not study the ancient languages, women remained largely barred from the realm of ideas in the classical world of the eighteenth century.[2]

The Revolutionary period changed the nature of education for both sexes. Academies sprang up in cities and towns, especially in New England. In addition to classical departments offering Latin and Greek, as preparation for college, the academies created the English curriculum: history, philosophy, modern languages, the natural sciences, and certain practical arts, such as surveying. During the school years in which the college-bound studied the ancient languages, students who took the English course completed their more worldly education. Academies had many different forms and sponsors. Towns organized and supported some academies; private endowments, religious groups, or combinations of the three sustained others. In many cases provisions for boarding opened access to rural young people. What is significant is that alongside academies for boys appeared academies offering the English curriculum to girls and to both sexes together.[3]

The Revolution had begun its work for women. As their lives changed during the tumultuous years following Independence, a new appreciation of the value of women's traditional tasks elevated their sphere. American women ceased to be merely helpmeets. They became the Mothers of the Republic. They nurtured the future electorate and representatives of the polity. The keepers of the nurseries of the new nation needed not only the virtue necessary for moral guidance, but also the ability to understand the world of political discourse.[4] As schools multiplied, they required teachers. Labor-scarce towns turned to older daughters who had guided younger siblings in the rudiments. Academies gave girls additional training to prepare them for teaching. Fires of religious enthusiasm intensified the calling of evangelical academicians who saw their schools as accomplishing the Lord's work.

Republican motherhood and the academies founded in the Revolutionary years ended completely the age-old division that had given men the world of culture and women the world of nature.[5] American women became culture-bearers. Through them, sons imbibed the milk of citizenship and virtue. To women—not just unusual individuals, but potentially the sex as a whole—the entire world of thought and expression opened. While efforts to impose barriers along the way and to channel women's minds hardly ended at the turn to the nineteenth century, American women reached a new watershed from which they never turned back. American women became "heiresses of the ages."

Schools also introduced girls and young women to the new discipline. New England villages and towns had common schools almost from their foundings. In the early nineteenth century, interest in the common school grew markedly and reformers set out to bring all New England children under its aegis for longer periods of each year and to extend it to the West. The school took on a new task. In addition to the rudiments, it taught pupils the requirements of an urban and industrial order: clocks and the school bell divided the day; rigid rows of desks divided the space. Students learned to work silently under the rule of the teacher. By the nineteenth century, girls attended the common schools alongside boys and thus confronted the new discipline. The bright girl with a school to keep had the responsibility of imposing this discipline on others.[6]

In the early nineteenth century the word *seminary* began to replace the word *academy*. The new word connoted a certain seriousness. The seminary saw its task primarily as professional preparation. The male seminary prepared men for the ministry; the female seminary took as its earnest job the training of women for teaching and for Republican motherhood. The curriculum and the quality of female academies and seminaries varied enormously. Some specialized in polite accomplishments, others promised skills useful for housekeeping. The female seminary never offered the classical option of the male academy, Greek and Latin, nor its extension into the classical element of the liberal arts college curriculum. At its best, the female seminary offered the English curriculum of the academy—history, philosophy, modern languages, and natural sciences—designed to prepare women for teaching. The most ambitious female seminaries carried some course work to early college level.[7]

Four female seminaries offered to young women unusual opportunities for intellectual development: Emma Willard's in Troy, New York (founded 1821); Catharine Beecher's in Hartford, Connecticut (founded 1828); Zilpah Grant's in Ipswich, Massachusetts (founded 1828); and Mary Lyon's in South Hadley, Massachusetts (founded 1837). Each, the creation of a remarkable educator and organizer, upheld high standards and demanded original thought. While Catharine Beecher left an important legacy in her writings on education and household economy, her seminary declined after her departure in 1833.[8] Emma Willard's influence remained profound, shaping the lives of generations of graduates. The institution itself remains today as an important independent preparatory school.[9] Zilpah Grant's and Mary Lyon's combined impact, however, was unique. Ipswich and Mount Holyoke, which can be seen as their joint creations, became the model for many other female seminaries and for the female departments of coeducational colleges, such as Oberlin and Knox.

Because its endowed founding and capable direction insured a continuous life, Mount Holyoke remains the more important of the two. The women's colleges that emerged after the Civil War, while offering to women the full curriculum of the liberal arts college, turned to Mount Holyoke for guidance.

What made the work of Zilpah Grant and Mary Lyon so important was that it linked the highest available course of study to a system of discipline and a form of building that propelled its students outward into the world. Mary Lyon created Mount Holyoke to turn daughters who were acted upon into women capable of self-propelled action. She broke into a woman's life—governed by tradition and natural rhythms, ruled by the heart and the demands of the flesh—to transform it into a life that could be planned.[10] She drew together key elements: academic subjects to train the mind as an instrument of reason; domestic work and a carefully regulated day to meet material needs and to protect health; a known, clear sequence of each day to lend order and predictability; a corps of transformed teachers who provided proper models for imitation; and a building shaped like a dwelling house as the proper setting for study, prayer, work, and rest. The results were extraordinary. Seventy percent of Mount Holyoke's graduates became teachers. Ipswich and Mount Holyoke gave to coeducational colleges their female leadership and to Vassar and Wellesley their first female heads. When Mount Holyoke extended to the first women's colleges its system, the seminary transferred to them its transforming power.

I I

Years of preparation shaped the design of Mount Holyoke. Its contours lie embedded in Mary Lyon's biography. She created Mount Holyoke out of her own inner needs and her hopes for women. She had a difficult early life, for family tragedy forced her to rely on her own resources while she was still a girl. With the help of friends and teachers, she set out to train her intellect, and in the process she gained inner peace and grace. In establishing an endowed seminary for young women, she drew on her experiences to create a school to transform others as she had been transformed.[11]

Born in 1797, Mary Lyon was one of eight children of Aaron and Jemima Shepard Lyon. Her father, a farmer in Buckland County, Massachusetts, died when she was almost six, and her mother added the chores of a man to that of a woman to keep her family and farm together. A second loss followed: when Mary Lyon was thirteen, her mother remarried, taking her youngest daughters with her. The single surviving son took the farm, and for two years Mary Lyon became her brother's housekeeper. She attended district school and at seventeen took her first teaching position in nearby Shelburne Falls. Saving her wages—$1.00 a week from her brother, $.75 a week from the school—she began her formal education at Sanderson Academy. Snatching four hours' sleep at night, eating hastily, Mary Lyon performed prodigious feats as a student, such as memorizing an entire Latin grammar over a single weekend. A leading citizen, the father of her friend Amanda White, offered her a second term at Sanderson, as well as lodging and board in his home. There began her first lessons in dress and manners which, unlike Latin, Mary Lyon never mastered.

In the succeeding years, Mary Lyon taught and studied at a variety of schools in Western Massachusetts. A term at Amherst Academy gave her an important friend, the young preceptress Orra White, who later married Amherst professor Edward Hitchcock. These were rough years for Mary Lyon. She had to learn how to gain students' attention and respect. She moved constantly, and her brother's departure with his family for New York State left her without a room of her own. Everything she saved went to buy more formal training. She experienced inner turmoil as well. During this period she "would yield to great depression, and even depend on indulging in long seasons of weeping." [12] Her greatest trial was her uncertainty of God's grace. The Puritan tradition was very much alive in her heart, and she felt deep despair that, as she wrote to a friend, "I am far from him, and walk on in darkness." [13]

In 1821, Amanda White's father decided to send his daughter to the new school opened in Byfield, Massachusetts, by Joseph Emerson. Mary Lyon took her small inheritance and all her other money and went also. Byfield changed her life forever. One of the early nineteenth century's originals, Emerson had trained at Harvard for the ministry, turning to school-keeping when his health failed. He brought to his students an unusual appreciation for women's minds, intellectual excitement, and a fervent belief in mental system. [14] At his school Mary Lyon found intellectual mastery.

And here, too, she found order. Zilpah Grant, an older student, became Emerson's assistant the year that Mary Lyon studied at Byfield. A handsome, gracious woman, three years Lyon's senior, Zilpah Grant had that influence over students and inner strength that Mary Lyon was struggling so hard to attain. [15] Mary Lyon admired her teacher from the beginning. Zilpah Grant became Lyon's inspiration and guide and ultimately her adored friend. Their friendship flourished within the early nineteenth century's acceptance of intimacy between women. [16] Mary Lyon wrote to her sister several years later, "I love Miss G.'s society more than ever, and I believe we may love our friends very ardently, and love them according to the principles and spirit of the gospel." [17] Zilpah Grant became a beloved surrogate mother to Mary Lyon, taking the place of the real one who had left her at thirteen.

Out of Mary Lyon's adoration of Zilpah Grant came imitation of her. At Byfield, Grant worked out a unique system of discipline. Lyon attempted Grant's methods in her own classes with marked success. After several years as pre-

ceptress at Sanderson Academy, Mary Lyon joined Zilpah Grant at the Adams
Academy in Londonderry, New Hampshire. From 1823 until 1834, Lyon worked
under Grant at Adams and at Ipswich Female Seminary. Ultimately the two
refined the seminary system in a way that powerfully shaped women's higher
education in America. As they did, Mary Lyon applied Zilpah Grant's principles to her own life, regulating her day in the manner required of her students. The inner transformation that this wrought propelled Mary Lyon outward
as her seminary system's best propagandist.

During these years of the 1820s and early 1830s, family crisis struck repeated blows. Zilpah Grant's mother, who suffered severe depressions, committed suicide in 1827.[18] Death stalked the houses of Mary Lyon's sisters. Lovina
Lyon Putnam, who lived in Buckland where Lyon taught in the winter, broke
down during the illness and death of her husband. Mary Lyon assumed "personal and financial responsibility" for her sister, who entered the Hartford
Hospital for the Insane.[19] Several months later Lovina Putnam came home,
and Mary Lyon wrote to Zilpah Grant that her sister's "calmness, self-government, and settled resolution to go forward in the path of duty . . . give me a
very important lesson."[20] Sanity proved to be short-lived, and Lovina Putnam
went back to the Hartford Retreat, where she ultimately died. What is tanta-
lizing here is Mary Lyon's close brush with insanity and with a new kind of
institution for its treatment, at the very time that she was re-creating herself
and, with Zilpah Grant, was shaping the ordered life of the seminary. The
parallels between the asylum and seminary are strong.

New theories about insanity were widely discussed in New England in the
early nineteenth century. In this period of rapid change, certain reformers saw
disorder as the critical cause of psychic distress. In the asylum they attempted
to restore the minds of the afflicted through the creation of places of perfect
order. The Hartford Retreat separated patients like Lovina Putnam from their
families; put them in a sylvan setting; and required a daily regime of therapeu-
tic labor, silence, enforced periods of private devotion, and the rule of the
clock. Asylum designers believed that putting patients under strict outer order
re-created in them inner order. Its advocates hoped the insane might pass from
external government to the "self-government" Mary Lyon saw momentarily
in her sister.[21]

The seminary system that evolved under Mary Lyon and Zilpah Grant mirrors the asylum regime. It developed slowly during the 1820s and 1830s, each
piece a response to a specific need. When taken as a whole, however, the seminary system bears a marked resemblance to the structure of asylum life.

Young women, freed from farm routine, did not automatically rise at an
early hour. Mary Lyon began to work with them, admonishing them to early
rising, but allowing them to determine their own time. Gradually she stan-
dardized an early awakening for all: the bell rang at five o'clock in summer,

six in winter. Lyon emphasized the virtue of a clear schedule and punctuality as a way of meeting one's own inner standard.[22] She insisted that sober judgment, not whim, regulate the tasks of each day and the hours in which each occurred.

Students boarded in the homes of local townspeople. At Ipswich the trustees converted a tavern into a boarding house for thirty students and several teachers. Both Zilpah Grant and Mary Lyon lived there. Communal life presented new problems—noise, crowding in the halls, meals that waited on the tardy.[23] Grant and Lyon met each situation with an injunction or a rule and developed a system of bells to mark the periods and tasks for the day. In time they prescribed almost every act and set the task of nearly every moment of the day. The value of life under a common roof became clear, for it allowed greater oversight over students' lives and control over their actions. The sequestering of all students in a single building under the watchful eye of teachers became central to Mary Lyon's plan.

The young women whispered in the classroom, Zilpah Grant spoke to them about how this undermined proper order and asked each individually to stop whispering for a week. Grant then asked each student to give an account of her success or failure at the end of her trial. Thus began the self-reporting system whereby each student monitored her own efforts to abide by rules, ultimately ritualized in a daily public confessional called a section meeting.[24] Self-reporting turned external authority inward, making Zilpah Grant and Mary Lyon's scheme of discipline that of each student. As Grant so clearly put it, the system established "the real authority of the Principal in the hearts of the pupils. . . . government . . . rather *in* them than *over* them."[25]

At some point during these years, Mary Lyon felt confident of her own salvation. In 1822, she was baptised in the Congregational Church in Buckland, forsaking the Baptist Corner of her family. While she did not experience any single moment of grace, over time her religious despair fell away.[26] Mary Lyon became an effective minister of the gospel. She herself never claimed such a masculine prerogative; but, in fact, within the walls of her school, minister is what she was. Joseph Emerson asked his students to divide themselves into the saved and the doubting. Upon those who experienced anxiety and some hope, he exerted his greatest energies, with the kind of success he enjoyed as a minister. Despite their gender and lack of training, Zilpah Grant and Mary Lyon continued Emerson's practice. They scheduled two periods of private devotion each day and held communal worship each morning, afternoon, and evening.[27] The seminary became the place of conversion. New England was experiencing the waves of religious revival known as the Second Great Awakening. Mary Lyon saw her school as God's agent, bringing women to Christ.[28] She measured her success each year by the number of souls won for the Lord.

While the seminary system evolved to meet the social and religious needs of communal living, it was also ordained by the psychic needs of its creators. It gave to Mary Lyon what she had missed. Under it, her own bouts of depression dispelled, and she became able to direct and focus her energy. Those who knew the mature woman of the 1830s testified to her seemingly boundless good health and her ability to sustain unremitting labor. Her co-workers contrasted the young Mary Lyon with the mature. They attributed the change to her self-control.[29] Mary Lyon found inner order from the external order she required of her scholars. She kept herself on the rigid schedule of meals and early retiring of the seminary even when she lived on her own, outside academy walls.[30] The regime of the Hartford Retreat failed to cure Lovina Lyon Putnam, but, applied within the seminary, it transformed her sister.

In their belief that the asylum might cure the disordered and return them to an ordered life in society, reformers assumed the uniformity of psychic experience. Different ways of life, once tolerated, now appeared deviant. This assumption of psychic sameness underlay Mary Lyon's plan for the female seminary. In the early nineteenth century, men and women increasingly lived quite separate lives, celebrated in the doctrine of separate spheres. Since the eighteenth century, men had been moving into the transforming impersonal rhythms of work-time; but women within the household remained within the realm of tradition, governed by daily and seasonal tasks and the unregulated calls of motherhood and care for sick. Ministers' sermons and articles in the new women's magazines, such as *Godey's Lady's Book*, encouraged a new self-consciousness about women's special nature and destiny.

Significant changes, however, were altering the experience of some young women, especially in New England. The common school brought to girls the new discipline. The new factories which employed young women insisted upon it. Mary Lyon's religious intensity prevented her from perceiving herself as an agent of women's modernization. She abjured the new egotism and she saw the times as degenerate. However, in her "detached thoughts"—the injunctions she gave to students to govern their daily lives that students wrote down and later published—she imparted to her female students the worldly wisdom of Benjamin Franklin that underlay the new order. She exhorted students to rise early, schedule each moment, and plan carefully. The seminary system that she devised with Zilpah Grant gave institutional form to these maxims.

Through her chapel talks and rules, Mary Lyon took women out of the world of tradition and brought them into modern times. The seminary system broke into a woman's life, previously governed by natural rhythms, and imposed on it the new order of her father and brother. It set up a clear schedule for each day, protected certain hours from intrusion and noise for study, regulated meals and sleep, set aside time for recreation, and, through a rigorous program of study, gave a sense of mental mastery. Posing itself in opposition to the farm, the seminary took traditional daughters and turned them into nineteenth-century individuals.[31]

Ironically, the female seminary brought to this task the most important family relationship for young women, that between mother and daughter. Mary Lyon's love for Zilpah Grant transformed her. The school she created drew on female bonds to reshape the lives of its students. A daughter's most intimate tie was to her mother; in seeking to imitate her, a daughter normally reproduced her mother's life. In the seminary Lyon re-created the mother-daughter relationship in the link between teacher and student. However, unlike the mother, the teacher offered an alternative way of life: rationality, rather than tradition; the order of the clock, rather than the rhythms of nature. To win the love of one's teacher, one imitated her. Intimate friendships, such as that between Grant and Lyon, flourished between teacher and student. The most successful and most loved students became assistant teachers. The seminary harnessed the power of the mother-daughter bond, not, however, to the reproduction of motherhood, but to the creation of disciplined women oriented to the external world.[32]

At Ipswich, Mary Lyon and Zilpah Grant had unimpeded freedom to develop their educational methods. Ipswich Female Seminary prospered and took shape. It offered forty weeks of instruction yearly, established minimum standards for admission, and attracted serious students. The seminary divided students into three classes by their level of knowledge. It further divided them into sections, and placed each under the moral and religious oversight of a teacher who had risen from the ranks. In daily afternoon meetings with her section, the teacher ("the friend and adviser" of each student) received "from each member an account of her performance of her duties in and out of school during the day."[33] While Ipswich offered the standard English curriculum of the time with no frills—mathematics, sciences, philosophy, history, and religion—its education differed markedly in one respect.[34] Teachers asked students not only to comprehend but to question. "In the exercises in intellectual philosophy particularly, there is great scope for freedom of discussion. The text-book is examined critically, and pupils are led to exercise their own judgment in respect to the correctness of the author's views."[35] Beginning in 1830, Ipswich took the name "Seminary" rather than "Academy" to signify its serious intention as a school that trained students for professional positions—in Ipswich's case, teaching.[36]

Ipswich's success made Mary Lyon dissatisfied. The seminary made a difference in young women's lives, graduating self-governed, professing Christian women eager to teach and convert. Yet its large fees prevented Lyon's favorite students, the daughters of poor New England farmers, from attending. As Mary Lyon pondered this she turned to the one solution she had fought up to this time: endowment. Earlier she had denied the value of "brick and mortar," when she had "living minds to work upon."[37] Now she saw the need of an endowed building to reduce costs. She began the difficult and ultimately unsuccessful effort to convince friends of Ipswich to endow the school.

Meeting failure, Mary Lyon began to cast her eyes west. In 1832, she confided in Edward Hitchcock, who had become a professor at Amherst, that she hoped to reestablish the seminary in the "genial soil" of the Connecticut River valley.[38] She directed her efforts away from the rich to the real friends of the seminary, "the more humble in life, led forward by their own ministers. . . . the same class of Christians who support our missionaries." To reach this class Lyon felt that "the style of the whole establishment should professedly be plain, though very neat."[39]

It was at this point that Mary Lyon devised one of the distinguishing features of her scheme. One way to cut costs was to run the seminary without servants. The students themselves became responsible for the care of the building in which they resided and recited. They also prepared and served their own meals. Lyon clearly had learned something about the economies of communal labor. While it took one woman, full-time, to care for a single household, a hundred young women, properly organized, accomplished all daily tasks in a single hour. To make an even stronger appeal and to reduce charges to the absolute minimum, Lyon declared that she and her teachers were missionaries who worked for only subsistence.[40] In a building erected through benevolence, organized as a cooperative household, and staffed by minimally paid teachers, the new seminary needed to charge only $60 a year, one-third to one-half the fees of Ipswich.[41] Mary Lyon knew her audience well: her plain style and missionary spirit appealed to "the more humble."

Mary Lyon grew close to Eunice Caldwell, one of her former students who became a teacher under her. This gave her support that allowed her gradually to separate from Zilpah Grant and establish her own seminary.[42] Lyon returned to Ipswich, but divided her time between her former duties and her new mission. She thought through her scheme, publicized it, and gathered interested men for its realization. She wrote several circulars, emphasizing the distinctive qualities of the future seminary. She stated the importance of an endowment held by a board of trustees to insure permanency, the value of the domestic system to reduce costs and provide healthful exercise, and the purpose of requiring all students to board as a means to "greatly facilitate the improvement of those for whom it is designed."[43] The circulars set out the rationale for public support, and they also attracted students.

Mary Lyon carefully described the kind of student she desired. She sought mature, serious students, capable of the Ipswich curriculum, who wanted futures different from their domestic pasts. "In laying out the minutiae of the plan," Lyon wrote in 1836, "great care is taken to furnish points of attraction to those who would gladly become benevolent, self-denying teachers, should the cause of Christ demand it, and points of repulsion to the more inefficient and self-indulgent, and to those whose views and desires are bounded by themselves and their own family circle."[44] The seminary trained Christian teachers to assist the ministry in the work of redemption. It took the "daughters of fairest promise," drew forth their talents, "to give them a new direction, and to enlist them permanently in the cause of benevolence."[45]

Mary Lyon attracted men to her cause, such as Theophilus Packard, minister of the Congregational Church in Shelburne, who promoted the seminary in neighboring towns and in the ministerial associations, and Roswell Hawks, a pastor who left his pulpit and took to the road as the seminary's agent. Lyon joined Hawks in 1835. For the next two years they laid the object of the seminary before any audience willing to listen, and gradually raised the money necessary for the seminary building. Mary Lyon braved criticism of those who disapproved of her forward behavior. Recalling her friend's independence and confidence in her cause, Eunice Caldwell summed up Lyon's jaunty rejoinder to her critics:

> What do I that is wrong. . . . I ride in the stage coach or cars without an escort. Other ladies do the same. I visit a family where I have been previously invited, and the minister's wife, or some leading woman, calls the ladies together to see me, and I lay our object before them. Is that wrong? I go with Mr. Hawks, and call on a gentleman of known liberality at his own house, and converse with him about our enterprise. What harm is there in that? If there is no harm in doing these things once, what harm is there in doing them twice, thrice, or a dozen times? My heart is sick, my soul is pained with this empty gentility, this genteel nothingness. I am doing a great work. I cannot come down.[46]

Edward Hitchcock brought Mary Lyon into the circle of Amherst College. She had a room in his house, as did several Amherst instructors who boarded with the Hitchcocks. Lyon attended Hitchcock's lectures on the college campus. Hitchcock himself took up his pen in the seminary's behalf, inadvertently creating a storm of publicity over the Greek name he proposed—*Pangynaskean*, for whole-woman-making. A trustee himself, he brought to the board Heman Humphrey, president of Amherst, and other Amherst colleagues.[47]

Principal financial support came from the churches, as Mary Lyon anticipated. Money also came from unexpected sources: Deacons Daniel Safford, Andrew W. Porter, and Joseph Avery, a blacksmith, a farmer, and a manufacturer, who had grown prosperous in the expanding economy of the era. More than economic mainstays, these practical men of affairs supervised the erection of the seminary.[48]

Several towns vied for the site. South Hadley won, on the condition that it raise $8,000 for the privilege. The seminary found its name, Mount Holyoke, in one of the hills gracing the town's borders. Trustees secured a site in the summer of 1836, and although they failed to gather all the needed funds, work began on the seminary building.

Mary Lyon's indifference to dress always embarrassed her friends. She coupled an inattention to fashion with a frugal nature. Both her artlessness and her thrift are apparent in the seminary building. Mount Holyoke Seminary arose as plain and unpretentious as its founder. Its creators planned it simply, so that it yielded the most for the $15,000 available: "plain, though very neat."

Northern view of Mount Holyoke Female Seminary.

The seminary in 1838; engraving by John W. Barber
Mount Holyoke College Library/Archives

The straightforward four-story red brick Georgian building, 94 feet long by 50 feet wide, rose on a ten-acre pasture next to South Hadley's church. In these years in provincial settings such as South Hadley, very little differentiated building types. With its plain rectangular form, Mount Holyoke could have been a factory, an inn, or a college. However, it soon acquired the distinctive decorative feature that marked it clearly as a dwelling house—a two-story white wooden piazza across much of its façade, with the entrance doorway in the center.[49]

More significant than this decorative element is the internal plan. Unlike the dormitory buildings at men's colleges, the seminary took the plan of a house. In a nineteenth-century private house, while the entrance gave access to the public rooms on the lower floors, the stairway protected family privacy upstairs by acting as a symbolic barrier. Once upstairs, family members, other than husband and wife, had little individual privacy, sharing bedrooms that opened on to a central hall. Mount Holyoke took the house plan and magnified it to fit a household of one hundred women, adding the rooms necessary for the running of a school.

To suggest that Mount Holyoke Seminary followed the form of a large dwelling house is not to deny that it took as its model the asylum. The asylum, too, drew on the dwelling for its building, as well as on domestic rhetoric to describe its system of governance. Yet founders designed the asylum to establish the basis of proper order, in contrast to the family which had failed its inmates. In asylum rhetoric "family government" meant the strict ordering of hierarchical relationships. Similar to the asylum, the seminary building contained appropriate symbols of authority and rank. The doorway at the center of the piazza led to an entrance hall and stairway. The major public rooms of the seminary flanked both sides of the hall. The seminary's double parlors, the primary place of internal contact with the outside world, opened to the left, as did the library. To the right was Seminary Hall, the main room for assembly (50 feet by 40 feet), looking much like the interior of a meetinghouse. Rows of settees, each to hold six students, faced a raised platform and the desks of the principal and her assistant. The teachers sat at ground level in a row to the left, facing the students. Clear separation of students and teachers and the hierarchical ordering of faculty established the proper basis for government of the seminary "family." The raised basement floor below held the dining room, as ordered as Seminary Hall above. A teacher headed each of the five rectangular tables, which were placed parallel to the width of the room. Mary Lyon presided over the sixth, which flanked them all. The basement also housed the principal workrooms of the domestic department: kitchen, washroom, ironing room, kneading room, and baking room, all carefully organized by Lyon's own hand.[50]

A central stairway led to recitation rooms and science laboratories on the second floor and to some private rooms for students and teachers on the second, third, and fourth. Mary Lyon wanted to give each student a bedroom. Her many years without a home convinced her of the value of a place of seclusion. In addition, Mary Lyon's encouragement of secret devotions, codified into the twice-daily silent period, made separate space necessary. Zilpah Grant had opposed single rooms, believing that a woman destined to share her abode with a mate ought not lose the habits of accommodation in her seminary years. In her ideal scheme she designed a separate closet for devotions by one of the roommates.[51] The need for economy prevented Lyon from realizing her hope for separate rooms, and Grant's plan prevailed. Two students normally shared a room, 18 by 10 feet—unusually generous by the standards of the time—which included a closet of 5 or 6 feet square lit by a window from the room. A diagram of a room shared by three students shows a large space broken into by two closets. There was room for the three beds and for a table, bookshelves, four chairs, and several rugs.[52] Each of the top two floors held eighteen rooms, placed on both sides of a central hallway, running the length of the building. In 1837, the seminary had no internal water closets or bathrooms:

privies were outside to the rear; students carried all water from the basement.

For the first time since she became an adult, Mary Lyon had her own rooms—bedroom, parlor, and library located on the first floor behind the double parlors. While a private suite on the first floor may seem an exception to the house plan, it is not, for the suite was in the location of the room for guests or convalescents in a New England house, the place that Lyon had occupied for many years.[53]

Mount Holyoke's appropriation of the house form is clear when one looks at men's colleges. While, in the seventeenth century, Harvard attempted to replicate Cambridge University's common life by housing faculty and students together, paltry resources limited the college to plain red brick structures on open land. As other colleges for men built halls, they adopted the form of Harvard's Stoughton Hall of 1698. Separate entrances led directly to student suites. The strength of the Georgian façade of Princeton's Nassau Hall of 1784 made it the stylistic model for the colleges which followed.[54]

Despite the many ties that bound Mount Holyoke to Amherst, the Western Massachusetts men's college did not inform the seminary's building plan. As a plain brick building, South College, Amherst's first building, dating from 1821, looks at first glance quite similar to Mount Holyoke; but unlike the seminary, its façade carried no piazza. More importantly, it had two entries on each side. From these entrances stairways led to student rooms on all four floors. South College had no dining room or kitchen in the basement, as students took board in the village. Recitation and meeting rooms found temporary quarters in student rooms in the first days, but by the next year they moved to the vacant rooms of North College, a building identical to the first which contained a large room on the fourth floor for chapel and lectures. Amherst did not group its public rooms around a central entrance, as in a house, but put them on upper floors as well as on the first. The president lived in a separate house, also completed in the second year. In 1827, Amherst erected a third building between the two dormitories. Called the Chapel, it held recitation rooms, laboratories, library, and scientific cabinets, as well as a room for worship. Adorned with white columns and pediment, it clearly asserted a dominant position in Amherst's academic village.[55]

Half of Amherst's initial student body came from Williams College, and they brought with them the college traditions that they had enjoyed in Williamstown. Amherst was as deeply rooted in evangelical Christianity as Mount Holyoke; but the fact that Amherst equipped village sons for the ministry did not inhibit the growth of literary societies, one of which became secret in 1827. These societies provided frequent occasions of irreverence and satire. Though on paper Amherst's regulations and schedule looked similar to those of Mount Holyoke, college men lived under far less supervision than seminary women. Young men moved from college chapel to village board and found

A corner of the dining room in the Seminary Building (ca. 1892)
Mount Holyoke College Library/Archives

Domestic work in the Seminary Building dining hall (ca. 1893)
Mount Holyoke College Library/Archives

their way to recitation, chapel, and society meetings in different buildings. Their president lived with his family in a separate house, as did mature faculty. Recent graduates served as instructors and lived among the students, but they might be allies rather than figures of authority. Unrestricted movement away from watchful eyes gave the men a realm of freedom. Even within the dormitory, many entrances and rooms grouped around stairwells diminished possible supervision. The college did not tolerate open breaches of its rules, such as a secret club whose residues of food and wine were found in the cellar of North College; but from the beginning college men led lives separate from their faculty and sensed college rules as external. Within a few years of Mount Holyoke's founding, Amherst fraternities sealed off student life from the campus, and rebellions and riots made clear that outside the classroom faculty could not make its will prevail. A men's college, such as Hamilton, which tried to enforce regulations, faced student uprisings serious enough to threaten its very existence.[56]

Mount Holyoke's building would have inhibited the growth of an autonomous student life had its inmates ever imagined such a possibility. The single structure, designed like a house with central entrance and stairwell, contained all components for learning, working, and living. It held no places for retreat, no interstices for freedom. The seminary's system of governance confirmed its control, further preventing the development of student independence. The principal reassigned roommates and room locations and, though students could express preference, the seminary placed sober students with the spirited and immature. With the day divided into small segments of time, and each given its task, the schedule left almost no time free for visiting. Rules required students to extinguish their lights at ten in the evening and leave their doors open. The principal lived in the building, the teachers along the corridor. Daily, public self-reporting coupled with chapel talks and two periods of silent devotions broke the distinction between external and internal authority.[57] Mary Lyon was principal; Eunice Caldwell, her assistant; the teachers, former students. Love, as well as position, joined these women, and they formed new bonds with their students. Neither space, time, nor will allowed a separate student culture to emerge in the seminary.

Thus while Amherst men created a lively college life, apart from faculty and president, their sisters at Mount Holyoke submitted to the demanding discipline of the seminary. Letters show considerable discussion about the schedule, rules, and self-reporting system. While an occasional student experienced discomfort in living according to rule—"O I shall be so glad to get home where I can speak above a whisper and not have to move by a line and plummet"—students did not resist outright, and they typically expressed satisfaction in meeting the rigors of the system.[58]

Mary Lyon got the students she sought. To Mount Holyoke came serious,

mature young women. To such students Mary Lyon offered intellectual mastery, inner system, and the hope of faith. She created a total institution that
promised to turn outer structure into inner order, transforming New England
daughters into nineteenth-century individuals. To do this, Mary Lyon drew
on the oldest resource in women's education, the mother-daughter tie, re-creating
within the seminary a new bond between teacher and student. Mount Holyoke
designed its seminary building as a well-governed home, its internal organization allowing the oversight within a strict family and its associations con-
firming the link between mother and teacher. Yet students led a new life. Their
teachers were women transformed, capable of clear thought and self-directed
action toward righteous ends. Students came and submitted because they believed in what Mary Lyon promised. They came to receive "a new direction,"
one "to enlist them permanently in the cause of benevolence."

                                    I I I

Mary Lyon died in 1849. While her death occasioned deep grief, faculty and
students never doubted that Mount Holyoke had a future. Mary Lyon intended
to build a seminary more durable than the life of its principal, and she
succeeded.
    The seminary did not stand still. It changed gradually as growth demanded
building and as new generations of students enrolled. The early years of Mount
Holyoke confirmed the fitness of its larger design. Willing students flocked to
its doors, exceeding 250 by the 1850s. Increasingly they came from far afield.
In 1856–57, in addition to 75 students from Massachusetts, 42 from New
York, and 35 from Connecticut, 13 came from New Jersey, 9 from Pennsylvania, and 5 each from Illinois and Indiana.[59] Principal and faculty raised standards for entrance and requirements for graduation; in 1861, the trustees granted
the privilege, long sought by faculty, of extending the course to four years.
On paper the curriculum resembled that of Amherst, with the exception that
it lacked Greek and some upper-level work in Latin and mathematics. Until
the 1870s, domestic work kept tuition and board low: the trustees did not raise
fees until 1857, and then only to $80; during the Civil War, inflation forced
fees up to $125. Three shared rooms designed for two; roommates took turns
sleeping outside in separate sleeping rooms.[60]
    Mary Lyon had shared the nineteenth century's general concern about the
state of women's health. She believed in exercise and justified domestic work
partly in its terms. She required students to walk a mile a day and introduced
calisthenics. Health posed an additional concern for the seminary, because large
institutions carried the real danger of epidemics. Responding to criticism, the
trustees appointed a woman doctor to care for students, teach physiology, and

Bird's-eye view, between 1889 and 1896; *Mount Holyoke College Library/Archives*

reexamine the regimen of the seminary. The physician introduced the system of gymnastic pioneer Dio Lewis and recommended a proper room for exercise. In 1863, the gymnasium met this newly felt need. Proximity to Amherst, where Edward Hitchcock's son first introduced physical training to American colleges as a basic element of the college course, increased Mount Holyoke's awareness of the importance of exercise.[61]

Despite these changes, continuity characterized Mount Holyoke during the 1850s and 1860s. Bells continued to divide the day into small units, setting aside time for twice-daily regular worship and private devotions. Students submitted to the self-reporting system. Graduates became teachers and principals. As the faculty and student body grew, the trustees added space not through new buildings but by extending the central structure and attaching wings. The gymnasium turned the building into a rectangle surrounding a courtyard. As the structure grew to an unwieldy size, the notion of the house form still dominated its plan. The piazza across the front exterior served as a reminder of Mary Lyon's effort to link the seminary with the symbols of home.[62]

The spirit of Mary Lyon still lived in some daughters of New England. In 1856, Louisa Dickinson, an older student from Amherst, after an absence of ten years from the seminary, returned to Mount Holyoke to complete her course. Her weekly letters to her husband-to-be, John Morton Greene, chronicled her intellectual efforts and her spiritual growth. She described recitations, domestic work, religious meetings, and study. She looked to her teachers for inspiration and approval. She struggled to do well in her studies, "for I know the teachers expect a great deal of me." By spring, when the principal asked her to preside at a dinner table, Louisa Dickinson knew that she met their expectations. The full mark of success came with the invitation to return to the seminary the following year as a teacher. Her life took a different course, however, important in the founding of Smith College. Instead of becoming a teacher, she married Rev. John Greene, when he received a call to Hatfield, Massachusetts, the home of Sophia Smith.[63]

From Mount Holyoke emerged generations of teachers not only for its own work but also for that of evangelical seminaries and colleges. If one looks at Mount Holyoke alumnae between 1838 and 1850 as a whole, 82.5 percent of its graduates taught school, but generally for a period of less than five years. What set them apart from women in their era was that they normally delayed marriage for five years, marrying at median age twenty-six rather than twenty-one. These gross figures obscure the importance of particular biographies, especially those of the 26 percent who taught for ten years or more and those 19 percent who did not marry. The extraordinary influence of Mary Lyon and Mount Holyoke came largely from among this number.[64]

By 1859, sixty Mount Holyoke graduates had entered foreign missionary work. Within the American field, Mount Holyoke spread its own kind of mission. Seminaries relied on Mount Holyoke for advice and for initial staff. Before he established Monticello Seminary in Illinois, Rev. Theron Baldwin called on Mary Lyon. Milo P. Jewett of Alabama's Judson Institute wrote asking for information on the seminary building. Jewett later emerged as the catalytic agent in the founding of Vassar College. "Daughter" seminaries, explicitly modeled after Mount Holyoke, were founded from Norton, Massachusetts, to Benicia, California. Even the new coeducational colleges of the West felt the influence of Zilpah Grant and Mary Lyon, beginning with Oberlin in 1837, where Byfield and Ipswich graduates set up its female department.[65]

To hire a Mount Holyoke graduate guaranteed not only a level of competence but also a commitment to Mary Lyon's seminary system. The women whom Mount Holyoke transformed knew exactly what to do. As they went forth, they promoted self-reporting, evangelicalism, domestic work, intense involvement of female teachers in the lives of students, and a seminary building. As Mount Holyoke graduates replicated the seminary's design, they multiplied the impact of Mary Lyon's effort manyfold.

2

More Lasting Than the Pyramids

V A S S A R

The opening of Vassar College in 1865 signalled a new era for American women. With full consciousness of its innovative leap, this true college boldly offered the full liberal arts curriculum to women. But along with Vassar's courageous breakthrough came fear of its consequences. Out of anxiety, Vassar's shapers turned to the seminary for its system of female protection.

Mount Holyoke took the name "seminary" to emphasize that it prepared teachers.[1] The seminary offered the standard English curriculum of the academy, an educational form that extended beyond the boundaries of secondary training but did not presume to cover the college's classical course of study. In the decades that followed Mount Holyoke's founding, the liberal arts college found new definitions among men. On the one hand, older institutions, such as Yale, extended classical training, formerly designed for the learned professions, to young men preparing for business or public affairs. They justified the traditional curriculum as the proper arrangement of the best furniture of the mind. On the other hand, the practical arts and the more worldly curriculum of the academy shaped newer institutions such as Union College in Schenectady, New York. Debate ensued between the partisans of the classical and the modern courses of study. By the 1850s, modern languages and the natural sciences gained general acceptance as part of the collegiate curriculum. Through the extra-curriculum of college literary societies, undergraduates made the study of literature and debate a meaningful part of the unofficial course of study.[2]

Though educational leaders increasingly agreed about what constituted the college curriculum, many schools had assumed the name "college" quite indiscriminately. Verbal inflation characterized the nineteenth century as well as the twentieth, and all sorts of schools claimed to be colleges or universities. In 1844, for example, the girls at Rev. Solomon Howard's school in Delaware,

Ohio, were told not to come. The fifteen boys became the first students of Ohio Wesleyan University.³ Some of these new schools calling themselves colleges were for women. Georgia Female College in Macon received a charter in 1836, but nothing justified the use of its appellation. Nine years after the founding of Ohio Wesleyan, women students got their Female College, housed appropriately enough in a large seminary building, Monnett Hall.⁴ By 1860, over fifty schools for women in the South called themselves colleges.⁵ A female institution with a more legitimate title is Elmira College, founded in 1855 in Elmira, New York. Its creators copied the design of Mount Holyoke so closely and had such modest resources, however, that the claim is tenuous.⁶

Vassar was something else. Here the aspiration existed from the beginning "to build and endow a College for young women which shall be to them, what Yale and Harvard are to young men."⁷ In taking the bold step of creating the first college for women, the shapers of Vassar experienced deep anxiety. Critics charged that the higher education "unsexed" women, turning them away from their feminine aspirations and graces to masculine hopes and demeanor. In addition, those entrusted with the care of young women had the responsibility of protecting them from inappropriate suitors. How could the college organize its inner life to preserve the femininity and purity of its students? How might the college guard their health, threatened by the demands of study? These basic questions shaped the original provisions at Vassar for communal life, the choice of the college's location, and the shape of its main building. In answering them, Vassar's founders drew on the building tradition of the female seminary and its plans of governance. Quite unanticipatedly, by reproducing the forms of Mount Holyoke, Vassar inherited much of its transforming spirit.

Vassar College's beginnings sprang not from the educational impulses of the day but from a self-made man's wish to insure his immortality in a great building. When Matthew Vassar was on the Grand Tour in 1845, he saw the Guy's Hospital in London, given by a distant cousin.⁸ Here was the way to be remembered by posterity! The Guy's Hospital was a solid, handsome Georgian building: three stories of London brick flanked a central portico of stone. In a prominent spot stood a monumental statue of Thomas Guy, the London bookseller who, "Warm with Philanthropy" and no heirs, in 1721 gave the hospital to his city.⁹ The sight inspired Matthew Vassar, and he paid $300 in gold for plans and sketches of the building and took them back to Poughkeepsie.

Born in England in 1792, Vassar had come with his parents as a child to the town along the Hudson River. His father's failures as an ale-maker were made good in the son's life. Matthew Vassar became Poughkeepsie's leading citizen, a part of every venture for improvement and growth of a village struggling to be a city. Civic and personal prosperity went hand in hand, and Vassar's brewery grew to considerable dimensions, as did his fortune.¹⁰

Vassar spent his later years working to enjoy his wealth, a task he took very seriously. Andrew Jackson Downing created a country estate for him in the manner of the English gentry.[11] Thomas Guy's example gave Vassar a larger purpose, and he began consulting with others on his plan for a hospital. He had already donated a sizeable sum to build the Baptist church where he attended services. There in 1855 he met a new friend, Milo P. Jewett, who surprised him with blunt words. Vassar might as well throw his money "into the Hudson River" as use it for a hospital; a hospital belonged in a great city, not a provincial town. The would-be benefactor asked for an alternative. The newcomer was prepared: while many female colleges existed in name, there was not "an *endowed* College for young women in the world." Vassar should establish the first "real college for girls" to "be to them, what Yale and Harvard are to young men."[12]

Unlike Vassar, Jewett had a clear purpose for an endowment, but no resources. A Vermonter, he had attended Dartmouth College and Andover Theological Seminary and was one of the band of four faculty sent out in 1833 to the newly founded Marietta College in Ohio. Licensed as a Presbyterian minister, in 1838 he "yielded all" and became a Baptist.[13] Resigning from Marietta, he went south, where he learned of Baptist efforts to found schools. In 1839, he opened a "School for young ladies" in Marion, Alabama, which took the name The Judson Female Institute when the Baptist Convention became its official sponsor.[14] Though physically removed from South Hadley, the links between The Judson and Mary Lyon's Mount Holyoke were strong. The Baptists named the school for Rebeccca Hasseltine Judson, the missionary sister of Joseph Emerson's wife at Byfield, where Lyon had studied. Jewett knew at least three former students of Lyon. In December 1838, he wrote to her asking for a drawing, with specifications, of the Mount Holyoke building to aid him in planning "on an extensive scale" schoolroom accommodations for 100 and boarding for 50.[15] Erected in 1841, The Judson's seminary structure was 150 feet long; with a main building of four stories, extending back 100 feet, and two wings of three stories. With its dominant columned central pavilion and two projecting wings, it was an imposing edifice.[16] The seminary prospered under Jewett's direction. Despite the influence of Mount Holyoke, the curriculum included ornamental subjects, such as embroidery and waxwork, as well as the more substantial English literature. The rules were strict, and the students wore uniforms. By 1852, the student body grew to 190; and the Baptist Convention valued The Judson's property at $30,000.[17] Once again, Jewett's views made it impossible for him to remain where he was. This time his anti-slavery sentiments forced him north, and, in 1855, he bought a small school for girls in Poughkeepsie, formerly kept by Vassar's niece, Lydia Booth.

Jewett's novel idea intrigued Vassar from the outset. Though it took patient urging and long letters to get Vassar to put all his wealth into a single benefaction during his own lifetime and turn it over to a board of trustees, there was no real turning back after 1856. Why did a women's college appeal to this uneducated, practical man with no particular interest in women and little respect for colleges? He himself gave no real answer when the early feminist Angelina Grimké Weld inquired about the source of his interest, only replying, "I am no monomaniac nor enthusiast who by dwelling long on a *single idea* have arrived at certain results."[18] Vassar was the kind of self-made American that Henry James understood so well: shrewd and calculating on the one hand, yet naive and romantic on the other. As the future president of his college later described him, Vassar had a heart "as large as an elephant's and as tender as a babe's."[19] The novelty of the idea impressed him—here was a chance to do something no one else had ever done. All the reservations and constraints college men might throw up about women's inability to sustain a college course were absent from his mind. In his later correspondence he used the phrase "Young America." The words are telling. A product of the early nineteenth century, Vassar was imbued with the optimism of a confident age.[20] Finally, a women's college gave Vassar the excuse for a grand building. Jewett promised him that a women's college was a monument "more lasting than the Pyramids."[21] Vassar knew that it was to be as fine a structure as the Guy's Hospital.

Soon after their first conversation, and long before Vassar firmly committed himself to a women's college, Jewett got in touch with Thomas A. Tefft, a Providence, Rhode Island, architect. Some years earlier Tefft had been recommended to Jewett as "the best School architect in the United States," and Jewett had secured his designs for the Richmond Female Institute in Virginia.[22] Tefft made preliminary drawings for Vassar and sailed for Europe to observe models at first hand. There he died in 1859. Vassar and Jewett turned to a more noted practitioner, James Renwick, Jr., the New Yorker famed for his Gothic St. Patrick's Cathedral and his picturesque Norman Smithsonian Institution. Educated at Columbia College where his father was a noted professor, but self-trained as an architect, Renwick received important commissions to design churches, hotels, commercial buildings, and houses during the decades surrounding the Civil War. Perhaps the most significant precedents for Vassar are his hospitals and asylums on Blackwells, Wards, and Randalls islands in New York.[23]

In 1858, Renwick designed Charity Hospital, the first of five such commissions for the Board of Almshouses and Charities in New York. The building incorporated the basic elements of asylum planning, drawing on the medieval tradition of the hospital as modified by an enlightened age. Designed to be places of perfect order, the asylum expressed hierarchical relationships to the outside. At its center, behind the portico and under the cupola, the superintendent lived and worked and the staff carried on its primary duties. Projecting wings housed inmates in long, straight factory-like barracks.[24] Jewett's Judson

Institute had just such a building. When Renwick designed Charity Hospital he gave it the basic plan of the asylum, embellishing its exterior with the decorative motifs of French Second Empire style, just coming into vogue. Its steeply pitched roof and dormers and its grand entry staircase gave palatial touches, quite in contrast with the lives of its humble inmates.[25]

Renwick was a fashionable architect, and Charity Hospital proved his experience with large buildings to house inmates and staff. To a philanthropist seeking a monument comparable to the Guy's Hospital, Renwick was an obvious choice. No design necessity, however, governed Renwick's form for Vassar College. In his other commissions, Renwick linked the style of the structure to the building's purpose. If he made churches Gothic, why did he not make Vassar look collegiate? In addition to the brick buildings, generally Georgian, carefully placed in open-ended quadrangles or in rows at older colleges, such as Harvard and Yale, Renwick would have known of two nineteenth-century men's colleges shaped by master architects. In Schenectady, New York, Joseph Jacques Ramée had created for Union College, in 1813, "the first realized campus plan in the United States," an elegant neo-classical form that circled a pantheon with buildings linked by a colonnade. In 1825, Thomas Jefferson had planned an "academical village" for the University of Virginia. In this handsome composition, a great rotunda capped two parallel lines of classroom pavilions, linked by a colonnade.[26] In his scheme for Vassar, Renwick looked to no men's college for precedents. Rather he returned to his plan for Charity Hospital and confirmed the association, reaching back to Mount Holyoke, of women's higher education with the asylum.[27]

While Mary Lyon wanted her seminary to change the consciousness of the young women under her charge, Vassar and Jewett returned to the forms she created because they promised safety. While daring to offer the full liberal arts curriculum to women, the two pioneers feared its potential consequences. They looked to the seminary tradition with its connection to the asylum as a means to protect the virtue of the first female collegians. A structural form that once suggested hope became at Vassar a structure representing fear.

The first practical task was the choice of location. Like planners of asylums and of colleges for men, Jewett did not want Vassar's monument to be in a city, with its immoral influences. As well as rural simplicity, a country site offered grounds for physical education: "spacious play grounds, extensive walks, facilities for appropriate outdoor labor, as gardening, and the cultivation of flowers and fruits: Gymnastics in the open air." Yet something else was at work. Jewett urged a country site, as it allowed both "the grand" and "the picturesque." Vassar was familiar with the picturesque, for its principles governed Sunnyside, his country estate, designed by Downing. Jewett perceived the picturesque as linked with nature: in his mind was that contrast between city and country that lay behind the early development of the suburb. In this dichotomy, pure women and virtuous families lived in the country. The city street was the place of commerce, hectic pace, and loose women; the country protected feminine chastity. Jewett urged a site that was accessible, but secluded. If the college building were "placed directly on some great thoroughfare, it seems to challenge the impertinent stare of the curious vulgar and invite a familiarity at variance with the character of woman." The ideal location was "a little retired from busy marts of commerce, from the hurrying multitudes, the rush and the roar of travel." Separate from the city, "embosomed in Sylvan Bowers, protected by shady Avenues, the site would be in harmony with the modesty and delicacy which are always associated with the gentler sex." [28]

Jewett's arguments prevailed. Vassar chose a picturesque site, the grounds of a former race course two miles from Poughkeepsie. The "grand" then followed. Vassar wanted two things of his building: that it be magnificent and that it be healthful. For the latter he required a twelve-foot corridor along the front side of the building as a well-lit place for exercise in inclement weather. [29] Jewett had many ideas coming out of his earlier experiences, which he reinforced by trips to seminaries (including Mount Holyoke), hospitals, and asylums to study their arrangements. [30] According to his own account, he furnished "all the plans for the interior . . . form, dimensions and fitting up." [31] He determined the orientation of the building as well. Rejecting an aesthetically governed placement, Jewett insisted that the four corners of the building match the four points of the compass to provide students with a lesson in practical geography. [32]

Renwick designed the building in 1860 and 1861, before the first trustees assembled. Matthew Vassar always insisted that he meant to provide only the externals, the "materialities," and that he intended the board and the president to create and govern the internals, the organization of the college, its system of governance, its curriculum, and its faculty. [33] Whatever Vassar's expectations, the building he caused to be erected did presume an inner system.

In his effort to create a true college for women, Jewett emphasized the difference between his plan and that of the seminary. While such institutions as Mount Holyoke offered a solid English curriculum, they had neither the equipment nor the faculty to offer true college work. Vassar was creating the first real college with "necessary buildings, libraries, Cabinets, Apparatus &c" and he intended to gather "a full faculty of Instructors men of learning, ability, and reputation." [34] It was basic to Jewett's design that the professors be men. In addition, Jewett presumed from the beginning that he was to be president of the college.

Vassar himself assumed that college officers ruled assistants and students. He combined the seemingly contradictory traits of the American manufacturer. Open to new possibilities, direct, even bluff in speech and manner, capable of enthusiasm and warmth, Vassar also presumed to govern. This did

Vassar College, ca. 1865; *Vassar College Library*

not mean that he dominated Vassar College, for he respected his board and president as peers, not subordinates. But Vassar assumed that governing officers ruled students, as owners ruled foremen and workers. With its clear hierarchical order, Renwick's building expressed Vassar's authoritarian side most clearly.

Renwick's design for Vassar College encased Vassar's and Jewett's requirements in a grand form. On his 1845 tour Vassar had admired the Tuileries as well as the Guy's Hospital. He brought home a view of the French palace, on which he later penciled "Similar to Vassar College."[35] Drawing on the Tuileries, Renwick designed for Vassar an ornate version of his Charity Hospital. A dominant four-story central pavilion with a dome atop its mansard roof was connected to two matching end pavilions by long three-story wings. The three-part central pavilion housed the center of power and the most important activities of the college. The entrance vestibule looked imposing. A great double stairway adorned with squared columns dominated an area 12 feet by 30 feet, opening on to the corridor at both ends. Double parlors, separated by sliding doors, flanked both sides. On important occasions, the doors opened, creating a great space 100 feet long. The president had a complete house on three floors in the south portion. His office was across the corridor on the second floor.[36]

The dining room and chapel, the two other great communal spaces, lay behind the central pavilion in a projection to the rear. On the principal floor, the dining room, 94 feet by 45 feet, was undecorated except for supporting columns. Directly above, the chapel rose for two stories. Capable of seating six hundred in benches, it served as an auditorium for all the college's ceremonies, secular and religious. A large copy of a Raphael Madonna adorned the back of the semicircular recess which served as pulpit and stage. The painting hid the organ from view. The music rooms of the college occupied the areas that lay behind the organ.[37] Opposite the upper floor of the chapel was the art gallery, a grand room, 96 feet by 30 feet. Lit by the great dome rising 40 feet from the floor, by skylights, and by the large windows along the college front, the art gallery was the most handsome room in the college and its collection a source of pride. Vassar purchased the art works from Elias L. Magoon, a Baptist minister and trustee from Albany, to raise the teaching of art to collegiate status.[38] Vassar's creators built into the design of its building serious attention to both music and art, elevating traditional seminary accomplishments to college grade.

Equally prominent were the cabinets of science and rooms filled with scientific apparatus. The medical lecture room, filled with instructional devices, adjoined the parlors on the principal floor. The Cabinet of Natural History was immediately above it, while the Cabinets of Geology and Mineralogy and the Cabinet of Lithography, with their systematic teaching collections, took the attic floor.[39] The college built a separate observatory to the north of the Main building, a small, rather elegant dwelling capped by a working dome. Vassar gave ample space to the study of the natural sciences.

The central pavilion held the recitation rooms, clustered on the principal floor. A modest room, 30 feet by 35 feet, contained the library. No one intended it as a place for reading and research.[40]

The exterior of this central pavilion—housing the academic, communal, and ceremonial activities of the college as well as its president and Lady Principal—was ornate. A massive double-turning staircase leading to the second and principal floor signalled the importance of the center of the college, as did the high windows and paired brick pilasters and the dome with its ornate curved French-type windows.[41] Pavilions at each end balanced the center. Four stories tall, these masses did not look quite as grand as the center, but were nonetheless imposing. Had economic difficulties not forced cutbacks, the end pavilions would have had impressive entrance stairways. Within each pavilion

Calisthenium; *Vassar College Library*

lived four male professors and their families in separate apartments. The wings
which connected center and ends were as plain as any factory, with the exception of their mansard roofs. Behind the western front lay the great exercise
corridor. Its other side held the rooms of students and women teachers. In
addition to the corridor, provision for health included a riding stable and gymnasium housed in the Calisthenium, a charming red brick building to the south,
erected during the first year. Beyond the observatory lay the Circle, where
students cultivated flowers and took their strolls out-of-doors.

In the months following the organization of the board of trustees, while
Renwick sketched out the design, Vassar sorted out the elements of his scheme.
Jewett taught him much. In a most revealing letter, Vassar discussed his objections to a trustee's plan to include day students. Vassar disliked the proposal.
College was like an army, where "furloughs & passes are never granted without *absolute necessity*." He explained his reasoning in words that Mary Lyon
would have understood, "What I regard as an essential element of our Institution is the perfect *Control* of the pupils during the period of their instruction
in the College." Like Jewett at Judson, Vassar wanted to "even go further and
insist upon a *Uniform* Costume for all the young ladies to be furnished by

VASSAR 37

the College."[42] Vassar had clearly imbibed the main features of the seminary system, with, however, one critical exception.

Jewett's insistence that Vassar College's professors be men negated a key feature of the seminary's system of control: the close relationship between female teachers and students. Criticism of this came from an unanticipated direction. As a good businessman, Vassar quickly sought to advertise his product, and he found a willing mouthpiece in *Godey's Lady's Book*. Two Vassar trustees were close associates of the magazine's editor, Sarah Hale: James Harper published her books; and historian Benson Lossing, whose works were also published by Harper, was a close friend. *Godey's* first notice about Vassar appeared in 1861, and in the following years the magazine regularly reported on the college's progress.[43] The attention of such "Literati" flattered Matthew Vassar, and the publicity pleased him.[44] Thus the hard-hitting article in *Godey's*, written in 1864 by Horatio Hale, the editor's son, shook Vassar. It challenged the all-male faculty. The "one defect" in Vassar College's organization was that "not only the President, but all the Professors are to be men. The only women for whom offices are proposed are some 'assistant teachers!'" This was wrong. Though appropriate that the president who handled the external and business affairs of the college be a man, "there should also be a *Lady* Superintendent, who should have the more immediate control of the pupils," and women should normally compose the faculty. The proper organization of a college mirrored the organization of the home. A mother was a rightful teacher of her daughter; if she relinquished her position it should be to a woman. "It is peculiarly proper that woman should be the teacher and guardian of her own sex. The different qualities of mind and character in the two sexes render this imperative."[45]

Sarah Hale never liked Mount Holyoke and was not really urging that Vassar imitate it. She had a more worldly vision, and one that fostered a sharp separation between women's and men's spheres. When Vassar wrote to Hale about his plan for student uniforms, perhaps along the line of a modified "Bloomer Dress," the editor was horrified: "Children are not taught to walk well by keeping them in leading strings. . . . Is not the training in your institution intended to prepare the young ladies for their duties in the world?"[46] Evidently Hale was unaware that a faculty of women did not always lead its students into the true womanhood that she envisioned for them.

Horatio Hale's article immediately convinced Matthew Vassar of the need for women faculty, and he had copies printed. It was a critical moment for the nascent college: the workmen had almost completed the building, and the board was ready to deliberate and decide on plans for organization and curriculum, expecting the college to open in the fall of 1864. Conflicts raged as various men close to Vassar struggled to dominate. Milo Jewett snapped under the pressure and wrote a letter to certain trustees insulting Matthew Vassar, which, when shown to Vassar, forced Jewett's resignation.[47] At such a time, strong words from *Godey's Lady's Book* had their effect. From this point onward, Matthew Vassar supported quite firmly the appointment of women, using language that rang of feminism. "Let us prove the certainty of woman's higher possible future by the best examples from the present. Let us recognize and honor her existing talent ourselves first."[48] Professorships for women gave them a chance to use their knowledge in a practical way: "for it is vain to educate woman's powers of thought, and then limit their operation. Give her a present confidence, and not push her back again upon a future hope."[49] Matthew Vassar enthusiastically hailed the appointment of Maria Mitchell as professor of astronomy.

Along with its advocacy of female faculty, *Godey's* commended Vassar College for its intention to offer its students a home. In 1864, the magazine praised Vassar's plan to house all its students "under the college roof. It is plain that the independence which young men may, in college life, enjoy without injury, would be pernicious to young girls. Boldness and daring, desirable in the one sex, are not becoming in the other. *The home life* is an essential element in woman's education. . . . Therefore, the plan of making this collegiate institution a pleasant HOME, for all who are educated under its privileges, was wise and beneficent."[50] The trustees turned to one of their number, John H. Raymond, the head of the Collegiate and Polytechnic Institute in Brooklyn, to serve as president in Jewett's stead. A close friend of the leading minister to the Gilded Age, Henry Ward Beecher, who immediately became a trustee, Raymond shared Sarah Hale's cast of mind.[51] While women were full partners with men in matters of culture and the arts and letters were their appropriate domain, their sphere of activity centered around the home and the care of children. The education of men and women was to be common, but their paths separate. The college was a family: the president, like the father, had final authority and faced outward to handle the business affairs; a college mother governed the daily life of her pupils, regulating their conduct, shaping their habits, and guiding their religious life. *Godey's* put it this way: the president was like a widower with a house of girls. He needed a governess to take charge of "the inner sanctuary of woman's nature, the heart and the conscience, as well as the outward semblance of manner and costume."[52] Vassar thus received from Sarah Hale and her son a mixed message about why women should hold responsible positions within the college, one potentially feminist, the other maternal. The tension this posed about the meaning of higher education to women remained central to Vassar College, surfacing again in the early twentieth century.

President Raymond's first and most difficult task was to choose a Lady Principal. In Hannah Lyman he found her quickly. Their correspondence in the following months is a fascinating record of their "wooing," as step by cautious step each revealed personal tastes and concerns.[53] Born in Northampton, Massachusetts, Lyman attended Ipswich Academy, where she began her teaching under Zilpah Grant. Over thirty eventful years had passed since Lyman had left Ipswich. But time and distance were nothing to her. Even though the new institution was a college, not a seminary, and Matthew Vassar founded it not in stony New England but in the lush country of the Hudson River, at Vassar College, in 1865, Hannah Lyman re-created the seminary system of the pioneers in whole cloth. Bells marking a day scheduled from 6 a.m. rising to 10 p.m. retiring, two periods of silent devotions each day, rules governing details of deportment, corridor teachers monitoring their charges, weekly self-reporting, and chapel talks all came to Vassar with Hannah Lyman.[54]

Her mentor Zilpah Grant had differed from Mary Lyon on several matters, and Vassar reflected that difference. She had disapproved of Mount Holyoke's requirement of domestic work; Vassar never introduced it. She had believed in a more ladylike standard of dress and deportment; at Vassar, rules regarding etiquette and dress were as important as those establishing religious practices. Lyman ordained that students change their dresses for dinner, and she personally measured hem lengths before important occasions. While Jewett intended that each student have a single room, Zilpah Grant's disapproval of this luxury many years before fit the actual practice of four-fifths of Vassar's students forced by lack of space to share a bedroom. The very small space of each bedroom meant that these students shared a bed as well.[55]

Neither Grant nor Lyman would have arranged student rooms as did Jewett and Renwick. Public controversy about the building centered on the failure to provide closets in student rooms.[56] Renwick's oversight here is revealing, for it suggests he unthinkingly repeated his hospital plans, equating college women with unwilling inmates. The lack of closets was remedied more easily than the building's most serious fault. Matthew Vassar required the extra-wide exercise corridor. Renwick placed this behind the western exposure. This had the advantage of providing extra privacy, as no bedroom window opened on the front of the building. Students lived in suites of three bedrooms and one parlor. From the corridor one entered a hallway that led to a student parlor. Around each student parlor were grouped three student bedrooms which housed five students.[57] Thus two bedrooms had no outer exposure to give light and fresh air. While students found this hardly conducive to health, the Lady Principal and her monitoring teachers also found that the arrangement went against their ability to maintain control. The suite arrangement, with rooms opening on to each other but not to the corridor, meant that students had places of privacy and retreat protected from the oversight of monitors. This had a critical impact on the student life that was to come.

Raymond secured his faculty. Before his appointment, the college had hired two professors: Maria Mitchell, the famed woman astronomer, and Charles Farrar, Elmira College's professor of natural science. Despite Matthew Vassar's desire to appoint women, the strong opposition of many of the trustees meant that the college largely adopted Jewett's plan, so sharply criticized by *Godey's*, of hiring men for the professorships.[58] With the exception of Mitchell, all important professorial positions went to men. Men got the apartments in the pavilions. Mitchell lived separate from the faculty through her own wish to share the observatory house with her astronomer father.[59] Interior planning may have governed the gender of faculty positions, for while Matthew Vassar did not share the common assumption that all women professors were single,[60] in fact, the men did come with families and the women—with the exception of Mitchell—without. And excluding Mitchell, Lyman, and the resident woman physician, the women were of a lower rank. They constituted the corps of teachers who lived in the end rooms of the student corridors. They were subordinate to the professors for their academic work and to the Lady Principal for their oversight of students' lives. Each woman teacher headed a table at mealtime and monitored her charges closely. She checked rooms, maintained quiet hours, and even regulated baths, which were to be no more nor less than two each week. The seminary system of discipline and control extended to the women teachers. Generally young women, they felt obliged to get permission each time they wished to leave the building.[61] While Sarah Hale may have failed to get many examples of highly educated women to inspire her sex, she certainly did get the governesses to take charge of "the inner sanctuary of woman's nature."

The seminary system was tried and tested in 1865; what was genuinely new was Vassar's explicit commitment to the college course of study. It was for the latter that 353 women, between the ages of fifteen and twenty-four, flocked to the doors in September 1865.[62] The first few weeks were confusing ones, for the students came with wrong information. *Godey's* had published the initial course of study devised by Milo Jewett. Based on the "university system" of Southern colleges, this plan set up nine schools within the college: a student passed from one to the next, satisfying its requirements; when she collected certificates from five, she received the B.A. degree.[63] When Jewett resigned, the "university system" went with him. Raymond's polytechnic years had been preceded by teaching at Hamilton College and the University of Rochester. In his mind a women's college had enough difficulty to face without making it "an *omnium gatherum* of all ages, studying on all plans." Instead he intended to "make an honest effort at organizing a liberal education for women."[64] The curriculum Raymond devised was a thoroughly conventional one for an American college in 1865, unusual only in its emphasis on the fine arts and the natural sciences—and that Vassar College offered it to women.

In the next year Raymond learned that it proved to be a difficult task to convince "*female* Young America" with "a will of her own" to subject herself to such a course of study.[65] Because female seminaries did not offer adequate preparation, the new college was forced to do the work of the secondary school. Raymond classified two-thirds of the first group of students as irregular and created a preparatory department to get them ready for college work.[66]

On September 26, 1865, all was in place. Vassar College's first students arrived to begin the great experiment. The opening days went well. Raymond wrote to his wife: "It seems like a dream, the sudden transmutation of this great lumbering pile of brick and mortar, which hung on my spirit like mountainous millstone, into a palace of light and life." He went outside in the evening for the first time. The gaslights were "ablaze," many blinds and windows open, "and everywhere fair young forms were moving around, and merry voices were heard in conversation and song."[67]

The seduction of the September evening notwithstanding, Vassar College's beginning was jerky and uneven. The example of Matthew Vassar's distant English cousin applied to American education had a basic flaw: endowing a building was not endowing a college. When first asked to assume the presidency, Raymond wrote to Matthew Vassar that he had put too much into "mere material provisions, compelling us to begin the ungracious work of retrenchment and enforced economy just as we reach the vital part—the men and women." Raymond saw that this displacing of resources required that he "pinch and starve the College at its heart."[68] Vassar's later generosity eased the situation somewhat, but the college suffered in its first years from its grandiose beginnings. To fill the building, Raymond had to lower the standard of admission and curriculum well below the desired college grade.

And the building itself, handsome as it was, posed its own problems. Grand enough to satisfy Matthew Vassar's desire for immortality, it took the form of a Charity Hospital and the façade of a French palace. To this had been fitted a college curriculum and a scheme of seminary governance. The result was a bad fit. Raymond once compared Vassar College to a turtle. In responding to the president of the University of Rochester, who had asked for the plans of Vassar College's building, Raymond advised against copying the structure and strongly urged Rochester not to erect a permanent building before "the internal organization had been matured." He summarized his experience at Vassar College: "The shell should be *grown by*, that it may be *fitted to*, the animal. It is an awkward thing, as I have learned by much & trying experience, to fit a live & vigorous animal to a shell manufactured to order, in advance."[69]

3

That Beauty Which Is Truth

In 1875, on a country estate outside Boston, Wellesley College received its first students. Ignorant of Vassar College's problems, Wellesley's founder brought its great building to New England. But if Henry Fowle Durant borrowed the shell of Vassar, he wanted to fill it with the soul of Mount Holyoke. He tried to create another Mount Holyoke not out of fear but out of admiration.

Henry Fowle Durant needed no Milo Jewett to tell him about Mount Holyoke. He had travelled there many times, welcomed into its parlors and hall as a lay preacher. Mount Holyoke Seminary proudly appointed this prominent man of wealth as a trustee. Durant knew at first hand the wonderful work of the seminary in educating Christian women as teachers and missionaries. "There is no danger of having too many Mount Holyokes," he was heard to say.[1] He decided to put a Mount Holyoke on his estate in Wellesley, Massachusetts. Only, he wanted to do what Mary Lyon, with her plain style and limited means, could not and would not: he meant to make his female seminary the most beautiful the world had ever seen.

Durant had always loved beautiful things. As a young man at Harvard, fellow students knew him more for his "refined and luxurious tastes" than for his studious nature.[2] A college classmate remembered him as "handsome, well-dressed, quiet and good natured. There was an impression that he was dissipated."[3] Born Henry Welles Smith, in 1822, in Hanover, New Hampshire, he moved with his family while a child to Lowell, Massachusetts. His parents were liberal Christians, and he prepared for Harvard at the private school that Samuel Ripley, the Unitarian minister of Waltham, and his wife kept in their home. Once settled in Boston as a lawyer, the need to distinguish himself from the other eleven Smiths practicing law caused him to substitute two names from his mother's socially prominent family for Welles Smith. As Henry Fowle

Durant he began a brilliant and successful career as a trial lawyer. He married his first cousin on his mother's side and bought a house in Boston and a country estate that bordered on a distant cousin's property in West Needham. Handsome and with a dashing style, Durant seemed poised to enter Boston's elite. Yet it was not to be. In some ways he was too effective: there was something unseemly in the way he gained power over juries, and, though never proved, a hint of scandal sullied his name.[4] A client later recalled how praise of his talents was "accompanied by slurs at his mode of practice," serious enough to raise the threat of his being disbarred.[5] And then, in 1863, when his young son died, an event happened which cast him forever outside Boston's Unitarian Pale: he became converted to evangelical Christianity.[6]

Seized with fervor, Durant reexamined his life to find that the law was incompatible with the Gospel. "He seemed to forsake it as if it were a sin," a contemporary recalled.[7] Durant's growing business affairs suffered under no such opprobrium, and he and his wife left Boston for New York, where he engaged in war production for the Union army. He turned his skill as an advocate to new ends and held religious meetings, where he argued for Christ. Beginning in 1865, his zeal took him to South Hadley, and the seminary received him warmly. He stayed for several days at a time at Mount Holyoke and acted as a preacher. He conducted morning devotions and the weekly prayer meeting and occupied the pulpit on Sundays.[8] Following the well-worn tradition of the seminary, he met separately with the unconverted. "Nearly all of these seemed touched and expressed a desire to become Christians," Mount Holyoke's letter to its missionaries related.[9]

As Durant forswore the conflict of the court to work for the Lord, he increasingly entered the realm of women. As early as the eighteenth century, secularizing forces had begun to reshape the consciousness of men, and fewer of them experienced the fire of religious conversion. Church membership started the long process of feminization. In the nineteenth century, the influence of women in the churches grew as ministerial power lost the support of the state, and ministers became dependent upon their increasingly female congregations. In holding revivals at Mount Holyoke, Durant struck that alliance with women that ordained ministers were making in their churches. In the seminary's female faculty and students he found a responsive audience which satisfied his vanity and the desire for approbation he had once looked for in the world. Yet, in allying with women, Durant did not take the smooth route. While the New England clergy shifted its sermons to glorify the domestic realm, turning theology into sentimentality, Durant sought to overturn conventional notions of womanhood. He shared his age's assumption about women's greater purity, but he stood inalterably opposed to female frailty and dependency.[10]

Durant committed himself to Christian education for women. As had Mary

Lyon, he envisioned the woman teacher as the agent of national reformation. He once asked, "What would Massachusetts be if our 9,000 women teachers were all of them Christians?"[11] Yet Durant's ideas differed from Lyon's in significant ways. A new awareness of women's position emerged in the decades that separated the two founders, as well as a new form of subordination. Wellesley's founder understood both developments. He claimed that "the real meaning of the Higher Education of Women" was "revolt." "We revolt against the slavery in which women are held by the customs of society—the broken health, the aimless lives, the subordinate position, the helpless dependence, the dishonesties and shams of so-called education. The Higher Education of Women . . . is the cry of the oppressed slave. It is the assertion of absolute equality. . . . it is the war of Christ . . . against spiritual wickedness in high places." An outsider never accepted in elite Boston circles, Durant condemned society's denigration of women, and declared his "outspoken opposition to the customs and the prejudices of the public."[12] He attacked its notion of feminine beauty, which was "pretty . . . a confused compound of vanity and sentimentality and shams . . . the old loathsome ideal of the gushing story paper and silly novel, with the baby face and the small waist and the small brain and the small sentimentalities." Instead he admired the "noble, beautiful form, healthful, vigorous, graceful."[13] The goal of higher education was the "unfolding of every power and faculty"—reason, imagination, emotion, and religion—to create "the crowned queen of the world by right of that knowledge which is power, and that beauty which is truth."[14]

Durant became a trustee of Mount Holyoke in 1867, and material blessings began to flow. His wife, Pauline Durant, joined him as a full partner in giving to the seminary. They sent a supply of oranges for the supper table and books for the library. In 1868, Pauline Durant gave $10,000 to Mount Holyoke for books, on the condition that a suitable building be erected.[15] A significant appropriation by the state legislature made this possible and the Durants engaged Boston illustrator and architect Hammatt Billings to design the library building. At his hands emerged an elegant small structure, slightly to the north of the seminary building, linked to it by a covered corridor. Durant served as an active member of the building committee.

Durant's success as a preacher within the seminary and his enthusiasm for the work there quickly shaped his resolve. In 1867, he made up his will, "consecrating" his country place "to the service of the Lord Jesus Christ, by erecting a seminary on the plan (modified by circumstances) of South Hadley." With the loss of their only heir, the Durants had originally thought of an orphanage, and in 1867 made provision for it on the same grounds as the seminary.[16] Spurred on by the realization of Mount Holyoke's library, the Durants' enthusiasm grew, and they lost interest in the orphanage. The library was a small jewel. A large hexagonal bay with handsome tall arched windows adorned

Library, Mount Holyoke Seminary; *Mount Holyoke College Library/Archives*

its basic rectangular form. Details, such as stone stringcourses and arches, den-
tils at the cornice, and wrought-iron railing at the ridge, conveyed restrained
elegance. Within the single large room with its high ceiling and well-lit alcoves, carved black walnut bookcases gave warmth to the classical detail. What
a contrast the library posed to the hard, painted surfaces of Seminary Hall.

Durant had found his calling. In 1870, he petitioned the legislature for a
charter for Wellesley Female Seminary and called together a board of trustees.
Durant chose five of his original eight trustees from the Mount Holyoke board.[17]
While Wellesley was never a proprietary school in the manner of Hollins Seminary and, later, College, whose president, faculty, and staff belonged to the
Cocke family, Pauline and Henry Fowle Durant totally dominated the Wellesley board during the latter's lifetime.[18] By putting his wife on the board, however, Durant made a unique provision which was an important omen for
Wellesley's future: he appointed women, as well as men, as trustees. Within a
few years, other women joined the original female member. Some came as
wives of members, but one held the position alone.[19] In contrast, Mount Holyoke
did not add women to its board until 1884, when it yielded to organized alum-

nae pressure.[20] Though agitation for alumnae representatives began at Vassar as early as 1871, it took until 1887 for three alumnae to join its board.[21]

Durant found fulfillment in the next four years as the diverse sides of his nature came together in the planning and erection of Wellesley's principal building, College Hall. Durant again chose Hammatt Billings as his architect. What Billings achieved on a small scale at Mount Holyoke, he accomplished on a grander, more elegant scale at Wellesley. Born in 1818, Billings had engaged in architectural practice since he was apprenticed to Asher Benjamin at age seventeen.[22] After assisting Ammi Young, Billings opened up an office with his brother in Boston in the 1840s. While the two designed a considerable number of Boston buildings in a wide range of styles, Hammatt Billings began a more notable career as an illustrator. In the years of Durant's lay preaching, Billings depicted scenes from Tennyson poems. It is intriguing that the scene he selected from *The Princess*, Tennyson's fantasy of a feminist and man-hating women's college, was the one in which a wounded fawn reminded a collegian of her maternal feelings.[23] At Wellesley, Billings tried to create a landscape in which women living without men kept their womanliness. While Billings knew Mount Holyoke well, he did not draw on its domestic plan or symbolism. Rather he shaped a consciously beautiful building set in nature, embellished by Christian motifs.

Through Billings' design, Durant fully indulged his love of beauty and magnificence, now dedicated to the service of his Lord and Savior. As his own contractor, Durant turned his nervous energy and drive for command to useful ends. College legend abounds with Durant's zeal in those days, arriving before workmen, watching their every move, prohibiting them from profanity, and handing out Bibles. Pauline Durant shared in the work, walking miles of stairways to determine the best heights, sitting in countless chairs to find the most comfortable.[24]

In 1873, Durant petitioned the legislature once again, this time to change the name Wellesley Female Seminary to Wellesley College. His sense of his mission was growing. In addition, he was learning much about Vassar College.[25] To Mount Holyoke's basic scheme, Durant added the new elements of Vassar College. One can see this clearly in the design of College Hall.

To fit Matthew Vassar's wish for a personal memorial, Renwick blew up the seminary building to mammoth proportions to house and serve four hundred students and faculty. Wellesley imitated Vassar's scale in a building of roughly the same dimensions and materials. Like Main, College Hall rose four stories high, with five-story towers. Its length of 475 feet was only slightly under its predecessor's 500 feet. Red brick pointed with black mortar and trimmed with stone served both as building material. Gatekeepers' lodges on the two campuses guarded entry to picturesque grounds.[26]

Imitation went beyond scale, materials, and setting. An early sketch by

College Hall; *Wellesley College Archives*

1894 class crew, College Hall in background; *Wellesley College Archives*

Hammatt Billings followed closely Renwick's design for Main.[27] Like his New York contemporary, Billings envisioned a four-story building with central pavilion, end pavilions, and towers. Over the pavilions he put a slightly modified French Second Empire roof. Imagined from the front, Wellesley, as originally projected, looked almost identical with Vassar.

Yet, as the plan developed, Billings made important departures from Renwick to suit the taste and program of his client. Durant in the 1870s had more money than Vassar in the 1860s. The Civil War enriched rather than reduced the resources of Wellesley's founder, and Durant could afford to embellish the scheme, rather than cut back. His country estate lent itself to picturesque possibilities. This West Needham land had no equal among the women's colleges: three hundred acres of varied terrain with hills, woods, and meadows, fronting a magnificent lake. The rise above Lake Waban became the site of College Hall. With the lake to its long south exposure, Billings extended the center and end pavilions to the rear, which greatly increased the living space with sunny views of the lake and meant that the back of the building cast a handsome reflection.

There are reasons more profound than the picturesque temptations of the site that determined Wellesley College's plan. Both Vassar and Durant agreed on certain fundamentals: while the grounds offered space for healthful recreation, students' primary existence took place within a single building where they lived, dined, worked, studied, and prayed. Durant knew Mount Holyoke well and felt nothing but admiration for the seminary's work. In planning his college, Durant assumed Wellesley's building would take seminary form. Yet like Matthew Vassar and Milo Jewett, Durant intended that Wellesley be a college, and thus, as had they, he eschewed the domestic imagery of Mount Holyoke's building with its original organization as a house and its adorning piazza. Wellesley College borrowed its plan from Vassar. The central pavilion housed many of the college's important functions: its president's office, reception room, and classrooms.

Wellesley differed from Vassar in one important respect: Durant believed in Mount Holyoke's tradition of female leadership. He decided to hire only women as teachers and president. With all officers of the college women, there was no need to build a house for the president or apartments for male faculty within the college building. Just as at Mount Holyoke, Wellesley's president had her quarters on the first floor, and the faculty lived along the corridors, taking their board at tables with students. Freed of housekeeping needs, the center and the two transepts of College Hall took on grand tasks: entrance hall, chapel, library, dining hall, and drawing room. A fourth projection to the west, separate from the main building and designed somewhat later, held the service areas of kitchen, domestic workrooms, gymnasium, and servants' quarters.

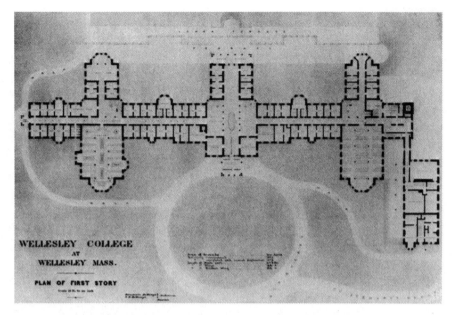

Plan of first story, College Hall; *Wellesley College Archives*

Vassar's Main conveyed a sense of hierarchy in its dominant center, its secondarily important end pavilions, and its subordinate wings. Wellesley contained no such hierarchy. The transepts and wings held equally important weight with the center. The plan of College Hall suggested Durant's Christian purposes, for it took the form of a double Latin cross. In addition, Gothic elements joined the original Second Empire design: atop the mansard roof jutted arches, towers, pinnacles, and finials. A cross adorned the keystone above the entrance, and cross-shaped finials stood atop pinnacles and towers. To 1876 eyes, the addition of these Gothic elements gave to the grand and potentially ponderous building "a certain feminine delicacy." "The combination of such masses in a form so light and airy must be set down as a rare achievement of architectural skill." [28] In the early twentieth century, critic Montgomery Schuyler said the building "scattered," that, lacking a clear focus, it seemed a mélange of discordant elements. [29] Durant wanted it just this way. The Gothic embellishments broke up any sense of hierarchy. Durant wanted every part of College Hall to be an expression of beauty.

When one entered College Hall through the porte-cochère on the north, one stepped into the Centre, a vast open space five stories high, illumined by skylights. Ten granite columns connected by graceful circular arches sur-

The Centre, College Hall; *Wellesley College Archives*

rounded a marble floor that held a basin filled with tall palms. Stairs with large
windows on the south opened to upper floors embellished with handsome
carved balustrades, punctuated with columns. "Standing by one of the polished granite pillars, two rows of which flank the court, and by means of
arches support the ceiling above, one looks up through the great opening to
the very glass-capped roof, story rising above story, column ranging upon
column, balustrade crowning balustrade." [30] Another contemporary witness to
the building in its early years found that the Centre reminded him of "the
cloistered gardens of mediaeval convents . . . the airy courts of southern pal-
aces." [31] Such a reference is provocative in a college for women; yet the Centre's
placement at the main entry, accessible to all visitors, hardly suggests the seclusion of a cloister. Rather the Centre is, in the best fashion of the day, an
intended beauty spot, a conservatory designed as a public space, recalling such
festive settings as the Crystal Palace.

A reception room, the president's office, and the principal recitation rooms
surrounded the Centre. Wide corridors ran from the Centre to the ends of the
building. Arched doorways and wainscoting of ash, benches along the walls,

and paintings and statues broke up the great length and made it interesting. In the east transept, the library and chapel provided elegant settings for study and worship. Designed to hold 120,000 books, the library expanded Billings' design at Mount Holyoke. The two shared an alcove plan, black walnut finish, and large bay windows to let in the sunlight. Yet the scale and rich decoration of Wellesley's library made the seminary's look chaste by comparison. On both sides of central reading tables, ornate capitals adorned the opening of the alcoves, springing to joining arches. A molded ceiling suspending thin, graceful chandeliers topped the whole. The flanking alcoves rose two stories, the second reached by a wrought-iron circular staircase. Great arches framed the windows. Busts and portraits of poets and prose writers crowded the walls. Our 1876 commentator found it "the very ideal of a library for young ladies, with cozy nooks and corners, . . . with sunny windows, some of them thrown out into deep bays; with galleries, reached by winding stairs, where the girls seem to have deep delight in coiling themselves away in such mysterious fashion that you can only see above the balustrade a curly head bending over some book."[32] A sunny reading room for American and foreign periodicals adjoined the library across the corridor.

Above the library, the chapel made full use of the great bay on the north side of the east transept. The bay, set on three sides with tall windows, framed by rounded arches, served as a chancel. A center mullion rising to tracery of circular forms divided these windows. Above them niches with pointed arches held small quatrefoil rose windows. A carved wooden semicircular arch, giving the effect of a chancel arch in a medieval chapel, set off the bay. Stained glass embellished the center window. Within a few years frescoes adorned the white walls. A donor gave a handsome pipe organ. The chapel went as far as a New England evangelical client and his New England Protestant architect could go in appropriating Gothic forms in the 1870s.

The dining room on the west corresponded to the library on the east. It conveyed a contrasting simplicity. Long tables covered with white tablecloths stretched between the thin white columns supporting the ceiling—clearly a place to eat, but not to linger. Student hands soon obliterated the one concession to luxury, the handsome Wedgwood service chosen by Pauline Durant. The plain white crockery that replaced it harmonized with the dining room's plain style.[33]

Other public rooms awaited time and donors. In 1880, the Durants furnished a reception room honoring Elizabeth Barrett Browning in a manner recalling her Italian sojourn. They spared no expense. A dark red imitation Venetian leather covered the walls: its embossed, hand-painted figures copied a medieval pattern. A twenty-four-panel frieze of flowers added color.[34] Mrs. Browning's poems served as subjects for windows and paintings; and statues commemorated her. Some years later Harvard scientist and inventor Eben

Browning Room, College Hall; *Wellesley College Archives*

Horsford, whose gifts aided the faculty in numerous and unusual ways, had the large faculty drawing room redecorated in the grand manner. Flowers and foliage set on a rich gold background covered the walls above ebony book-cases.[35] How far in only a few decades from Mary Lyon's vision of "plain, though very neat"!

While grandeur and luxury increasingly characterized the public rooms of College Hall, Durant wanted living quarters for faculty and students to be comfortable and pleasant. Billings arranged in suites the 350 rooms, each generally 14 feet by 20 feet. The corridor ran through the center of the long east-west axis; the rooms formed a single line on each side, giving each a window to the outside. College Hall had thus neither the dark quarters of Vassar's inside rooms nor the unanticipated privacy of Vassar's four-room suites. Generally two students shared a bedroom and an adjoining parlor, though occasionally a large parlor served two bedrooms for four students. Choice locations overlooked the lake on the south side. Students especially desired those rooms that had a circular parlor shaped by the exterior tower. The president resided in the extreme east wing, beyond the library and chapel. Professors had bedroom and parlor suites, scattered throughout the building, enabling them to supervise students. Each room had handsome black walnut furniture set on patterned carpets.[36]

Wellesley's College Hall was a distinctive building. Knowledge of Mount Holyoke and Vassar influenced its form. Yet Wellesley departed from its precedents in significant ways. It abandoned all effort to pattern internal space after either the house or the asylum. Public rooms did not group on lower floors or at the center but occupied all floors and the east and west transepts. No piazza connoted domesticity. The rich and varied Gothic additions broke up any external expression of the hierarchical organization of public space. The building "scattered" in part because Durant did not have a vision of dominance and subordinance befitting an asylum, but wanted each part to be perfect and beautiful. Richly decorated library, chapel, and parlors took handsome large spaces, shaped by great bays. The Centre was like nothing seen in a college before. Its vast lit space, devoted to no specific use, conveyed a luxury and taste for pleasure that would have aroused the envy of Matthew Vassar and the scorn of Mary Lyon. Durant intended Wellesley for the "calico" girls, the hardworking daughters of modest means, each one of whom in his mind was worth "two velvet girls."[37] But unlike his unassuming predecessor in South Hadley, he saw no contradiction in offering them silk accommodations. As a true man of mid-century America, Durant saw no necessary tension between wealth and piety. Durant believed that material goods, rightly used, were an aid to the spirit.

Durant held serious spiritual aims. While he drew on Vassar's building and its sense of being a college, Durant relied on Mount Holyoke for his basic understanding of its purposes and its form of organization. He recruited Ada Howard, a Mount Holyoke graduate and former teacher and the principal of the female department of Knox College, as Wellesley College's first president. Too much has been made of the fact that Durant appointed the first woman ever to be a college president in the United States. In reality, Howard served as president in name only. Even her title suggested limits, for it was "President of the Faculty." Durant's dominance as founder, treasurer, and payer of deficits meant that, whatever her title, Howard served as a Lady Principal under his headship.[38]

While he might undercut the power of a female president, Durant believed in an all-women faculty without reservation. As he explained to a male applicant in 1874, because "all the Professors + teachers are to be ladies it will not be possible for the Trustees to consider your application although the very eminent references that you give would have made it very desirable in other circumstances." Durant then added, somewhat tactlessly, "it may be that you know of some learned lady whom you could suggest as fitted for the position."[39] Durant employed quite extraordinary measures to find the women he wanted. With Howard's guidance, he recruited trained women from Mount Holyoke, Oberlin, and Vassar, even stealing Vassar's teacher of Latin, Frances E. Lord. He drew most heavily on the University of Michigan, which had admitted its first women in 1870. When Durant faced the reality of 1874, that he could not find thirty learned women for college positions, he did a truly innovative thing: he found good teachers and paid for their training to do college work. Susan Maria Hallowell taught high school in Bangor, Maine; Sarah Frances Whiting, at the Brooklyn Heights Seminary. Durant hired both and let Hallowell spend the first year and Whiting the first two preparing. Durant's close friendship with Eben Horsford, professor of chemistry at Harvard's Lawrence Scientific School, encouraged his commitment to experimental science. He sent his science faculty to study research laboratories at universities and gave them a free hand to acquire appropriate equipment in the United States and abroad. In 1878, in the organ loft on the fifth floor of College Hall, Sarah Whiting opened a student laboratory in physics, the second such in the United States.[40]

Durant coupled his commitment to the development of the intellect with an underlying religious motive, similar to that of Mount Holyoke. The original statute of the college announced that "The College was founded for the glory of God and the service of the Lord Jesus Christ, in and by the education and culture of women." A necessary corollary followed: "It is required that every Trustee, Teacher, and Officer, shall be a member of an Evangelical Church, and that the study of the Holy Scriptures shall be pursued by every student throughout the entire college course under the direction of the Faculty."[41] Durant meant this literally. Ministers from Boston and New York evangelical churches and colleges formed his first board of trustees. All his teachers submitted to his religious tests, strict enough to prevent Vassar's Unitarian astronomer, Maria Mitchell, from employment. Lay preaching hardly ended with Wellesley's founding. Not only did each member of Wellesley's faculty include Bible in her repertoire of courses, but Durant saw the college as the appropriate field for his labors. He regularly spoke at chapel and he found occasions in the course of the day to admonish students' behavior or pose questions about their religious state.[42]

Mount Holyoke's daily schedule came to Wellesley along with its domestic department. The first day opened without that crucial element for communication, the college bell. College legend has it that a woman in town lent a brass dinner bell, and at six the next morning two students walked through all the corridors ringing it to wake up the college. What makes this significant is the importance all attached to that necessary bell. Wellesley required a period of silent devotions when roommates separated, one to take the bedroom, the other the study. Section meetings followed chapel, but teachers discussed the Bible with students, not their personal failings. A second chapel service came after the evening meal, followed by another period of silent devotions. Lights went out at ten. There clearly was "no danger of having too many Mount Holyokes." Yet important differences separated the two institutions. While students gave an hour to domestic work, servants performed the most difficult tasks, including all food preparation. Faculty monitored the corridors, but ruled students with a lighter hand. "Being out of one's room in Silent Time or after ten was considered reprehensible, although no penalties were attached": the teachers greeted coming in after ten in the evening and "undue noise" only with "admonition."[43] Wellesley enforced its rules more gently than Mount Holyoke and kept them external. No system of self-reporting crossed the Berkshires to West Needham.

Yet Wellesley did transport in full a crucial element of Mary Lyon's successful plan. By having only women teach women and by housing students and faculty within the same large building, Durant re-created the totally female world of Mount Holyoke Seminary. Vassar went partway in its compromise between a seminary of female teachers and a college of male faculty. The Main building gave expression to this curious hybrid in its long plain wings behind which women lived, contrasting with the more ornate pavilions which housed the male faculty. Wellesley went the whole way, placing women in all positions including those of professor and president. Like Vassar's teachers, Wellesley's faculty lived along the corridor and headed a table at meals. While on the one hand Wellesley constrained its faculty by a religious test, it eased their monitorial duties and emphasized their prestige as professors. When faculty women later vied for influence, they fought from a position of strength, compared to their counterparts at Vassar.

One can see the greater strength of women faculty in the exterior of College Hall. Male professors lived in the pavilions at Vassar, while at Wellesley the library, chapel, and dining hall took their place. The east-west stretch of building, where faculty and students lived, did not recede into subordinance. In modifying Billings' original design, Durant added towers, pinnacles, and finials, breaking up any hierarchical organization of space. In his scheme Durant placed as much importance on living space for women faculty and students as on any other element and wanted it to receive equal external embellishment. The façade of College Hall portended Wellesley's future. In designing the College Beautiful, Henry Fowle Durant not only expressed his evangelical hopes, he also created a world where women attained a special place.

4

Acting a Manly *Part*

THE BEGINNINGS OF COLLEGE LIFE

What effect did college have on young women? Were they protected from all danger by the great buildings and the many rules? In the 1870s, this question increased in significance as college education became a real possibility for American women.

Women were entering seminaries and colleges in increasing numbers. In 1870, the United States Commissioner of Education estimated that 11,000 women currently attended seminaries or colleges. While the bulk of this number enrolled in seminaries, 3,000 matriculated in college. The women's colleges claimed the greatest number, 2,200; only 600 attended the coeducational colleges; and only 200, the state universities.[1]

The number of colleges open to women began to grow significantly after 1870. Many former seminaries claimed collegiate status. Wells, for example, founded in 1868 as a seminary, began to call itself a college from that date. Formerly male institutions became coeducational: the University of Michigan and Cornell both opened their doors to women in 1870. While these numbers and foundings reflect a growing interest in women's higher education, they obscure real differences among educational institutions. Coeducational colleges and state universities did not necessarily allow women to take the liberal arts course. Despite the impact of Mount Holyoke and Vassar, the labels *female seminary* and *women's college* did not insure standards or curriculum. It has been estimated that, in 1875, out of 209 schools "for the 'superior' education of women" only a half-dozen met "accepted college standards."[2]

Geographical distance and local traditions limited contact even among this handful of schools which offered high-quality instruction to women. Thus in 1875, when Wellesley and Smith opened, only two institutions mattered to their founders: Mount Holyoke and Vassar. Henry Fowle Durant knew Mount

Holyoke well and admired it without reservation. While Durant never saw Vassar College at first hand, he intended to create an institution its equal. In imitation, he changed his seminary's name to Wellesley College. Renwick's building fit Durant's sense of scale and desire for impressiveness. Dedicated to a dream of the College Beautiful, Durant did not examine closely the Vassar experiment or raise questions about Mount Holyoke.

In contrast, the men who brought Smith College into being were experienced educators—professors and alumni of Amherst College. Aware of the gap between the actual life of Amherst collegians and college rhetoric, they knew enough to look behind official statements to examine closely the seminary and college. Proximity to Mount Holyoke fostered a critical perspective; and while these New England evangelicals regarded Vassar as far away, news of the first great college for women filtered in through observers. Smith was the first women's college designed in reaction. The men who planned its program and buildings hoped to avoid the mistakes of Mount Holyoke and Vassar.

What were the negative lessons that Mount Holyoke and Vassar taught? From the beginning Mount Holyoke had detractors, critics who challenged basic assumptions behind its plan. One scorching attack came from the editor of *The Religious Magazine*, E. A. Andrews, who also headed Boston's Mount Vernon School for Girls. Responding in 1837 to a pamphlet written by Mary Lyon, Andrews mocked her grammar and systematically questioned every element in the seminary's design. While he intended his article to demonstrate a Boston man's cultural, social, and intellectual superiority over a self-educated Western Massachusetts woman, one aspect of his criticism deserves consideration, for it involves the central question of separate seminaries and colleges for women.

Andrews remarked at the end of his tirade, "We must . . . express our doubts of the expediency of separating a large number of young women, for a considerable period from all but female society, and immuring them within the walls of a boarding school." He compared such "a rash and unpromising experiment" to the "monastic course" of the much-despised Catholics: "Human nature is the same, whether confined to a Catholic or a Protestant nunnery, and whether subject to the control of a lady abbess or a maiden schoolmistress." He judged women-run boarding schools "hurtful and often disastrous." A young woman needed to remain in the care of "her natural guardians, with all the influences of home clustering around her, and where her best affections can be daily cultivated by exercise." If this proved not possible, she should "board in some private family in which we had entire confidence."[3] Obviously the plan of the Mount Vernon School for Girls.

Andrews' argument was more than a competitor's effort to defend his enterprise. The issue Andrews posed resurfaced throughout the nineteenth and early twentieth centuries and is fundamental to understanding both the original design of Smith and the efforts to shape and reshape the other women's colleges after 1875. Andrews raised the old spectre of the unsexed woman. "The tendency of female education at the present day" is to develop the mind to the neglect of the graces. "In place of all which is most attractive in female manners, we see characters expressly formed for acting a *manly* part upon the theatre of life. . . . Under such influences the female character is fast becoming masculine."[4] When Andrews went on to describe this manly part, he gave as example the teacher who ventured west "on a half missionary, half school keeping expedition to the *Great Valley*, 'in search of a husband.'"[5] Andrews clearly connected the Protestant nunnery under the maiden schoolmistress to the graceless Western schoolteacher, intent on an active, though not necessarily a masculine, life.

At a certain level Andrews understood Mary Lyon's plan for Mount Holyoke very well, perhaps far better than some of her supporters. By removing students from home influences and natural affections she did intend to transform them, to give students "a new direction" to turn them from private concerns "to enlist them permanently in the cause of benevolence." She did not see this as making them less womanly, but rather turning them into a different kind of woman, whose greatest satisfactions lay in the public realm. She took pride in the missionaries and teachers that Andrews so derided.

Andrews and Lyon disagreed not on the relation between the means and ends of the seminary but rather on the nature of those ends. Andrews correctly perceived that female governance in Lyon's proposed seminary might develop new, unconventional expectations in its students to act "a *manly* part upon the theatre of life."

Mary Lyon built the discipline of Mount Holyoke on intense, intimate friendships among women. The house plan of the seminary reinforced female closeness. Yet out of the spectrum of possibilities that the world of the home allowed, Mount Holyoke drew on only one form of female relationship, that of mother and daughter. When Zilpah Grant took the place of the mother Mary Lyon "lost" to a stepfather at thirteen, Lyon gained the strength to reshape her life. Mary Lyon became that same mother to other young women, creating an army of disciplined workers for Christ. Mary Lyon demanded that her students focus their entire energies on intellectual and moral training under the guidance of a teacher. She countenanced no other important tasks or relationships. That Mount Holyoke allowed no fathers, brothers, or lovers is obvious. What is not so obvious is that there were to be no sisters. The seminary did not let close friendships develop among students. Mary Lyon continued the practice of Ipswich of changing roommate groups every four weeks to prevent intimacy.[6] The seminary schedule itself deterred friendship: in the hours between five o'clock rising and nine o'clock retiring, it left only a few short periods free; otherwise it secluded students in their rooms for study or devotions or brought them all together under supervision for meals, chapel, recitation, domestic work, or recreation. Mount Holyoke harnessed the power of women's friendship to but a single object, the relationship between the student and teacher.

Matthew Vassar, Milo Jewett, Hannah Lyman, and John Raymond did not bring Mary Lyon's religious and psychological drives to the founding of Vassar College. Out of a mixture of egotism, ambition, fear, memory, sense of duty, and commitment to the liberal arts, Vassar's creators drew on many of the forms and practices of Ipswich and Mount Holyoke and applied them to a broad range of students. Raymond and Lyman were conservators by nature, called on to be pioneers. Aware of the criticism initiated by such men as Andrews, they determined to prove that a Vassar education made a young woman no less ladylike. Raymond neither shaped the college's building, hired certain of its faculty, nor encouraged the publicity that attracted the college's first students; but he found himself forced to live with the consequences.

Above all else Raymond wanted his students to appear feminine. In his report to the trustees after the end of the fourth year, Raymond spoke of the anxiety he shared with them "lest by too close an imitation of the forms & studies and too much cultivation of the Spirit, of ordinary colleges, we should impair womanliness of character in our students, & encourage the formation of those mannish tastes & manners which are so disgusting to every right mind & feeling." By the 1860s the old danger held a new dimension: women's rights. Raymond warned that at the point when Vassar as represented "by its seniors and its alumnae, becomes popular with the vulgar and extreme woman's rights people, and disgusts the wise," the college would know it had failed.[7] Feminism became Raymond's central fear. The system of control that Hannah Lyman had learned from Zilpah Grant at Ipswich Female Seminary and Lyman's emphasis on propriety in dress and deportment gave Raymond great reassurance. Nothing else explains the importance he attached to the Lady Principal's office or the reverence he gave to its first occupant.

While ties between Vassar and the seminary tradition go back to Jewett's awareness in Alabama of Mount Holyoke, the strongest link to actual practice came through Lyman's memories of Ipswich. To Vassar College Hannah Lyman brought Ipswich Female Seminary's schedule, chapel talks, system of corridor teachers, and rules. Yet she learned that she could not re-create a New England seminary of the 1830s along the Hudson in 1865.

Raymond and Lyman spoke at chapel, exhorting students to right attitudes, proper behavior, and appreciation of their opportunities. Other speakers instructed as well, such as J. G. Holland, a doctor known for his books of advice for young men and women. Vassar did not permit everyone to speak. In 1869, the Students Association invited the abolitionist and reformer Wendell Phillips to address them, but Raymond, fearful of Phillips' radicalism, forbade

his appearance.[8] Try as Raymond might to control outside influences, an occasional feminist broke through the lines. The writer Grace Greenwood offered her lecture, innocuously titled "Indoors." To Raymond's horror, it turned
out to deal with "the domestic relations & family life from the 'Woman's Rights'
point of view." Raymond wrote to his wife that the talk presented "a coarse
worldly view, altogether below the Vassar standard of delicacy & seriousness
in treating such themes."[9]

Raymond failed in his efforts to control the thoughts and feelings of his
students. His regular exhortations to students succeeded only in boring them.
Sarah Glazier, a student in the second year, wrote to a former classmate a
knowing comment about a chapel talk by Dr. Raymond: "like no other man's
long speeches." His importation of safe speakers backfired. J. G. Holland's
conventional view of marriage and women's sphere infuriated Glazier. She
sputtered to her same friend.:

> Do *you* believe, Belle, that the only *end* of woman is *marriage*—that she who
> fails of that may be happy in another world, but never in this. . . .&c, &c?—
> And to have a man stand up and tell a person of common sense that the only
> remedy for the great social evil [prostitution] . . . is *marriage*, is enough to make
> one feel that the world which will allow such a man to be tolerated hasn't
> advanced much since the time of my Biblical namesake. . . . Pardon my inco-
> herency . . . believe me it is but a slight expression of my disgusts for Dr. H.'s
> views.[10]

Raymond's refusal to allow Phillips to speak awoke a spirit of rebellion in Ellen
Swallow who, as Ellen Richards, later became the leader of the home economics movement. She and her friends planned to get around Raymond by having
the faculty invite Phillips and then selling tickets to the students. As she wrote
to her mother, she wearied of "poky lectures."[11]

Clearly the future Ellen Richards saw the faculty as on her side. And certain of them were. When Raymond barred Wendell Phillips, he outraged Maria
Mitchell, Vassar's renowned astronomer. Raymond had nothing to do with
her appointment or with that of Charles Farrar: both were legacies of Jewett's
administration. A Unitarian of Quaker origins and a pronounced feminist,
Mitchell bowed to no one's rules. She refused to submit to "police work," as
she called it, and did not take attendance or give serious attention to grading
students. She rebuffed a teacher who asked to use her telescope to identify a
student seen outside college grounds.[12] And yet Mitchell took pride in Vassar
and insisted that the college created "the best educated women in the world."[13]
At her observatory home north of the Main building she received noted feminists and scientists and brought them into the college. Though extremely
reticent, she lectured to students, inspiring them to achieve. She got exemp-
tions for her students from the ten o'clock rule so they could search the heav-

Maria Mitchell with students on the stairs of the Observatory parlor
Vassar College Library

ens. She demanded the highest standards of direct observation and reporting and encouraged her students to become scientists.[14] Charles Farrar had an important influence on early Vassar students as well. In his laboratory course he proselytized for the natural sciences, drawing Ellen as a recruit by calling her "Prof. Swallow" in class.[15] When Raymond cancelled Farrar's planned student excursion because taking students close to West Point might make the newspapers, Farrar let Swallow know that such interference by the administration made him "indignant."[16]

Mitchell and Farrar were unusual because they fought openly and stayed. The other professors, all of them men, either left quickly, because they refused to accept Lyman's presumption of authority, or they undermined her in more subtle ways. The high spirits of the Dutchman Henry Van Ingen, the first professor of art, as he encouraged his students in the studio, implicitly challenged notions of propriety. When a critical student questioned the way another used both hands to draw, Van Ingen retorted, "I don't care . . . if she rubs the crayon on with her nose too, just so she gets it on right."[17] Vassar could not count on its professors to insure ladylike behavior.

Lyman did have a large staff of teachers who taught under the professors but who reported to her in monitoring the corridors. These teachers lacked the educational qualifications to command respect. When Raymond asked the board of trustees to grant Vassar B.A. degrees to teachers who had instructed in the college for two years and whose professors certified their work to be equivalent to the undergraduate course, he found only one "among the large corps . . . whose education is as yet sufficiently broad & complete to endure the test."[18] Yet as Raymond sought to upgrade the teaching staff, academic qualifications proved to be less important than personal ones. Failures in maintaining order among the "College Family" led Raymond to seek more "mature & experienced women" for teachers. He stated his intention to choose women with "accompanying qualifications for what we call corridor-work . . . with increasing care."[19] When able he followed the Mount Holyoke practice of hiring those who came up through the ranks. In 1871, he wrote to a man whose daughter sought employment as a teacher that the college preferred its "own alumnae, whose familiarity with our methods of instruction and the whole college life gives them from the beginning a great advantage."[20]

Yet while Raymond tried to duplicate Mount Holyoke's system of hiring from within, he hardly recaptured the seminary's spirit: from the first, Vassar's 350 students were made of different stuff from that of their Mount Holyoke predecessors. Mount Holyoke had drawn its homogeneous students from the descendants of Puritan settlers in Western Massachusetts. Vassar students enjoyed a remarkable diversity. What they first remarked about themselves was that they came from all sections of the United States. "Gracious, cordial, talkative Southern girls," six in the first class, physically distinguished by their "almost universal use of powder," mixed with fifty-five independent Westerners, with brash manners, "stencilled brows and eyelids," and eyes dilated with belladonna.[21] The wife of a Civil War officer killed in battle wore her widow's weeds. With some exaggeration a member of the initial class recalled, "Every state in the Union was represented at Vassar."[22] For the students, who had generally stayed close to home circles, this afforded an altogether new experience, a source of endless fascination.

Vassar students also differed widely in age and in educational background. They came as young as fifteen and as old as twenty-four. Raymond estimated that only one-third had been well taught. They came expecting the rather free university system as advertised in *Godey's Lady's Book*. When Raymond created a preparatory department to bring them into a traditional liberal arts course, many bucked. Raymond's bland official history breaks through the genre to bristle with the memory of the first students' impertinence. "That the young lady 'liked' this study or 'disliked' that was the reason [for wanting to go outside the required curriculum] perhaps most frequently assigned. If its force was not at once conceded, she strengthened it by increased emphasis, declaring that she was *'passionately* fond' of the one and *'utterly detested'* or *'never could endure'* the other."[23]

When Vassar students wanted a literary society like their college brothers, Raymond obliged. A literary society, after all, was one of the marks that distinguished a college. He helped them form Philaletheis—from the Greek for "truth-loving"—and served as its first president. The society met in "Society Hall," the room above the Riding Academy in the Calisthenium. In the second year, the society passed completely into student hands and divided itself into three chapters, Alpha, Beta, and Delta. Each chapter met weekly for literary exercises, designed to be interesting and witty. While such literary societies at men's colleges evolved into fraternities, Philaletheis had a different history. Within a few years each chapter became a dramatic society which presented plays to other chapters, the preparatory students, and eventually the faculty.[24]

While ultimately formal organizations became quite important at Vassar, in the early years college life meant largely spontaneous informal gatherings. Boxes of food from home (including such perishable delights as turkeys) or ice cream and cakes ordered from a Poughkeepsie confectioner provided occasions for parties of friends called "spreads." A student described to her parents such an impromptu feast sparked by a sermon so solemn "we girls were obliged to do something quickly to counteract its influence." The ice cream tasted delicious but paregoric laced the fruit cake. The nine revelers invited their two corridor teachers to join in, dividing the ice cream and "generously piling the dish with that nice fruit cake also."[25] Other spreads were not so inclusive, for a contemporary later remembered that the spreads occasioned by the huge box from home "almost always" took place "after the 'retiring hour.'"[26]

Vassar's diverse, spunky collegians hardly responded to Hannah Lyman as she had to Zilpah Grant at Ipswich. From the outset students regarded corridor rules and monitors as nuisances to be evaded. As at Mount Holyoke, Vassar had a schedule designed for control. It attempted to isolate students from each other during study hours, devotional periods, and after ten in the evening. While one such Western student nicknamed Lyman "the All-seeing Eye," the college life the student described in her letters home suggested Lyman saw very little.[27] The Western letter-writer recounted a November 1869 night in her first year of college:

> After the ten o'clock bell rang I got out of our window and ran two doors up the corridor to Belle and Fannie's room, climbed their window and perched on the upper sash. They were nearly frightened out of their wits at first and I had to say "peace, be still" before they found out who it was. Then they begged me to come in but their window made such a racket I ran back for fear of

alarming the corridor teacher. Soon there was a sound as of one running and
into our bed fell Belle. In a moment the sound was repeated and in piled Fannie,
then we were bombarded by Clemmie.[28]

Later Clemmie paid a visit to Fannie during study hours. A teacher, who came
to call on a sick Belle, surprised them: "Fan opened the closet, pushed Clem
in and closed the door," where Clemmie smothered for half an hour.[29] Teachers
intruded rarely and only accidentally: the amusing life of visits, sharing a bed,
spreads, and high jinks went on at Vassar relatively free of monitors in the self-
contained student suites.

Supervision extended to the dining room, where, as at Mount Holyoke, a
corridor teacher presided at the table. Seniors, however, gained the privilege
of conducting themselves without the outsider's presence, and an alumna later
remembered with relish the discussions uncensored by a monitor.[30] Miss Lyman presided over the first table, attended by Maria Mitchell and Avila Avery,
the resident physician. (Raymond and the men on the faculty ate with their
families in their separate apartments.) As students filed past the Lady Principal,
she scrutinized their dress and demeanor. Lyman's rule was not complete even
in the dining hall: despite her express prohibition, at the moment after the bell
for announcements before Miss Lyman began to speak, students broke the
silence by "moistening the rims of their tumblers and rubbing till a clear, bell-
toned ringing filled the great, echoing hall."[31]

Hardly farm daughters from Western Massachusetts willing to submit their
wills to Mary Lyon, Vassar's spirited collegians clearly learned how to operate.
Keeping their independence, they obeyed enough forms to stay out of trouble
but lived their own lives outside Lyman's structure of rules. High jinks were
serious business. They signal at Vassar the beginnings of college life for women.
Like their brothers at the men's colleges, Vassar students began to see themselves as separate from college authorities. While they noticed distinctions among
the faculty and between faculty and administration, their primary realm of
reference became other students. They created a student culture with its own
codes of behavior, its own social hierarchy.[32]

Not all collegians partook of the spirited group-life just described. A serious student such as Ellen Swallow had no time for "chitchat and gossip." She
had quietly done her work, rather than enter the "rushing, foaming stream"
of student life. As she reflected in her final year, she sensed it wise that she had
stood aloof, because as a "thorough-bred democrat" she would have collided
with the "aristocracy and particularly monarchy, in the air of the College," a
reference not only to the administration but to the cliques among the students.[33] She, however, had her own kind of independence from authority. She
enjoyed country rambles out-of-bounds. Her criticism of Lyman and Raymond made her mother fear for her standing. Ellen Swallow reassured her

Vassar students in their room, ca. 1890; *Vassar College Library*

mother: as a prompt, well-prepared student, with "no intimate friend," she could afford to break a rule or two.[34] Her self-description is interesting, for it suggests a new fear about the women's college, that in a setting of seclusion from men, women students might direct their passionate feelings toward each other.

In 1882, a committee of the Association of Collegiate Alumnae studied the health of women college students. Alice Stone Blackwell, Lucy Stone's daughter and a feminist in her own right, reported that the committee "gave it as their strong opinion that one thing which damaged the health of the girls seriously was 'smashes'—an extraordinary habit which they have of falling violently in love with each other, and suffering all the pangs of unrequited attachment, desperate jealousy &c &c, with as much energy as if one of them were a man."[35] Educated outside the women's colleges, Blackwell said that she would have found the discussion exaggerated "if Maria Mitchell hadn't told me, when I was visiting at Vassar, what a pest the 'smashing' was to the teach-

ers there—how it kept the girls from studying, & sometimes made a girl drop
behind her class year after year."[36] Mitchell's indirect remark is interesting, for,
if remembered accurately, she did not freight the issue with moral overtones.
Rather she was distressed by the distraction that took women away from their
studies.

Hannah Lyman took an altogether unequivocal view of "smashing": she
disapproved completely. The Westerner wrote to her parents that Miss Lyman
gave some students new room assignments. She did not move students "on
account of bad behavior." Rather, "if any grow fond of each other they must
look out or they'll be separated. She does not take much stock in school-girl
intimacies."[37] In addition to following the Mount Holyoke practice of reas-
signing rooms, Lyman lectured to the students against forming quick friendships and against open displays of affection, especially kissing.[38]

As a good Victorian gentleman, President Raymond never alluded directly
to "smashing" in his public writing. But knowing the concern with it at Vassar
enables us to read between the lines of his annual reports to the trustees. Even
with the college's high fees, Vassar's Main proved too costly to operate. To
bring in more revenues, the trustees packed more students into the building.
Along with the Lady Principal and resident physician, Raymond fought against
this, year after year. Adding students to the building denied the administration
the flexibility that it needed to deal with problems among students. In 1872,
Raymond sought twenty free rooms. His language suggests that "smashing"
was one of the problems which he confronted. He sought the unoccupied
rooms "to break up injurious associations, to relieve deserving students from
incongenial companions, to provide for those afflicted with delicate ailments."
His handwritten report demonstrates his obvious discomfort. Raymond corrected his own prose, but fortunately left legible the phrases he chose not to
read to the trustees. "We cannot save our students from many of the inconve-
niences & privations of our artificial college life," he wrote and then crossed
out. "The trial to these young & sensitive organizations of living always in a
crowd," he read to the trustees (then added but thought better of "& always
by rule & by the clock"), "is much severer than is generally appreciated by
those who are not in daily contact with them." In enumerating the consequences of living in a crowd, Raymond listed "many sleepless nights, many
meals untasted for want of appetite, many nervous headaches, many fits of
uncontrollable spleen, temper & despondency, many hours of mental languor
& incapacity."[39]

While college authorities, worrying about "artificial college life," disapproved of "school-girl intimacies," students at Vassar during its first decade
clearly recognized and accepted them. In letters home they did not define the
"smash" to their parents: they assumed their parents understood what the term
meant. For example, the Western correspondent described an evening when

Trig ceremony; Vassar; *Vassar College Library*

she and her friends looked out the window and saw two of the men on the faculty walking together "with an arm over the other's shoulder." One of the girls set the others to uproarious laughter when she said, " 'Oh, look out the window, there is a smash.' "[40] In 1873, for the uninitiated male collegian the *Cornell Times* reprinted a letter to the *Yale Courant* which gave a full definition of the "term in general use at Vassar. . . . 'smashing' ":

> When a Vassar girl takes a shine to another, she straightway enters upon a regular course of bouquet sendings, interspersed with tinted notes, mysterious packages of "Ridley's Mixed Candies," locks of hair perhaps, and many other tender tokens, until at last the object of her attentions is captured, the two become inseparable, and the aggressor is considered by her circle of acquaintances as —*smashed*. The mortality, so to speak, resulting from these smashups, is frightful to contemplate. One young lady, the "Irrepressible," rejoices in more than thirty. She keeps a list of them, in illuminated text, framed and hung up in her room like a Society poster. . . . Vassar numbers her smashes by the score.[41]

While this description by a male writer may have distorted the intense female friendship that Vassar students recognized as the "smash," the tone of the report is nonetheless interesting. In the 1870s, neither male nor female students brought to their mention of "smashing" moral judgment. Acceptance and humor characterized student statements. While mentioned and joked about, the phenomenon was not underscored by students as particularly important.

That students found amusement in a practice condemned by college authorities suggests the real issue at stake. "Smashing" dramatized the threat to presidents and Lady Principals of student autonomy. Emerging college life, with its independent standards, was the problem, not student sexuality. Vassar collegians had begun to shape a way of life separate from the official culture as represented by the administration. Chapel speakers sought to influence students, and corridor teachers attempted to monitor behavior according to the rules, but students developed their own ideas about how they ought to behave and what they should feel. Vassar authorities had little power to curb an autonomous student life. Locked in an enormous seminary building, whose room arrangement hid much from view, and saddled with deficits rather than endowments, Lyman could only exhort and switch roommates, Raymond could only hire more mature monitors, seek a few extra rooms, and pray.

At Wellesley, with his eyes focused only on Mount Holyoke, Durant was oblivious to college life developing at Vassar. He knew better than to create internal suites enclosed from the corridor, and he did not countenance a Maria Mitchell or her male colleagues on the faculty. But he did assume that only obedience and purity would characterize his students and faculty. Thus he created College Hall in the image of Vassar's Main. Understandably, Wellesley's college life came to have much in common with that at Vassar.

In Northampton, however, in these same years a quite different story was unfolding. The men entrusted with planning Smith College were aware of the emerging student culture both at Amherst and at Vassar. Like their counterparts at Vassar and Wellesley, they regarded protecting the femininity of women seeking higher education as all-important. Their knowledge gave them an additional challenge. How could they organize the inner life of Smith College to insure proper feminine behavior? How could a women's college seclude women, yet keep them within the patriarchal world?

5

To Preserve Her Womanliness

SMITH

Sophia Smith was the first woman in America to endow a college for women, but the college that took her name is, like Vassar and Wellesley, a male creation. Unlike Matthew Vassar and Henry Fowle Durant, the men who shaped Smith College were experienced practitioners of higher education. All critical actors—Sophia Smith's pastor and confidential guide, the co-workers he engaged as trustees, and the president they selected—were Amherst men. As alumni and powerful faculty, they knew the standards for admission and the curriculum of a New England college. While they were unusual in that they wanted to make college education available to women, they were thoroughly conventional in their desire to protect nineteenth-century femininity. The original buildings and plan of Smith College reflect this tension between innovation and conformity. Not only did Smith's initial scheme shape the college until the turn of the century, the other women's colleges felt its influence. Those already established attempted to remodel themselves after Smith's example. The men responsible for planning Bryn Mawr set about to copy Smith in whole cloth.

Sophia Smith turned to John Morton Greene when her brother Austin died in 1861, leaving her with the bewildering responsibility of a large inheritance.[1] Unmarried, she had lived with her single brother and sister in their parents' homestead in Hatfield, Massachusetts. Austin prospered, Harriet kept the house, and Sophia depended upon them both. Harriet's death in 1859 left her bereaved; Austin's death left her with a fortune. Then a young man, Greene was Smith's pastor, and despite the obligation to counsel the philanthropic which his ministry entailed, he only reluctantly agreed to advise her, recalling the acrimony that followed the creation of the Smith Charities by the will of her uncle. Greene imposed one condition on his petitioner. Miss Smith was not to try to fathom the wishes of her mean-spirited late brother. Greene agreed to help her, but only if she accepted the decision to dispose of Austin's fortune as her own—with God's guidance, of course. She accepted the terms, and Greene began laying out the options.

He thought first about the needs of his alma mater, Amherst, where he tutored in 1855–57, before assuming the Hatfield pastorate, and of Mount Holyoke Seminary, where his wife, Louisa Dickinson Greene, studied. But Miss Smith refused to consider either institution. So adamant was she that she declined to visit both the college and the seminary, despite the fact that she had seen neither. Greene then presented her with the choice between a college for women and a deaf-mute institution. Influenced by her own deafness, her first will endowed the latter, as well as an academy and public library in Hatfield. In 1868, when another benefactor gave Western Massachusetts a school for the deaf, Greene wrote to Miss Smith and urged her to endow a women's college. Greene enlisted the aid of two powerful Amherst professors, William S. Tyler, the redoubtable professor of classics who had assisted at the birth of Mount Holyoke, and Julius Seelye, then professor of mental and moral philosophy (and soon to be Amherst's president). They, in turn, worked on George W. Hubbard, who succeeded Greene as Miss Smith's confidential advisor. Miss Smith capitulated, and Hubbard drew up her will, using Greene's language.

Sophia Smith left the bulk of her estate to accomplish "the design to furnish for my own sex means and facilities for education equal to those which are afforded now in our College to young men," through the founding of Smith College. She affirmed that while she did not intend the college to be sectarian, she wanted it "pervaded by the spirit of evangelical Christian religion." She then specified a full curriculum, including ancient languages and mathematics, the distinguishing marks of a college as opposed to a seminary. And in a crucial sentence she tried to reconcile the claims of higher education with womanhood: "It is not my design to render my sex any the less feminine, but to develop as fully as may be the powers of womanhood & furnish women with means of usefulness, happiness, & honor now withheld from them." She closed by listing the trustees chosen by Greene: though she rejected President Stearns of Amherst, she agreed to Tyler and Seelye and to Edwards A. Park, a professor at Andover Theological Seminary who once taught at Amherst.[2] Greene and these three among the eleven initial trustees made the critical formative decisions.

Greene determined to get the future college out of Hatfield and to Northampton. Not only did he dislike the specific site that Miss Smith had chosen, he thought Northampton offered him a greater chance to realize his conception of a women's college. Greene's letter to Sophia Smith of April 1869 gave the first inkling that he did not like elements of Mount Holyoke's plan. He reminded Miss Smith that they agreed that her college would differ from the seminary in "two prominent particulars." It would not "put the pupils into one large building" but instead build "several small ones, or cottages." And it would bring "the pupils more into the social life of the town," keeping them in touch with "real practical life. They will be free from the affected, unsocial, visionary notions which fill the minds of some who graduate at our girls' schools." Greene urged Northampton as the larger, more varied, and more interesting town within which Smith College might keep its young collegians practical.[3]

Greene's letter reveals far more than the official history usually allows. Greene knew Mount Holyoke well. In the interval between his courtship and marriage, he had urged his future wife to return to the seminary to complete her course of study. Louisa Dickinson spent the year 1856–57 at Mount Holyoke, while John Greene tutored at Amherst and awaited a ministerial pulpit. Though two decades had passed since the seminary's founding, Louisa Dickinson adhered to its original spirit, meeting fully the expectations of teachers and principal. In the years that followed, John Greene developed doubts about the seminary, disapproving of a key element of Mary Lyon's plan. Lyon had intentionally created an environment to remove students from the "real practical life," which limited their horizons to the private familial world. She had wanted her students to have "visionary notions" of benevolent action in the public arena. Seclusion in the seminary home under the total influence of teachers was a necessary means to this end. In the spirit of E. A. Andrews' early criticism of Mount Holyoke's plan, Greene opposed secluding young women in a cloistered setting. He wanted to keep them within the vital life of a New England town.

An obvious solution to this Amherst man might have been coeducation. Amherst's most influential alumnus, Henry Ward Beecher, lent his powerful voice to urge opening Amherst College to women. Edwards Park led the opposition.[4] The strong interest in Smith by loyal sons of Amherst can be seen as a means to protect their alma mater as a male bastion. But in their minds, they were also protecting the young women, whom they perceived as daughters. The gap at Amherst between official piety and student carousing was alarming. Fraternities established beachheads in town, free from the oversight of college authorities.[5] Whereas some might have naively repeated the adage that the presence of women made college men more moral, these realists knew better. The hedonism of the Amherst man threatened the virtue of any young woman entering college gates.[6]

Greene successfully convinced a reluctant Hubbard to get Miss Smith to change the site of the college to Northampton. After his death and the resolution of her will, the trustees met for the first time on April 12, 1871. Greene discussed with them the elements of his plan which Miss Smith had found "pleasing," but did not include in her will. Greene recommended that students be housed in cottages, that the president be a man, and that men as well as women be chosen as faculty and members of governing boards.[7] All these recommendations must be seen as part of the effort to make Smith different from Mount Holyoke. Park wrote Greene that he had difficulty convincing others that Smith was "nothing more than *other* Female Seminaries": "I am asked often who is to be the President-ess."[8] To signal to the public that Smith was a college, not a seminary, the trustees agreed to seek a male president and faculty.

The board approached several men about the presidency without agreement or success until July 1872, when it chose Professor L. Clark Seelye of Amherst, the younger brother of one of their number, Julius Seelye. Clark Seelye refused: Miss Smith's bequest was too small to create a college. Greene left his pulpit, now in Lowell, Massachusetts, for six months to devote himself full-time to raising money, especially in Northampton. While Greene failed to gain funds, his speeches and articles in the press generated interest in the nascent college. The investments grew, and in the summer of 1873, L. Clark Seelye accepted.

Seelye's accession caused no abrupt change in direction. He came from the Amherst world that selected him, and he shared the basic assumptions of his colleagues about the appropriate design of a women's college. He and his brother Julius were descendants of the first Puritans, two of ten children of Seth and Abigail Seelye of Bethel, Connecticut. Clark was the youngest surviving child. His four brothers preceded him into the professions, two into the ministry. Clark attended Union College in Schenectady. His uncle was the college's president, and his brother Julius had just taken a pulpit in the town. Study for the ministry at Andover Theological Seminary followed, but after a year and a half, pneumonia forced Clark Seelye home. In the following years he travelled to Egypt and the Holy Land and to Europe. In 1863, Seelye became pastor of North Church in Springfield, Massachusetts. There he met and married Henrietta Chapin, the cousin of parishioner J. G. Holland's wife. In 1865, Seelye accepted a call to become Williston Professor of Rhetoric, Oratory, and English Literature at Amherst and moved into a house opposite that of his brother Julius, who, in 1858, had come to Amherst and was emerging into its most powerful force.[9]

In 1821, the sons of Connecticut Puritans founded Amherst to protect orthodoxy against Harvard's Unitarianism. By the 1860s, the college tempered its religious zeal with Romanticism and a growing emphasis on learning. The college no longer aimed to produce orthodox Congregational ministers, but Christian gentlemen. Classics remained the most important course of study, interpreted through the evangelical lens of William S. Tyler. Clark Seelye came to Amherst as its first teacher of English literature. Into a curriculum without art or music, Seelye brought a love of vernacular English.[10] As the youngest child, his large family treated him with unique affection; he spent important years of his early manhood abroad. Perhaps these influences set Clark Seelye apart somewhat from his older, more severe Amherst colleagues. The memory of a graduate of 1866, "seeing 'tears of joy' stream down" Seelye's face "as he read to his class the coarsest parts of Chaucer's 'Miller's Tale,'" suggests this.[11] Seelye made one addition to the circular that first presented Smith College to the public:

> More time will be devoted than in other colleges to aesthetical study, to the principles on which fine arts are founded, to the arts of drawing and the science of perspective, to the examination of the great models of painting and statuary, to a familiar acquaintance with the works of the great musical composers and to the acquisition of musical skill.[12]

Perhaps the opportunity the new women's college offered for a richer aesthetic experience helped lure Seelye to its presidency.

On all other matters Clark Seelye agreed with Smith's Amherst creators. He spoke for them when he addressed the American Institute of Instruction in 1874. Seelye based his advocacy of women's higher education on a ringing defense of the liberal arts. All arguments against college training for women dissolved when learning aimed only to develop mind and spirit. Just as a man might enter law, a woman might marry, but the college prepared neither: education opened to the student "that all-perfect Mind, which is neither male nor female."[13] Woman, like man, aspired to perfection in imitation of God.[14] Moreover, domesticity alone did not define her future life: "Woman is a member of society. She has duties to her race as truly as to her family."[15] Those duties did not normally include professional life. Seelye had a strong distaste for the professional woman, in whom "the gentle-woman is lost in the strong-minded":

> Is it mere prejudice which causes so general a feeling of aversion to some women whose energy, heroism, and ability we cannot but admire? Has not their training repressed their amiable qualities, made them bigoted, what the English would call bumptious, and very frequently excessively conceited?[16]

Women could not get the liberal arts training they deserved in coeducational colleges. The "animal passions" of young people when "the appetites [are] most inflammable"[17] made that dangerous. "Would prudent parents," Seelye asked, "who have large families of sons or daughters, introduce into their homes large numbers of the opposite sex . . . [and] go away for four years, and leave young people thus associated to keep house by themselves under the general supervision of their pastor and school-teacher?"[18] In addition, a college meant more than instruction: "it has its traditions, its sports, its esprit de corps, its intellectual and moral atmosphere, which mould and stimulate all who are connected with it."[19] The strength of male college culture left no room for the development of women's colleges. "What if the same climate which strength-

ens the pine blasts the rose?" "What if the same forces which develop all that
is most manly in one sex repress and dwarf all that is most womanly in the
other?"[20]

The separate college for women was the only solution. Yet it held dangers
as well. Seelye shared his Amherst colleagues' sense that Mount Holyoke instructed by negatives. What did they find so distasteful about the seminary?
The official college documents state simply that Louisa Dickinson Greene urged
her husband to oppose the single large building because climbing stairs drained
women's health.[21] Much more was clearly at issue.

By the 1860s, those outside college circles, responsible for hospitals and
asylums, were questioning the proper form of institutional care. The large
setting, or "congregate" system, came under attack as dangerous to the physical and mental health of its inmates. As early as 1832, an outbreak of ophthal-
mia, an eye disorder, among the pauper children at Bellevue caused authorities
to disperse the inmates among Long Island farms for their protection. By the
late 1860s, several experiments in caring for delinquent boys demonstrated the
value of placing them in homes under the care of surrogate parents.[22] After
Samuel Gridley Howe, the chairman of the Board of State Charities of Massachusetts, visited European asylums, he returned committed to the vision of
Gheel, Belgium, where the mentally ill lived without restraint in a village.
Study and travel taught him that the institution created its own forms of disorder. The creators of the large asylum believed that by imposing external
discipline they could remold the troubled psyche. Howe saw that this did not
work; instead asylums begot merely different forms of psychic distress. Beginning with the state board's annual report in 1867, Howe worked to break
up existing asylums and to board patients out or house them in small-scale
cottages.[23]

How did this apply to women's colleges? In 1869, John Greene wrote to
Sophia Smith against the "affected, unsocial, visionary notions" of girls' school
graduates. Intriguingly, he connected this to their isolation in a large building,
secluded from "the real practical life" of the town. An editorial in *Scribner's*,
immediately after Seelye was selected president, added the issue of sexuality
to Greene's concerns about keeping women's expectations down-to-earth. Its
author was *Scribner's* editor J. G. Holland, Seelye's cousin by marriage and
close friend. Author of books of advice for the young, Holland had lectured
to the first Vassar students, offending some of them by his conservatism. In
his article on Smith he used quite frank language. The seminary and Vassar
brought together large numbers of students under one roof. Those in "charge
of large bodies of girls" know what "mischiefs" this causes:

> No consideration would induce us to place a young woman—daughter or ward—
> in a college which would shut her away from all family life for a period of four

years. The system is unnatural, and not one young woman in ten can be subjected to it without injury. It is not necessary to go into particulars, but every
observing physician or physiologist knows what we mean when we say that
such a system is fearfully unsafe. The facts which substantiate their opinion
would fill the public mind with horror if they were publicly known. Men may
"pooh! pooh!" these facts if they choose, but they exist. Diseases of body, diseases of imagination, vices of body and imagination—everthing we would save
our children from—are bred in these great institutions where life and association are circumscribed, as weeds are forced in hot-beds.[24]

Nineteenth-century readers would have understood that Holland's overheated
language meant that he was talking about sexual matters. The new danger that
higher education for women posed was that in protecting young women from
men in large seminary structures, colleges exposed them to each other. Separated from their families, students were developing an autonomous life, unregulated by authorities. College life as it was developing at Vassar, with its
independence and intense female friendships, allowed such spunky students as
Sarah Glazier to question a world that tolerated J. G. Holland's conventional
views of marriage. Such an environment was unnatural and unsafe. In such a
setting vice and disease could flourish unregulated. Holland urged Smith to
avoid the large asylum and to place students in households headed by faculty
families, the "cottage" as opposed to the "congregate" system.

Seelye never spoke in such fashion. He made only positive statements. But
from the beginning he insisted that Smith protect femininity. His inaugural
carried this commitment: "it is to preserve her womanliness that this College
has been founded."[25] Womanliness for him, as for John Greene, meant that
students remained within the culture of the family and the town. The danger
was not men, even Amherst collegians; it was the college culture developing
at Vassar. Undoubtedly influenced by asylum reformers such as Samuel Gridley Howe, John Greene, J. G. Holland, and L. Clark Seelye all shared a solution quite wonderful in its simplicity. Educate women in college but keep
them symbolically at home. Erect a central college building for instruction
and surround it with cottages where the students live in familial settings. Keep
them in daily contact with men as president and faculty. Build no chapel or
library to encourage them to enter into the life of the town. Place students
under family government as members of the town and prevent the great harm
of the seminary—the creation of a separate women's culture with its dangerous
emotional attachments, its visionary schemes, and its strong-minded stance to
the world.

In September 1875, when Smith College opened, it looked exactly as one
might expect. The trustees had purchased the homesteads of two prominent
families close to the center of Northampton. They placed on the hill an impressive Victorian Gothic administration and classroom building. Next door

College Hall; *Smith College Archives*

stood the president's ample house. The trustees moved one house to a new location and expanded it to serve as the first residence of Smith College students. Smith College's initial campus had every element important to the new vision: the dignified setting for intellectual life; the male patriarchal presence; the domestic dwelling house; placement on a central street; and no library or chapel.

When the trustees chose an architect for College Hall they looked eastward to Peabody & Stearns, the young Boston firm that had designed the Smith Academy in Hatfield.[26] In the tradition of the "Old Main," the primary building of male and coeducational colleges, College Hall provided spaces for college work and assembly—classrooms, laboratories, a meeting hall, an art gallery, and the president's office. An "Old Main" stood traditionally atop a hill: thus the trustees removed the Lyman house from its prominent position to give College Hall a dominant place. The Victorian Gothic building that arose boldly asserted its power over the setting. It is a nervous, vital building. A clock tower rising ninety-five feet, topped by four turrets, strongly emphasizes its verticality. Gables, dormers, and finials draw attention to the steeply pitched roof. The tall clock tower, the primary entrance to the building, sits atop the juncture of the two rectangular wings which meet in an L, giving the building an asymmetrical appearance when seen from the front. Bays and the tower create an irregular exterior outline, emphasized by the polychromatic red and white stone trim. An extraordinary variety of windows adorns this rich surface. The boldest have Gothic pointed arches like the doorway, surrounding stained-glass rose windows. Links with British Victorian building and the architectural credo of John Ruskin are everywhere apparent—though nowhere more directly than the stone columns with capitals of plant forms at the entrance.[27] College ivy has enhanced the organic interplay. In its specific details, its decorative scheme, and its basic massing, College Hall expresses perfectly the muscular Christianity of its Amherst sponsors: vertical, irregular, nervous, and symbolic. Nothing in the formal education—curriculum or academic building—suggested the gender of the student body.

In keeping with the injunction against stairs, classrooms occupied the first floor. The sizes of the recitation rooms varied, though each had a platform to emphasize the authority of the instructor. The second story held the central meeting spaces of the college. Social Hall occupied almost all the west wing and could be expanded to almost the entire floor by separating the wide doors of the large recitation room and art gallery. The president's room opened on to Social Hall at the raised platform.[28] Students went to Sunday services in town, but each morning they attended chapel in Social Hall. As the president conducted the morning service, the placing of his office thus signalled his ministerial position in the college.

Dewey House stands in sharp contrast to the main building. Its associations came not from the power of Christian learning but with the life of Northampton through the adaptation of the handsome residence of one of its most prominent early-nineteenth-century families. Designed in 1827 for Charles A. Dewey by Thomas Pratt after the example of Ithiel Town, its four Ionic columns adorned a solid two-story box to which a three-story ell was added to the back.[29] The Dewey House contained all the components of a family residence. The porch opened on to a hall with parlors and led to the large dining room in the ell. Students lived privately upstairs. The number of rooms suggests that at least initially each student had a separate room. The only significant difference from a single-family house is the scale—visually hidden from the front—and the provision for the receiving room and bedroom for the lady-in-charge near the entrance.[30]

Seelye and his trustees symbolically chose a prominent existing house for the first student residence. By definition they gained a dwelling with its familial plan. When they came to erect new buildings, they copied the Dewey House's domestic form. Peabody & Stearns designed Hatfield House, built in 1877, for thirty-two students, Washburn (1878) and Hubbard (1879) for approximately fifty.[31] They planned these three brick buildings of increasing size to look like family houses. Though sometimes labelled Gothic,[32] they are really vernacular dwellings with steeply pitched roofs and gables. Welcoming porches stretch along one wall. Doors and windows open on to lawns. The houses sit somewhat informally placed in back of College Hall. In the nineteenth century, curving walks connected them with each other and the central building. The downstairs held the public rooms and the bedrooms and receiving rooms of both the lady-in-charge and the faculty resident. Upstairs, student rooms of different sizes and shapes group irregularly around a hallway stretched into a corridor.[33] The scale is larger than that of the Dewey House, the materials somewhat more solid, but the Hatfield, Washburn, and Hubbard houses feel like family homes.

Smith's creators wanted to avoid the mistakes not only of Mount Holyoke Seminary but also of Vassar College. There the "congregate" system demonstrated economic as well as moral liabilities. Greene knew that Matthew Vassar had overstretched his resources to build a grand main building. To fill it, Vassar created a large preparatory department, seriously diluting its offerings and lowering its tone.[34] Greene suggested to Sophia Smith that she include in her will the provision that "not more than one-half of the sum appropriated by me to this object, shall be invested in buildings and grounds." The other half she stipulated the college trustees invest "for furnishing teachers, library, and apparatus, for the higher education of young women."[35] Seelye and his coworkers were determined to keep admission standards that of the men's colleges, no matter how small the entering class. He hired only two teachers to aid him and drew on part-time instructors from the immediate region.[36]

In September 1875, fourteen young women presented themselves for admission to Smith College and were received by the "ardent young President" and Sarah W. Humphrey.[37] Smith repeated the Vassar pattern of male president and female Lady Principal. Determined to insure that Amherst standards of femininity prevail, Seelye brought the daughter of a late Amherst president to oversee the manners and morals of the students as director of social culture. Seelye created this department and found "an accomplished lady" to fill it, who, "accustomed to the best society, will make it her special work to organize the social life of the institution, and to preserve and increase those graces of manners and of social life which we justly esteem so highly."[38] Sarah Humphrey remained at Smith only briefly, and her official title went with her, but her presence in Dewey House established a Smith tradition: each house had a lady-in-charge and a female faculty member. The matron added to her domestic tasks Humphrey's concern for the personal and social life of the resi-

The cottages of Smith, taken from College Hall; *Smith College Archives*

Hatfield House, 1888; Mary Augusta Jordan at far right; *Smith College Archives*

dents; the teacher (nineteenth-century Smith avoided the title "professor" for a woman) set the intellectual tone. J. G. Holland did not get exactly what he wanted—"a real family in every house." [39] The imitation one, however, came provocatively close: a houseful of young women and two parental figures—only both were women.

Only one written rule governed the first years—the "ten o'clock rule," setting the bedtime hour of students. The daily schedule of chapel, classes, gymnastics exercises, and meals established order, as did the students' own sense of decorum. [40] "Most of the students come from refined families and have been well-bred in their homes. They have been granted the liberty common to such families. . . . They have been free to walk or ride whenever and wherever young women can safely do so without escort." [41] A student commented for the press on the freedom from regulation that she found so pleasing. At Smith, she lived in "neither a nursery nor a nunnery." No rules regulated her life at college, nor bells, except for "the *door*-bell. That may sound when and for whom it will, each student receiving her friends of both sexes as freely and independently as in her own home." Smith treated a student as a "sensible, honorable woman," and allowed her the pleasure of "walking, rowing, riding, driving, attending musical or dramatic entertainments, or accepting invitations from friends in town as she will." [42] Social freedom broke with seminary traditions. It formed an essential part of Smith's experimental design to protect students' femininity by keeping them within the heterosocial culture of village life.

Seelye found himself pleased with the outcome of Smith's first years. He remarked to his trustees on the wisdom of starting small, which allowed "harmony and homogeneity" of teachers and students. "The different experience" of Wellesley "shows very clearly the dangers incurred in attempting to organize, satisfactorily, a numerous body of students and teachers when all are strangers to each other and most of them unacquainted with collegiate methods." [43] Two years later he gave his full approval to Smith's experiment. Offering women higher education did nothing to lessen their "feminine modesty" or their religious faith. Smith College students did not "copy the distinctly masculine traits of male institutions. On the contrary there seems an increasing sensitiveness and repugnance to that coarse effrontery which has given to the epithet 'strong-minded' so frequently its opprobrious significance." [44] In Seelye's eyes, Smith College worked. Its founders had created a college fostering "a refined, intelligent Christian womanhood." [45]

Though Smith College proved to be a more complex institution than Seelye recognized in such public statements, its design appeared just right to its age. Coping with the daily dilemmas of caring for four hundred students and competing for those few young women with adequate academic preparation for college work, Vassar and Wellesley learned the advantages of Smith's plan.

To the conservative Quaker gentlemen outside Philadelphia, thinking of the educational needs of their sect's daughters, the Amherst shapers of Smith had the right solution for Bryn Mawr. Even the originator became the follower: when Mount Holyoke Seminary decided to become a college, it assumed that Smith defined the women's college's proper form.

6

The Advantages of the So-called "Cottage System"

WELLESLEY, VASSAR

I

Smith College made Vassar and Wellesley seem immediately behind the times. Yet what could a women's college with a large seminary building do? While critics judged the main building at Vassar and College Hall at Wellesley inflexible and expensive to operate, both Matthew Vassar and Henry Fowle Durant had confused erecting them with endowing a college. However appealing the domestic vision of Smith's cottages, neither Vassar nor Wellesley could afford to tear down its principal building to begin again.

The thought that College Hall had a basic flaw in its design never occurred to Durant. Both he and his wife experienced disappointments in the first year. Teachers whom Durant hired as loyal workers in the cause of Christian education for women turned out to have their own ideas about a women's college. Durant wanted to reproduce Mount Holyoke. Instead of unquestioning devotion, he got several outspoken, independent faculty. Sarah Glazier, who had kept her own mind as a spirited undergraduate at Vassar, came into conflict with Wellesley authorities as a teacher. Durant summarily fired her and two others at the end of the first year, because "they conflict[ed] with the government of the Coll.," causing great consternation among the students. One student, hardly the respectful daughter that Durant had anticipated, wrote to her mother that she "could not bear the thought of coming back next year; to find those teachers gone; the only ones we loved and respected to be under the thumb of a man and woman that I despise."[1] The beautiful Wedgwood service in the dining hall did not survive student handling: the Durants replaced it with plain white crockery. Durant found it hard to comprehend that students

82

did not value and conserve all his gifts, but instead carelessly broke dishes or turned down the leaves of valuable library books.[2]

Though saddened, Durant remained undaunted. Far from questioning his plan, Durant wanted to expand it. College Hall was just a beginning. Just as his aspirations grew in the period of building from seminary to college, so they swelled from college to university in the years that followed.[3] "Do you see what I see?" he once asked Louise Manning Hodgkins, Wellesley's professor of English: "On that hill an Art School; down there a Musical Conservatory; at the furthest right a Medical College."[4] In 1880–81, two new buildings expressed Wellesley's vaulting ambitions, Stone Hall and Music Hall. At the end of the decade the Farnsworth Art building completed the scheme.

From its inception Wellesley stressed its special mission to educate Christian teachers. Along with a preparatory department for younger students needing courses prior to undertaking college work, Wellesley established, as had Vassar, a category of special students for older women who, while generally prepared, lacked certain courses required for entrance. In 1877–78, the college circular announced a new program for "teacher specials," which let women already established as teachers take courses at the college in the area of their greatest interest. Wellesley made it possible for them "to pursue any course of study which they prefer, and to give all their time to their chosen work," bound by no requirements.[5] College opening in 1878 demonstrated the need for such a flexible program, for fifty-one "T. Specs" enrolled. Wellesley oversaw the building of Dana Hall in the village to house those special students who required residence; when it proved too small, the preparatory department, no longer needed by the college, became a private school and took the Dana Hall building and name. In 1880, Mrs. Valeria G. Stone, a widow dispersing her fortune for good works, gave $100,000 for a separate building to house the Teachers' Collegiate Course and its students. Stone Hall opened in September 1881.[6] During the planning period Wellesley trustees called a conference with the Massachusetts Board of Education in the State House, where representatives from New England normal schools and colleges advised about the teachers' department.[7]

The architectural firm of Ware & Van Brunt designed an imposing building for Stone Hall on the low hill to the west of College Hall, overlooking the lake. Hammatt Billings had died before the college opened. Wellesley turned to one of Boston's most prominent architectural firms for its second large building.[8] For Wellesley, Ware & Van Brunt created a ponderous four-story brick structure with five-story towers. Flemish gables of varying sizes adorned the top stories, made the more nervous by tall conical roofs atop the towers, weathervanes, a Georgian cupola, and decorative chimney stacks. By the time planning for Stone Hall began, Wellesley had experienced an unpleasant aspect of its initial building, that the single dining hall for all students and faculty created an overpowering din. Stone Hall provided four small dining rooms for its hundred students. Perhaps because intended for older students, it gave each woman a single room. Despite these generous provisions, a stately two-story parlor, and a separate library, the very existence of Stone Hall symbolized the separation of the "Normal College" and its students from the regular liberal arts program, whose students always assumed superiority.[9]

As did the other women's colleges, Wellesley had to resolve the question of the relation between the liberal arts curriculum and the fine arts. Traditionally, music and art formed part of women's education, foremost among the necessary accomplishments to "finish" a woman for polite society. Even excellent schools, such as the Augusta Female Seminary (later to become Mary Baldwin College), gave primary attention to the fine arts, devoting half of the faculty positions to music, painting, and elocution.[10] Those who wanted to distinguish institutions of collegiate grade from the seminary either had to eschew education in the arts, establish it on a different basis, or insist that students taking fine arts add them to a full liberal arts curriculum. Wellesley took the latter course, and, in 1878, founded a College of Music and a College of Art, each requiring a five-year program to allow work in the fine arts in addition to the regular course of study. Durant himself gave the College of Music a building, which opened in 1881. For Music Hall, Ware & Van Brunt designed a companion for neighboring Stone. Though smaller than Stone Hall, the two shared many design elements: a symmetrical plan of Flemish gables and towers with tall conical roofs topped by finials, steeply pitched roofs and chimney stacks, all done in red brick trimmed in red stone. After twentieth-century fires destroyed College and Stone halls, Music remained as the oldest large building on the Wellesley campus, a rather sombre reminder of Durant's architectural taste. When built, it contained thirty-eight music rooms, a hall for choral singing, pianos, and an organ.[11] In 1881, a music course consisted of mastering an instrument. The Music building provided no rooms for lectures, for musical theory and history did not form part of the music curriculum.[12]

With the death of Isaac D. Farnsworth, a close friend of Durant, the third separate college within Wellesley attained in 1889 a building. Farnsworth left $100,000 to Wellesley for an art building to house a museum and the College of Art. Placed on the lake side of Norumbega Hill (named because of benefactor Eben Horsford's interest in the Norse exploration of America), Farnsworth looked utterly different from any other Wellesley building. Boston architects Arthur Rotch and George Thomas Tilden, both trained at the Ecole des Beaux Arts, designed a classical structure in cream-colored Berea sandstone that appeared to its age as a light, elegant jewel set among Wellesley's dark, heavy brick. Demolished in the mid-twentieth century to make way for Jewett Art Center, this symmetrical building contained a museum, a lecture hall with stereopticon, a library, two laboratories containing art material related to courses, studios, and exhibition rooms for student work. Unlike the study of music in its first decades at Wellesley, the art course consisted of a program both of "general art culture" and practical training.[13]

Its founder's ambitions that it become a university meant that Wellesley grew rapidly in its early years, both in its student body and in its academic offerings and faculty. Great numbers of students applied. While the college accepted only a portion, it turned away only the unqualified, for in the late nineteenth century, Wellesley felt committed to taking every student who met its standards.[14] Durant's mission encouraged growth; so did his economic worries. Even though Durant, Stone, and Farnsworth gave their buildings as outright gifts, the low fees charged to students did not cover operating costs, and the college ran a deficit from the beginning. Committed to the "calico" girls, Durant did not consider raising tuition. In the early years he cheerfully made up the deficits, which averaged $50,000 each year. But his own finances met with some reverses. Beyond land and buildings, the college had no endowment.[15] Increased numbers of students would bring in more revenues, especially if they occupied the same space (in 1880, Thomas Wentworth Higginson found in College Hall three beds in a room twelve feet square)[16] or the college found a less costly way to house and board them.

Ironically, Durant's hopes for a women's university allowed for a competing vision to take root and flourish. Pauline Durant saw the college in a manner different from her husband. She focused on the individual student and her needs. She understood the problems of the great seminary structure. A loyal wife, Pauline Durant never criticized the realization of her husband's dream in College Hall, but she cared for those who found living with so many others too great a strain. She welcomed into her home students who needed quiet and isolation. And she came to envision a Wellesley that looked much like Smith. While Henry Fowle Durant "saw every rise of ground in our spacious campus crowned with the stately buildings of the university-to-be," his wife "beheld home-like cottages nestled in every glade."[17]

With the aid of an important ally, Pauline Durant partially realized her dream for Wellesley. When Ada Howard resigned, young Alice Freeman became acting president and then president in her own right. While her predecessor held the title "President of the Faculty," Freeman assumed the more inclusive one of "President of Wellesley College." The board of trustees made her a member, a position usual for the male presidents of Smith and Vassar, but not for the Lady Principal of Mount Holyoke.[18] Henry Fowle Durant died in 1881, and Pauline became treasurer in his stead. Gradually power began to shift from the office of treasurer to that of president.

As one of the early women graduates of the University of Michigan recruited by Durant, Alice Freeman had experienced the unique independence of that pioneer coeducational university. In the first years of coeducation, the

Junior Tree Day, 1887, with honorary class member Lyman Abbott and his wife;
Alice Freeman and Eben Horsford in window; *Wellesley College Archives*

university allowed women the complete freedom of men, letting them attend
all classes (except in the Medical College) and live in boarding houses without
supervision. As a Wellesley faculty member, Freeman demonstrated her competence, poise, and evangelical spirit. As president, she moved quickly to organize Wellesley on a collegiate basis. On taking office, Freeman abolished the
preparatory department, at the same time that she encouraged the development of private secondary schools, such as Dana Hall. She reorganized the
faculty into departments with a head for each and created standings committees of the college. She replaced the daily Bible class taught by teachers of
other subjects with a formal, examinable course in the Bible. She fostered the
formation of alumnae clubs and spoke about Wellesley throughout the country. The college raised tuition to $300. A new, crisp secular tone replaced the
more long-winded and morally freighted language of college reports and
circulars.[19]

Yet while Alice Freeman moved the college several steps toward becoming
a modern, secular institution, she shared with Pauline Durant a belief in the
moral and social purposes of women's education and a commitment to nurtur-
ing Christian faith. At Wellesley, at the same time that she removed religion

Freshman Tree Day, 1885, class of 1888; Lyman Abbott, second row, fourth from left;
Sophonisba Breckinridge, second row, fifth from left; *Wellesley College Archives*

from the curriculum, Freeman founded the college's extra-curricular Christian
Association. Alice Freeman was one of the late nineteenth century's heroines,
for she seemed able in her own life to reconcile the claims of profession and
power with femininity. She brought the metaphor of the home to the college,
and a sense of its importance.[20] An organizer and administrator, Freeman
counseled individual students on personal and academic matters as well, developing close relations with a number of them. In her letters, Sophonisba
Breckinridge, a member of the class of 1889, addressed Alice Freeman as "my
other mother" for the rest of Freeman's life.[21]

    In the cottage, Alice Freeman found the perfect instrument of her hopes
for Wellesley, an aid both to the secularization of the college and its domesti-
cation. The cottage separated residence from instruction. This freed the academic side from moral and religious constraints, focusing the spiritual mission
of the college on the domestic environment. Like the home in the same period,
the cottage served as the repository of values, a feminine refuge from the challenges of contemporary life. Under Alice Freeman's presidency, Wellesley acquired or erected four cottages; upon her resignation to marry Harvard
philosopher George Herbert Palmer, the college built a fifth and named it for her.

Eliot House group, ca. 1895; *Wellesley College Archives*

In 1881, Pauline Durant gave Waban, the first cottage. The following year, with a gift from M. H. Simpson to honor his wife, the college built Simpson Cottage. Here Van Brunt & Howe broke from their red brick institutional mold to fashion a Tudor dwelling house "destined to be a quiet temporary retreat for pupils who may become unwell or fatigued by the nature of their studies." At the dedication of the cornerstone President Seelye of Smith gave the prayer: he must have felt a twinge of triumph at Wellesley's avowal that its magnificent building created such threats to student well-being.[22] In 1886, Pauline Durant helped purchase a boarding house formerly for young women working in the local shoe factory, which the college remodeled as the Eliot. Outside the Wellesley gates in what came to be called the Village, the Eliot housed forty-seven students who worked at the college for reduced fees. In 1886 and 1888, Frank W. Hurd designed Norumbega and Freeman, two sizeable cottages placed on Norumbega Hill. As at Smith, each house held faculty residents and a matron. The cottages were self-contained units where students dined as well as slept. While Smith built its cottages of brick, Wellesley erected large rambling wood structures with the informal look of summer homes along

Norumbega, ca. 1891; n.b. threesome in window; *Wellesley College Archives*

the coast. The interiors complemented their shingle-style exteriors, comfortable and filled with home-like associations.

Students gravitated toward the cottages, so much so that not all who wanted to live there could be satisfied. The college promised each student that she could have "one year of cottage life" during her college course.[23] Alice Freeman preferred to live in a cottage rather than in the great building. She moved the presidential suite from College Hall to Norumbega's ground floor. There, in her sitting room adjoining her bedroom and bath, she saw and counseled students; in the dining room, she entertained college visitors.

Norumbega quickly became a major center of college life and tradition. It attracted unusually able and engaged faculty residents, some of whom, like Sophie Jewett, enlivened the dinner table with their "wit and . . . rich mental gifts." Presidential visitors added a certain excitement. The house became noted for its plays, especially the annual fund-raising effort for Dinah Pace's school for Negro children in Atlanta. Norumbega's warm and friendly environment made it the choice for foreign students, especially those from the Far East. While other building forms supplanted the cottage in the twentieth century,

Norumbega, surviving until the 1950s, regarded itself as the repository of the true Wellesley spirit. As one of its first gifts, the Alumnae Association donated $10,700 to free the cottage from debt.[24]

Wellesley transformed the cottage system. The Amherst shapers of Smith saw cottages as a means to keep a women's college protected by a patriarchal presence. Smith's cottages broke up the all-female community of the seminary and dispersed students among situations of home, integrated into a New England town. The women of Wellesley, by contrast, saw the cottage as a natural environment for women within a women's community. Isolated on a great country estate, the cottages remained as separate from the world as College Hall. Guided by a female president and faculty, students stayed within the world of women, whether housed in the large congregate building or smaller dwelling houses. At Wellesley, cottages altered the scale of Durant's vision and created domestic, rather than institutional, environments. Left intact was the power of female influence.

II

Vassar had some of Wellesley's needs without its flexibility or resources. Despite his impassioned pleas in 1872, President Raymond's fight to reduce the number of students in Main did not succeed. As long as there were students willing to fill the building, the trustees accepted them to increase revenues. This pioneer women's college faced a peculiar handicap. When Matthew Vassar died he left two nephews on the board of trustees who never sympathized with their uncle's scheme for a women's college. Both Milo Jewett's reminiscences and those of trustee Benson Lossing angrily recall the brothers' treachery as they attempted to jettison or diminish their uncle's college before the endowment was secure. It was the brothers who balked at a female professoriate. And it was probably the brothers whose insistence on economy packed Main too tightly with students. In the 1880s, a truce of sorts was effected, but on the brothers' terms. They gave Vassar its first building since the opening of the college: the Vassar Brothers Laboratory for chemistry and physics. But they coupled this gift with the most hostile bequest ever received by the women's colleges: in 1882, Matthew Vassar, Jr., endowed chairs in Greek and Latin and in physics and chemistry, on the condition that no woman ever occupy either; in 1891, Guy Vassar's will established chairs in modern languages and natural history, on the same terms.[25] These vengeful endowments at the end of narrow lives clarify the nature of the opposition Vassar's president faced as he attempted to make even modest changes in Main.

Declining enrollment due to competition, rather than concern with students' mental or physical well-being, changed the minds of trustees. Smith made an economic impact on Vassar, not a moral one. In 1874, Vassar had 411 students. Ten years later, with Wellesley and Smith flourishing in Massachusetts, the number fell to 275. The real decline is more startling than these numbers, for the enumeration included almost 100 preparatory students. While Raymond's successor, Samuel L. Caldwell, lacked the imagination to bring Vassar out of its slough, he made modest improvements in students' living conditions. He increased the number of detached single rooms, the choice most in demand, and reduced the number of students sharing a suite from five to three, allowing each to have a separate bedroom. A trimmed-down Main accommodated 280 students and 23 teachers.[26]

Vassar's difficulties in the early 1880s involved more than overcrowding. While growth at Wellesley enabled it to add cottages in the 1880s, shrinkage at Vassar prevented new building. Caldwell comforted himself with the thought that Smith's system was merely a fad of unproven value.[27] When continued decline threatened to reduce Vassar to a preparatory school, an open campaign by alumnae forced Caldwell to resign. In 1886, Vassar acquired the energetic educator to take it into the twentieth century, James Monroe Taylor.[28] Taylor brought from his pastorate of the Fourth Baptist Church in Providence, Rhode Island, a fresh perspective and new energy to attack Vassar's problems. Under Taylor the college emerged strengthened and sure. Endowments from new sources and vast building programs transformed the campus into the landscape we know today.

By 1886, the college was not only troubled; it looked oddly anachronistic. Built to conform to the seminary ideal, Main held all classrooms, laboratories, the library, the chapel, and the dining hall; in addition, it housed all students and their female teachers along wide exercise corridors. Most backward-looking of all, the male faculty had apartments for themselves and their families in the end pavilions, while the president's "house" lay within the central pavilion. This was intolerable. It personally offended Taylor's feeling for family privacy, and it also created an unwholesome dependence of faculty households on the college. In addition, time turned darling faculty children into unruly adolescents, who posed threats to college property. Immediately on assuming the presidency, Taylor began a campaign to have the college build professors' houses outside the college hedge.[29] When he first broached the subject he suggested that the vacated apartments be kept as separate entities to become "cottages" within Main. "Whatever may be the advantages of the socalled 'cottage system,' it is now in favor, [and] one must in some way meet the popular want."[30]

Taylor's vision for Vassar was close to that of Smith's creators. This is clear in his plans for faculty houses. He wanted his male faculty outside college property, but close by. He saw the men on the faculty as rescuers in case of an emergency, a possible volunteer fire department. In addition, the men had an important social role to play. Like the shapers of Smith, Taylor wanted to keep students in contact with heterosocial family life while in college. He envisioned a cluster of "homes distinct from the college building, open to the students, and adding a normal element to their lives." Professors' houses, staffed by professors' wives, provided a necessary refining agent, important to the proper social development of college students.[31]

Beginning in 1891, the college built houses for male professors across Raymond Avenue. Conventional large frame houses, surrounded by four strips of green, they faced the campus with images of normality. In 1895, Vassar built a president's house, a generous red brick structure designed to keep on college grounds a firm patriarchal presence.[32]

Taylor found an enthusiastic donor in Frederick Ferris Thompson, a new member of the Vassar board of trustees. A Poughkeepsie native, he was president of the First National Bank of New York. Thompson gave the first two college houses, to which the trustees added an additional two.[33] These were unusual gifts for Thompson to make, for he normally thought of students, not faculty. Thompson was a benefactor who delighted in gifts that enhanced enjoyment of college life. He initiated a "Good Times" fund to pay for freshman festivities. He presented each senior with a silver Vassar spoon, and sometimes gave them an oyster supper to commence its use. He paid for the annual Mohonk excursion that took freshmen and seniors away from campus for a day in the hills. Thompson's vision of Vassar endeared him to students. In 1891, he wrote to the librarian that while "hard study" might be necessary, "personally, you know, if I could have my own way, I would like to just make the girls' life in college one long picnic." He did what he could to bring that about.[34]

If the college demanded hard study, Thompson decided to make it as comfortable as possible. In 1893, he gave a new library to Vassar, on the condition that he could choose its location. Against Taylor's urging that it be a separate building named for its donor, Thompson insisted that it be built as an annex to Main: he meant it not "for the glory of Fred Thompson, but for the comfort of these Vassar girls." He wanted them to go to the library in the evenings without having to step outside.[35] Thompson won, and the library emerged as a porte-cochère of Main, affectionately dubbed "Uncle Fred's nose." For the next sixty years, the large proboscis on its front façade disfigured Main. Interior elegance gave the library its second nickname, "The Soap Palace," in honor of its rose and gray marble stairs.[36]

The library was a curious throwback to the early conception of the college as seminary that Taylor was working to change. While, as a realist, Taylor recognized that he had to accept the physical fact of Main, he understood the popularity of the cottage. Initially it had cost too much to house students in small units. But after building its first cottages, Smith had shifted to erect much larger versions, more appropriately called residence halls or dormito-

ries. Taylor began a campaign for residence halls, which the alumnae enthusiastically supported. Ellen Swallow Richards, now established at M.I.T. as a
scientist experimenting with practical applications of technology for the home,
became actively involved in the campaign to raise money to make a hall possible and to see that it proved both hygienic and attractive.[37]

As a prominent Baptist, Taylor caught the ear of America's wealthiest Baptist layman, John D. Rockefeller. Vassar offered to Rockefeller a safe haven for
his daughter Bessie, who came as a special student from 1886 to 1888. Taylor
attracted Rockefeller to the Vassar board of trustees in 1888, insuring at least
annual visits. At the point in which Rockefeller was turning from the making
of money to its distribution, Taylor became one of his principal advisors.[38]
Taylor worked with his Chicago contemporaries and William Rainey Harper
to urge Rockefeller to endow the University of Chicago. At the same time that
Rockefeller committed himself to the advancement of higher education in Chicago, a gift that ultimately cost him $35 million, he began his smaller, but
significant, gifts to Vassar, which he later extended to the other women's colleges. In 1893, Rockefeller gave a residence hall, which he named in honor of
Bessie Rockefeller Strong. Nine years later, he gave a second dormitory, Eliza
Davison House, named for his mother. At the southern end of the group of
ultimately four residence halls—Strong, Raymond, Davison, and Lathrop—
he contributed Rockefeller Hall, a much-needed lecture and recitation building.

Vassar hired the Boston architect Francis R. Allen to design Strong. This
was the first of twelve buildings that Allen's firm planned for the college over
the next decades. Allen followed the precedent set at Smith by Peabody and
Stearns: he designed residential halls for students as overscaled dwelling houses
in the prevailing domestic vernacular of the region. It is revealing that Raymond carries its original name above the entryway—Raymond House. Strong
is a large plain brick dwelling, four stories tall under a gable, with a projecting
dining hall. The unornamented façade is punctuated by regular window openings topped by simple brick-colored stone lintels. Only the roof carries decoration: gables, cupolas, and Jacobean chimney stacks.

Internal planning followed along the lines set at Smith: public rooms grouped
around the entrance; the dining room and kitchen formed a wing off to the
side with servants' quarters above; a few student rooms were interspersed on
the lower floors, but the bulk of them ranged above. Vassar carefully avoided
the overcrowding of Main. Each student had a separate bedroom; doubles were
three-room suites, where two students shared a study room.[39]

Strong faced east toward the gardens. Later in the decade, when the college
decided to add more residential buildings for students, it called on the great
landscape architect Frederick Law Olmsted to place them. He advised an "éch-
elon plan" that staggered buildings in a step-like fashion toward the road forming
the western border of the campus. Francis Allen argued against this arrange-

ment. The trustees agreed with him on a "quadrangle plan" for Strong, Raymond, Davison, and Lathrop.[40] "Quadrangle," however, is a misnomer: the
word connoted to its age a composition of connected buildings surrounding
an inner court, following English collegiate precedents. At Vassar, the Quad
consists of four identical large residence halls, each built as a free-standing
house, completely separate, placed two on a side. The four halls are oriented
outward: the primary entrance to each is on the side facing away from the
inner court.

In the late nineteenth century, Smith's vision prevailed at Wellesley and
Vassar. Within the limits set by immense seminary buildings, each college adapted
as best it could. Henry Fowle Durant's vision of Wellesley as a women's university helped realize his widow's hopes for home-like cottages. When revived
under Taylor, Vassar moved its male faculty into houses, built a president's
house, and began erecting large cottages for its students. In 1865, and even
1875, the great seminary structure seemed just right; after 1875, a women's
college had to have cottages to be up-to-date.

7

As Unnoticed as the Daughters of Any Cambridge Residents

RADCLIFFE

Radcliffe College started simply enough. On December 23, 1878, Arthur Gilman wrote Charles W. Eliot, president of Harvard, asking if Gilman was "correct in supposing" that the relations of Harvard professors "to the university are such as to permit of their giving instruction to those who are not connected with it." Gilman was working out a scheme to "afford to women opportunities for carrying their studies systematically forward further than it is possible for them now to do in this country, except possibly at Smith College," and he thought it prudent to inform Eliot and get his clearance.[1] Gilman planned to gather qualified women in Cambridge and arrange for Harvard faculty to offer them the courses they taught to men at Harvard College. It was a clever scheme and it worked. Within nine months, twenty-seven women were studying with Harvard professors under the auspices of "The Society for the Collegiate Instruction of Women," familiarly called the Annex. In 1893, with an endowment and a legal relation to Harvard, the Annex emerged into Radcliffe College.

Yet the Annex/Radcliffe began and remained a curious entity. While it stood officially opposed to coeducation, it also never wanted to become a separate women's college. Harvard and Harvard's faculty gave the Annex its only reason for being. Thus it made no separate appointments. As a result, only men taught its women students. Only gradually did Harvard's annex become a physical place, acquiring and building administrative and academic structures and finally dormitories. Until the twentieth century, Radcliffe resisted building, for its founders felt an aversion to anything that smacked of the seminary associations of women's colleges.

While a negative evaluation of the seminary had shaped the design of Smith College, the founders of the Annex felt a heightened distaste. They predicated all their efforts on the importance of Harvard. The university's "relation to the intellectual world outside, its maturity of thought and methods, its claim on cultivated minds everywhere, give it a hold on our respect and affection which women share with men."[2] In the eyes of literary Boston and Cambridge, only Harvard really mattered. In the 1870s, a son of Boston society did not go to Amherst. Boston regarded itself as liberal, enlightened, and urbane. It judged the evangelical colleges, such as Amherst—and therefore Smith—provincial, narrow, and sectarian. Nearby, Henry Fowle Durant's omnipresence continued to taint Wellesley.

Even a reformer as liberal as Thomas Wentworth Higginson, the editor of the feminist weekly *The Woman's Journal*, reflected these attitudes. In 1876, Higginson responded to the question "Which College?" for a young woman. He considered only three single-sex institutions: Vassar, Wellesley, and Smith. As a seminary, not a proper college, Mount Holyoke no longer counted. A close, firsthand observer of colleges, Higginson considered the various strengths and weaknesses of the three. While he found that Vassar had excellent departments in mathematics and English and a fine president, he perceived Main as "an evil in itself, besides being ill-arranged." Wellesley offered both higher academic standards than Vassar (he later stood corrected on this) and a better planned building, but Higginson found that its discipline retained "too much of the boarding-school order" and its all-female faculty only enhanced "the special evil of separate education."[3] Two years earlier Higginson had spelled out what he meant by "evil." What disturbed him was not the "smash," but the larger context in which it occurred, the all-female world of the women's college: "So forced and unnatural does the whole policy of separation seem to me, that I would almost as willingly send my daughter into a convent for education, for four years, as into a Protestant palace of celibacy, called a college."[4] A friend of women's higher education, Higginson shared some of John M. Greene's and L. Clark Seelye's views; thus it is not surprising that Smith had the solution that Higginson preferred. It provided an education equal to or better than Wellesley's, it had no preparatory department, and its "family system" of governance and residence was the best plan yet devised for colleges.

Higginson framed his discussion of the three women's colleges in a curious manner. He actually disapproved of them all. "As to patronizing all separate colleges," he could only say "like Punch to his young people about to marry— 'Don't!' But to those who do," he recommended Smith.[5] Essentially Higginson believed in coeducation and in university rather than collegiate training. He was a son of Harvard, a maverick reformer who, except for his heroic stint in the Civil War as the officer of a black regiment, remained close to his Cambridge home. As he repeated frequently from his editor's chair, he wanted to see Harvard open its doors to women.[6] He applauded the founding of coeducational Boston University under Methodist auspices. But to Higginson, as to others of his Brahmin caste, Harvard was simply the only institution of higher education that counted.[7] In 1869, the young, well-born scientist Charles William Eliot had become president, with a clear mandate to bring the college into the modern world. By the late 1870s, many changes were already transforming the venerable institution into a great university. Eliot set out to attract scholars engaged in research and nurture their creative work. He introduced the elective system to open up the older curriculum to the new lines of inquiry and theory.[8] But long before these great days, Higginson felt that Harvard had offered excellent instruction in modern languages and literature. As a feminist who believed in coeducation, Higginson fought valiantly for women at Harvard.

It was not to be, at least not in the manner that Higginson envisioned. While Eliot was committed to turning Harvard into a modern university, he had real doubts about the forms and nature of higher education for women. To Higginson's scorn, Eliot used the occasion of Smith College's first commencement to applaud an unfounded assertion that coeducation "finds no acceptance in New England, with the most insignificant exceptions."[9] Eliot scandalized academic women some years later by a speech at Wellesley suggesting that the great traditions of learning from the time of the Egyptians were the creation by and for men and served as no guide in educating women.[10] Eliot's vision of the separate intellectual nature and culture of women hardly fostered opening Harvard to them.

In addition, like the other older colleges for men, Harvard saw its mission in the late nineteenth century to be a nursery of leadership and scholarship. In the minds of the men who composed the boards of trustees of the Ivy League universities, women had no place in either realm. As Mothers of the Republic and teachers, women were to receive the higher learning, but not at the sacred grove reserved for the future ruling elite and intelligentsia. Trustees did not want precious resources designated for men dissipated in this way. Nor did they approve of mixing the sexes during the college years. The young men agreed. In part, class considerations dominated male collegians' desire to avoid women as coeds. While upper-class men set the tone of undergraduate life in the Ivy League in the nineteenth century, the women seeking higher education came from more modest backgrounds, and they brought a more serious approach to college. In addition, college men aspired to the club life of the urban upper class, a completely male preserve. At coeducational universities such as Cornell, the men did what they could to segregate the women into a separate realm to imitate better the manly life of the older Ivy League.[11]

Given these forces, no direct effort to make Harvard admit women could succeed. A gentler, indirect approach was needed, one calculated so that it "stirs no prejudices, excites no opposition, involves no change of policy for the University."[12] The creators of Radcliffe College were masters of indirection. They devised a means to offer women a Harvard education at no expense to the university and without introjecting the unwanted women into male college life.

As a proper citizen of Cambridge, Arthur Gilman, a writer and editor, found himself troubled about the future education of his daughter. A widower with three children, in 1876 he had married Stella Scott, a teacher at Bradford Academy. She urged upon him "the need that exists in Cambridge for an institution for the higher education of women."[13] Gilman wrote to England to inquire into the workings of Girton College outside Cambridge, England.

In 1865, a small band of women and men in England had successfully opened the Cambridge Local Examination to women. One of their number, Emily Davies, took the next step and organized a college for women with standards identical to the men's colleges at Cambridge. She gathered influential support, leased a house outside Cambridge, and opened with five students in October 1869. Lecturers from the university came to the college, and the students prepared for the Cambridge examinations. While the university refused officially to permit the women to take its examinations, it allowed the college to make separate arrangements with the examiners. Victory came when three candidates passed with honors the Tripos, the B.A. examination. As numbers grew, the college began building at Girton, two miles outside Cambridge. The initial structure by Alfred Waterhouse set a new standard in college residence for women, giving to each student a bedroom and a sitting room. In addition to quarters for twenty-one students, the building included rooms for the hall mistress and for a resident lecturer, as well as classrooms and a dining hall.[14]

A letter to the *Nation* in January 1876, by Eliza Theodora Minturn, an American woman in residence at Girton, stressed the identity of Girton with the university. The university determined Girton's course of study, its regulations, its calendar, and its examinations. Upon passing the final examinations, students received a degree certificate. "The highest aspiration of Girton is incorporation in the university; but these hopes it scarcely yet dares to breathe audibly." For the present, however, Girton offered the best education possible to a British or American woman. In contrast to the existing American women's colleges which Minturn insulted as "little more than high-schools," with unrecognized degrees, a narrow life, and an onerous discipline, Girton "brings women into direct competition with men, under the auspices of an institution of high character and wide reputation," attracting women of the highest social status and offering a life "delightful to the most fastidious."[15] To Arthur Gilman, who shared all Minturn's prejudices about women's colleges in the United States and who lived in the shadow of Harvard, how perfect Girton's solution must have seemed.

Arthur and Stella Gilman began to think through a plan to gather women

Private Collegiate Instruction for Women.

The ladies whose names are appended below are authorized to say that a number of Professors and other Instructors in Harvard College have consented to give private tuition to properly qualified young women who desire to pursue advanced studies in Cambridge. Other Professors whose occupations prevent them from giving such tuition are willing to assist young women by advice and by lectures. No instruction will be provided of a lower grade than that given in Harvard College.

The expense of instruction in as many branches as a student can profitably pursue at once will depend upon the numbers in the several courses, but it will probably not exceed four hundred dollars a year, and may be as low as two hundred and fifty. It is hoped, however, that endowments may hereafter be procured which will materially reduce this expense.

Pupils who show upon examination that they have satisfactorily pursued any courses of study under this scheme will receive certificates to that effect, signed by their Instructors. It is hoped, nevertheless, that the greater number will pursue a four years' course of study, in which case the certificates for the different branches of study will be merged in one, which will be signed by all the Instructors and will certify to the whole course.

The ladies will see that the students secure suitable lodgings, and will assist them with advice and other friendly offices.

Information as to the qualifications required, with the names of the Instructors in any branch, may be obtained upon application to any one of the ladies, or to their Secretary, Mr. ARTHUR GILMAN, 5 Phillips Place.

Mrs. LOUIS AGASSIZ	*Quincy Street.*
Mrs. E. W. GURNEY	*Fayerweather Street.*
Mrs. J. P. COOKE	*Quincy Street.*
Mrs. J. B. GREENOUGH	*Appian Way.*
Mrs. ARTHUR GILMAN	*Phillips Place.*
Miss ALICE M. LONGFELLOW	*Brattle Street.*
Miss LILIAN HORSFORD	*Craigie Street.*

CAMBRIDGE, MASS., *February 22, 1879.*

Circular, 1879; *Radcliffe College Archives*

in Cambridge, Massachusetts, to be taught by Harvard professors. When Annie Johnson, Bradford's principal, came for a visit, the Gilmans talked over their ideas with her, and she applauded their scheme as "practicable and desirable."[16] As in England, a group had opened up the Harvard examinations to women as a standard of merit. Gilman's sister served on the New York committee administering the examination: the committee offered to Gilman's scheme "material encouragement."[17] Gilman next approached James B. Greenough, Harvard's professor of Greek and Sanskrit, who, with Professors Francis J. Child and William W. Goodwin, was giving private instruction to Abby Leach, a woman who had made arrangements with the professors on her own. Gilman's courage almost failed him here, for he knew that powerful members of the Harvard faculty had to join in his plan wholeheartedly. To his delight, Greenough was enthusiastic. Gilman had drawn up a list of those Harvard professors who might prove receptive to teaching women. Greenough gave him his own more informed list, with the names of future supporters, such as William Elwood Byerly, and began to sound out colleagues individually.[18] Gilman and Greenough fleshed out the essential elements: Harvard professors were to offer to women exactly the same courses they gave to Harvard students; at the end of four years, students would receive a certificate testifying that they had done identical work to the Harvard B.A.; and professors should create an academic board to determine the courses and settle all academic matters.

When the two men and their wives next met, they decided to form a "committee of ladies to manage the matter." They chose carefully, selecting, along with the women present, two unmarried daughters and two wives and a widow of Harvard professors.[19] Elizabeth Carey Agassiz's name proved particularly potent. A daughter of Boston's elite, she had married the great naturalist Louis Agassiz. During his lifetime, she had aided his research in the field and had organized and run a school to supplement his Harvard salary. A widow, she first joined the ladies' committee and then became the Annex's president. Her tact and her position in society helped smooth the way for the Annex at crucial moments and opened the access to philanthropic Boston.[20] Gilman's official position became secretary to the ladies' committee, a spot from which he gave the Annex his undivided attention.[21] Gilman and Greenough carefully framed a circular that went out under the names of the lady managers—after President Eliot read, corrected, and approved of the text.

How cautiously they proceeded! The circular announcing "Private Collegiate Education for Women" described the new venture in this modest form: "The ladies whose names are appended below are authorized to say that a number of Professors and other Instructors in Harvard College have consented to give private tuition to properly qualified young women who desire to pursue advanced studies in Cambridge."[22] Such discretion was necessary. Harvard, as represented by its president and official bodies, emphatically did not

Carret House, Appian Way (first building used by the Annex)
Radcliffe College Archives

Tutorial session; *Radcliffe College Archives*

want women students and took care to avoid any official recognition of the new body. Eliot, in editing the circular, added to the title the word "Private."[23] The circular promised nothing beyond instruction. After a four-year course, a certificate testified to the courses taken. The education cost dearly, perhaps as much as $400 a year for tuition alone. The circular contained no discussion of any of the nonacademic matters that normally filled such announcements, only that the ladies of the committee promised to help arrange lodging and assist the students "with advice and other friendly offices."[24]

Gilman sent the circular to fifty-four members of the Harvard faculty with a letter asking each if he were "willing to give any private tuition to young women for the year 1879–80."[25] Forty-one agreed and set the number of hours they could give and their hourly rate. The list included the most distinguished members of the Harvard faculty, as well as their younger colleagues. As had Louis Agassiz, many faculty found they needed to supplement Harvard salaries by other work, including teaching women if it meant "a regular addition to their incomes."[26] Some warmly supported the project and proved to be mainstays of the academic board.

The committee of ladies initiated fund-raising activities, one of their main responsibilities. By August 1879, they had raised almost $16,000. In September, twenty-five students presented themselves, and two more joined them by the end of October. They included three members of the ladies' committee and Gilman's daughter. Most enrolled as special students; only three took the regular course. Abby Leach became one of the regular students, continuing her studies under legitimate auspices.[27] Those students living away from home arranged to lodge and board in Cambridge houses. The Annex rented rooms in a private house on Appian Way for classes and a study room.

It is intriguing that buildings occupied no part of the original conception of the Annex. Unlike Matthew Vassar's college, no monument perpetuated a name. In fact, the founders desired just the opposite. Above all else, they wanted the Annex to be inconspicuous. An early report proudly stated, "Our students are scattered by twos and threes in Cambridge families, their lodgings being chosen for them by their friends, or by the ladies of our Executive Committee. . . . They quietly pursue their occupations as unnoticed as the daughters of any Cambridge residents."[28] Finding itself in the position of an uninvited guest, the Annex tried to take from the table as unobtrusively as possible so that its unwilling host might allow it to stay.

In addition, Annex founders had no wish to offer students anything beyond the intellectual element of college experience. They were thinking of their own kind and attempting to open to the polite daughters of literary families the full taste of Boston culture. Given in their minds every other advantage, such daughters needed only systematic training under Harvard professors. Young

Fay House (before reconstruction); *Radcliffe College Archives*

Fay House library; *Radcliffe College Archives*

women from the provinces required only substitute homes in which to lodge and board; mature, well-bred, and grateful, they needed no supervision.

Thus the Annex proceeded for four years. Students came largely from Massachusetts, more frequently to take special courses than a regular undergraduate program. Only a tiny minority received the certificate of B.A. equivalency. As numbers grew, stretching the rented rooms on Appian Way beyond their limit, the Annex came to a decisive juncture. In 1883, the ladies' committee decided to strengthen the Annex by acquiring a distinguished house on Garden Street, the former residence of Judge Fay. This fine old Federal house was filled with Harvard associations: a member of the class of 1811 wrote "Fair Harvard" there. It fit perfectly into the founders' conception of the Annex. "Although a private dwelling, it has that touch of dignity which belongs to an old-fashioned house; and it can easily be adapted to the more general purpose of an educational institution without losing the character of a home. It must, however, be understood that by a home is not meant a dormitory."[29] In taking possession of a house, the Annex remained inconspicuous to the outside. Inside, its parlors and bedrooms became offices, classrooms, and library. Previously, students had only limited opportunities for fellowship. Fay House gave them places in which they could visit and meet. But unlike Girton, the Annex did not use Fay House as a residence hall or as a setting for female residents or fellows. While Elizabeth Agassiz had once favored this, by 1882 she opposed it as leading to the "building up of another female college, distinct from the University."[30] In the 1880s, no one associated with the Annex wanted any resemblance to a women's college.

In the liberal, urbane world of Cambridge, the women's colleges carried the taint of sectarian provinciality. Their buildings symbolized their backwardness. To the Annex's founders, residential structures offered only the option of seminary dwelling or domestic cottages, and each carried undesirable associations. Only in the 1890s, after Bryn Mawr pioneered a new type of architecture appropriate to a cosmopolitan, secular college, did it become possible to consider residential life at Radcliffe and the building of a strong institution separate from, yet drawing on, Harvard.

8

A Certain Style of
"Quaker Lady" Dress

Bryn Mawr had a great advantage. Opening in 1885, a decade after Smith, it drew on the Northampton college's experience and advice. Yet the narrow confines of Amherst did not limit its conception. Coming as it did after the founding of the Annex and shaped by a woman familiar with Cornell, Johns Hopkins, and German universities, Bryn Mawr offered its students a unique blend of university and women's college.

In 1877, when Joseph Wright Taylor decided to found a Quaker college for women, he had a ready group of advisors.[1] He had pondered questions regarding the education of young men since 1854, when he joined the Board of Managers of Haverford College, founded by orthodox Quakers in 1833. Born in 1810, and trained as a doctor, Taylor prospered in his brother's tanning business in Cincinnati. A bachelor, he retired in 1851 and moved with his sister to Burlington, New Jersey, where members of his family had settled. His fortune grew with wise investments. Taylor came to know his colleagues on the Haverford board: the Baltimore banker Francis T. King and James Carey Thomas, King's physician cousin. In 1876, when Johns Hopkins, a Baltimore Quaker, left $3.5 million to found a university and an equal sum for an affiliated hospital, King and Thomas became members of his board of trustees.

In 1877, these men called a conference in Baltimore to discuss Quaker education, and Taylor attended. He asked himself an important question: Who educated Quaker women? Swarthmore College outside Philadelphia was coeducational from its beginning in 1864, but, founded by the Hicksite Quakers, it was no place for conservative Friends. A bright daughter, such as Martha Carey Thomas, one of James Carey Thomas' many children, had to venture to Cornell, a thoroughly secular university linked to the faith only by the religion of its founder, for the higher education she wanted. Joseph Taylor talked this over with Francis King and decided to found a Quaker college for women. Taylor consulted with President Thomas Chase of Haverford and with President Daniel Coit Gilman of Johns Hopkins. On one of his trips to Baltimore to see Gilman, he visited with James Thomas and talked with his Cornell daughter. She discussed her pessimistic fear that a coeducational institution would never include women on the faculty, despite their importance to women students.[2] In 1877, Taylor made up his will, which set the outline of his future college. He named a board of trustees to gather after his death, designating Francis King president. Taylor appointed James Thomas and several of his relatives to the board: in addition to King, his cousin, there was Thomas' wife's brother, James Whitall, and another cousin, David Scull, Jr.

As president of the Johns Hopkins Hospital board, as well as a Hopkins and Haverford trustee, King naturally became Taylor's closest advisor. In addition King had a talented daughter just returned to Baltimore from the Howland Institute, a Quaker boarding school, where she had roomed with her cousin and closest friend, Martha Carey Thomas. Taylor saw his college as a female Haverford placed near his New Jersey estate. Aware of Girton at Oxford, King initially suggested that Taylor's college adjoin Haverford, repeating to Taylor the suggestion of an Oxford graduate that the two "use the same observatory, lectures, laboratory, gas, and water—but have separate courses of study, charter, endowment, and management . . . [and] divide the time of certain professors who can repeat the same lessons." Such a college had the advantage of "a large city" and "kindred influences," unlike Vassar "which in its isolated situation . . . will never rise to a high position."[3] King later questioned the wisdom of such close association between Haverford and its female copy and urged a spot five miles away. Another advisor, later to play a very important part in the life of the college, James E. Rhoads, saw the value of propinquity to Philadelphia "where the benefit of professors and literary and scientific aids could be had, also some social influences." He wanted some separation from Haverford, where he, too, was a trustee. Rhoads did not want Taylor's college to be an annex, but fully separate, allowing "more untrammelled and vigorous growth of both Institutions."[4]

King helped Taylor select a site, a thirty-two-acre parcel in Bryn Mawr adjacent to the Pennsylvania Railroad and five miles from Haverford. King also recommended Addison Hutton, a Quaker architect who had just designed Barclay Hall at Haverford, a source of great pride to its trustees. King did not, however, approve of Hutton's Bryn Mawr residences in "very fancy style."[5] In June 1879, in a letter to Hutton, King expressed the trustees' wishes for college buildings, hoping to tone down any excesses:

There is a certain style of "Quaker lady" dress, which I often see in Phila, which tells the whole story—she has her satin bonnet—her silk dress—her kid gloves—

her perfect slippers—but they are made to harmonize with the expression of her face which is both intellectual and holy—so may "Taylor College" look down from its beautiful site upon the passing world and we hear them say "just right."[6]

President Gilman suggested to Taylor that he travel north to visit Mount Holyoke, Smith, and Wellesley. Taylor made two such trips, accompanied on the first occasion by King and James Thomas, and on the second by King and Hutton. On the later trip, the three men "conferred very fully with President Seelye of Smith upon plans for building."[7] King was convinced that Smith had the best plan. Answering Taylor's query "as to merits of Cottages or a congregated building," King wrote, "I think Barclay hall is adapted to boys—but Cottages for girls—as they have less nervous strain."[8] After his return Taylor wrote to Seelye for advice on academic and domestic organization. Seelye replied in a long, detailed letter of November 27, 1878, of great interest both because of its summary of Seelye's intentions for Smith and because of its influence on the future Bryn Mawr.[9]

Seelye emphasized the importance of adequately prepared students and the traditional liberal arts course. Smith had insisted upon requirements equal to Amherst. Though few currently met this standard, if women's colleges persisted "good preparatory schools will speedily arise."[10] Seelye believed Taylor's college ought to require Greek for entrance and base the college course in classics and mathematics, with electives in language and natural science, music and art. Seelye urged against preparatory departments, such as at Vassar and Wellesley, which required seminary discipline, in turn harming the collegiate program: "The lower school degrades the higher."[11] The design of Smith assumed adult women, who needed little formal supervision. College students set the right tone at the outset: "It is a great advantage to a college to have its traditions, its social and literary influences created exclusively by those who are prepared for its culture."[12]

Seelye advised Taylor against Wellesley's policy of hiring only women faculty. He found it difficult to get qualified women and keep them. Because "marriage . . . makes the vocation of women naturally more uncertain," a mixed faculty proved "more permanent and efficient."[13] Having men on the faculty in no way lessened the moral responsibility of the college, however: "It does seem very important, especially in a woman's college, that manners and morals as well as learning should determine to a great extent a teacher's fitness for the position."[14]

Smith's president wrote with great confidence about its plan for building, adopted after "a careful study," its "excellence" proven by experience.[15] "Our plan has been to erect central academic buildings which shall be devoted to the more distinctive intellectual work of the institution" and around them "at con-

The early Bryn Mawr campus: from left to right, Merion Hall, Taylor Hall, the Deanery

Bryn Mawr College

venient distances, in grounds laid out as a private park, smaller dwelling houses.
. . . as homes for the students. Each dwelling house is organized as a private
household," presided over by "a lady of culture and refinement to direct its
social and domestic life."[16] Everything about this plan spoke to its advantage.
Beyond the strong practical aspects, such as flexibility and less danger from
fire, Seelye stressed the moral effect. While a women's college should adopt
"studies which have been of greatest benefit in the intellectual culture of men,
I do not advise you to treat women as men." Smith's cottages, re-creating the
"refined home," secured the "desirable moral and social influences."[17] Small-
scale dwellings gave students "greater comfort and less nervous excitement."[18]

Seelye's letter confirmed Taylor's intentions. He had already instructed Hutton
to design buildings "similar in its purposes and appliances" to those of Smith
College.[19] Hutton's three buildings for the new college re-created Smith in the
appropriate dress of a Quaker lady. Imitating Smith, he sited the academic
building on high ground, open not only to the campus but to the surrounding
community. King had stated very clearly his feeling that he "would face the
building as it is on the Smith plan, towards the hotel, the depot, the town, and
the natural approach," giving a good view from the railroad coming from
Haverford.[20] Like Peabody and Stearns' College Hall, Hutton's Taylor Hall is
a strongly vertical building. In its more muted gray tones of local Fairmont
stone, it lacks the rich polychromy that accentuates College Hall's Victorian
Gothic, but it shares steeply pitched roofs ending in gables, tall chimneys, and
varied window treatments. Tall square clock towers, irregularly placed, dominate both. Taylor Hall copied College Hall's internal plan. Taylor's irregular
rectangular form does not make College Hall's dramatic L, but like its precedent, the first floor originally held lecture rooms, and the second, the primary
assembly room with the president's office at one end. Taylor also had a full
third story from the outset, with administrative offices and classroom on both
sides of the top of the assembly room.[21]

Partway down the hill, the first cottage also demonstrates Smith's influence. As had Peabody and Stearns in Hubbard House, Hutton designed Merion as a large vernacular dwelling with steeply pitched roofs and gables. While
local gray stone replaced brick, Merion had similar welcoming porches, trimmed
in wood. The internal arrangement of rooms, with public areas on the first
floor, partly resembles the Smith houses, but important differences mark Bryn
Mawr's distinctiveness. Because of Taylor's commitment to "the higher and
more refined classes of Society," from the beginning Bryn Mawr paid greater
attention to privacy than any of the other women's colleges, allocating much
more space to student rooms. Hutton's Barclay Hall offered to Haverford students a choice of suites for two students, with a study connecting two bedrooms, or large rooms for individual students.[22] Similarly, his Merion had 19
suites and large single rooms, several of unusual size. In contrast to Washburn

House at Smith, built in 1878 with 28 rooms for 50 students, Merion at Bryn
Mawr had 75 rooms for 55 students.[23] In addition, Hutton followed the usual
plan of the men's dormitory, eschewed by most women's institutions: Merion
had two entries, a principal one leading to the hall and drawing room, a secondary one to the dining area. Student rooms on the first floor connected these
public areas, an unusual arrangement in a women's college where generally a
single entrance opened on to public areas, and private spaces remained quite
separate.[24]

Seelye advised putting the gymnasium and music rooms in a different
building. While Smith initially provided for both within College Hall, the
noise from these activities made them incompatible with academic work. While
it would be a long time before a Quaker college allowed space for music, the
trustees recognized that the health of students required a gymnasium and Hutton designed a simple structure in red brick.[25]

In 1882, Hutton submitted to the board a plan for a symmetrical grouping
of four cottages, not unlike the siting of the Morris, Lawrence, Dickerson,
and Hubbard houses at Smith. While the board adopted Hutton's scheme, it
never went beyond paper. Between 1882 and the actual opening of Bryn Mawr,
a new and unpredicted force emerged to transform the "female Haverford"
into a quite different—and unprecedented—institution for the higher education of women. M. Carey Thomas created the college of 1885. While Bryn
Mawr retained its initial Smith-influenced "Quaker lady" design in Taylor and
Merion halls, the buildings constructed in the years that followed gradually
gave architectural form to Thomas' quite different conceptions.

Taylor died in January 1880, and his board gathered the following May to
ponder his lengthy will. Taylor envisioned his college as a small one "for the
advanced education and care of young women and girls of the higher and more
refined classes of Society." He wanted to offer them an orthodox Quaker education, "the doctrines of the New Testament as accepted by Friends and taught
by Fox, Penn, and Barclay." Taylor specified that orthodox Friends "in a close
corporation" control the college.[26] He never envisioned a denominational college, whose ruling body was appointed by the Meeting. In the Women's College of Baltimore, later renamed Goucher, the Methodist Episcopal Conference
established such a college in 1885: the conference itself founded the college and
appointed one-third of the trustees.[27] Rather Taylor conceived of his board as
a self-perpetuating body whose initial members he selected. Meeting after his
death, this board chose as vice president James Rhoads, a retired physician,
active as an advocate for the American Indian, as the editor of the *Friends Review*, and as a Haverford trustee. They turned to the first business at hand, the
completion of the buildings. Rhoads and David Scull, Jr., took over Taylor's
supervisory work, which occupied the next four years.

In 1883, Rhoads got a remarkable letter. M. Carey Thomas, who had just received her Ph.D. *summa cum laude* from Zurich, wrote to suggest herself as "a candidate for the presidency of Bryn Mawr."[28] It was a bold step, but one thoroughly characteristic of a woman unusual since her girlhood.

In March 1872, when she was fifteen, Minnie Thomas confided to her journal the dream of the future that she shared with her cousin and closest friend Bessie, the daughter of Francis King. They had gone to the Sewing Meeting of the Society of Friends, and because there were no "horrid boys," after supper they went into the Meeting House alone. In the "solemn gloom" and "dim uncertain shadows" of the quiet room "it was just the very time to build air castles and we walked up and down the aisle and talked of what we wanted to be and do and formed plans." The daughters of prominent Quaker families, their ambitions soared far from the domestic accomplishments of their mothers. These two hopeful and spunky girls exchanged their given names for ones more suited to their imagination. Young Minnie Thomas took the tough, energetic name Rush; Bessie, Rex. The two decided that they would go to Vassar and win high honors and "would do everything." Rush and Rex would become scholars and "live together, have a library with all the splendid books, with a bright wood fire always burning, dark crimson curtains and furniture, great big easy chairs where we could sit lost in books for days together." They would have a "great large table covered with papers" and a laboratory for scientific experiments. "There we would live loving each other and urging each other on to every high and noble deed or action and all who passed should say 'their example arouses me, their books ennoble me, their ideas inspire me and behold they are women!'"[29]

What is extraordinary is not the dream of adolescent friends, but its relation to the reality that Thomas created. Details changed: the tough name became Carey, not Rush; Mamie Gwinn and Mary Garrett came to hold a more intense claim on her affections than Bessie. But Carey Thomas acted out the larger dream, her "wildest fancies," on a national stage. The library and laboratory emerged as the remarkably beautiful Bryn Mawr campus. She had the aid of a distinguished faculty to arouse by their example the well-qualified students who passed through, to ennoble them by their books, and to inspire them by their ideas. She always kept the purpose in mind: "behold they are women."

Carey Thomas did not go to Vassar.[30] After two years at the Howland Institute, a Quaker school for girls outside Ithaca, New York, Cornell seemed to offer the greater challenge. The university had just completed Sage Hall, the residence for women, and Thomas entered in its first class of women, graduating in 1877. In its early years of coeducation, Cornell offered to its women students the full freedom of the elective system and the excitement of a young but excellent university.[31] Carey Thomas thrived.

Thomas' Cornell years were followed by that painful period of indecision and anxiety that so many educated women of the late nineteenth century endured. Reluctantly, Johns Hopkins accepted her as a graduate student, though denied her access to the graduate seminar. Undeterred, she got private tutoring from a willing professor, but found that without the fellowship of other students and the stimulation of the seminar, she could not carry out her program of study. The home years gave her one critical element of her later success. Carey Thomas' close friendship with Bessie King expanded to include Mamie Gwinn, Mary Garrett, and Julia Rogers. Bonds of affection among the five women lent Thomas crucial support; in later years the five collaborated on a number of educational projects for women, not the least of which was Bryn Mawr.

In 1879, sobered by her difficulties in obtaining graduate education and troubled by the mounting conflict with her parents over the loss of traditional Quaker faith, Carey Thomas set sail for Germany with Mamie Gwinn. The three-year absence toughened her considerably as she tested her talents and independence abroad. In 1883, when she passed her doctoral examinations *summa cum laude*, she felt she had fulfilled her promise. Relishing her victory, she immediately sent off letters to promote her candidacy for president of Bryn Mawr. To her mother, Carey Thomas wrote that as president she could make Bryn Mawr "the very best woman's college there is."[32] She planned her campaign well, enlisting her influential family in her behalf, including her powerful aunt, Hannah Whitall Smith. Carey Thomas even suggested that she had returned to the Quaker fold, a timely, if not altogether sincere, profession.[33] What an extraordinary coincidence: the opening of a Quaker college for women at the moment that a brilliant, determined, feminist Quaker woman returned from Europe with a Ph.D. in philology, the daughter, niece, and cousin of members of the board of trustees.

How could the Bryn Mawr board resist? In retrospect, it all seems inevitable. Yet at the time Carey Thomas had three strikes against her. She was a woman, and the board was and remained for many years all male; she was untried; and there was some perception by the trustees that she was not quite the Quaker daughter that she appeared to be, a suspicion time proved true. So the board hedged: in a plan worked out by Hannah Whitall Smith, they chose James Rhoads president and M. Carey Thomas the first member of the faculty and dean. Rhoads and Thomas enjoyed a congenial, effective collaboration, largely because Rhoads gave Thomas full authority on important matters while he protected her from a sometimes questioning and querulous board of trustees.

Carey Thomas took as her first task a tour of the prominent existing women's colleges to learn everything that she could about their methods, buildings, strengths, and weaknesses. She was not an altogether unprejudiced witness: she had chosen Cornell over Vassar on the advice of her Howland teacher that Cornell offered the better education; and her journal abroad is sprinkled with distaste at the prospect of becoming "a wretchedly paid, overworked shadow of a professor at Wellesley or Smith like Miss Whitney."[34] The diary that she kept on this fact-finding trip and her letters to Mary Garrett provide a splendid view into the other women's colleges from the prospective of a harsh, feminist critic.

Thomas fumed with rage at Smith, which she described to Garrett as "a chance wasted. I dislike to think about it—these 250 girls getting husks." The spirit of the students impressed her; but this just caused her to "despair over women, so clever, so enthusiastic & so little chance." They did not come with adequate preparation; and at Smith "their education is in the hands of men who *do not care.* There is not one strong woman in the place not even one really well educated woman." "I am conscious of a strong impulse . . . to wring the necks of most of the profs. & teachers in Smith College."[35]

Carey Thomas admired practical aspects of Smith, however. She initially approved of the cottage system of student residence. Her diary noted that while Vassar's Lady Principal felt that the "Cottage syst[em] has not proved itself yet," a clear "place where strain felt is in din[in]g hall. If possible break up dining room into six rooms for 50 each."[36] In Stone Hall, Wellesley had set up four dining rooms of twenty-five "so had the nervous effect of eating in a crowded dining room been felt in the Central College Building." Thomas also learned that applicants to Wellesley favored Simpson Cottage and that it was requested by "the parents of delicate girls."[37] While Carey Thomas might later wish that Bryn Mawr had selected another architect initially, upon her return home she expressed her satisfaction with the plan of Bryn Mawr's first cottage, declaring the bedrooms and studies of Merion Hall "far beyond any woman's college."[38]

She also approved of the manner in which Smith separated tuition from self-supporting room-and-board fees. Unlike Wellesley, Smith charged different rates for different room accommodations, arguing that as "the principle" governing "all other matters of the student's lives," economic inequality created no unnatural distinctions. Carey Thomas' own experience in Sage Hall at Cornell served as an example: "It made no social difference whether a girl had one, two, or three rooms. I had three: many of my friends had but one."[39]

Carey Thomas returned from her tour filled with useful information: gentlewomen supervised cottages more effectively than housekeepers; varnish covered floors better than other finishes; Smith had a "very nice kind of bench in one recitation room."[40] Her report to the trustees acknowledged this technical aid at the same time that it asserted that the women's colleges had nothing to offer when one turned to the curriculum and faculty.

Vassar and Wellesley held a surprise. At Vassar, Carey Thomas rankled at the rules and loathed the Lady Principal ("little souled, not lit[erary] or scholarly—too f[on]d of rules & system"),[41] but found it nonetheless "monastic &

charming. I can't express how it impressed me, but unlike anything else I had
ever seen." She had the thrill of sitting opposite Maria Mitchell, the astronomer, and going to her study to see "her lying on the couch at full length
speaking sarcastic, rather bitter, wholly loyal things."[42] Wellesley affected her
powerfully: she sat in chapel and looked down "upon a woman president,
reading prayers to an audience of 500 women and 70 profs. & teachers—all
women, not a man's influence seen or felt" and observed the gym with "the
girls in trowsers swinging on rings, twirling on bars, a newer race of ath-
letes—ushers in a new day." She was impressed by "the devotion to study of
these girls & women profs. in this Princesslike community of Wellesley."[43]
Carey Thomas' trip heightened her sense of the possibilities of a college dedicated to the higher education of women. For the first time she experienced the
potential power of a community of women. Yet the poor quality of the faculty,
the constraints placed upon them, and the weakness of their teaching distressed
and saddened her. "In none of the three colleges; Smith, Wellesley and Vassar,
are there many professors who can lay claims to original scholarship, or who
are fit to guide the students in original work."[44]

Carey Thomas ended her tour in Boston. Stella Gilman, the wife of Arthur
Gilman, gave a reception for her, where she met the professors connected with
the Annex. While Thomas made no comments on the Annex in her letters to
Mary Garrett, her report to the trustees candidly summarized her views. The
Annex had the benefit of Harvard, which, like Columbia, Yale, and Johns
Hopkins, offered students "higher teaching" with professors immersed in
original work. While the Annex provided the best education available to women,
it could not serve as a model, for it contained "none of the attractions of
college life."[45]

M. Carey Thomas composed a clever solution for Bryn Mawr: she created
a college for women that adapted the best elements of its sisters and yet had
the standards, curriculum, and scholarship of Johns Hopkins. This was an
astounding new element. Carey Thomas did not hope to re-create Smith, the
equivalent of the best colleges for men. Rather she intended to offer to undergraduate women the highest standards of university training available in the
United States. She recruited a young, largely male faculty, newly trained in
the German universities. She limited their teaching time to encourage study
and research, and she added a graduate school to keep them stimulated and
aware of new research in their fields. To matriculate, a student first presented
a comprehensive preparatory course which included Latin and Greek, and then
passed a rigorous set of examinations, modeled on the Harvard exam. An
upper-class student elected her courses, grouping them in two related specialized areas. Thomas offered to a new generation of women what she had been
denied seven years before. Yet, aware of that special something she could not
describe at Vassar and Wellesley, she consciously shaped Bryn Mawr into a

female community where women's influence predominated. While insistence on graduate training required a faculty of young, single men, her presence as dean, the careful selection of residence supervisors, and the establishment of fellowships for talented young women scholars would encourage the best efforts of the young undergraduates.

It was a grand scheme. However, it hardly matched the vision of a "female Haverford" that Joseph Taylor bequeathed to his board. Carey Thomas was not certain that she could convince these Quaker gentlemen to substitute Johns Hopkins as their model. She confided to Garrett that she would write her report and print it and "endeavor to be resigned if the Trustees do not vote affirmatively to each resolution," happy to return to her books.[46] She did not have to practice the arts of resignation. She won on every major issue and spent an intense summer rounding up an extraordinarily capable faculty, taking pleasure in the abundance of talent from which to choose. She gloated to Mary Garrett that she had "to decide between two men & three women all with Harvard or Cornell degrees[,] high recommendations & at least one year's study abroad. . . . Which of them will teach Latin the best?"[47] Each appointment, each decision, had the firm support of President Rhoads and carried the board, liberally sprinkled with members of Carey Thomas' family, two of whom were on the Johns Hopkins board. In 1884 and 1885, Thomas convinced them of the value of scholarship linked with female influence, and from this Bryn Mawr never retreated.

In the fall of 1885, Bryn Mawr opened its doors to thirty-six young women whose initial faculty included Paul Shorey, Charlotte Angus Scott, Edward Keiser, Edward Washburn, and Woodrow Wilson. In the years that followed, M. Carey Thomas fought to strengthen the intellectual quality of Bryn Mawr's faculty and academic offerings and demanded a new architectural setting as an appropriate symbol of the life within. The Jacobean quadrangles that emerged at Bryn Mawr at the turn of the century gave new architectural expression to the women's college.

In 1885, this lay still in the future. Bryn Mawr opened with its building and its academic programs premised on incompatible notions of higher education for women. University training of the highest quality, modeled after Johns Hopkins, took place in college buildings designed to look like Smith in the dress of a Quaker lady. Taylor and Merion remain today as reminders of the original intention of the founder. They symbolize the opposition M. Carey Thomas faced as she turned what began as a Quaker college for women into a secular and cosmopolitan institution.

9

Behold They Are Women!

BRYN MAWR

M. Carey Thomas built in stone as effectively as she did in academic policy. She shared her era's belief in the power of the physical environment to shape communal spirit and individual character. She brought to Bryn Mawr a strong, feminist commitment to the needs of young women scholars. However inimical to Quaker traditions, she added a love of pageantry and drama. All of this is visible in the Jacobean quadrangles of Bryn Mawr.

In 1885, Carey Thomas convinced the board of trustees of the value of original scholarship in a college for women. She had the full support of Bryn Mawr's president, James Rhoads, who advocated her views to a body liberally sprinkled with her relatives. In 1893, when Rhoads' failing health forced his retirement, Carey Thomas staked all on becoming president. After a bitter and intense struggle, she won the following year. Mary Garrett offered Bryn Mawr $10,000 a year if the board chose Thomas, a gift that her beneficiary called "a sweet & clever attempt to use Mammon for righteousness." [1]

During her long incumbency, M. Carey Thomas fought and refought the same issues. Increasingly her protection on the board disappeared, as age and death removed her father, uncle, and cousins. At stake was the commitment of the college to scholarship in an increasingly secular and materialistic age. As devout Friends, certain members of the board repeatedly sought to return Bryn Mawr to James Taylor's original conception of a female Haverford. They tried to redefine the college as sectarian, to block its physical growth, and to restrain its profane communal life. Carey Thomas never relented. She insisted that only growth could sustain the standard Bryn Mawr had set and that identification with contemporary thought and life—not adherence to Quaker traditions—made the college a powerful force in the higher education of women. [2]

The resignation of a senior trustee followed M. Carey Thomas' accession to the presidency, and, until 1902, the board refused to appoint her as a member of its body, a position her predecessor had held. The board fought unsuccessfully to keep costs down and to change the language of college publications to express Quaker commitment. While Thomas tried to contain public expression of student hedonism, such as smoking and nude swimming, the growth of pageantry on campus and the acceptance of theater clarified what Bryn Mawr had become. Ultimately her building program caused the dissident trustees to try to bring her down.

The Bryn Mawr campus remains as a monument to M. Carey Thomas' hopes for women. During her deanship and presidency the talented young Philadelphia architectural firm of Cope & Stewardson gave form to the residence, library, and laboratory of her adolescent daydream.[3] In the two decades following Bryn Mawr's opening, building after building encircled the original Taylor Hall, creating splendid spaces for living, studying, teaching, and playing. Walter Cope—the nephew of board member Francis Cope, brother of a member of the first class, and a Friend—was the ideal designer for Bryn Mawr. While he worked as an apprentice in Addison Hutton's office, Cope had a more cosmopolitan and sophisticated sensibility. He travelled in Europe and on his return formed a partnership with John Stewardson. The two were from a similar Quaker background, and Stewardson was also related to members of the Bryn Mawr board. He had trained at the Ecole des Beaux Arts. With Cope as the major design partner, the firm of Cope & Stewardson gradually came to its mature style, a Jacobean Gothic that combined dignity with a festive air. Bryn Mawr offered Cope and Stewardson their first experience with college buildings. Well-publicized success led to important commissions at the University of Pennsylvania, Princeton, and Washington University in St. Louis.[4] The firm worked in close collaboration with Carey Thomas, who always guided and, at times, fully outlined the plan.[5] Cope and Stewardson created a fitting setting for the realization of her girlhood dream of a life as an exemplary woman among women.

At fifteen, "Rush" Thomas had envisioned surroundings that hardly suggested a woman's parlor. Her dream library had "dark crimson curtains and furniture" and "great big easy chairs," a "bright wood fire always burning" and a "great large table covered with papers."[6] Unlike the men who planned domestic places at Smith or seminary settings at Vassar and Wellesley, Carey Thomas had no desire to adapt feminine spaces to academic uses. Rather, she wanted to appropriate the library and the laboratory of men. Though her closest relationships were with women and she became the moving force behind a women's college, Carey Thomas held no belief in a separate women's culture. The curriculum of Bryn Mawr made no genuflections to women's special nature or domestic future. She argued that courses generally deemed appropriate for women either lacked the necessary intellectual content, as did domestic science, or they equally fit men and women, as did infant psychology. The life of the mind was neuter: "Science and literature and philology are what they are and inalterable."[7] Bryn Mawr created special opportunities for women to enter the sacred groves of scholarship, but the groves had no gender. "Given two bridge-builders, a man and a woman, given a certain bridge to be built, and given as always the unchangeable laws of mechanics . . . it is simply inconceivable that the preliminary instruction given to the two bridge-builders should differ in quantity, quality, or method of presentation because while the bridge is building one will wear knickerbockers and the other a rainy-day skirt."[8] As the visible sign that truth had no sex, the Bryn Mawr campus gave no clue as to the gender of its student body.

Nothing about Bryn Mawr suggested a home. Smith's President Seelye linked domestic forms and scale with women's college residence in the cottage. But domesticity in all its forms was anathema to Carey Thomas. After she returned from her years abroad, she had felt acutely uncomfortable in her parents' house with its informal, child-centered ways and its lack of privacy and order. The college that she envisioned had nothing of home. Unlike Mount Holyoke and Wellesley, students performed no domestic work during their four years, not even the making of their own beds. They wore a special dress on campus, the traditional mark of scholarship worn by men, the cap and gown.[9] They enjoyed privacy unusual to young women: each student had a single room at the minimum. Carey Thomas carried from the visit to Girton the standard of a bedroom and sitting room, with wood-burning fireplace: whenever possible Bryn Mawr's halls contained two-room suites.

Like Smith and the Annex, Bryn Mawr eschewed the structure of rules and the daily schedule bequeathed by the seminary. Bryn Mawr had no desire to imitate the Annex's avoidance of common residence, but Carey Thomas needed an alternative to Smith's simulation of family governance. Because young, unmarried men largely composed the faculty, she could not give them rooms within college residence halls or any responsibility over students' lives. More strikingly, Carey Thomas never considered such an abuse of women faculty. She insisted that female as well as male professors have full control of their time outside the classroom for the pursuit of scholarship. Following Smith's lead, Bryn Mawr installed a gentlewoman as resident mistress of Merion, in this case a Quaker lady; but in time Thomas replaced her and added to the other residence halls young Bryn Mawr graduates, increasingly outside the fold.[10] In 1901, she renamed the mistresses "wardens," in imitation of their British counterparts.[11] In addition, the graduate fellows, women despite the appellation, lived among the undergraduates to inspire them by their scholarly example. The students themselves regulated behavior, at least in principle. In 1892, when growth in numbers made the informal system of the first years unworkable, Bryn Mawr instituted the first plan for student self-governance

The economics and history library in Taylor Library; n.b. students in academic dress
Bryn Mawr College

in a women's college.[12] Students held only limited power: collegians never made rules, they only enforced them. Controversy remains over their actual control even here. Carey Thomas' need to protect the college from the outside caused her to intervene to uphold conventions in which even she did not believe. For example, while she had to halt nude bathing, she confessed to Mary Garrett, "there is really no harm in it."[13] Her love of power may have led her to create a spy system among students, a charge her critics made.[14] But, however limited, self-government remained an ideal and took architectural form. Cope & Stewardson designed halls for Bryn Mawr scholars as distinctive as their caps and gowns, bearing the same mark of scholarship as the traditional colleges for men.

This signalled the critical divide in the building history of the women's colleges. Before M. Carey Thomas' leadership at Bryn Mawr, women's colleges had distinctive structures designed to protect young women as they received the higher learning. With Bryn Mawr's decision to take the forms of traditional male institutions of higher education, buildings at the women's colleges entered into the mainstream of collegiate architecture. Architects accepted college commissions, indifferent to the gender of the student body. Cope and Stewardson moved from their triumphs at Bryn Mawr to Princeton, the University of Pennsylvania, and Washington University.

But what were these collegiate forms to be? In the past, at such colleges as Harvard and Yale, men had received their education in separate buildings dotting the center of the campus. Yale had "Old Brick Row," two lines of buildings that opened to the campus and then to the New Haven Green. In the 1870s and 1880s, Russell Sturgis designed buildings at the perimeter of the campus. Yale tore down "Old Brick Row" and built the Old Campus, a wall of buildings separating gown from town. Sturgis argued in the *Nation* and elsewhere for colleges composed of quadrangles, based on the English model of Oxford and Cambridge. He was America's most articulate follower of John Ruskin. Carey Thomas proclaimed herself a Ruskinian.[15] As a reader of the *Nation*, she would have been aware of Sturgis' arguments. Moreover, she shared with Sturgis the Ruskinian beliefs that buildings expressed the life of the community, that they had the power to shape that life, and that organic medieval forms had a special beauty.

Ruskin, however, found the early years of Gothic the most compelling, years when religious fervor united craftsmen and turned them into artists. To him civilization slid on a downward arc and Europe moved toward decadence in the later Middle Ages. Carey Thomas savored just these years. She took special delight in the Jacobean period with its love of theater and pageantry and an architecture that evolved from theatrical stage settings at the hand of Inigo Jones. What a curious choice for one who professed Quakerism, a faith born in rejection of the popery and worldliness of those same years, the practice of which required abjuring theater. Carey Thomas was no Quaker, at least not on the inside. During a time of conflict with her board, she became increasingly sour about her heritage. When a generous donation went to another women's college, she remarked to Mary Garrett, "I think most people really dislike Friends. Indeed I do not see how they can fail to."[16] Carey Thomas professed the faith in order to gain control of Bryn Mawr. Her testimonials of religious loyalty were of a piece with abjuring smoking and requiring abstinence from cigarettes of students and faculty in public settings. When retirement freed her from the necessity of appearances, Carey Thomas joined the Episcopal Church and returned to cigarettes.[17]

Carey Thomas loved the theater. Her correspondence with Mary Garrett is filled with her passionate responses. Sarah Bernhardt in *Cleopatra* "was divine . . . the very serpent of old Nile, the courtesan. . . . I think I told you of my desire, granted once that I were a man, & to a man fallen from grace, to have her once for my mistress; well, the long act in her Egyptian palace where

Anthony & she, in her diaphanous robe of course, lavish countless caresses upon one another entirely satisfied my desire."[18] In 1900, after some initial scepticism, she enthusiastically endorsed Bryn Mawr's initial elaborate May Day festival, an Elizabethan extravaganza staged by students under the supervision of Evangeline Walker Andrews, a recent alumna, married to Charles MacLean Andrews, a Bryn Mawr professor. First observed at Earlham, a coeducational Quaker college in Indiana, this re-creation of English traditions, complete with Maypoles and theatricals, gave students an acceptable alternative to the dancing forbidden by religious practice.[19] Carey Thomas admired Shelley and the Romantic poets and delighted in opera.[20] The three offspring of her aunt, Hannah Whitall Smith, brought Carey Thomas into the international circle of aesthetes: Mary Smith lived with and married Bernard Berenson; Alys Smith was Bertrand Russell's first wife; Logan Pearsall Smith became a minor literary figure in his own right. Thomas' Smith cousins provided her with her natural aesthetic habitat, available during her travels.[21]

In her mature years, as Carey Thomas came to love Mary Garrett deeply and passionately, she must have sensed a sharper cleavage with a faith which placed such an emphasis on family life. All Thomas' energies, including her sexual ones, focused on women. A reading of her daily letters to Mary Garrett makes it unmistakable that though she professed sexual attraction to men as well as women, she felt committed to a professional life that excluded marriage. This did not mean a life without intense and committed love. By the mid-1880s, Carey Thomas regarded herself as bound by love to Mary Garrett exclusively and forever.[22] Earlier commitments to Mamie Gwinn stood in the way, but, in 1904, Gwinn eloped with Alfred Hodder, freeing Thomas. Mary Garrett moved into the Deanery, and the two realized the joint life so long desired. As a side consequence, as the wealthy daughter and heir of John Garrett, Mary Garrett provided Carey Thomas with the means to indulge fully her love of acquisition both in private and in the college setting.

Bryn Mawr gave Carey Thomas a landscape in which her non-Quaker aestheticism took solid form. The initial building designed by Cope and Stewardson suggested a few signs of what followed. Radnor Hall forsook the domestic imagery of the cottage. This frankly institutional building bore some resemblance to Taylor in its verticality, but its façade of irregular stone was much cleaner. The shape of the building gave a slight feeling of enclosure over the entrance. The great octagonal room carried battlements. However, following the lead of Hutton's initial buildings, Cope & Stewardson sited Radnor in the middle of the campus. Bryn Mawr had asked Calvert Vaux, the experienced landscape architect who designed Central Park with Frederick Law Olmsted, to create a plan for the campus. He reaffirmed earlier locational decisions, though he suggested encircling the campus in trees as an arboreal barrier to the surrounding neighborhood.[23]

May Day, 1900: Maypole dancing; Taylor Hall in background; *Bryn Mawr College*

May Day, 1900: The St. George Play; *Bryn Mawr College*

Denbigh Hall; *Bryn Mawr College*

The real breakthrough occurred in 1891. Cope & Stewardson designed
Denbigh, the third student's residence, as a long, low, elegant structure placed
at the perimeter of the campus. Its irregular gray stone façade was punctuated
by the bay windows of the students' sitting rooms; its roof, by their chimneys.
The cornice line carried the battlements that established most clearly its English antecedents. One entered on the side, into a three-sided bay topped with
battlements. Despite its decorative emphasis at the roofline, Denbigh is a calm
horizontal building with clean lines and repetitions conveying order and regularity. Most important of all, its placement created courtyards between Denbigh and Taylor and between Denbigh and Dalton, the science building. With
Denbigh, Bryn Mawr not only shed its Victorian skin, but bones as well;
monumental masses gave way to walls that enclosed.[24]

Cope & Stewardson reached their mature style with the building of the
double dormitory Pembroke East and West. The long line of buildings of
the two residence halls walled off the campus on the south. At the joining of
the two residences, an arched gateway framed the carriage entrance on to the
campus and created a strong perpendicular axis. This powerful square entry
carried Jacobean decoration and four battlemented towers. Its impressive windows sheathed the great dining hall of the double residence. A more vital
composition than Denbigh, Pembroke Hall is a courtly building, dignified yet
festive. It formed a wall that defined the campus from the outside and enclosed
it from the inside. With the library, it shaped handsome courtyards.

Pembroke Arch with Taylor Hall on left; n.b. 1901 banner on Pembroke
Bryn Mawr College

Rockefeller Hall dining room, 1910; *Bryn Mawr College*

Rockefeller, the last Cope & Stewardson residence hall, continued the line of Pembroke West, turning the corner to define the southwest point of the campus. Variations in setbacks and the resulting L-shape added a needed variety to the long building. At the turn, a tall tower held a massive arch that provided a pedestrian entrance, Owl Gateway, approached by stairs. When the library was constructed, the gateway framed perfectly its delicate form.

In 1895, Frederick Law Olmsted confirmed Cope & Stewardson's basic plan. In 1893, the college had purchased land to the west of the campus. Working with his stepson, John C. Olmsted, the great landscape designer laid out athletic grounds in the informal northerly section of the campus that sloped down to Roberts Road and determined that future buildings frame the western perimeter as they had the southern. While the college never carried out the many specific plans for athletic fields and plantings, the firm set the location of new buildings and roads until 1928.[25]

Each dormitory grouped near its entrance a drawing room, student sitting room, and dining room. The college guaranteed to each student a single room, at the minimum. But beyond this and the common rooms, students lived under quite varied conditions. They had rooms of different shapes, sizes, and locations, some with a shared or an individual study. A modest single room in an unfortunate location went as low as $100 for the year; a two-room suite or a room of unusual size cost as high as $350.[26] In Carey Thomas' eyes, this great differential only mirrored students' experience in other realms. Recalling her own luxurious three-room suite in Sage at Cornell, she argued that differences in housing did not affect students' judgments about each other.[27] She dismissed the notion that students' economic backgrounds shaped college social structure because she identified with the affluent student, not the one forced to live in pinched surroundings. As time went on, Bryn Mawr attracted more wealthy students, and successive dormitories held an increased ratio of expensive rooms. Rockefeller, the most luxurious, had thirty-nine single suites, each with bedroom and sitting room. In addition, its basement had service rooms for sewing and hairdressing and a students' grocery store.[28] Carey Thomas always hoped to attract the daughters of wealth. Bryn Mawr became increasingly successful in doing so.

Joseph Taylor intended from the beginning that his college educate "the higher and more refined classes of Society,"[29] but he expected them to be Friends. By 1897, the incoming class had only two Quakers, the same number as entering Roman Catholics, in contrast to thirty Episcopalians and twenty-four Presbyterians,[30] a disturbing ratio to trustees committed to James Taylor's vision. Little wonder that they came into conflict with Carey Thomas. They fought her on a number of grounds; but because trustees held ultimate responsibility for buildings, they took their strongest stand there. By the turn of the century, they turned against her building program. While Thomas argued strenuously that buildings provided a preferred form of investment with a high annual return, the trustees forbade further use of Taylor's endowment for buildings.[31] Yet, while trustees created hurdles, they failed to block Carey Thomas. The attempt to stop growth merely forced her to venture outside to beg for funds. A large gift from John D. Rockefeller built a residence hall with his name and encouraged alumnae gifts for the library, Thomas' most intense fund-raising effort.[32]

In the library, Carey Thomas found her crowning symbol of Bryn Mawr. As she planned the library, her attention to detail became obsessive, and she came into conflict not only with her trustees but with her architects.

Cope & Stewardson designed the library according to very explicit instructions from President Thomas. Its main reading room copied the dining hall of Wadham College, Oxford, while Oriel College provided the model for the entrance. Thomas wanted an enclosed cloister at its center and seminar rooms adjoining professors' offices for graduate work. The architects agreed to work within these limits and to accept her requirement that the library could not be used in their designs for other colleges. (Cope & Stewardson had repeated their Bryn Mawr residence hall successes at Princeton and at Washington University

Reading room, Thomas Library; *Bryn Mawr College*

Cloister archway, Thomas Library; *Bryn Mawr College*

in St. Louis.)[33] The firm created an elegant plan, perhaps unsuitable for a library—the librarian complained that the central reading room was larger than that of the British Museum—but certainly befitting the dignity that Carey Thomas demanded for Bryn Mawr.[34]

Walter Cope died before building began. While Carey Thomas was travelling abroad, Herbert Tatnall, the chairman of the buildings and grounds committee, decided that the proposed library was thirty feet too close to Taylor Hall and detracted from its dignity. Cope's successor agreed to shift the building back. When Thomas heard, she turned livid with rage: she insisted that laymen had no right to make decisions about location and that the college should trust Cope's judgment, not some unknown with whom it had never worked. Through a barrage of long, agonized letters, she sought and gained a delay and then the restoration of Cope's plan.[35] By 1904, Tatnall and the conservative trustees had lost on every major issue: the siting of the library was their last-ditch effort to protect the symbol of their vision of the college, Taylor Hall. A library built like a Jacobean college chapel with towers and battlements threatened to encroach upon the "Quaker lady."

M. Carey Thomas won not only on the site but also on every detail. This required both a change in architects and a messy lawsuit.[36] In Thomas' eyes the victory justified the struggle, for it produced a library that matched her pedagogy and taste. The Johns Hopkins–influenced seminar method, where professors and students gathered around a table in the presence of books to engage in mutual research, required seminar rooms in every graduate subject. Along with their long tables surrounded by chairs or laboratory equipment, the rooms contained shelves of specialized books for graduate students' use.[37] Senior professors' offices adjoined the seminar rooms, emphasizing by their location the importance of research and graduate teaching. Undergraduates read their books in a more splendid setting, at one of the 134 tall desks in the great and ornate reading room. This vast open space, reproducing an Oxford dining hall, with light pouring in from tall windows adorned with tracery, fit Carey Thomas' vision of the dignity of scholarship. The rectangular cloister with its handsome groined-vault passageway and courtyard arcade offered an appropriate setting for the monastic renunciation that Thomas associated with the life of the mind.

These were embattled years for M. Carey Thomas. She emerged triumphant against trustees and architects on the library, only to face, in 1916, a faculty uprising against her dictatorial rule.[38] She could no longer count on alumnae, who felt a different stake in the college. She confronted a new generation of students, whose goals she found difficult to understand. Carey Thomas herself changed as well. She remained a brilliant feminist; but where she had once moderated her materialism and sensualism by a Quaker upbringing, she now unleashed her desires. In time her enjoyment of power became an habitual exercise. What began as leadership became autocracy. In the twentieth century, M. Carey Thomas turned formidable. Her own dwelling, the Deanery, mirrored these changes.

Bryn Mawr had acquired several houses along with its land. These it used as homes for president, faculty, and dean. With her strong distaste for the life of the woman professor boarding in student residences, and perhaps in imitation of Maria Mitchell, Carey Thomas took one of the cottages at the outset and named it the Deanery. There she lived, saw students, and transacted college business. Mamie Gwinn, who joined the English faculty (with an appointment coterminous with Thomas' tenure), moved into the Deanery. When M. Carey Thomas assumed the presidency, the house proved too small. In 1896, she oversaw its first expansion. By this time, her own scale of living had grown, for Mary Garrett added $5,000 a year to Thomas' Bryn Mawr salary.

The purchase of land on the western edge of the campus shifted the relative location of the Deanery from the border to the center of the campus. The library's placement meant that it almost adjoined the cottage, a symbolic touch that would not be lost on Carey Thomas. When Mamie Gwinn's marriage to

M. Carey Thomas greeting students from the porch of the Deanery;
Mary Garrett under the umbrella; *Bryn Mawr College*

Alfred Hodder opened the way for Mary Garrett to join Thomas, Garrett
brought to the Deanery her handsome possessions. In 1907, she had the house
completely rebuilt at her own expenditure of $100,000. Lockwood de Forest,
brought in to finish the library after conflicts severed the college's relationship
to Cope and Stewardson's successors, redesigned the Deanery in the manner
befitting a railroad heiress. The brother of Mary Garrett's close friend and a
member of Tiffany's firm, de Forest was a turn-of-the-century aesthete who
revelled in the intricate patterns of India and in the finishes and textures of
wood. He once wrote that Americans needed to regain their sense of touch
and learn to see before they think: "Design should appeal directly to our mind
through our eyes."[39] He copied Dorothy Vernon's Gallery in Haddon Hall for
the Deanery's vast entertaining room and made it a feast for the eyes. Carved
chests from India, Persian rugs, and Tiffany glass filled a room decorated with
the tile floors, leaded windows, and copper-beamed ceiling of the arts and
crafts movement. M. Carey Thomas' biographer remembered it as having "the
fairy-tale quality of an extravagant dream."[40]

While the shingled cottage's exterior remained unpretentious, the Deanery
grew to an immense size. A great rambling house on three floors, its bulk
equalled Merion, which housed fifty-five. De Forest planned its sprawling

The Deanery's Dorothy Vernon Room; *Bryn Mawr College*

rooms for entertaining on a grand scale, something in the manner of an English country house. When converted to a college guest house in 1934, it slept eighteen persons on the second and third floors in addition to those sharing a large open "dormitory," probably the maid's quarters.[41] Under Carey Thomas, the Deanery required a staff of six to clean, cook, and serve. Callers rang so constantly that though Thomas once hired a butler, she found he "got so exhausted that she had to give him an assistant," and turned to two "waitresses" instead.[42]

However busy and public the Deanery, Carey Thomas and Mary Garrett possessed a retreat of quiet beauty, the Deanery garden. "Secluded, intimate and charming,"[43] the garden gave them that protected out-of-doors space, in which Thomas' generation of academic women took special delight. John C. Olmsted planned it and determined its evergreen plantings. De Forest, Garrett, and Thomas decorated it with statuary, fountains, and tiles from travels abroad, but kept the garden restrained and quiet.[44]

The Deanery and garden gave Carey Thomas ample scope to indulge her acquisitiveness on her travels with Mary Garrett. It expressed Thomas' love of

The Deanery Garden; *Bryn Mawr College*

luxury and service. And yet it stands for more than self-indulgence. The Deanery made a statement about a woman's power in a materialistic society. Its grand scale and elegant furnishings gave frank avowals of the pleasures of success enjoyed by an extraordinary woman. M. Carey Thomas richly fulfilled her adolescent daydream.

Bryn Mawr's president had always exerted care to set and maintain the "Bryn Mawr standard," a phrase frequently found in her reports and addresses. The Bryn Mawr campus, created in her years, did just that. Its residence halls, groupings of buildings and spaces, late Gothic forms, library, and president's house set a new standard for the women's colleges. With its buildings and landscapes went Bryn Mawr's system of self-governance, which, however limited, opened up new possibilities for organizing communal life. Bryn Mawr broke with the building and governance traditions that had marked the women's college and claimed for women the academic setting and way of life of men. Bryn Mawr ended the distinctive building tradition of the women's colleges: within a short span, quadrangles rose in New York, Poughkeepsie, Wellesley, Cambridge, Northampton, and South Hadley.

IO

The Stately Columned Way

To a young, privileged woman, New York offered every advantage but one—the chance for a liberal arts education in the city. Vassar took her away to Poughkeepsie. City University's normal school, later called Hunter College, lacked the standards and curriculum of liberal learning. Columbia University provided the obvious solution, but its trustees refused all petitions to admit women. President Frederick A. P. Barnard, with all his persuasive powers, failed to convince them of the simplicity and justice of opening Columbia to women. No one could accuse the board members of wholesale misogyny, for some of them promoted women's education in other places. As conservative men they saw their task as administering Columbia College; admitting women unnecessarily complicated their duties and threatened to deplete resources. That was why Annie Nathan Meyer's plan appealed to them. In 1889, the "Certain Committee of Friends of the Higher Education of Women," which she had called into being, asked the trustees to establish a female annex for Columbia, a college for women within the university. The committee agreed to maintain a separate building in which the Columbia faculty offered instruction to women. Although never mentioned, the Harvard example provided a precedent. The Cambridge annex's invisibility reassured the New Yorkers that educating women did not necessarily put heavy demands on the host university.[1]

Once empowered by Columbia, the new Barnard College created a prestigious board of trustees. However energetic and effective, the early movers knew that to be successful in New York City the college required names that counted. Despite her matronly position as a doctor's wife, Annie Nathan Meyer was very young. She had attempted for one year "The Collegiate Course" at Columbia, an early effort to satisfy women's aspiration by offering them Columbia exams and degrees, without, however, the preparation of lectures or recitations. In the years after she withdrew to marry, the unequal contest she had waged with men for an education rankled her. Encouraged by Melvil Dewey, Columbia's librarian, she determined to win for New York women what Arthur Gilman had won for those of Boston. She interested Ella Weed, a Vassar graduate who served as principal of the fashionable Miss Brown's School for Girls in New York. Working through Ella Weed's contacts and her own, Annie Nathan Meyer drew up an impressive list of supporters to petition Columbia and later serve as trustees.

A member of a prominent Sephardic Jewish family, Annie Nathan Meyer understood the rules of power and prestige in New York. Her list therefore included Arthur Brooks, minister of the Church of the Incarnation, and such prominent New Yorkers as Mrs. Joseph H. Choate and George A. Plimpton. With such supporters promising an independently financed and managed institution under Columbia's academic control, Meyer gained early acceptance of her plan. In fact, she learned that she had read the Columbia trustees' minds. Six years earlier, a select committee of the board had recommended that when an association independent of Columbia established a separate college according to "the laws of physiology and hygiene, and reverence for the principles of the Christian religion," the board would find a way "to connect it with the University system, and to secure to it the advantages of the personal attendance of our College faculty."[2]

Barnard began plainly. The original agreement with Columbia stipulated that Barnard be responsible for a building used for instruction, not residence. In contrast to the handsome buildings that received the first students at the "country colleges," Barnard offered, as had Radcliffe, the modest quarters of a converted house. In September 1889, the doors of 343 Madison Avenue opened to receive the first thirty-six students, twenty-two of them science specials. Their faculty came over from Columbia at Madison and Forty-ninth Street. As at Harvard, before an annex existed, Columbia faculty had taught women students for additional income. The establishment of Barnard allowed them to teach college women gathered conveniently nearby.

From the beginning, Barnard treated its students as responsible adults, though legend has it that the janitress acted as chaperone, making her presence all too clear when a student lingered in conversation with a male member of the faculty.[3] The initial budget provided for a Lady Principal. No one ever took the title or assumed a Lady Principal's duties. The assumption that the students would be New Yorkers greatly simplified early planning. Day students who gathered for classes and then returned to their parental homes needed little of the anxious care expended by Vassar or Wellesley.[4] Ella Weed served as the paid chairman of the Academic Committee, while keeping her principalship at Miss Brown's. Ella Weed was the guiding spirit in the first four years, and at her death the college called her successor dean. She brought high standards and a sense of humor to her tasks. Under her leadership Barnard did not repeat Vassar's mistakes. In language reminiscent of President Raymond, Ella Weed set out the rationale for the liberal arts at Barnard. She wanted only students who met Columbia's entrance standards, which included Greek. She required students to take the regular sequence of courses. She fought against imitating Radcliffe's policy of accepting special students who came only for a few courses. Because New York provided no opportunity for the study of the sciences, Barnard did agree initially to accept science specials; but it moved quickly in the following years to eliminate them.

Both Ella Weed and Annie Nathan Meyer wanted to convince the public of Barnard's high standards. When a Columbia professor allowed an assistant to write a special examination for Barnard students, Meyer rushed to Columbia to persuade the professor that only the same examination for women and men insured the public's perception of Barnard's academic equality.[5] Annie Nathan Meyer insisted that Barnard accept no graduates from the normal school of City University, even the daughter of a friend. She preferred to have only a few students than to lower the standard.[6]

Radcliffe insured quality by never hiring a professor outside Harvard's faculty. Barnard, by contrast, hired some separate professors. The Columbia faculty appointed the Barnard faculty, however, and Columbia also lent all examinations. Given Columbia's assumption that its own professors be male, the provision for a separate Barnard faculty made it possible for women to teach female students. In 1890, Emily L. Gregory, a distinguished botanist, became the first professor in Barnard College. The risk a separate faculty involved intensified Barnard's insistence on standards.

While Barnard and Columbia had to work out many details over time, unlike Harvard the Manhattan university encouraged its annex. Columbia's librarian, Melvil Dewey, had vigorously endorsed Annie Nathan Meyer's efforts; the library welcomed advanced students to use its books. Columbia granted Barnard students the B.A. Presidents Seth Low and Nicholas Murray Butler supported the enterprise unequivocally. Mrs. Seth Low became a Barnard trustee. Even in the early years, Barnard never had to imitate Radcliffe's cautious tread.

Supported by Columbia, but fiscally autonomous, Barnard College needed money. For a four-year trial period, the nascent college struggled with small donations begged from its friends. Columbia was preparing to move uptown to Morningside Heights. Barnard wanted to follow, but it could not even raise enough to pay the annual rent of $1,800 on the modest brownstone house at 343. Pessimistic about the future, Jacob Schiff resigned as treasurer. He found it too "undignified to carry on an educational institution of such high aims by begging from door to door."[7] George A. Plimpton took his place, to remain Barnard's chief fund-raiser until 1936. When Ella Weed died in 1894, Plimpton decided that Barnard needed "the strongest woman in this country" at its head.

He wondered if Alice Longfellow, the poet's daughter, might accept, bringing to the post her administrative experience at Radcliffe, her fund-raising ability, and her famous name.[8] The trustees offered the position to Alice Freeman Palmer's protégée, Marion Talbot of the University of Chicago, but she refused. The deanship went to a brilliant member of Bryn Mawr's first class, Emily James Smith, who had continued her classical studies at Girton and the University of Chicago. The unusual opportunity to head Barnard came to her when she was twenty-nine.

Gracious as well as brilliant, Emily James Smith brought to Barnard a commitment to the higher education of women, nurtured under M. Carey Thomas, and an ability to work strategically and effectively with Columbia's president. Dean Smith needed both qualities for the dual task of upholding the integrity of Barnard and opening to its students the resources and offerings of Columbia. She sought to lead women into the university, not to replicate its offerings at Barnard.[9] Insisting, as had Ella Weed and Annie Nathan Meyer, that Columbia College's standards be Barnard's, Dean Smith sought Columbia's supervision on all academic matters.

Barnard felt certain constraints keenly. The university opened its graduate courses to Columbia College seniors, but only the Faculty of Philosophy extended this privilege to Barnard students; other departments refused. When the University Council tabled consideration of the question of admitting women to advanced courses in mathematics, political science, and history, President Low wrote to Dean Smith that only "Time, and the growth of Barnard in strength and importance," would open Columbia's doors.[10] By a brilliant stroke, Low himself provided the means of growth. Anonymously he gave the salaries of three full professors to bring to Barnard three distinguished scholars: John B. Clark in political science, James Harvey Robinson in history, and Frank N. Cole in mathematics. They in turn lent their time to the graduate faculties in exchange for courses at Barnard by other members of these faculties. Once Barnard had something to offer, barriers to Columbia began to give way.

Barnard's campus provided the symbol of growth. Unlike Radcliffe's need for invisibility in its early tenuous years, Barnard College learned the importance of presence. Supporters of Barnard not only had to convince Columbia of Barnard's strength, they had to teach New Yorkers that the women's college existed. Annie Nathan Meyer recounted the time when, after hearing Barnard's case in an audience of prominent New Yorkers, a woman apologized for not contributing to Barnard—on the grounds that so many New York City institutions claimed her loyalty that she could not give to anything so far away.[11]

In 1896, Barnard hit a streak of luck. With a few exceptions, its trustees added prestige rather than wealth to the board. At the critical moment, the trustees demonstrated their influence. Three women offered gifts of land and

Barnard in 1906, Grant's tomb on left; n.b. rubble in foreground

buildings for a campus adjacent to Columbia's property in Morningside Heights. Cultivated by her lawyer, Barnard trustee Frederick Wait, Mrs. Van Wyck Brinckerhoff promised $100,000. This caught Plimpton completely off guard, and he learned the identity of the unknown donor from a newspaper reporter.[12] No other motive than trust in her attorney's judgment proved forthcoming. Barnard gained a sizeable theater and classrooms. After a campaign for land encouraged significant gifts, including $25,000 from John D. Rockefeller, Elizabeth Milbank Anderson, a parishioner of Arthur Brooks, gave $170,000 for a second building in honor of her parents, Mr. and Mrs. Jeremiah Milbank. In 1896, on Broadway between 119th and 120th streets, construction began on Brinckerhoff Theater and Milbank Hall. Within a year Mrs. Josiah M. Fiske gave Fiske Hall, which served for three years as a dormitory before its conversion into a science building.

The daughter and heiress of a wealthy investment broker, Elizabeth Anderson originally intended to give a medical pavilion to Roosevelt Hospital. She chose Charles A. Rich, of the New York firm of Lamb and Rich, as architect and sent him abroad to study European hospitals. He drew up plans, and the hospital broke ground, but the trustees ultimately refused to accept the conditions surrounding the gift. Guided by Arthur Brooks, Anderson turned to Barnard and offered a building. The architect of her hospital became the architect of the "three buildings in one" which constituted the initial Barnard campus: Milbank, Brinckerhoff, and Fiske.[13]

The triple building composed three sides of a rectangle. The original design, never realized, called for a colonnade to enclose the courtyard on the fourth side.[14] Milbank, the center building, housed administration, classrooms, and a library reading room. Students found it elegant, a "stately col-

Entrance Hall, Milbank; *Barnard College Archives*

Aerial view of Barnard, with Columbia in muted background, upper half
Barnard College Archives

umned way."[15] A contemporary described entering the building: "A fine entrance hall leads up by double marble stairways to a beautiful foyer corridor, finished in tessellated marbles, and opening into the spacious and artistic library and handsome suite of offices apportioned to the use of the dean." Brinckerhoff—the east wing—held theater, gymnasium, science laboratories, and classrooms. Decorated in "Colonial red and white," the theater was the scene not only of chapel, lectures, and classes but also of college dramatics, dances, and teas.[16] Fiske—the west wing—contained dormitory space for sixty to sixty-five graduate students from outside the city. Four years later when the college converted the building into science classrooms and laboratories, student residences moved to Teachers College.

Across Broadway, Charles Follen McKim was designing the new campus of Columbia University. The plan of Columbia is an important milestone in the evolution of the college plan. When Russell Sturgis inspired Yale and Bryn Mawr to model themselves after Oxford and Cambridge, he not only advocated an enclosing wall to separate college from town, he also encouraged harmonious design and the conception of the campus as a composition. In 1893, a great boost to comprehensive college planning came with the World's Columbian Exposition in Chicago. A group of architects, trained in Beaux Arts principles, created the Court of Honor, the famed White City of the fair. Renaissance-inspired buildings with a common cornice line, symmetrically arranged around an impressive domed structure, framed an open area.

In the years surrounding the fair, its principles inspired such diverse settings as the New York Zoological Park, the redesign of Washington, D.C., Cope and Stewardson's campus for Washington University in St. Louis, and Columbia University.[17] Charles Follen McKim of the pre-eminent New York firm of McKim, Mead & White created in Columbia a masterful Beaux Arts design focused on Low Library, a great classic domed monument.[18] After McKim's achievement at Columbia, Beaux Arts principles dominated college planning. Other campuses might choose collegiate Gothic rather than classic, but the plan remained dominated by Beaux Arts massing, symmetry, axial planning, and key focal points.[19] Women's colleges, in the mainstream of collegiate architecture after Bryn Mawr, confronted Beaux Arts planning advocates at every turn.

Barnard's Milbank group suggests Beaux Arts principles in its massing and symmetry. In materials, scale, and decorative treatment, Barnard harmonizes with the classroom buildings of Columbia. But Barnard lacks the grace and power of Charles Follen McKim's elegant design. All accounts describe the building group as in the style of Henry II.[20] Its portico with four double columns of Indiana limestone, its quoined corners, its windows crowned by stone, and its medallions connote French grandeur; but they adorn a rather plain four-story brick structure that suggests New York institutional architecture more than anything else.

It is possible that Rich merely adjusted his design of a hospital pavilion to Barnard, for there is nothing to convey that these are college buildings. In Barnard's early years, its guiding forces showed little concern for architecture. In contrast to the excruciatingly detailed oversight that M. Carey Thomas gave to Bryn Mawr structures, Barnard's form did not matter. Barnard's Milbank group simply made a statement of dignity and solidity: the college existed, fully established. Placed to the side on its own axis, Barnard's campus spoke of its independence.

Barnard's founders created Columbia's annex to meet the demands of intelligent and well-trained New York women for a college education. Its moving spirits had no thought of changing the consciousnesses of young women and redirecting their lives, as did Mary Lyon or M. Carey Thomas, nor any desire to protect them from the dangers of higher education, as did Matthew Vassar and L. Clark Seelye. Thus the planners of Barnard lacked the intense concern for moral oversight and physical planning that accompanied the design of the other women's colleges. Only in the twentieth century, when Barnard attempted to transform itself according to its image of a proper women's college, did questions of student life and college buildings hold any genuine significance.

PART TWO

Experience

The founders of Mount Holyoke, Vassar, Wellesley, Smith, Radcliffe, Bryn Mawr, and Barnard boldly offered to young women the higher learning. To their task they brought particular hopes and fears about educated women that shaped the system of moral government within the institutions and their physical structures. Each successive founding captured the notion of higher education of women appropriate to its era.

While different conceptions shaped the varied plans of the women's colleges, each institution projected a vision of an ordered college community where protected young women, guided by professors in the world of books, grew in intellectual power. By the turn of the century, however, events rudely shattered these dreams. Students developed their own culture which gave meaning to their college experience and reshaped their consciousness. In the process, female collegians turned buildings and landscapes into the settings of their own dramas of college life. Faculty women, assumed to be loyal and dependent allies of founders, asserted themselves as autonomous professionals. They severed the prescribed connection between themselves and students and demanded a private life of their own, lived outside college gates. As students and faculty created their own separate worlds, they changed inalterably the schemes of the founders who had once brought them together.

I I

The Life

STUDENT LIFE

I

In 1903, a Vassar student examined the college as might a friendly visitor to an asylum and offered to the *Miscellany* "An Institution Report." Under the heading "Inmates," she described the "*Class for whom intended*": "The institution was originally intended for young women interested in the pursuit of knowledge, but has lately been usurped by some whose avowed aim is something they call 'The Life.'"[1] Throughout the women's colleges, presidents, professors, and students recognized the change. As a writer in *The Lantern* at Bryn Mawr lamented, "One might be even justified in fearing that the love of learning, for its own sake, . . . has ceased to permeate the life of the college . . . while the main stream of our enthusiasm flows in other channels—into our clubs, our committees, our friendships, our athletics and dramatics." Not the serious student, but "the gayest and most spectacular members of our community . . . set the standard for the life of the whole college."[2] What began at Vassar when plucky, independent young women began to subvert rules grew to engulf the women's colleges by the turn of the century.

A new element joined the old. Despite differences in emphasis, founders intended the women's colleges for one kind of student, Durant's "calico" girl, the serious, hardworking daughter of the middle class preparing to teach. These formed the backbone of the early classes, leavened from the beginning with some scholarly daughters of the more wealthy. By the 1890s, the women's colleges attracted a new clientele—young, well-educated women of the wealthy strata who had no thought of a career after college. As a Bryn Mawr instructor saw it, these women "with no need to coin their brains, and no definite aim in life" changed the tone to "enliven the college atmosphere."[3]

147

Because college presidents did not give economic breakdowns of their student body, the best evidence is indirect, the denominational affiliations of students. Smith, founded in the heart of evangelical Protestantism, had 92 Episcopalians by 1892–93, no threat to the 260 Congregationalists and 72 Presbyterians, yet a clear indication in New England that the college was drawing students outside its original base. Perhaps as significant, Smith attracted 83 Unitarians, suggesting that liberal Boston society was sending its daughters there.[4] While President Seelye admitted that "it has not yet become the fashion among the wealthy to send their daughters to college as it has to send their sons," he recognized that "each year they are more largely represented."[5]

Yet it is wrong to equate in a simple way the development of college life for women with the entry of the leisure class. At Vassar the beginnings of student culture anticipated wealthy students by decades. As we will see, society introduced new dimensions into the college scene: wealth brought style and panache, along with new tensions. But just as society changed college life, so, too, did college life transform some of the daughters of wealth.

Students agreed that college life absorbed them completely. As one story writer put it, when her principal character said goodbye to a male friend without sorrow: "Vassar's all-sufficiency was working within her."[6] In their letters, students wrote parents of their eagerness for vacations and their desire to return to the comforts at home, but this generally came at the end of a letter packed with the details of full days. When they longed for home, they wanted the rest and ease that came at the close of a time of struggle and activity. "How glad I shall be to come home to a quiet life, next summer, to my own dear home," a student wrote. "Whenever I am very tired I always think of home as the place of rest; and how happy we shall all be."[7] Akin to a businessman's desire for the home peace of a Sunday off, there is no question in the minds of these collegians where the real life lay: in the fray. Students wrote of how quickly time—a term or a year—passed, and how busy and happy they were. They sensed difficulty in explaining to an outsider the importance of the internal events of college. Their emphasis on clubs, parties, dramatics, and rituals baffled parents who had sent their daughters to college for an education. As a Vassar student explained, she did not write about trigonometry, German, and essays, because they were "ordinary occurances, and one gets used to them and does not think anything about writing about them."[8]

Seen from the perspective of the administration, college life offered more threat than promise. Not only did it violate the primary educational goals of the instruction, it posed a clear and open danger to college authority. While college life accepted the formal limits laid down, it saw regulations as external and withheld inner consent. The evangelical spirit of Mount Holyoke, Wellesley, and Smith assumed that students shared their college's official understanding of the way and that they desired to do good. College life created a different

Page from a student's scrapbook, Bryn Mawr; *Bryn Mawr College*

standard, one that was secular, even hedonistic. It recognized different qualities for achievement. It offered a new system of rewards for success and punishments for offenders. While college authorities kept one essential weapon, the right to expel students for academic failure or a serious breach of the rules, they lacked the ability to shape behavior within this broad limit. Thus, following the precedent set at Bryn Mawr, several of the colleges turned to student self-government, enlisting certain students to monitor the behavior of others.[9] And equally important, colleges relaxed their discipline, leaving fewer regulations to break. By 1910 the hand of authority weighed much less heavily than it had in the founding days.

Fewer rules monitored by student representatives lessened clashes between college authorities and students and thus made their differences less apparent, but it did not affect the basic reality, that college life opened up to students possibilities different from those intended. While founders of most of the women's colleges meant them to be "non-sectarian, but distinctly Christian," college life became increasingly secular.[10] Students may have willingly observed the forms of religion by attending chapel, but the spirit changed. Chapel provided a place of meeting where students recognized and confirmed the prerogatives of college status. At Vassar, where members of the four classes sat in assigned sections, the first confirmation of senior rank came when students took the front rows in chapel. "It seems awfully queer to be up just in front of Dr. Taylor, in the Senior seats this morning," a student commented.[11] Students electioneered and applauded the victors in morning chapel. As they gathered there in the evenings they admired each other's gowns on the occasion of special dinners and festivals. A Vassar senior wrote that after supper at the Lady Principal's apartment, "when we came out to go into Chapel, all the freshmen stood back forming admiring throngs of spectators, looking with awe at the Seniors' sweeping gowns. My pink gown was much admired."[12]

The subverting of chapel to serve communal rather than religious ends suggests the hedonistic quality of college life. If a student went to college for "the life," the experience itself, then she did not see it as a means to the higher end of intellectual or spiritual growth. She did not expect to defer gratification until after graduation, but intended to enjoy the present. That the pleasures of the turn of the century seem relatively innocent—sports, dramatics, teas, spreads, all-female dances, and festivals—should not make us forget the essential fact that they were pleasures. Students anticipated them eagerly, planned and prepared for them incessantly, and seemed to enjoy them thoroughly. College events punctuated the calendar. Even a very serious student such as Edith Rickert conceptualized time at Vassar by the succession of the opening of Senior Parlor, plays, honors, elections, and Founder's Day. Her letters, which also treat her scholarly concerns and achievements, focus largely on her preparations for these events, her decision about which dress to wear, and her relish in the memory of the occasions after they had passed.[13] Student scrapbooks gathered the extensive paraphernalia the events generated: invitations, programs, snatches of decorations, and flowers.[14]

Students created their own standards of success in this world. In the harsh cruelty of youth they divided their classmates into four basic types, two of whom they admired and two they rejected. The "swells" and the "all-around girls" dominated the college. They tolerated the inoffensive "grinds," but regarded the "freaks" as beyond endurance. The natively intelligent "brains," potentially a fifth type, floated throughout the four categories, depending upon how they exercised their natural gifts.

To be a "swell" was either easy or impossible. Entrance into this large group came with money, clothes, contacts, and a fun-loving spirit. Social life at the women's colleges had both a formal and an informal organization. Dances, receptions, concerts, and plays filled the official calendar. The students' private calendars added teas, "at homes," and spreads. The label "swell" required more

A senior birthday, Vassar, 1896; *Vassar College Library*

than money: it applied to the debutantes attuned to society and its rituals. While some daughters of such families chose not to follow family patterns, those who did turned college into a lively world of constant festivity.

Such students came into college knowing other students. A Vassar story described the "swells" as "a clan, loyal to itself, sufficient to itself, yet admired by the 'Uitlanders,' the leader of all the good times, of all the 'society.' " [15] An "endless chain" of connections bound them together. As one of the "swells" in a Vassar short story explained to a friend,

> You and I had met before we came. Sally Dean was your school friend, Barbara Sterling's sister and yours were pals. Lois Duncan is Bab's cousin, Arna Kellar rooms with Bab. Margaret Uhler went to school with Lois, Emily and Nan room with Lois. Betty's sister is a Senior: when she was a Freshman, she was Margaret's sister's best friend. It's a regular House that Jack Built. [16]

Quiet and from a modest New England background, Lydia Waitley longed to be part of the clan. "They amazed her,—those gay, jolly, happy-go-lucky beings who laughed and joked and played through the livelong day." [17] Social, not geographical, distance separated her from them. Lydia lived among the clan along the fourth-floor corridor in Main. They did not snub her, they simply ignored her. Quarantined in the infirmary with one of the clan leaders, who became fascinated by a girl "who had never owned a visiting card, never heard of a golf tea nor a Paris hat nor a theatre party,"[18] Lydia became a social success: "When 'the swells' became friends of Lydia, the girls in all the sets of the class discovered how desirable an acquaintance she was."[19]

This informative tale lays bare the social structure of the women's colleges at the turn of the century. Students divided themselves into sets, or cliques, which formed a hierarchical scale which "the swells" sat atop. Vassar gave no recognition to student cliques in its rooming policy, keeping room prices equal and forcing its students to draw each year for their next year's place. Groups of friends worked together to gather along a corridor, but bad luck occasionally forced them apart.[20] At Vassar, propinquity did not assure familiarity. Two students from different social worlds who lived next door to each other did not meet unless properly introduced.

While Vassar tried not to let social differences sort out students spatially, Bryn Mawr encouraged distinctions. Room fees varied a great deal, and the affluent enjoyed extra-large single rooms or suites with fireplaces. The college gave students the choice of rooms in the order in which they applied for admission, favoring elite daughters whose mothers sent their names in at birth. The society girls clustered in Pembroke East and West, making those halls less comfortable for serious students or the less affluent who retreated to Radnor and Merion.[21]

Wellesley's residential policy unwittingly segregated the modest from the wealthy. The Durants' commitment to the "calico" girls held fees down and kept them uniform. When it became necessary to increase board, the college opened the Eliot. Appropriately converted from a rooming house for the women workers of a shoe factory, this cottage enabled students to reduce their board fee by $75 by serving as waitresses and performing other domestic chores.[22] In a Wellesley short story, only a sense of charity to a bewildered freshman led senior Hannah Moore to accept an invitation to the Eliot: "Hannah looked across at the bare walls of the Eliot, where the ancient woodbine which lent the only line of grace to the ugly house, now shook the moisture from its long, leafless sprays. None of Hannah's friends had lived here."[23] In admitting students who had to earn part of their way and giving them a separate residence, Wellesley unintentionally isolated them.

At the other end of the spectrum, college organizations which began as literary, debating, or drama societies, became socially exclusive sororities in all but name. All the seven women's colleges except Bryn Mawr had such organizations, but only Wellesley granted them separate buildings. Starting in the 1890s, Shakespeare, Phi Sigma, Zeta Alpha, Agora, Alpha Kappa Chi, and Tau Zeta Epsilon petitioned the Wellesley board of trustees for the right to build society houses. The trustees granted their petitions, partially and provisionally. The board denied a request by one society to build a residential cottage and reserved the trustees' right in all cases to reclaim the land if needed for college purposes.[24] While Barnard and Mount Holyoke banished their societies in the early twentieth century, the clubs remained at Wellesley, possibly because they had built substantial houses. Never residential, the society houses, which formed "Society Row" along the lake, offered amenities missing in College Hall. To the outside they presented the façades of elegant houses. On the inside, dens, libraries, and kitchens offered unpretentious settings for informal entertaining, such as hot chocolate and sandwiches before ice skating on the lake. Properly chaperoned, the society houses provided ideal small-scale places in which to welcome male guests come to call.[25] Yet however pleasant for their members, the exclusive societies intensified distinctions among students. In a Wellesley short story, a College Hall senior "strolled into the student's parlor after dinner, and remained there in animated talk with certain attractive freshmen whom she entertained royally while she considered in another lobe of her brain, whether they would do as members of her society."[26]

Divisions at Wellesley grew so great that certain society members saw the need of a club to provide regular recreation for the "non-society students . . . most of the poorest class, who cannot buy amusement, and the 'digs,' who cannot make it." Here the "hindrances to participation in so much of the social pleasure of college, namely lack of attractiveness and lack of money," had no part, for the organization welcomed all. Given a barn on campus recently vacated by Jersey cows, Barnswallows provided fortnightly entertainments. In stating the value of the club to the trustees, leaders of Barnswallows inadvertently laid bare the depth of divisions at Wellesley. Barnswallows gave a "new element of unity" to student life divided among "village freshmen, and upperclass girls, society members and non-society members, rich and poor, prominent students and obscure." Working together, the "less-known students" learned that "the prominent girl is not always a snob" and the "prominent girl that the obscure girl is not always stupid."[27]

Smith presents the most interesting case of the gap between college rhetoric and reality. The domestic vision of cottages linked to town and church contained a commitment to the democracy of the New England college. During President Seelye's long tenure—1875 to 1910—his words never wavered from this ideal, but the nature of Smith's student culture changed completely. Like Vassar and Wellesley, Smith took in more students than there were college rooms, but while freshmen at the other two colleges lived in town and village, by the turn of the century one-half of Smith's student body, including the upper classes, lived in rooming houses outside the campus.

While the college regulated these off-campus boarding houses, the conditions they offered varied considerably. One joined them through a network of

Haven House dining room, Smith, 1904; *Smith College Archives*

friends: invitations to tea developed into invitations for residence. A friend
took Kate Keith to Mrs. Pomeroy's for a dance, and she found it "a lovely
house, with girls from all classes in it."[28] If she could not live in a campus
house, she hoped she might move there. Ruth Sessions returned to Northampton in 1900, to open a house to help support her family, allowing her husband
to write. Her establishment grew as she added student rooms and a large recreation room, the "Hilarium," whose ceiling had tiny lights to turn it into
a ballroom. Sessions observed campus customs in full measure—dancing
after supper followed by the reading of Dickens, Sunday vespers, and a dressy
dinner.[29]

When a group of students set up their own house, renting it and hiring a
matron, they created an Invitation House which chose the next year's occupants through a formal vote. While never receiving the name "sorority," White
Lodge and Delta Sigma linked residence and social selection in much the same
manner as did the Greek societies on coeducational campuses.[30]

Smith got something of the Gold Coast of Harvard as well. De Witt Smith,
a speculative builder from New York and a Yale man, erected the Plymouth,
a handsome Richardsonian-Romanesque apartment house adjacent to the campus. With its grand marble-encased public rooms, expensive suites for sixty-

four students, gymnasium and swimming pool, and dining room equipped
with a stage, the Plymouth created a new level of extravagance and exclusion
among college women.[31] Smith's residence policy allowed students to sort
themselves out economically and socially: cliques embedded themselves in residential groups, giving spatial form to distinctions within the student body. In
addition, college societies with their highly competitive process of selection
further intensified divisions.

Whatever their economic and social differences, students assumed that they
shared an ethnic heritage. The women's colleges of 1875 were white Protestant. Without any recorded discussion, Roman Catholics and Jews entered by
ones and twos in the late nineteenth century. The colleges extended their welcome to a few fully assimilated non-Protestants, as long as they offered no
challenge to college life. When a Bryn Mawr parent bore her daughter's com-
plaint about being placed with a Jewish roommate, President M. Carey Thomas
opposed forcing the Jewish student to move because to do so "the college . . .
[would] take part in what has grown to be a religious controversy, and our
great desire is to show the strictest impartiality." After this statement of official
toleration, however, the college found a way for the two students to live apart.[32]

Such "impartiality" did not extend to black students, except at Wellesley.
In 1913, when a controversy erupted at Smith over the right of a black student
to room on campus, letters went out to the other Seven Sister colleges asking
about their policy in regard to Negro students. Only Wellesley stated that it
did not discriminate in admittance or housing. Not knowing that she was
Negro, Smith had accepted Carrie Lee from Washington, D.C. She arrived on
campus in the fall and met her roommate, who came from Tennessee. The
roommate complained, and the college barred Lee from its housing. The col-
lege-certified boarding houses in Northampton refused her except as a servant
who entered through the back door. Her incensed parents alerted Joel E. Spin-
garn of the NAACP, who threatened embarrassing publicity. Julia Caverno,
Smith's professor of Greek, took Carrie Lee into her own home, as she had
taken in other Negro students over the years.

With the exception of Wellesley, the other women's colleges sympathized
with Smith's problem. Vassar had only learned after their graduation of the
presence of Negroes whose complexions had been fair enough to pass for
whites throughout their college years: the college never knowingly admitted
Negroes. Mount Holyoke took a similar line. Bryn Mawr answered fully:
because of the presence of Southern girls, Bryn Mawr advised Negro students
to go elsewhere "on account of the student herself and on account of the life
in the College Halls."[33] As Bryn Mawr reveals, the stance of college officials
compounded their own prejudices and notions of expediency with their per-
ceptions of student codes within the residence halls. In all the women's colleges
at the turn of the century, Negroes were outsiders: while Wellesley officially

welcomed them, white students parodied Negro dialect and sang "Coon songs" on their mandolins and banjos.[34]

College students cruelly labelled outsiders "freaks." A painful short story set at Wellesley captured the tensions between its society daughters and the residents of the Eliot. A well-meaning philanthropist had given a factory worker the chance to go to Wellesley. Charlotte Johnson lived at the Eliot, and wore wool dresses rather than silk. Friendless, cut out from college social life, Charlotte had only prayer meetings and tutoring sessions to give her human contact. Tree Day allowed her a moment of community, as she joined others in costume on the college green. Charlotte's dream of being accepted was shattered when students found a letter she had written, exaggerating her part in the festivities, and branded her a "freak."[35] While modest background alone did not lead to ostracism, difference did.

A modest background, combined with a quiet manner and a studious nature, had its own derogatory name: "grind" or "dig." In Georgia Oberley, a Vassar short story described the grind: "Georgia was the typical grind, pale, worn, and nervous. No one knew her. In her Junior year her class were still calling her Miss Oberley."[36] The poor collegian moaned, "I can't stand my life here. I'm not like most of the girls, I don't care for parties, or athletics, or the class, or any of the things they get so excited about. I just want to study."[37] Because she planned to teach, she tried for honors, the importance of which required explanation: "You know outsiders set so much more value on those things than we do."[38] Given the high level of participation in college activities, such noncombatants in the field of college life must have felt in the distinct minority.

While the "swells" sat atop the social life of the women's colleges, they competed in esteem with the "all-around girls" who dominated campus organizations and set the public tone of student life. The "all-around girl" was the one who "worked for the college." She filled her days with service to class, campus organizations, and the college as a whole. A Wellesley alumna who taught at Mount Holyoke contemplated "The Crowded Hours of the College Girl." Knowing that the average collegian spent 36 hours a week at her studies, she questioned her own students about the use of their time to learn that they were "organized to death." More important than social engagements, what filled their days was "executive work"—student government, clubs, the newspaper, and literary magazine. Her own advanced students averaged, in addition to athletics and social life, between 5 and 14 hours each week in college organizations; one student confessed to over 22 hours the preceding week.[39]

Both administrators and students worried that "a few girls received most of the honors and performed most of the work." To avert this, Smith initiated a point system which spread to the other colleges: the college made a list of the most important and burdensome honors and activities, assigned each of

Office of Monthly and Weekly, Students' Building, Smith, 1915
Smith College Archives

them points on a scale of one to six, and limited a student to fifteen points a semester. The list allows us to see the major channels in which "executive work" flowed. The highest number of points went to the heads of student government, the Christian Association, the newspaper, and the leads in the senior play. Class presidents came right behind as did the editor of the literary magazine and the head of the athletic association, followed by the captains for the major team sports.[40]

The question of who rose to the top dominated college fiction. To be successful, one did not have to be a "swell," but it helped. Cliques at Vassar had their candidates: the clan divided the spoils with a rival group, both of which "did try to manage the class for its own interest and did trample down the mild, unassertive grinds."[41] As a clan member expressed it, the class president should be one of its own, who had every qualification: "She's bright, chock full of business, and popular with every one. And isn't she a stunner to look at! She's done heaps for the class."[42]

The natural leader, in fiction if not in life, deserved office because of her special gifts. Tom Jefferson's Wellesley class wanted her for president not because she was "brainy" or "swell," but because she held the class together: she

1906 Bryn Mawr Class President, Mary Richardson;
snapshot from student album; *Bryn Mawr College*

Student government, Barnard, 1916; *Barnard College Archives*

was "the girl who had made them remember their unity while they disagreed."[43] Elected freshman president, she gave up her office because she failed a class exercise and received a condition. As she explained to her classmates, "a president, you know, ought to be an all-around girl; and first of all she ought to have brains."[44] She worked hard in the next three years. The vice president took her place, but knew "that she was not the leader. Every girl in the class knew that the one girl who could lead them and hold them together, and represent them, was the girl who had been honorable enough to throw up her leadership."[45] They watched her in the following year and when she proved herself, "they forced their real leader into her proper position."[46]

An "all-around girl," such as Tom Jefferson, scarcely fit conventional feminine stereotypes at the turn of the century, in manner or in nickname. No ivy looking for its oak, she was a young woman in control. President Jefferson conducted a meeting "with perfect self-confidence. Her familiarity with parliamentary order astonished the girls . . . but more than that, the force of her personality, the undeviating directness of her judgment, and a strange new poise and purpose in her manner, dominated the minds of her admiring subjects."[47] Tom Jefferson may have had no real counterpart, but she clearly expressed in fiction the collegiate ideal of clarity, direction, and force. What is intriguing is the possibility that life in the women's colleges at the turn of the century helped foster these very traits, that it gave to young women an education in independence and power, that in encouraging the "all-around girl," it transformed her.

Three areas dominated official campus life: organizations, athletics, and dramatics. Each had its specific lessons. In college organizations the "all-around girl" first learned how to serve and then how to lead. She conducted meetings according to parliamentary procedure, debated in public, handled money, made decisions, solicited advertisements. Emphasis went to group loyalty—to the class, the college, the literary magazine—whose needs took precedence over personal routine or self-cultivation. Where women once worked privately and individually, they learned to work publicly and collectively.

In athletic competition the college woman learned team play, developed strength and endurance, and tested herself in open physical combat. While students played a wide range of sports, basketball captured the imagination of turn-of-the-century college women. Each class had its team and each year entered into a major competition with its rival class. Intense class loyalty gave no quarter to the weak. College women played rough, competed keenly, and cheered passionately. One story of heroism involved a student who escaped from the infirmary, where she was recovering from a burn, to lead her class to Field Day triumphs.[48] M. Carey Thomas described to Mary Garrett the Bryn Mawr junior-senior supper at the end of a match: "The wounded heroes were carried in on stretchers & hobbled in on crutches."[49] Sports pulled spectators into the

Basketball game in Alumnae Gymnasium, Smith, 1904; *Smith College Archives*

Bryn Mawr playing fields; Constance Applebee on left; *Bryn Mawr College*

Athletic spectators, Vassar; *Vassar College Library*

fray in class cheering (so intense in Bryn Mawr dining halls that it repeatedly came under regulations), jostling, and celebration.

While many played and tried out, the major college sports became so competitive that even enthusiasts sat on the sidelines for the major games. By contrast, dramatics saw almost universal participation in the women's colleges. Through Philaletheis, almost two-thirds of the student body of Vassar belonged to a dramatic organization. The Greek-lettered chapters divided up a proportion of the members into competitive societies, whose function, beyond the pleasures of exclusive membership, included producing plays.[50] By the early twentieth century, house plays and the elaborate senior play so crowded the calendar of dramatic productions at Smith that the college continually tried to limit student participation and create an ordered system.[51] All the colleges presented Shakespearean plays, which offered a range of interesting and challenging characterizations.

As she learned to play important roles in organizations, athletics and theatricals, a college woman had a chance to wear various unconventional attire. While she generally changed into a silk dress for dinner and a gown for special occasions, a good part of the day she wore a gym costume, generally a modified bloomer that freed her movement, or a tailored shirtwaist and golf skirt, shortened several inches from the floor. College theatricals opened up a whole spectrum of possibilities, from the comic animals of *A Midsummer Night's Dream* to the frock coat of *Le Bourgeois Gentilhomme*. Formal photographs captured the young college thespians in the costume and make-up of men as well as women.

Students resorted to role-playing and costumes in their parties and rituals, as well as in their dramatic productions. At the all-female dances, upper-class students took the part and sometimes the attire of men. At Smith the sophomores welcomed the freshmen at the annual Freshman Frolic in a gymnasium transformed into a ballroom. "Each soph constitutes herself a cavalier for the freshman to whom she is assigned. She sends her flowers, calls for her, fills her order of dance, introduces her partners, fetches ices and frappés between dances and takes her to supper. . . . Every soph sees her partner home, begs for a flower and changes orders for souvenirs, and if the freshman has taken advantage of the opportunity and has made the desired hit, there are dates for future meetings and jollifications, and a good night over the balusters, as lingering and cordial as any the freshie has left behind her."[52] Wellesley and Vassar held similar entertainments. At Vassar "those who fill men's parts at the dances" wore "bloomers, sack-coats disclosing a wide expanse of shirt-front, white lawn ties and buttonhole bouquets."[53] At a rustic ball for Halloween described in a Vassar story, the seniors, dressed in farmers' overalls and cowboy hats, played the role of "attentive swains . . . hovering . . . in mimic masculine devotion" about the calico-clad freshmen, "their sweethearts."[54]

College authorities experienced acute anxiety about the adoption of male attire and made elaborate rules to limit it to occasions where no men observed. Rules forbade photographs, though student scrapbooks contain elaborate ones.[55] Bryn Mawr, which feared such breaches of decorum most keenly, was shocked by a student going about in pants and required students to change into skirts before leaving the place of theatrical performance or dances.[56]

Exposure threatened to reveal the most carefully guarded secret of the women's colleges, that in a college composed only of women, students did not remain feminine. Through college organizations, they discovered how to wield power and to act collectively; through aggressive sport, to play as a team member and to win; through dramatics, to take male roles. In a society in which

Dance Program of a Smith student, sophomore reception, October 15, 1902; *Smith College Archives*

gender differences attributed aggression, strength, and directness to men, the "all-around girl" of the women's college learned how to act as a man. One critic later characterized the early-twentieth-century women's college campus as dominated by "the gang spirit": "To stride about the campus, excel in athletics, serve as cheer-leader or play hero in dramatics represented the *sine qua non* of group idealism."[57]

Did the adoption of masculine attire or attributes involve more than social role-playing? College fiction usually insisted that it did not, that the Vassar senior dressed as a farmer shined in a ball gown from a box at the Metropolitan Opera the previous week.[58] One intriguing story suggests that role-playing had an erotic side. Set at Smith, it focused on the Pygmalion-like transformation of a plain freshman into a campus leader. When her sophomore escort found her country clothes and demeanor unacceptable and enlisted an artistic

House of Commons, Wellesley, 1888; upper floor, Centre College Hall;
Professor Katharine Coman in white wig; *Wellesley College Archives*

Dramatic production, the Idler, Radcliffe's dramatic club, ca. 1896
Radcliffe College Archives

Vassar dramatic production, before 1900; n.b. hidden skirts
on "male" characters; *Vassar College Library*

friend to create for her a more appropriate dress and style, Evangeline became a stunning beauty whose success at the freshman-sophomore dance made her college career. "Her milk-white shoulders rose magnificently from folds of auburn velvet that her wonderful hair repeated in loose waves about her face. . . . Her long, round arms gleamed against the black of her skirt."[59] She became the girl everyone wanted to know, and in the following year a society invited her to join and her class chose her president. Designed to mock the false nature of collegiate success, the story unwittingly exposes the play of sexual attraction among women students in the setting of college dances.

Wellesley Lyrics is even more explicit. This collection, which included faculty and alumnae contributions as well as those of students, contains poems expressive of a wide variety of emotions. While some invoke nature, heterosexual love, maternity and death, several are love poems of women to each other. A few, such as "My Sophomore," are set within the college frame.[60]

College mores insisted that only immature college students formed erotic attachments with other women. The shift from the word "smash" to "crush" at the end of the nineteenth century involved a change in focus from the dominant to the subordinate actor. As a Smith clipping clarified, this "distinctly woman's collegiate word" described the situation when "one girl, generally an underclassman, and usually a freshman, becomes much attached to another girl, ordinarily an upper-class girl. The young girl is 'crushed' on the other, sends her flowers, and tries in various ways to give expression to her admiration."[61]

Official student opinion turned against the "crush" and tried to label it a holdover from childhood that college students should abjure. In 1893, a writer in *The Wellesley Magazine* wrote scathingly of the "disgrace to our students, to our college, that the sickly sentimentality of a boarding-school should be carried out in the use of the word, and in the fact that there are in college, 'crushes.'" She urged her colleagues to frown on "these unwholesome attachments," to condemn those who encouraged them, and to isolate those afflicted in the hope of eliminating "crushes" or shipping them "to some preparatory school where the students could take them as they take whooping-cough and so be proof against them when they enter college."[62] Yet the author admitted in her condemnation that "crushes" existed. In contrast to college newspaper articles, student letters to family and friends suggest a wide acceptance of female infatuation. Edith Rickert wrote to her parents during her junior year in an unembarrassed fashion: "Dear, ridiculous old Ellen! She and I having [*sic*] been having quite a 'spoon' tonight." Yet Rickert perceived such behavior as a holdover from an earlier time, adding, "It seemed quite like old times when we were 'crushes,' when I was a Freshman and she was a prep."[63]

The "crush" linked an erotic element to a power relationship. However official opinion might condemn the sexual feelings college women had for each other, from the beginning the women's colleges built into their design the dominant-subordinate relationships which fostered these feelings. In 1837, Mount Holyoke harnessed the power of women's friendship to the bond between teacher and student. As college life developed in the women's colleges, students perceived faculty as naturally antagonistic to their interests, and distance replaced familiarity. Undergraduates looked askance at close relations between faculty and students: "Many girls," a writer in *The Wellesley Magazine* complained, "are afraid to encourage any personal relations with members of the faculty, from their dread of having to bear the accusation 'crushed.' "[64] The attachment younger women felt to their elders remained. It shifted downward to become that between upperclassmen and freshmen. Young freshmen, leaving their families, no longer sought to win love of teachers through imitation, but rather that of juniors and seniors.

However frowned on when it became excessive or explicitly sexual, the experience of dominance and subordination remained at the heart of the college experience for women. Each campus had its specific rules governing respect paid to upper-class students: at Bryn Mawr, freshmen opened doors for seniors and stepped aside on a path; at Smith, a freshman could not ask a senior to dance, but only await being asked.[65] Whatever the particular expression, these rules shared the purpose of enhancing social distance based on upper-class dominance. Students exercised power openly as well as symbolically. Though forbidden, hazing of freshmen continued. At Bryn Mawr, suspension followed a night of hazing so severe that it endangered life.[66] That encountered by Kate Keith at Smith in 1906 involved more humiliation than pain.[67]

Just as the relation between teacher and student transformed the Mount Holyoke student early in the nineteenth century, so that between upper-class student and freshman reshaped consciousness at the turn of the century. The feminine part in the dance marked the underclassman. As one grew into maturity, one acquired the prerogatives of the masculine role with its dominant postures. The Smith or Vassar freshman imitated the one she admired. Adoration was the first step in a process of transformation. College opinion against the "crush" demanded only that the upper-class student not misuse her position or the freshman take it too seriously.

The transformation of student consciousness is significant because founders intended the design of the women's colleges to protect femininity. Vassar's location, Wellesley's beauty, Smith's much-copied cottages, and Radcliffe's boarding houses were planned to insure that higher education not unsex women students. Thus the flowering of college life meant that the messages built into the landscape and structures went unheeded. So long feared, "acting a *manly* part" became a reality. While each women's college developed its distinctive form of student culture, once begun the basic process went on, regardless of whether students lived in Main at Vassar or the Dewey at Smith.

Suffrage parade; *Radcliffe College Archives*

Election night, Mount Holyoke, ca. 1908; *Mount Holyoke College Library/Archives*

Away from their homes, young women collegians of the turn of the century created an all-female community. While the outside world penetrated to reproduce the class structure on campus, the perpetuation of the structure of gender proved to be another matter with quite different consequences. In the single-sex society of the women's college, women re-created the social roles of men and women with their hierarchical relationships. But women took both parts, assuming masculine prerogatives as upper-class students. This encouraged the development of the forcefulness and direct stance of men rather than the tilts and smiles that marked female subordination. Buildings designed to protect femininity became places where women learned to act as men.

I I

At Vassar, Wellesley, and Bryn Mawr, college builders provided students with bedrooms and study parlors and large public parlors for entertaining. At Smith the cottages provided rooms of a middle size for comfortable gatherings of students and faculty, and these spread to the other colleges. When space became available, Wellesley and Vassar gave seniors a parlor and granted organizations meeting rooms in their grand buildings. As students created an increasingly elaborate college life unanticipated by college authorities, where could it take place? Private socializing—teas, spreads, and chafing dish parties—went on in student rooms. Just as it turned literary societies into sororities, so college life turned bedrooms and studies into parlors. The well-stocked tea table became an essential element of the college room, bedspreads and pillows changed beds into couches, screens hid private effects, and nets covered bare walls with memorabilia. Students learned to perfect the art of fudges, oyster stews, hot chocolate, and tea. Increasing numbers of wealthy students called in outside caterers for elaborate teas and florists for bouquets and corsages.[68]

Early classes at Smith and Vassar felt an acute need for a proper gymnasium. Alumnae at both colleges made an adequate facility their first major contribution. In 1889, Vassar erected its Alumnae Gymnasium; Smith followed in 1892. While properly stocked with the latest equipment and well suited to the new sport of basketball, the gymnasium's vast expanse of polished floor presented space adaptable for dramatics and dances. For college-wide occasions, students transformed the dining room or the gymnasium into festive settings with their private possessions. A character in a Smith story watched from her window "the file of girls loaded down with the pillows, screens, and palms whose transportation forms so considerable a portion of the higher education of women."[69]

Fanny Sinclair's room with floral tributes, Bryn Mawr, 1901
Bryn Mawr College

By the turn of the century makeshift arrangements no longer sufficed for college women. On each campus students began a campaign for a special building to house college life. By the late 1920s, all of the women's colleges had students' buildings. While minor differences separated them, each held small meeting rooms for college organizations, an auditorium for theatricals, generally with removable seats to allow a dance floor and banqueting hall, and a kitchen for special class suppers and banquets. While students' buildings took different architectural forms, from Jacobean at Smith to Colonial at Vassar, one feature distinguished their façades. An arcade or set of columns adorned the front of each building, creating an appropriate setting for strolls and promenades.[70] However serious the rest of the campus, the students' building carried this mark of festivity.

As significant as these buildings are, they hardly measure the impact of college life on the landscape of the women's colleges. College life did not confine itself to students' buildings. Rather students subverted the entire campus into a great stage setting for "the life." Just as student rooms designed for sleeping became gathering places around tea tables, so chapel became a place for the demonstration of status, campus politicking, or the celebration of the

Porch of Students' Building, Smith, dressed for a prom
Smith College Archives

victors. The dining hall added class cheering to meals or became the scene of banquets and promenades. Students not only reshaped the spaces contained in buildings, they claimed the places in between. Each college had its particular paths, its favorite haunts and retreats. The lake, the Circle, or even the stretches of countryside beyond campus bounds became special places for important conversations or self-examination.

College rituals which gave form to communal life cast a special aura over the landscape. Knowledge of the interworkings of student culture in the women's colleges allows us to understand that the focus of college traditions was the initiation of freshmen. At Wellesley, the freshman came to breakfast on the first Sunday of college to find a bunch of flowers at her plate, left by an upperclassman; in white she went to the chapel for Flower Sunday. Lantern Night at Bryn Mawr vividly dramatized the initiation ceremony. The freshmen donned for the first time the cap and gown, the distinguishing marks of student status, and formed two semicircles between Denbigh and Taylor halls. Coming from Pembroke Arch the sophomores sang *Pallas Athene Thea* and passed the lanterns they carried to the freshmen, symbolizing the light that illumined the way through college life. The freshmen then carried their lanterns through each college building while the sophomores waited outside. At the return to Pembroke, all classes joined in cheers and sang the college hymn.[71]

Yet conflict followed this promise of community. For the next twelve hours, Bryn Mawr freshmen guarded their caps and gowns from the sophomores, who attempted to steal them and prevent the freshmen from appearing suitably clad at the next morning's chapel. This mock battle had its analog on every campus. At Wellesley sophomores tried to rob the freshmen of their secrets—their song, class motto, and flower—intended to impress the older students at Tree Day. Technically Vassar reversed the process: the freshmen had to discover the time and place that the sophomores dedicated their class tree in secret ceremony; but in fact the sophomores turned it around, embarrassing and harassing the freshmen by sending them out on false leads.

Finally each college had its moment when the upper classes accepted the freshmen into the full ranks of community life. Wellesley held the most elaborate ceremonies with Tree Day. The college barred outsiders, and all students came in costume. The freshmen at Wellesley planted their class tree and established their legitimate place among the classes with songs, motto, and flower. Along with the seniors, they offered to the assembled college a dance. In 1901, they "dressed as Greek maidens, in exquisite delicate shades," and revived an old Greek dance with laurel hoops.[72]

Just as ceremonies marked initiation of freshmen into the college community, so did they surround the departure of seniors. The final step-singing, where seniors passed on their power to the class beneath them, the senior play,

Commencement, Mount Holyoke, 1916; *Mount Holyoke College Library/Archives*

Ivy exercises, Mount Holyoke, 1902; Frances Perkins
leading on left; *Mount Holyoke College Library/Archives*

Ivy Day, Smith, 1902; *Smith College Archives*

the festive dinner, and finally Commencement itself, celebrated the success of the graduating class and framed their transition to the world outside.

With the growth of rituals the campus assumed a new importance as a ceremonial space. When Katharine Lee Bates studied at Wellesley in the late 1870s, only once in her four years did she ever venture outside College Hall after seven in the evening, and that was when a faculty member led her to see a night-blooming cereus. In the twentieth century, the campus became a stage for ritual by night and by day. Florence Converse, a member of Wellesley's class of 1893, gave a vivid sense of how the campus became intertwined with the dramas and rituals of college life. "Every hill and grove and hollow of the beautiful campus holds its memories of playdays and midsummer nights," she wrote. "Those were nights when Rosalind and Orlando wandered out of Arden into a New England moonlight; when flitting Ariel forsook Prospero's isle to make his nest in Wellesley's flowering rhododendrons . . . . when Puck came dancing up from Tupelo . . . when the great Hindu Raj floated from India in his canopied barge across the moonlit waters of Lake Waban. . . . High noon is magical on Tree Day. . . . No wood near Athens was ever so vision-haunted as Wellesley with the dancing spirits of past Tree Days."[73]

Many of the rituals linked the students to the college landscape. On Bryn Mawr's Lantern Night, the freshmen not only put on college dress for the first

time, through their procession they claimed the college buildings as their own. Through tree plantings at Wellesley and Vassar and Ivy Day at Smith each class left a mark upon the land. Processions, such as Wellesley's Tree Day when students wound down College Hall's long hill and circled on the lawn, turned a stretch of green into an outdoor cathedral.

As the settings of memorable ritual, archways, hills, and lakes assumed a sacred quality. Rituals lent a special aura to the scene of the daily dramas of college life. What an alumna said of Bryn Mawr can be broadened to include the other women's colleges. A stranger to the handsome campus might be struck by "the grand old stone buildings covered with ivy, by the campus stretching far off into the distance, and by the great spreading trees." As impressive as the scene appeared, "how much more then must it mean to those who have lived in those halls, studied in the library under those trees, and discussed the problems of life, death and eternity in the Cloisters. . . . Each room, each tree, almost each corner is bound up with some special memory." When she attempted to capture those memories, she turned almost automatically away from personal experience to the rituals of college life. "The cloisters are forever sacred because there as freshmen we all received our lanterns." As she recalled various traditions and their locations, she focused on "Pembroke Arch through which the freshman enters college and the senior leaves it," the

Shakespeare Society's *Midsummer Night's Dream*,
Wellesley, 1893; Florence Converse on left;
Wellesley College Archives

Vassar Daisy Chain, led by the Wood twins,
1903; *Vassar College Library*

Tree Day, Wellesley, 1896; *Wellesley College Archives*

May Day, Wellesley, 1909; College Hall wing in background
Wellesley College Archives

scene of all the rituals and of communal singing and therefore "the spot especially dear to the whole college."[74] Rituals created to give symbolic form to the college experience became firmly rooted in the college landscape.

The college campus that began as a brewer's dream of glory or as Amherst alumni's scheme for preserving femininity thus became transformed both in fact and in consciousness. As students adapted given spaces and created new ones, they changed the college landscape into their own setting for parties, meetings, athletic contests, dramas, and ritual. Coming into a world created for them by others, students made the college their own. With few structural changes, they adapted their bedrooms, studies, parlors, chapels, gymnasiums, walkways, and lakes to their own purposes. Moralism cast aside, they enjoyed the present moment. Impelled by their status hierarchies, they sorted themselves out by sets. Where tolerated, societies separated out the "swells," increasing social distinctions. As they learned to wield power, win at play, or take the role of hero, the "all-around girl" leaders set the standard of manly behavior taught to freshmen. Buildings designed to protect femininity were subverted to its suppression. Students fought for students' buildings to house organizations and college and class functions. These special structures hardly measured students' impact on the land. College life encompassed the entire campus. Through ritual, students symbolically claimed college ground. Whatever the intentions of founders and builders, in the minds of students—and thus of future alumnae—the buildings and landscapes of the women's college became the material embodiment of college life.

12

Households of Women

When the frenetic busyness of college life broke the health of a fictional Welles-ley senior and she missed graduation, she could not toast the faculty, "that august body of severe, clever, kind, and droll individuals whom she had alter-nately mimicked and reverenced for four years."[1] College fiction captured the view at a distance that the "all-around girl" held of her professors. Faculty were others, playing only background parts in college dramas.

Students' views sharply contrasted with the intentions of the creators of the women's colleges. Mount Holyoke's system, adopted at Vassar and Welles-ley and modified at Smith, depended on intense involvement of teachers in the private lives and feelings of students. But just as a student culture developed that excluded faculty, so a faculty life developed apart from the mass of stu-dents. Less public and far more individualistic than the world of students, faculty life created a distinctive sense of its own needs and of the campus land-scape. The college life of students developed in antagonism to the wishes of founders and authorities; so, too, did faculty life violate certain basic assump-tions of those in command.

Autocracy characterized late-nineteenth-century colleges. Presidents made on-going decisions, not faculty or committees of faculty, students, and alumni. Ultimately presidents were responsible to their boards, who made long-range plans, including those involving buildings and landscape. While in extraordi-nary cases trustees intervened, normally presidents had a free hand in running colleges, and, as members of the board, many presidents had a strong influ-ence on the trustees. Professors gathered in departments whose heads had cur-ricular power and carried out the will of the president. From one perspective, the struggles of faculty women constitute part of the general struggle by the American professoriate to gain greater control over the college. For women faculty in the women's colleges, their residence in college buildings and the assumption that they had a special relation to their students made their battles more difficult.

One can see this by looking at the differential treatment of men and women within the women's colleges. Men as well as women taught at the women's colleges, especially at Vassar, Smith, and Bryn Mawr. From the beginning, men had no monitoring duties and lived in separate quarters. Vassar's curious arrangement of apartments for male faculty and their families in the end pavilions of Main proved short-lived. President Taylor quickly moved to get families off the campus and into single-family houses with their own yards, fighting successfully for a college-financed faculty row outside the hedge just across the public road from the campus. Bryn Mawr built a faculty row along the northern edge of the campus, fronting on Roberts Road. Smith gradually acquired houses adjacent to college grounds for faculty households.

The distinction between men and women involved more than just the provision of single-family houses for the men with their families. Women professors lacked professional respect and their private lives remained controlled by the assumption that they provided proper models for students. Even Vassar's distinguished astronomer Maria Mitchell found that, as a woman, her president presumed that she was second-rate. When President Raymond asked for a list of publications from his faculty, he inquired only of the men, incurring Mitchell's scorn. She and Avila Avery fought to raise their salaries equal to that of the men faculty because their unequal pay gave a "lesson . . . to young women . . . precisely the opposite of that intended by the Founder when he said 'Let us recognize and honor women's existing talents ourselves.' "[2] In the early 1890s, when Lucy Salmon began riding her bicycle on the Vassar campus, President Taylor promptly forbade her wearing the necessary divided skirt.[3] At Smith, official publications labelled women faculty of whatever rank teacher, while men held the title professor.[4]

Some faculty women suffered from a two-tiered system. With the exception of Maria Mitchell, eight men composed the initial faculty of Vassar, assisted by a corps of women teachers, many of them without college degrees. As women joined the faculty as professors, distinctions between professors and teachers continued. The women professors dined at a high table, seated in order of rank, while each teacher headed a table of students. Professors gathered in faculty meetings that barred teachers from participation.[5] At Bryn Mawr, M. Carey Thomas' determination to give women students a faculty of German-trained specialists caused her initially to hire unmarried younger men just emerging from graduate school. In time, Bryn Mawr's men matured, and women joined the faculty. With a few exceptions, however, Bryn Mawr unwittingly reproduced the two-tiered system of Vassar: Thomas hired graduates of Bryn Mawr as assistants, a position quite subordinate to that of the professors.

Wellesley's women did not face these discriminations, for Durant's initial policy of hiring only women meant that no male faculty ranked above them. In addition, Wellesley's professoriate had a benefactor. Eben Horsford, professor of chemistry at Harvard's Lawrence Scientific School, with a personal fortune from his invention of baking powder, showed rare imagination in his gifts to Wellesley. In 1888, he paid for the adaption of a large room overlooking the lake into an elegant faculty parlor, as a place of communal retreat. His larger benefactions gave faculty a respite from the college. He endowed a sabbatical fund that supported a year in Europe for senior faculty. He lent a house on his Maine property as a place of summer refuge. Ultimately he established a pension fund to protect Wellesley's faculty emeritae.[6]

Such backing gave Wellesley's female professors unusual privileges. Despite low salaries, they had handsome spaces within the residence halls, each seventh year abroad, and access to a summer cottage. Yet by the late nineteenth century, this did not seem sufficient. While Wellesley raised the seminary system to its most benevolent level, faculty women no longer found it satisfactory. They, along with women faculty in the other women's colleges, began to seek the professional respect and the autonomy enjoyed by the men on their campuses or in male colleges. This required them to challenge and overturn the legacy of Mary Lyon. Women faculty in the women's colleges fought a complicated battle. By 1920, they had largely succeeded in redefining their place. They lived apart from their students and had responsibility solely for a student's intellectual direction.

Mary Lyon's plan for Mount Holyoke assumed that teachers, sharing her evangelical zeal, accepted missionary pay and expected to have no private lives. The hours outside the classroom went to monitoring student behavior, heading a table in the dining hall, and counseling and advising students as "special friends." Vassar and Wellesley consciously adopted Mount Holyoke's plan, modified at Vassar by the provision for male faculty. Smith, while rejecting the Mount Holyoke model in theory, followed an important element in practice: each cottage included a faculty woman to set the intellectual tone of the house. While she enforced no formal code, she informally presided, setting implicit standards by her presence. Bryn Mawr explicitly rejected this pattern for its few women faculty, substituting in their stead graduate students to serve as models for students; however, M. Carey Thomas' insistence on propriety limited the freedom of female professors to dress and behave as they pleased.

Respect was a two-edged sword, involving not only the college but the outside world. The women's colleges initially gave their academic women the great gift of external respect. The unmarried professional woman of the nineteenth century was an anomaly because she performed the work of a man outside the context of marriage.[7] The public could understand a female academy teacher and place her within the social order, for she lived with her charges as a surrogate mother. The women's colleges stretched the concept of the academy teacher to the higher learning. By joining the seminary system to the women's college, Vassar and its followers created a clear and understandable place for its women faculty. It offered residence, responsibilities, and a reason for being. The first academic women to teach in the women's colleges were grateful.

Beginning in the 1880s, a new generation of professionally trained women scholars saw themselves in a different manner. While college teaching afforded women external respect not accorded by other professions, this contrasted markedly with their position within the institution. The minutiae of regulating students' lives robbed them of time for scholarship and allowed them no privacy. Alice Freeman, never one to complain, wrote to her mother early in her teaching career at Wellesley, "Unless you are careful in this great family, all your time goes uselessly. You accomplish nothing."[8]

The first public statement of the difficulties of women faculty came in 1889, when Emily Wheeler criticized the women's colleges in print. She contrasted the public impression of the women's colleges, based on appreciation of "the stately halls, with all conveniences and even elegances of life," with the private reality of "households of women." While newspapers and magazines glowingly reported on "the fine buildings, the libraries and laboratories" and on the decoration of student rooms, they failed to "enlighten us much as to the intellectual and social life nourished within their walls." While Emily Wheeler found students suffered from nervous strain and morbidity, she focused on the faculty living in residence halls. A teacher faced "steady strain . . . the vitality drained from her" in the constant presence of students. "A bright and cultured woman, college bred and having taught some years in a woman's college, recently resigned her position, saying she was 'utterly sick of living in households of women!'" Another confessed that while she liked to teach, "she did *not* like to 'eat girls and sleep girls.'" As a result the women's colleges lacked great teachers. Emily Wheeler understood the historical origins in the seminary system which required teachers to live with students to mold their "mind, manners and morals." While appropriate for an earlier time, "we recognize now that the life inside such walls was abnormal, unwholesome; that it narrowed both teachers and taught, gave them false views of the world, and encouraged a morbid sensibility."[9]

Emily Wheeler clearly caught the feeling of many women faculty. Despite Katharine Lee Bates' loyalty to Wellesley, she dreaded her return after a sabbatical to "*such* a busy, feverish place," beset by "girl-problems and girl-

Katharine Coman's table, Wellesley, 1887, in front of College Hall;
Professor Coman seated to the left of column
Wellesley College Archives

judgments," so destructive to her own health.[10] Lucy Salmon found life in Vassar's Main insufferable. When her health broke down, she took a leave of absence in Europe, extended to two years. Time away gave her a chance to reflect on her life. Anticipating her return from Europe she wrote a poignant expression of the constraints about to press in upon her. "I sigh for a quiet corner where I shall not have to get up by a bell, eat by a bell, talk by priority of appointment and dress according to other people's standard of propriety. I hate and loathe the friction of the college life and still more the restraint imposed on all who would seek to lessen it. I fear I long since joined the class of society bearing chips on their shoulders."[11] As she made ready to return home, Vassar loomed like a prison: "I already hear the clink of the chain and the key turn in the door!"[12]

Beyond the issues of involvement with students, constant demands on one's time, and college rules, women faculty sought to change the whole tone of the women's college. To this new generation of women faculty, the evangelical assumptions of founders and trustees did not hold. Even those with religious convictions fought institutional efforts to force conformity. In 1890–91, the Wellesley trustees debated reinstituting a religious test for faculty members. Katharine Lee Bates was travelling in Europe, but when word of the debate reached her, she wrote that she was outraged and considered resigning her position. While her own beliefs in the divinity of Jesus passed the trustees' test, she felt it wrong for "a college which is established to seek truth, to dictate its truth at the outset." Offered the chairmanship of the English department, she believed it degrading "to seem to buy the Department by theological pledges. . . . I feel that I should be making the most sacred things of life sordid."[13] The trustees backed down to require of its faculty only "Christian character," enabling Bates to return to Wellesley with her integrity intact.

At Bryn Mawr, M. Carey Thomas fought the religious battle for her faculty against trustees seeking to return to the college's Quaker origins. Such restraint on Thomas' ability to hire talented professors of whatever persuasion threatened her deepest hopes for offering university education to college women. Carey Thomas' later Anglo-Saxonism suggested anti-Semitism, but unique among the women's colleges, Bryn Mawr hired a male Jewish professor in the 1890s. Even at Bryn Mawr, however, "Christian character" applied to women on the faculty. Carey Thomas attempted to stop the geologist Florence Bascom from riding her horse astride on the campus.[14] When a student confessed that she smoked with Helen Ritchie, a young instructor, in Ritchie's apartment on college grounds, Carey Thomas agreed with Self-Government that Helen Ritchie be required to pledge never to smoke again while on the faculty. Faced with the alternative of resignation, Ritchie accepted. Thomas contrasted her sweet, contrite behavior with that of the young male lions on the faculty "roaring" over students' presumption in setting rules for faculty.[15] Women faculty accepted what the men rebelled against, for they lived by different rules that judged women faculty by external signs of character.

As women faculty gained the right to their own inner beliefs, if not their outward behavior, they wanted less to do with the spiritual well-being of their students. The earlier confidential relation between teacher and student disappeared not only because students in college lived within their own social world but also because their women faculty wanted less and less to do with them outside class. The withdrawal of faculty women took place gradually. They continued to receive students in their parlors, to listen to students' concerns, and to help them make choices for the future. But one senses among faculty women both the need to protect themselves from intrusion and the desire to establish an adult life among chosen friends. A key measure of growing distance from students is faculty women's departure from the residence halls to establish their own homes outside college grounds.

Several elements delayed this development into the twentieth century. First, the colleges needed a substitute for the corridor teacher who monitored students' behavior. Most of the women's colleges followed Bryn Mawr's lead and adopted self-government. Yet a faculty woman not only labelled and judged student misbehavior, she set an intellectual and social tone at the dinner table and in the parlor. In addition to a resident professor, Smith had a matron preside over each cottage. Bryn Mawr turned her into a college-educated warden for each residence hall. One of these alternatives became acceptable to each of the colleges. Unlike faculty women, the house mother or warden held no other duties: her modest income and board compensated her giving her sole attention to students' personal lives and communal well-being.

To live outside college walls required a step that colleges found far more difficult than selecting substitute presences—higher salaries. It is a truism that the greatest endowment of American colleges in the nineteenth century was the willingness of professors to teach for very low wages. As the universities arose to compete for faculty, men were able to command higher salaries. Their female colleagues in the women's colleges had no such bargaining possibilities. Their meager salaries did rise, but not enough to allow ordinary faculty women without private means to live in college towns, especially those like Bryn Mawr and Wellesley which were becoming fashionable suburbs. In the 1890s, Carey Thomas recognized this problem, possibly because her sister was one of the college's instructors. As she wrote to Mary Garrett, "the success of the college depends on our keeping them here satisfied on low salaries." [16] With the needs of younger faculty women particularly in mind, M. Carey Thomas pushed for a boarding house for faculty in "the English manner." Financed through the sale of bonds to members (Thomas subscribed $5,000 and served as president of the association), the Low Buildings (the irony of the name was unintentional) arose on the northeast corner of the campus down the long slope of the

Low Buildings, Bryn Mawr; *Bryn Mawr College*

hill. A long, rambling three-story shingle-style "cottage," the boarding house contained apartments of varying sizes to suit its diverse clientele, which included a few men among the women. Lucy Donnelly took a four-room flat with a kitchen and dining room, and brought with her a maid; sixteen others had only the minimum standard set by Girton—a bedroom and a study. The communal dining room's bentwood simplicity fit the relaxed style of the exterior. In the planning of the Low Buildings, certain amenities assumed great importance. Each suite had a bell, allowing its occupant to ring for service, including the luxury of meals brought to one's study.[17]

At Vassar, Lucy Salmon took Maria Mitchell's place as the champion of democratic principles within the college. A measure of change since the early years is that while Mitchell had only the power to rebel, Salmon fought from within and ultimately won. In her long tenure she opposed the seminary system as maintained by a Lady Principal, struggled for faculty governance, campaigned for an adequate library, and encouraged students to gain self-governance. Like Mitchell, she found college rules irksome, but had no observatory into which to retreat. President James Taylor fought her on each issue, including her campaign for the right of women faculty to live outside college halls.[18] In 1889, Taylor responded in print to Emily Wheeler. In condemning the "household of women," Wheeler had given no thought to the needs of students. She presented only the side of the faculty and did "not fairly . . . represent that." While Taylor had "found those who think such a life irksome; many others, who care as much for the general interests of the world, express themselves as greatly attracted by it."[19] By the turn of the century, Taylor relented and allowed women faculty the right to live outside college residences, but the college granted women $100 less than men for a rent allowance because women had the option of living in college. Taylor did not, however, allow women to take the college houses on faculty row: he intended these for men and their families to lend to the college "a more normal character," and protection from danger, something that women faculty could not provide.[20]

Soon after the Low Buildings' completion, Taylor urged Vassar trustees to build "suitable homes" for faculty women. He now presented their view. Many suffered from "the pressures of the life here": "I am persuaded that . . . a great many women . . . cannot long bear the strain of a life as intense as ours."[21] But other building needs took precedence at Vassar; it was not until the 1920s that the college built the faculty apartments Williams and Kendrick. Wellesley's women got their apartments, the Horton Quadrangle, in the same period. Designed by Eliza J. Newkirk, an alumna on the faculty in art, three modest buildings formed an open quadrangle in the area of freshman boarding houses between the college and the Village.

The three faculty residential buildings at Bryn Mawr, Vassar, and Wellesley shared certain features. While giving faculty easy walking access to academic buildings and library, the colleges placed faculty apartment houses at a distance from student residential areas. In contrast to the student dormitories of the period, faculty buildings were far more modest in scale and detailing. They had no elaborate parlors; the dining room provided their principal communal space. At Wellesley, Horton House became the faculty club for nonresidents, which brought them in for meals. Priority went to private space, allowing each faculty apartment, suite, or room to be completely separate.

A survey of faculty needs for housing taken at Wellesley in 1929 suggests that the faculty wanted college housing for economic reasons: it cost too much to buy or rent private real estate in the suburb that surrounded the college.[22] Faculty members, including women, did not seek in their residences to meet communal needs, satisfied in the round of daily work. Faculty residential buildings began and remained an alternative to salaries adequate for living costs.

Women college professors preferred the private house to communal living. At the turn of the century faculty women began to move outside residence halls and build their own houses. They had complex households: generally they lived in pairs, but included women members of their families, and in certain cases, boarded graduate students. With her brother's help, Katharine Lee Bates built a large shingled house in an area across the railroad tracks from the college, just opening up for development. Her beloved friend, Katharine Coman, joined her, as did Bates' mother and unmarried younger sister, who served as their homemaker. Returning from a trip to Egypt, Katharine Bates named her house the "Scarab" and placed a small green Egyptian stone beetle under the study mantel.[23] Other colleagues in similar households moved into the neighborhood. In a slightly different area to the east of the campus, Vida Scudder used her Boston-based wealth to build a house patterned after an English farmhouse for herself, Florence Converse, and their mothers. Scudder delighted in its hall opening to the garden and its large attic study with a high-beamed ceiling where she conducted her seminars in English literature. "If there is any happier game than building a house, I have failed to play it," she wrote.[24]

These houses built for Wellesley faculty women are indistinguishable in their façades and internal plans from the single-family houses of their neighborhood. Like professorial homes for men, they contain prominent libraries with fireplaces. One intriguing feature does mark them—their gardens. Both the Bates house and the Scudder house have English wildflower gardens to the rear, beautiful retreats on to which open the most important rooms of the house. These quiet enclosed places, like M. Carey Thomas' Deanery garden, offered privacy out-of-doors and beauty within that may best express the needs of the academic women who created them.[25]

Recently these women have received new scholarly attention. As historians and biographers have retrieved the public careers of this generation at the turn of the century, they have, sometimes unwittingly, uncovered their subjects' personal lives to find that these unmarried women were not selfless renunciating celibates, but passionate human beings who lived a rich and intense life within the emotional world of other women. Feminist historians committed to defending lesbian alternatives have claimed them. These scholars have reinterpreted this earlier generation in the light of the late-twentieth-century understanding that "women who love women, who choose women to nurture and support and to create a living environment in which to work creatively and independently, are lesbians."[26] This approach distorts the past. It poses a dichotomy unfamiliar to the late nineteenth and early twentieth centuries, dividing human beings into those who are heterosexual and those who are homosexual. It presumes that within each category those who choose each other as loving partners freely express themselves sexually. A nineteenth-century professional woman did not necessarily see herself as a person with sexual needs demanding fulfillment. Her primary concerns lay in different directions.[27]

Dewey House room, Smith, occupied by Vida Scudder and Helen Chadwick, 1880s
Smith College Archives

As she matured from girlhood, a young woman of the late nineteenth century first had to find herself. She had discovered in college her full abilities and
the satisfactions of creative work. Her family held high expectations of her.
They had often sacrificed so that she, marked as talented very young, might
go to college. If a man courted her, she had to ask a difficult question: should
she give up her future plans and abnegate her past (and her and her family's
sacrifice) by marrying him? The more wealthy added the obligations of social
visiting. Should she waste her time in such a manner? A professional woman
did not make decisions alone. Parents, siblings, and friends helped her think
about her future, argued with her, and ultimately supported her decision. An
opportunity arose: in the case of an academic woman, a call came from a college to teach. Here, too, family and friends made the connections and encouraged the daring move. A young woman came to a women's college to try it
out. Some stayed only a short time, finding academic life distasteful, and left
to go elsewhere or to marry. Those who stayed did so for varied reasons:
college teaching enabled them to be economically independent; the work chal-

lenged them; the college community offered friendships and stimulation; faculty position entailed respect.

To enter a women's college as a member of a faculty did not mean renouncing one's former life. Mothers, sisters, and friends came along, sometimes only through correspondence, sometimes quite literally. Faculty women made new friends within the college context. In the late nineteenth century, sexual segregation dominated social life. What made life in the women's college unusual was that this engendered communities of women geographically separate from all but a few men.

Friendships deepened. Women accepted a great range of emotional expression in their relationships with other women: intense love as well as simple familiarity. Women took comfort and pleasure in each others' physical presences: it remained common to hug and kiss intimates, to walk hand in hand, even to share a bed for the night. Women openly expressed their deep feelings about each other. They accepted some erotic components of female affection, such as the appreciation of physical beauty and the sensation of touch. The tradition of romantic friendship among women had elevated sensation and emotion to a high and noble plane.

By their mature years, many of the women professors within the women's colleges had committed themselves to other women. They had made choices, and in the process had formed deep and meaningful attachments to other women, which opened up realms of self-knowledge, emotional growth, and a shared life. As women left the residence halls, they generally withdrew in pairs of friends to apartments or houses, to which the women of their families were usually invited. They were the first generation of American women able to support themselves and buy houses. House-owning gave to some the most meaningful aspect of their lives. Faculty women dwelt on the details of planning and furnishing. They named their homes. These domestic structures provided them with physical confirmation of their existence, their independence, and their intimacy with other women. Their libraries, dining rooms, and gardens offered inviting places for stimulating talk, refreshment, and relaxation.

And their bedrooms? Here we simply do not know and probably cannot know. The real question, is why do we care? We do know that these women openly committed themselves to other women by their middle years, and that the academic world in which they lived accepted this and them. We know that they felt free to express their deep feelings about one another even in print. At Katharine Coman's death, Katharine Lee Bates published *Yellow Clover,* her memorial tribute to her beloved partner. In her deep grief, she did not hide in her poems the extent of her loss of Coman's physical presence.[28] Sent to her friends as an Easter gift in 1922, the poems elicited in their receivers the feeling that Bates had expressed their lives and relationships as well as her own.[29]

Wellesley is the one college where these friendships have been studied. Durant's policy created an all-female faculty who lived in College Hall in the early years. By the turn of the century, two-thirds of the sixty-six tenured women faculty (there were also three men) chose to leave college grounds. Their network of friendships forms no simple pattern. Dyads of friends sharing residences were close to some of their colleagues but had merely formal ties with others. What is significant is the permeability of individual households as they welcomed relatives, friends, and graduate students as guests or permanent residents.[30]

Most committed friends were peers. But occasionally they crossed the line between faculty and students. In 1900, Lucy Salmon at Vassar established her household with Adelaide Underhill, who had been her student in 1888. In 1901, Mary Woolley moved from Wellesley to the Mount Holyoke presidency with Jeannette Marks, a graduate of the Wellesley class of 1900. Woolley's correspondence gives no indication that she had any concern about how her colleagues or students perceived her devotion to Marks.[31] Lucy Salmon felt a great sense of responsibility for Adelaide Underhill's reputation and wrote her movingly of the need to establish an autonomous life in Poughkeepsie. Salmon's fears for her shy, beloved friend came out of her perception that her own combative relationships with colleagues might inhibit Underhill's friendships. Salmon's letters contain no suggestion that she feared criticism of their intimacy as such.[32] Letters from her former student Edith Rickert suggest just the opposite, that at least one student respected and appreciated the happiness that her teacher had found. Rickert bestowed on them her pet word borrowed from Robert Louis Stevenson—"twosome"—an appellation which she found "peculiarly applicable to your case."[33]

Yet this was the period in which official student opinion as represented by college newspaper editorials turned against the "crush." How did faculty women view their own relationships in the light of this public condemnation of student "crushes"? If M. Carey Thomas properly represents them, it is clear that she distinguished her own relationships from what she saw about her in the undergraduates. To Mary Garrett she related her experience of student "crushes" at the Howland School: "When Bessie and I reached Howland devotions were rife—Bessie was made love to by Harry Tilden [the nickname of a female student] and responded sufficiently to make me fly from our room when ever she appeared; and I of course was treated in just the same way by Libbie, who was seven years or more older . . . a few visits from her & a few sentimental remarks and a little teasing from the other girls, and I knew from a slight touch of personal experience what was going on about me." In the same letter she reflected on a student "crush" going on at Bryn Mawr. "As ill luck will have it," an exceptional student had grown miserable about "a perfectly ordinary

Lucy Salmon's study in the Main building, Vassar; third floor,
southwest corner; *Vassar College Library*

Lucy Salmon's kitchen, Poughkeepsie; *Vassar College Library*

girl whose whole mind is not worth one least corner of her own & my A[nglo] Saxon poet is spoiled."[34] What is interesting is that Thomas did not make a connection between her own devotion to Garrett and the crush held by the student. The latter disturbed Thomas (as it had Maria Mitchell at Vassar) because the student formed a destructive relationship. She understood her own love of Mary Garrett, the kind in which "a word or a photo does all and the pulses beat & the heart longs in the same old way," by contrast, as the source of her greatest happiness, underlying her ability to do work.[35]

Separate residence gave faculty women the chance to shape their private lives apart from observation and control of college authorities. It is a critical element in the development of autonomy, going hand-in-hand with the growth of professional respect and the right to their own inner beliefs. What began at Wellesley spread to the other women's colleges. Jeannette Marks brought with her to Mount Holyoke a conception of the woman professor's life, nurtured by her academic mentor Katharine Lee Bates.[36] Lucy Salmon visited Wellesley at the turn of the century and returned to Poughkeepsie with a plan to rent a house with Adelaide Underhill. Salmon's letters testify to the importance of privacy away from college walls. Once in her home, Salmon's depression of many years lifted and her letters to Underhill became comic exercises interspersed with housekeeping detail and plans for the continuing stream of guests that the two entertained.[37] For the academic woman, separate residence was the decisive step in overturning the seminary tradition and attaining professional position and its prerogatives.

One can see this through the question of academic freedom. It is clear that only with separate residence did academic freedom become an issue. Only then did faculty women have the strength to come into political conflict so intense that trustees infringed on that freedom and fired them for their beliefs.

An issue wracking campuses across the country at the turn of the century, academic freedom became significant for women faculty in the women's colleges when they gained the independence of their male counterparts. Pressure to be politically circumspect weighed on women faculty more strongly than on men. One index is women's suffrage. Women's college founders feared that opening higher education to women might unsex them. Thus the wives of Arthur Gilman and L. Clark Seelye appropriately joined the Massachusetts Anti-Suffrage Association, committed to fighting the extension of women's sphere to the ballot.[38] James Taylor's greatest controversies at Vassar surrounded his refusal to allow the suffrage issue to be brought on campus. Faculty women felt the pressure on them to be accommodating and conventionally feminine. Mary Augusta Jordan, a Vassar alumna, sister of a Vassar trustee, and a member of a wealthy, established family, accepted Smith's traditions fully. On a campus that allowed women faculty the many housing options offered to students, this head of the English department remained the faculty resident of Hatfield House during her entire teaching career. She not only joined the anti-suffrage association, she wrote in its behalf, arguing that the vote was superfluous for ordinary women and wrong for its advocates, those women of affairs who required "radical changes in the relation of women to an ideal society . . . at once undesirable and perverse."[39] Jordan represents what President Seelye wanted, and she felt comfortable living on campus. Lucy Salmon opposed President Taylor on Vassar campus matters and as an articulate spokesman for women's suffrage. Salmon felt tension living on campus and fought for the right to live in town.[40] At Bryn Mawr, living off campus allowed privacy for cigarettes and alcohol, but did not influence support of feminism—for M. Carey Thomas was the national president of the College Equal Suffrage League.

If political conflict provides a measure of autonomy, then the faculty women at Wellesley, living away from the college in their own houses, gained the greatest realm of action. Vida Scudder's membership in the Socialist party and especially her address to the Progressive Women's Club of Lawrence, Massachusetts, during the violent 1912 woolen mills strike created a storm of protest which reached the college's conservative trustees. Scudder presented to President Pendleton a copy of her speech and offered to resign, which proved not to be necessary.[41] Several years later, her colleague, friend, and co-worker at Denison House, Emily Greene Balch, argued forcibly against the United States' participation in World War I. When the nation went to war, the college granted Emily Balch's request following her sabbatical for a year's leave of absence, which she used to agitate for peace. She headed the Department of Economics and Sociology, an appointment renewable each five years, and her contract came up for review at the end of her second year away. The trustees postponed action, which meant depriving Balch of her position for a year. A year later, after an agonized debate, the trustees refused to reappoint her. Her pacifism during the feverish war years overstepped trustee bounds, and they fired her. Emily Balch's friends protested in the alumnae magazine and tried ineffectively to reverse the board's decision. All the alumnae and administrators on the board worked for her retention, but the businessmen had the majority.[42]

It is hard to recapture what this meant in the Wellesley community. Emily Balch was more than a brilliant and respected colleague, she was a devoted friend in a close-knit world. If her peace efforts measured the Wellesley faculty's strength, her dismissal painfully reminded her colleagues of the realities of conservative masculine power underlying the college.[43] In a curious way, however, Emily Balch's departure from the college demonstrated the autonomy and strength of faculty women at Wellesley. After several years of work in New York and travel for peace, she returned to Wellesley to remake her home within the world of which she had been a part, at the same time that she continued

Smith teacher Mary Augusta Jordan and five students pause on walking trip to pose in a photographer's studio, ca. 1890; *Smith College Archives*

Mary Augusta Jordan in class, Smith, 1915; *Smith College Archives*

her efforts for internationalism and peace. Because Wellesley's faculty women lived in their own dwellings, to be denied appointment affected only the workplace: it did not involve expulsion from the community of faculty women.

In their private, individual decisions to leave college grounds and take up residence outside, academic women transformed the landscape of the women's colleges as profoundly as had the students by their boisterous college life. In fact, the two processes were indissolubly intertwined. As faculty women struggled for respect and autonomy, they confronted head-on the seminary system bequeathed to the women's colleges by Mary Lyon. Female professors fought for the right to their beliefs and politics and for the control of their own time outside the classroom. This meant severing the prescribed connection between themselves and students. Faculty women reshaped the college landscape literally by taking themselves outside its gates to live, as did their male counterparts, in town. As they did so, they left the campus to students, who, increasingly independent, were developing the rich culture they called college life. As professors removed themselves physically and psychologically, they became increasingly dim presences to students, lessening chances for close relationships or personal influence. College life so fully filled all spaces that students sensed no change or loss.

While to students the campus became the theater of college life, to faculty it emerged into the workplace. With the new sense of autonomy came an independent view of the landscape. Whereas college presidents promoted physical expansion, faculty did not autonomically identify with growth. In the early twentieth century, as colleges added building after building, certain faculty withheld approval. Lucy Salmon campaigned for decades for an adequate collection of books for Vassar's library, creating her own support society among former students, the Alumnae Historical Society, to add to the history collection. President Taylor's emphasis on physical expansion seemed misplaced. As she wrote from Europe in 1899, she rejoiced over the new chapel, but "alas, I wish I didn't long more for equipment than for buildings."[44]

To women faculty members, the college also provided grounds for walks and communing with nature. In the years in which they themselves had been students, long walks or tramps, rather than the competitive games of their students, meant exercise. Wellesley's campus above all provided an endless source of pleasure in its lake and wooded areas. Katharine Lee Bates and Katharine Coman regularly walked on college grounds accompanied by their collie, Sigurd.[45] Faculty women came to feel responsible for the protection of college grounds. At Wellesley, in the years after the 1914 fire, they assumed an important role in planning to preserve its picturesque spaces.[46]

By 1910, women professors had already significantly reshaped the women's colleges. They had gained professional position with its accompanying personal privacy. In so doing, they had overturned the seminary system in all its manifestations. In separating themselves from students, faculty women created their own private world of house, garden, and neighborhood, in contrast to the college, which was for them both public arena and park. While working less publicly than college builders and less dramatically than college students, faculty women redesigned the college landscape with equal finality.

PART THREE

The Classic Design

At the turn of the century, three developments shaped the women's colleges into their classic design. M. Carey Thomas created at Bryn Mawr a campus that linked women to the Anglo-Saxon academic tradition, formerly a male preserve. This allowed the women's colleges to appropriate the Gothic forms of coeducational and men's colleges and universities, opening up the women's colleges to the mainstream of collegiate architecture in America. Students claimed possession of college ground and turned it into the setting for college life. Academic women developed professional autonomy and moved outside college gates. By the early 1900s, the women's colleges had a clear image of what they ought to be.

The results are visible on every campus. While seminary and cottage traditions constrained Vassar, Wellesley, and Smith, each college took advantage of growth to add those buildings that a common notion of a women's college required. Mount Holyoke required the most dramatic transformation. In the decades surrounding the turn of the century the seminary became a college modeled after Smith, and a new landscape emerged from the ashes of the old. Mary Woolley brought to Mount Holyoke the academic and building standards of Bryn Mawr and Wellesley. Despite their separate histories as annexes, Radcliffe and Barnard were not immune from the effects of the new conceptions. Enthusiasm for college life based on residence and Bryn Mawr's freedom from the old seminary associations encouraged both annexes to wage extensive building campaigns in the early twentieth century. By World War I, a decade before these women's colleges joined together in the Seven College Conference, they held a common conception of the women's college reflected in each campus's design.

13

The Necessities Peculiar
to Women of Today

WELLESLEY, SMITH, VASSAR

Wellesley, Vassar, and Smith emerged at the turn of the century from idiosyncratic histories that had shaped the original designs of their buildings and grounds. By 1910, each college had altered its landscape in ways that suggested common forces at work. The strength of college life, faculty women, and Bryn Mawr's example made themselves felt—in varying proportions to be sure—on the three pioneer women's colleges. By the United States' entrance into World War I, Wellesley, Vassar, and Smith had modified their original schemes to conform to a common conception of what a women's college ought to be.

I

In the late nineteenth century, Wellesley found itself hamstrung by its origins. The college's evangelical spirit fit the daughters of Western Massachusetts farmers, not those of urbane Bostonians. Just as polite Boston society shunned Henry Fowle Durant, so they ignored his college. As a professor of philosophy at Harvard, George Herbert Palmer understood the feeling well, yet did not fully share it. He could hardly avoid the college. In 1887, he married Alice Freeman, Wellesley's attractive and able president. At one level he felt he rescued her from a future of grinding labor in an all-female community; yet at another level, he knew he stole her from a college that needed her guidance and firm hand. From their courtship until his death in 1933, George Herbert Palmer involved himself in Wellesley to complete the process of secularization and modernization that Alice Freeman began. Enlisting friends as powerful as he, Palmer made Wellesley respectable. By the turn of the century, Proper

Alice Freeman Palmer Memorial
Wellesley College Archives

Bostonians regarded it as one of their places, suitable for their daughters and an appropriate recipient of their philanthropy. Palmer's ashes repose in Wellesley's Houghton Memorial Chapel alongside those of his wife. This is fitting, for the chapel was the signal he gave to Proper Boston that Wellesley belonged to it.

Yet the chapel symbolized more than Wellesley's appropriation by Boston's elite. Its siting aroused intense debate, which forced the trustees to listen to faculty women and respect their vision of the campus. With the accession of Caroline Hazard to the Wellesley presidency in 1899, faculty women found they had a powerful comrade, capable of protecting the College Beautiful. Caroline Hazard brought to the campus the wise and influential Frederick Law Olmsted, Jr., who shaped decisions about future building. Guided by Olmsted, Wellesley constructed the four dormitories composing the Quadrangle. Their Jacobean forms expressed the dignity of college life to the Wellesley community and the strength of the women's college to the outside.

Henry Fowle Durant died in 1881, but Pauline Durant lived on. The initial efforts to change Wellesley hurt her deeply. She kept alive her husband's memory in her labor for the college. The college grew in size and complexity and attracted able scholars. Pauline Durant scrutinized each faculty appointment as if it were 1875 and she the minister at the anxious bench searching for evidence of grace.[1] Truth adhered in Henry Fowle Durant's original vision: his widow experienced any deviation from his design as declension. While the original board of trustees accepted Durant's authority because they shared his evangelicalism and understood the right of the donor to determine the use of his gift, after Durant's death the composition and attitude of the board changed.

Alice Freeman Palmer left the Wellesley presidency to marry, but stayed on the board of trustees. She and her husband courted new men to join her: Horace Scudder, editor of Houghton Mifflin, came on the board in 1887; Phillips

Brooks, the rector of Trinity Church, in 1891; Edwin Hale Abbott, in 1892.[2] By 1894, Pauline Durant felt the college was out of her hands. She wrote to the president of Boston University to pray for Wellesley, for "we are in a difficult place. Many of the trustees do not wish to carry out the intentions of Mr. Durant, but their own very different ideas."[3] She observed correctly. The new members of the board wanted to break the identification of the college with the Durants. Many years later, George Herbert Palmer explained to a former president of Wellesley why he objected to labelling Eben Horsford as the Durants' friend on a memorial plaque. Horsford's generosity came from his commitment to the college, not from his friendship with Durant. The college belonged to the wider community, not to a single family.[4]

By 1899, the trustees abolished all the evangelical elements that linked Wellesley with the Mount Holyoke tradition. The special confessional relation between woman teacher and student, signified by an all-female faculty and their required residence in college buildings, did not fit a modern institution. New provisions encouraged faculty to live off campus. A man joined the ranks, and the college aided him in building a house. Unitarians and Episcopalians did not submit to required periods of solitary, silent devotions; in 1894, these were eliminated. Trustees made chapel attendance voluntary and opened the library on Sunday. In 1896, the college ended domestic work, requiring a significant increase in tuition.[5] By the turn of the century even M. Carey Thomas would have felt comfortable with Wellesley's new collegiate ways. In addition, these changes addressed all the objections to Wellesley's compulsory evangelicalism made by Thomas Wentworth Higginson.[6] Liberal Boston now felt at home.

In breaking with its evangelical past Wellesley remained Christian, but turned to the Christianity of Proper Boston—the enlightened Unitarianism that Henry Fowle Durant abjured and the newly fashionable Anglicanism preached from the pulpit by Phillips Brooks of Trinity Church. The chapel within College Hall no longer held the expanded college. In 1887, under President Freeman's encouragement, the students, led by Sophonisba Breckinridge, began a campaign to raise money for a new chapel. In 1896, Elizabeth G. Houghton and her brother, Clement S. Houghton, superseded this effort and endowed a chapel in memory of their father, former trustee William S. Houghton. This gift gave the liberal trustees the opportunity that they needed. Wellesley gained a chapel for its enlightened future.

In keeping with up-to-date practice, the trustees authorized an architectural competition for the new building. Leading architectural firms entered. Peabody and Stearns, who designed much of Smith College, offered a neo-classical design. A. W. Longfellow, Jr., responsible for many Radcliffe buildings, also submitted an entry, as did the Boston firm of Shaw & Hunnewell, and the New York firm of Heins & La Farge.[7] Heins & La Farge won. Graduates of

M.I.T., George Lewis Heins and C. Grant La Farge held prestigious credentials. In these years they designed private homes for wealthy clients such as Gifford Pinchot, held important public commissions that included New York subway stations and classical animal houses at the Bronx Zoo, and won the prized competition for the Cathedral of St. John the Divine in New York. C. Grant La Farge enjoyed the added distinction of being the aristocratic son of the painter John La Farge, whose stained-glass windows and stencils decorated Boston's fashionable Trinity Church. The two architects submitted a plan for a Gothic-inspired stone building in the shape of a Latin cross.

As the head of the building committee, Horace Scudder kept in constant contact with Boston minister Edward L. Clark, a member of his committee. Clark's letters suggest the wide authority held by the trustees in determining the form of the chapel. The donors played a minor role. They preferred another plan: after the trustees chose the Heins and La Farge design, the Houghtons expressed their "utter dislike" of it, feeling "that it is impossible to make any thing of it."[8] Clark's letters made no mention of Pauline Durant's wishes or those of Wellesley's president, faculty, alumnae, or students. The trustees presumed the selection, siting, and oversight of the chapel was their task alone.

The trustees themselves did not feel fully satisfied with the design. Clark hoped that Heins could rework the plan into something "less commonplace— more ecclesiastical."[9] To him the design suggested the "Sheldonian Theatre of Oxford," conveying no sense of a chapel's religious functions: "It would be a pity to have strangers ask 'What is that building?'" Heins needed guidance, for he lacked experience "in the necessities peculiar to women of today—or of tomorrow."[10] The trustees on the building committee—all men—would guide him. No real planning set the architectural program before the competition. Basic questions remained, with important implications for form: how many should the chapel seat? should there be a tower and carillon? ought faculty have seats in the apse separate from students?[11] Months later the trustees still had not decided the nature of the stone to cover the exterior walls.[12]

As they planned "the worshipping place of women under intellectual and religious training," the trustees confidently resolved each of these questions.[13] They set stakes in the ground in the Longfellow Fountain Woods to site the building. A letter from Pauline Durant came as a surprise: "I am sorry to be obliged to say I cannot & will not consent to the location of the Chapel." Faculty, alumnae, and students would "raise a storm," for "it would simply ruin that beautiful wood & the region near the Longfellow fountain." As one who had lived on the grounds since 1855, she understood that particular piece of land, and her husband had entrusted her "to protect" the grounds.[14]

Pauline Durant did not persuade the trustees. The storm then followed. Wellesley clubs petitioned the trustees, as did alumnae, faculty, and students,

Houghton Memorial Chapel; *Wellesley College Archives*

requesting that the board change the chapel's location.[15] Two alumnae on the faculty called on Lilian Horsford, the daughter of Eben Horsford and a member of the board since 1886. One of them, Ellen Fitz Pendleton, then a member of the faculty in mathematics, later played a major role in Wellesley's life as president during the critical years of rebuilding following the 1914 fire. "Representing a number of the faculty and of the alumna," the two asked her to present their protest against the siting of the new chapel. The location planned would destroy "the trees and the rural simplicity of the path. . . . The sense of freedom and beauty which comes from the wide prospect on either hand will be lost if this large building is placed as we plan."[16]

The protesters won. The trustees changed the site of the chapel to place it where it now stands on the knoll to the east of the Music building. The conflict is significant in two respects. Trustees learned that they did not hold unlimited power to determine the shape of the campus. When aroused, alumnae and faculty spoke with considerable force. Their protest made the trustees uncomfortable—Clark called it an "annoyance"—but the trustees could not ignore it.[17] Moreover, the conflict made manifest the vision of the college's landscape of Wellesley faculty women. They wanted it to embody elements of the English park, offering a feeling of unbounded space. They appreciated its rolling, sylvan beauty. While Cambridge critics snobbishly portrayed Wellesley as rural, Wellesley's women professors properly understood it as an English pastoral landscape in the manner of Capability Brown's aristocratic country houses.

The chapel, as it emerged, is a "Greek cross with a slightly lengthened nave" of buff Amherst stone with sweeping roofs of red slate. A square lantern tower rises from the crossing of nave and transept. Though described as Gothic and adorned with pointed arches and windows, the chapel's heavy, solid stone walls and low-pitched roofs suggest Spanish Romanesque. The interior forms a single vast unobstructed space. Gothic stained-glass windows adorn all major walls. An intricate oak vault springing from piers dominates the decorative scheme. Chandeliers scarcely relieve the deep shadows of the interior, even on the brightest of days.[18]

In many respects the building is a peculiar one. Montgomery Schuyler criticized the vault's "erraticisms of timber construction which one has difficulty in reconciling with elemental mechanical principles."[19] The exterior poses comparable problems, especially at its upper reaches. At the crossing of transept and nave, an added third plane opens up the space but creates an awkward exterior form, made more so by an ill-fitting spire. The roofs hang so low that the entrance takes the form of a squat triangle, repeated in the low drop arch of the doorway. The plain stone blocks surrounding the doorway and the Gothic stained-glass window create a ponderous effect. It is difficult to understand why the trustees chose this design. Two possibilities suggest themselves. Heins & La Farge's stature may have promised the trustees a fashionable, up-to-date design. And trustees may have associated the chapel outlines with H. H. Richardson's Romanesque masterpiece, Trinity Church, linked to the La Farge name.

Whatever its design flaws, Houghton Memorial Chapel served the trustees' purposes well. Its forms dramatically expressed Wellesley's break with the Durants and evangelical Protestantism. Quite unintended by the trustees, the building also testified to the growing power of Wellesley's faculty women. Its siting protected the grounds of their College Beautiful.

Before the dedication of the chapel, the trustees announced the selection of Caroline Hazard as Wellesley's fifth president. For the first time the trustees had seriously considered a man. Alice Freeman Palmer suggested the president of a Colorado college as "an earnest Christian man . . . with a very fine wife." Pauline Durant won perhaps her last victory, arguing, "If we get a man now we will never again have the place for a woman in all probability."[20] A male president appealed to the trustees because he came from the outside. Ada Howard brought Mount Holyoke traditions to Wellesley; all other presidents, including Alice Freeman, came from Wellesley's faculty. Julia Irvine, the most recent incumbent, had instituted the changes that cleansed Wellesley of Durant's evangelicalism. She also led the faculty into the new elective curriculum devised under her predecessor, raised entrance standards, and replaced older members of the faculty with promising younger scholars. What the college gained in academic strength, however, it lost in internal conflict, decline in enrollments, and rising debt. The trustees wanted both an outsider and one who could connect the college to new sources of philanthropy.

Caroline Hazard was the perfect choice. The daughter and granddaughter of wealthy Rhode Island industrialists, she had spent her adult years as a writer and historian and as an administrator of the family's charities. She and her brother Rowland Hazard had contacts with important givers, opening Wellesley to philanthropy in the twentieth century.[21] Because she never went to college, she possessed an unusual perspective on Wellesley's problems. Yet she immediately became an insider. A wealthy, single woman, generous and gracious, Caroline Hazard entered Wellesley's community of women as a friend and benefactor.[22] By her actions as president, Caroline Hazard guaranteed that the Wellesley campus reflected the vision of the college held by its increasingly powerful faculty women.

Alice Freeman Palmer had once again pointed the way. She suggested to Horace Scudder that he visit Caroline Hazard. Reluctant to leave her pleasant life for the trials of putting Wellesley on a sound financial footing, Hazard declined. Undeterred, Scudder convinced her of her opportunity for wider service.[23] Before her inaugural, Caroline Hazard made her first public appearance at the college at the dedication of the chapel. Scudder orchestrated her installation, turning it into a grand occasion. For the first time Wellesley invited the presidents from major colleges and universities to attend. The faculty and seniors donned cap and gown, beginning a tradition unbroken to this day. To signal the full ascension of Wellesley into the pantheon of Boston institutions, President Charles William Eliot of Harvard gave the inaugural address.[24]

In addition to her other attributes, Caroline Hazard had excellent taste. From its concentrated beginnings, the college campus had begun to spread in many directions in structures large and small. Henry Fowle Durant's dream of a women's university led to Stone Hall on a plateau to the east of College Hall; to Music Hall between Stone and College halls; and to Farnsworth Art building on Norumbega Hill. The cottages began in wooded seclusion. As the need for more residential space grew, Norumbega Hill at the center of the campus became the site for three substantial wooden cottage structures. In 1900, Wilder, a Georgian red brick building with white trim, joined them. The chapel sat on a knoll near Music. In the 1890s, the trustees gave permission to student societies to build houses. Between 1898 and 1904, the campus acquired six elegant society houses in scattered sites.

Caroline Hazard believed in growth as a means to put the college on a solid financial footing. This dictated new buildings, especially residence halls. The faculty shared a commitment to the natural beauty of the land. How could Wellesley retain its special landscape at the same time that it grew? On her initiative and at her own expense, Caroline Hazard asked three design firms to prepare plans for the campus: C. Howard Walker; Heins & La Farge; and Frederick Law Olmsted, Jr., the talented son and successor of the great planner.[25]

In one of its acts of wisdom the trustees chose the Olmsted plan, contained in a letter of 1902 to Caroline Hazard. It is an extraordinary document. It describes the unique landscape of the campus, states the need for its protection, and sets out the principles to govern the siting and forms of buildings. With its "glaciated topography . . . accentuated by the distribution of trees," Wellesley had a "landscape not merely beautiful, but with a marked individual character not represented so far as I know on the ground of any other college in the country." Human occupation had destroyed comparable landscapes in less protected settings. The land was "a delicate and intricate bas-relief," peculiarly vulnerable to scratches on its surface. Possessed of such a landscape of "intricate beauty" and geological significance, a college had a duty "to treasure it for future generations."[26]

To protect the land, Olmsted recommended grouping buildings rather than scattering them. The land took three forms: "irregular plateaus of slightly undulating surface rounding over rapidly into steep sloping sides"; small rounded hills; and meadows in between them. The college should never build on the meadows. Low and damp, the meadows provided unsuitable building sites. The unfortunate temporary Chemical Laboratory placed on the low land west of Norumbega Hill served as a convenient lesson in what to avoid. The little hills held room for single buildings only, which led to undesirable dispersion. The plateaus provided the college with its best building sites.[27]

College Hill and Norumbega were two such plateaus. The remainder of the report suggests ways to build on them, compatible with the natural terrain and the prevailing architectural idioms and uses of existing structures. Here College Hall, Wilder, and Farnsworth constrained Olmsted. He strongly urged that classrooms, laboratories, and academic and administrative offices be concentrated in College Hall, as "the conditions of life in great barracks such as the main building are not considered desirable." This allowed the removal of the kitchen wing and the possible erection in its place of the library.[28] Norumbega Hill became the natural place of residential expansion. Olmsted recommended the destruction of the wooden cottages and their replacement by brick structures. Wilder, built in brick, unfortunately had a "large, simple, uncom-

Wellesley College, aerial view, 1931; the Hazard Quadrangle in the foreground
Wellesley College Archives

promisingly formal and rectangular shape . . . out of harmony with the delicate intricacy of the topography." While Wilder's Georgian style required that future dormitories have classic or colonial detail, it did not dictate their form. Olmsted suggested that new residence halls have "a somewhat intricate and complex architecture" and "be built along the edge of the escarpment, following its curve with their length by various angles and breaks."[29]

Olmsted's 1902 report had little immediate effect on building. Its role lay largely in the future. After the 1914 fire, Olmsted's understanding of the Wellesley landscape guided the women faculty in their fight to protect the campus. Because the college lacked adequate residential space in 1902, the radical surgery that Olmsted suggested seemed impractical. As things stood Wellesley freshmen had to live in boarding houses in the Village. To remove the wooden cottages to build brick dormitories required destroying much-beloved student dwellings and threatened greater housing pressure during the long period of construction.

Caroline Hazard returned to Olmsted for a new suggestion of a site for a group of dormitories. A donor wanted to give a residence hall near the observatory erected by her sister. For the four structures known as the Quadrangle, Olmsted chose "the high plateau near the West Woods" on the northern border.[30] Boston architect J. A. Schweinfurth, who, in 1899, had planned Wilder Hall, won the architectural competition over his better known Boston contemporaries Coolidge & Carlson and A. W. Longfellow.[31]

In Schweinfurth's winning plan for the Quadrangle, two dormitories front the road, connected by a fence. Behind each is an identical dormitory, set back slightly, reversing directions to give a mirror image. Between the two sets of dormitories is a formal garden with a fountain. Each of the four buildings forms an elongated L, three and four stories high. The shorter end, facing the road, holds the service areas; the longer wing of student rooms faces inward to the courtyard and garden. At the juncture, a five-story tower encloses the public rooms. The tower carries battlements and four Elizabethan cupolas atop turrets. Repeated in each of the four buildings, the towers dominate the composition, giving it a ceremonial air. White stone enlivens the red brick surface of the walls in stringcourse, window frames, and quoins on the turrets. Dormer windows with Flemish gables add interest to the top floor.[32] Inside the buildings are study-bedrooms, lining both sides of the long corridor on three floors. A comfortable living room adjoins the entryway on the first floor. The dining room in the basement is straightforward and unadorned.

Between 1904 and 1909, Wellesley built four residence halls: Pomeroy, Cazenove, Beebe, and Shafer. The college rejected Schweinfurth's plan for a formal garden but did accept an alumna's gift of flower beds and landscaping, which in memory of her daughter was named the Alexandra Garden. Insufficient funds prevented finishing the composition until the years after the 1914 fire when Schweinfurth designed a link between the two outer halls, closing off the group from the street and creating more living space. In 1927, the college named the complex the Hazard Quadrangle, a fitting tribute to the president who ushered the buildings into being.

Designed by a man, accepted by a predominantly male board of trustees in a style dictated by a donor, the Quadrangle nonetheless represents a significant step in Wellesley's development as a women's college. Unlike College Hall or the cottages, the Quadrangle carried no distinctively feminine associations. Built on a public road and offering entry into college grounds, the residence halls announce the college to the outside rather than offering seclusion within the grounds. The energetic towers capped by green copper convey collegiate grandeur, while the internal courtyard suggests the dignity of college life. M. Carey Thomas had encouraged Bryn Mawr's architects to create an academic setting fitting her notion of the woman scholar. While the Hazard

Quadrangle offers nothing as aesthetically satisfying as Cope and Stewardson's design for Bryn Mawr, it suggests the same hopes for women.

Wellesley had travelled a long way from its evangelical origins. By 1914, it had become an essentially secular liberal arts college for women, characterized by an unusually talented female faculty. The Wellesley campus reflects this evolution. Through the efforts of Alice Freeman and George Herbert Palmer, Proper Boston claimed the college for its daughters. Houghton Memorial Chapel symbolized their usurpation, at the same time that its siting ultimately respected the growing strength of the women faculty. The Quadrangle brought Bryn Mawr's imagery to the Wellesley campus, suggesting the possibilities of women's strength.

In the years after the 1914 fire that destroyed College Hall, the Olmsted plan, which embodied the landscape values of faculty women, reshaped the college. In the process Wellesley's feminist commitments came to the fore. What was merely hinted at in the four residence halls of the first decade of the twentieth century was loudly proclaimed in the academic quadrangle which rose atop Norumbega Hill.

I I

Smith College ventured by a different path to a similar destination. By President L. Clark Seelye's retirement in 1910, Smith no longer resembled the modest collection of cottages around College Hall that had made such an impact on women's higher education. With almost 2,000 students, Smith had become the largest of the women's colleges. Seelye's patriarchal presence meant that women faculty remained relatively weaker at Smith than at its sister women's colleges. The large student body and the absence of formal regulations helped create a ripe college life, unsurpassed by the other institutions. While Smith had no trace of quadrangles, it did present to public view a large campus with impressive, if heterogeneous and ill-sited, buildings. All those elements that Seelye had once forsworn stood on campus: large residential halls; library; and assembly hall for chapel. They came to Smith less by conscious plan than as the unanticipated result of Seelye's vaunting ambitions, business acumen, and ability to charm philanthropists.

At the outset, Smith had made its entrance requirements equal to Amherst's, limiting itself to candidates who passed the classical secondary course. By 1880, 229 students enrolled. Many more wanted to enter but lacked the required classical training. Seelye never considered opening a preparatory school, but in 1880 he found a way to bring in more students. He created a School of Music and a School of Art. Unlike Wellesley, Smith did not integrate these studies into the college curriculum by requiring that students take an extra year of combined work. Rather, Smith created two largely autonomous schools, with their own program and their own diminished entrance requirements. A student needed only the equivalent of a standard high school course to qualify for the School of Music or of Art.[33]

Quite unexpectedly, Winthrop Hillyer, a Northampton resident with no known interest in Smith or in art, gave $25,000 for a building for the School of Art. In 1882, the Hillyer Art Gallery opened. Peabody and Stearns, responsible for the initial buildings on the Smith campus, designed Hillyer as well. By then the firm's approach to Gothic suggested a fortress.[34] When no donor appeared for a companion building for the School of Music, the college erected Music Hall to the southwest of College Hall where, as Pierce Hall, it still stands.[35]

Buttressed by the schools of Art and Music, Smith grew quickly. Increasing numbers of students meant a need for laboratories and classrooms. In 1886, the college put Lilly Hall of Science next to the School of Music. In the place of Peabody and Stearns, Smith hired the Hartford architect William C. Brocklesby, who ultimately planned nine buildings on the Smith campus. Brocklesby designed a building of dimensions, form, and materials similar to its neighbor. Lilly was a charming addition to Smith's evolving scheme.[36]

In the twentieth century, Smith added large functional buildings for classrooms, laboratories, and communal gatherings. The early academic buildings formed an external perimeter, fronting the street. In 1900, Seelye Hall, placed opposite Pierce and Lilly, started a second tier of buildings, which filled in the center of the campus, destroying internal vistas. Seelye Hall also broke with the shapes and materials that had unified the Peabody & Stearns and Brocklesby buildings. Its visual variety introduced a discordant note to the campus.

In 1875, Smith's distinctive design called for students to live in cottages in a simulation of family life. When Smith housed fourteen students in a converted family residence, domestic rhetoric bore some relation to reality. As increasing numbers of students enrolled, the college erected cottage after cottage, and they grew larger and larger. As the cottages swelled in size, a certain level of fantasy prevailed, in design language as well as in words. In the 1890s, Brocklesby planned a series of four cottages: Morris, Lawrence, Dickinson, and Tyler. Though intended for sixty students, these buildings preserved features of a house. Their public rooms are generous and spacious, while remaining warm and domestic. The wide stairway to the upper floors leads from the center of the building and opens on to short, wide corridors. Student rooms on the upper floors are varied in size and shape, with doubles and triples and upstairs parlors. No young woman had fifty-nine sisters; but if she did, her house might have looked like Brocklesby's cottages.

Waiting for admission to basketball game, Smith, 1904; Seelye Hall in far right
Smith College Archives

Basketball, 1904; Senda Berenson holding ball; *Smith College Archives*

Smith had turned to the cottage scheme as a way of breaking up the college life developing in Vassar's Main. Sprinkling the young collegians in houses integrated into a New England village promised to keep them from the visionary notions of Mount Holyoke seminarians and from the vices that grew in Vassar's hothouse. The cottage system hardly worked. Rather the large houses of Smith provided merely more comfortable settings for the most extensive student culture in the women's colleges to develop.

College life required its own special settings. In 1879, Smith had built a wooden gymnasium. Alumnae strongly supported physical training, and, in 1890, gave Alumnae Gymnasium. Brocklesby created a design for the gymnasium which harmonized well with its Peabody and Stearns antecedents. Like the early buildings, it is of red brick trimmed in brownstone. Small round arches enclose openings on the stair towers, and there is a Queen Anne stepped gable, added in 1892; but the gymnasium's steep roofs, gables, dormers, and cupola relate it to its architectural setting.[37] One of the few early gymnasium buildings to remain intact, its interior is a large open room with corrective apparatus lining the walls. It was here, in 1892, that women first played their own version of basketball, devised by Senda Berenson.[38] In 1903, the college erected the Students' Building with money earned and begged by Smith collegians. In Smith's one red brick nod to Tudor motifs, students had club rooms, a large smooth floor for dancing, and a makeshift stage for theatricals. The round-arched loggia which adorned its façade gave the proper setting for strolls during the all-female dances and the annual Promenade, the one event which brought college men on the campus. Following the universal custom in the women's colleges, Smith students took up step-singing, locating it at the entry to the Students' Building.[39]

Smith originally intended students to use the town library, an important component of their integration into Northampton. Rather quickly the college found that while students might rely on Northampton for special purposes, Smith needed its own reference collection for everyday use. When Hillyer opened, the art room in College Hall became Smith's first, quite simple library. The placement of the Forbes Library across the street from the campus proved quite convenient, but, by 1900, daily use of Smith's own books had grown significant enough for the college to build a small library within Seelye Hall. This charming two-story circular room created a bay on the southern side. Its alcoves, reached by wrought-iron staircases, lit by a dome, afforded pleasant places to browse through books.

As the student body grew, tension developed between the Forbes Library and Smith. In 1905, the Forbes insisted that the college support its heavy use of the library by paying an annual fee of $2,500. While the college made an annual contribution to the Forbes, it refused a required payment, fearing that it might begin a town policy of taxation. The Forbes retaliated by denying Smith students entry to the library, unless they each paid a fee of $5. Smith then decided to build its own library and turned to that known source of library buildings, Andrew Carnegie. He agreed to shift his gift of $62,500 from a biology building to a library, if other donors gave an equal sum. Alumnae responded generously, for a library had been a project of the Alumnae Association since 1894. The Faculty Library Committee presented a plan for departmental rooms and alcoves, which met their conception of small, specialized space. The librarian, Josephine Clark, held quite different notions, and she prevailed. Smith built a library around a great stack, with far fewer number of seminar rooms than the faculty had sought. Mary Augusta Jordan gave her private library to the English seminar room.[40] Lord and Hewlett designed the 1909 building. Unique on the Smith campus, the library took a classical form. Renaissance detail—such as dentils at the cornice, round arched windows, oculi, and Greek key motifs—lends delicacy to its rectangular red brick form. Low and dignified, the library is a serene note on an otherwise visually complicated campus.

In 1875, to encourage students into Northampton for worship, Smith had also forsworn a chapel. A room in College Hall served for college meetings in the early years. With its expanding numbers of students and faculty, Smith lacked a place for communal gatherings, including morning chapel. Smith built John M. Greene Hall, an auditorium seating 2,225, to serve the college community for daily chapel and for important gatherings. Designed by Charles A. Rich of New York, who planned Barnard's early buildings, John M. Greene Hall is a great rectangular red brick mass trimmed in brownstone, decorated in the classical manner. Its great Roman portico with brown stone Ionic columns fronts the street, making the clear statement to Northampton that the college welcomed the town to its public events.[41]

The Smith that, in 1910, L. Clark Seelye turned over to his successor, bore little real relation to the original design he had helped to formulate. As he encouraged growth, so quite inadvertently did he deviate from his vision of young women receiving the liberal arts surrounded by the healthy influences of a New England town. While student residences kept sentimental links to house design, they grew to the size of residence halls. Far from forcing college students into the patriarchal world of the New England village, Smith fostered a rich college life in its oversized cottages. Monumental academic buildings crowded the campus. Smith acquired a library and, for all practical purposes, a chapel. While Seelye's rhetoric always echoed his founding conceptions of 1875, the Smith that he left thirty-five years later resembled Wellesley far more than it retained any distinctive plan.

III

Under James Monroe Taylor, Vassar grew from a beleaguered and anachronistic pioneer in danger of sinking into a secondary school, into a thriving women's college in great demand. A distinguished faculty challenged students to confront the intellectual and social questions of the day. College life flourished, offering to students not only diversion but new possibilities for change. At the beginning of the twentieth century Vassar conformed well to Smith's vision of the women's college.

Quite ironically, in the years before World War I, Vassar assumed some of the trappings of Bryn Mawr. Wealthy donors contributed monumental collegiate Gothic buildings that framed Vassar's entryway. These stone buildings, so suggestive of the strength of a women's college, curiously sprang from deeply conservative sources. Vassar in 1914 is a study in contradictions that unwittingly demonstrate the power of the women's college idea in the early twentieth century.

Taylor's transformation of Vassar began with his clear conception of a liberal arts college. To be realized in campus buildings, this vision required donors. Taylor proved to be an adept fund-raiser. As one of the country's leading Baptist educators, he had a special appeal. He drew into Vassar's orbit wealthy Baptists, beginning with John D. Rockefeller. Frederick T. Gates, Rockefeller's most important advisor, served as trustee from 1893 to 1905; Bessie Rockefeller Strong's father-in-law, the important Baptist minister Augustus H. Strong, had joined the board in 1884 and stayed as a member until 1918.[42] In 1899, Taylor confirmed his ability to appeal to wealthy Baptists when the trustees of Baptist-founded Brown University asked him to become their president. Taylor surprised both Brown and Vassar by refusing. After much soul-searching he decided that while Brown offered him "the chance of directly influencing the life of one's time through the young men of a great college," at Vassar he shaped his era "indirectly" through wives and mothers and to "an increasing degree directly" as women involved themselves in school, church, and society.[43] His commitment to Vassar, unbroken until his retirement in 1914, sealed the affection of the community and clearly strengthened Vassar's claim to Baptist philanthropy.

Vassar's most important Baptist acquisition was Charles M. Pratt, the eldest son and namesake of one of Rockefeller's former competitors turned chief co-worker in the Standard Oil empire. Like Rockefeller a staunch Baptist and committed family man, the elder Pratt had given much of his fortune to education, endowing the Pratt Institute in Brooklyn. His eldest son graduated from Amherst and married Mary Seymour Morris, a Vassar graduate whose father had been the governor of Connecticut. With his father's death, Charles M. Pratt emerged as an important power in Standard Oil, ultimately its secretary and treasurer. The center of a faction within the trust, he was difficult to work with and "regarded by many Standard men as inclined to subordinate the Company's welfare at times to a desire for greater authority." He assumed presidency of the Pratt Institute as well as its board of trustees. In 1896, he began his service as a trustee of Vassar, becoming chairman of the board in 1917.[44]

Beginning in 1904, Vassar felt Pratt philanthropy in the first of many gifts to embellish the campus. Charles Pratt's wife, Mary Seymour Pratt, joined with her friend Mary Thaw Thompson, Vassar 1887, to give the college a new chapel. The two women commissioned designs and got estimates. They finally decided on the Boston firm of Shepley, Rutan & Coolidge—the Beaux Arts–influenced successor firm of H. H. Richardson—who offered them a plan "full of dignity & grace" for $175,000. When the two women corresponded about their gift, they assumed that they had all the choices to make. Unlike the other women's colleges, Vassar's president and trustees played little role in selecting architects or determining the nature of a building. Vassar College did not intervene in what it assumed was a private matter between donor and architect.[45] Mary Pratt and Mary Thompson discussed such questions as pew design and cushions, roof and wall material, and stained-glass windows. While neither ever stated the meaning of the gift, these two deeply religious, conservative women clearly saw the chapel as a pillar of order.[46] To Mary Thaw Thompson, plagued by the scandal created by her brother's murder of the great architect Stanford White, the chapel must have been an especially poignant exercise in devotion to a more comprehensible past.

Completed in 1904, the chapel itself reflects this in its Norman solidity. With expansion of the student body, the college had lost a place for the community to gather. Built to seat thirteen hundred, the new chapel gave this enveloping space. In many respects similar to buildings on the Stanford campus, designed by Shepley, Rutan & Coolidge in the years immediately preceding, the chapel is of irregularly shaded, rather smooth tan stone, a seamed Cape Ann granite, and has a low, sloping red tile roof.[47] The façade forms a broad triangle around a large circular stained-glass window. Its round Romanesque openings, flanked by a solid tower, suggest the abbey churches of Caen. The central room of the interior creates a vast interior, spanned by open-timbered Gothic construction.[48] Tiffany windows give color and light to an otherwise chaste setting.

A year later Vassar acquired its great Gothic tower with the Frederick Ferris Thompson Memorial Library, given by his widow and designed by Allen & Collens. The Beaux Arts–trained Boston architect Francis Allen had planned

Chapel; *Vassar College Library*

Taylor Hall dedication; from left to right, Charles Collens, Charles Pratt,
H. N. MacCracken, James Taylor; *Vassar College Library*

Strong and the three identical buildings that followed. During these same years Allen's firm, now expanded to include Charles Collens, designed buildings at Williams and Middlebury. For Vassar's library Allen & Collens appropriated perpendicular Gothic for a building that looks like a cathedral. Its imposing gray stone façade carries handsome windows and is penetrated by a great Gothic-arched doorway with medieval carvings. Rising 105 feet and adorned with battlements and crocheted pinnacles, the tall square tower quickly became Vassar's visual symbol.[49]

It was Taylor Hall, the art building, above all which gave Vassar its twentieth-century look. Charles Pratt joined with his wife to give this expensive entrance to the college. The gatekeeper's lodge, a charming reminder of Matthew Vassar's era, fell to the builder's ax. The Gothic arch in the art building's square tower served as the motor entrance to the campus. Named in honor of President Taylor the year after his retirement, the building itself housed galleries, lecture hall, and art library. Fashioned of light brown granite and Indiana limestone, the building carries whimsical gargoyles and academic emblems.[50] As MacCracken, Taylor's successor, suggested in his irreverent memoirs, the grin on the little grotesque tailors on the wall of the building was "slightly ironic, since Taylor did not favor Fine Art." Despite the important early history of art at Vassar, it had been largely ignored during Taylor's presidency. When Professor Van Ingen died in 1898, studio art went with him. While the new building gave gallery space and symbolic status to art, it hardly helped in a practical manner. As MacCracken explained, "Characteristically, the building, in the best college Gothic, has no studio, and its library was originally in its smallest room. A single classroom must suffice for instruction."[51]

What did Pratt intend Taylor Hall to be? MacCracken captured the nature of the relationship that Charles Pratt had with Vassar when he considered the trustees as he found them in 1915. Men in their mid-sixties, who ignored or scorned the three women among their number, the trustees enjoyed Vassar as "their playground. To visit it and its gardens was their holiday." They came to campus once a year, or once a month if members of the executive committee. They enjoyed their position and their authority. But they did not want to face difficult issues. "Often ruthless and quite arbitrary in action, they were utterly sentimental about Vassar life. It was a fountain sealed, a walled garden. Their lives did not have much aesthetic outlet, and the pretty college took it all."[52] Taylor Hall is the perfect expression of this relationship. It was meant to be exquisite: college photographs capture the central hall where delicate leaded windows create a luminous background for a white marble medieval tomb. The Pratts gave personal attention to every detail of the building. They wanted it to embellish the campus, not provide functionally for college needs. The handsome stairway, whose wood-carved railings give a lace-like effect to the wall, leads nowhere. Symbolically placed as the entry to the college, in its striving for beauty and disregard for use, Taylor Hall captures the meaning of Vassar to a wealthy, powerful, and wholly arbitrary trustee.

As Vassar received, so she became. Within Baptist circles Taylor was a religious liberal; within the political context of the Progressive era, he became a deep conservative. In the early twentieth century, Theodore Roosevelt challenged the consolidation of corporations. One of the first objects of "trust-busting" was Standard Oil. The trust was sued in many states; the federal government became a party to the suit in Missouri and named seven Standard Oil officers, including Charles M. Pratt.[53] By belief and by alliance with conservative donors, Taylor opposed Progressive social movements. He shared Pratt's Republicanism and fear of any reform that might threaten the corporate order. He took the position that a college was a haven devoted to learning, protected from political agitation, and that the college itself should take no stand. Thus he denied Jane Addams a Vassar platform when she travelled under the auspices of the Collegiate League for Equal Suffrage, and he refused students the right to hold a women's suffrage meeting on campus.[54] Taylor's "neutrality" fooled no one: his opponents saw him as the political conservative he was.

Try as he might, Taylor lacked the power to control political currents on his campus. Faculty, such as Herbert Mills and Lucy Salmon, actively engaged in the questions of the day and trained generations of reform-minded students. Julia Lathrop, a co-worker of Jane Addams at Hull-House and the first head of the Children's Bureau, became an alumna trustee in 1912, at the height of her political influence. Students turned into participants in the political fights of their time and wanted to form a women's suffrage organization on campus. When Taylor refused, they gathered in a nearby graveyard at midnight in support of suffrage.[55]

While trustees, aided by the college's president, tried to turn Vassar into a "walled garden," students and faculty rather successfully ignored them. Faculty labored under Vassar's distinctive pressures, but they nonetheless carried on independent lives in and out of the classroom. Students maintained the frenetic schedule of college life: some became transformed in the process. As the college added impressive buildings, it looked to the outside like a fitting complement of Bryn Mawr. The impressive façade of art building, library, and chapel suggested the power of a wealthy institution devoted to the liberal education of women. Just as President Seelye's ambitions for Smith took the college far from its protective beginnings, so did Taylor's success with donors create a campus that hardly fit his or their conservative intention. When Taylor retired in 1914, the college that he transmitted shared with Bryn Mawr, Wellesley, and Smith not only a landscape, but also a distinctive life. Vassar demonstrates that the strength of the women's college in the early twentieth century could overpower even the treasurer of Standard Oil.

14

A Larger School Room

Mount Holyoke had the greatest distance to travel before it entered into the ranks of the women's colleges at the turn of the century. In 1887, Mount Holyoke was still a seminary. By 1900, it had begun to catch up. The seminary had re-created itself into a college in the image of 1875 Smith. Mount Holyoke had a long way to go, however. In the years before World War I, Mary Woolley turned a weak sister college into a strong one, the equal of its peers. To make this double transition, Mount Holyoke reshaped curriculum, upgraded its faculty and offered them independence, created a full-blown student life, and built a new campus. The drama of its changes is visible in Mount Holyoke's buildings and landscapes.

I

In 1887, Mount Holyoke celebrated its first half-century. The outpouring of memory and pride was marred by a disquieting sense that Mary Lyon's great institution had a past rather than a present or future. In 1837, she called her school a seminary to emphasize its serious professional training for teachers. In addition to hard study and domestic labor, Lyon relied on a self-reporting system of discipline in which students accounted for their adherence to rules in public confessionals. Lyon meant to transform the consciousness of students, and she did so by a form of apostolic succession which elevated favored students to teachers and principals. This had an unintended result. What began as experiment hardened into orthodoxy. Teachers trained from within repeated Mary Lyon's methods, immured from outside influences. While growth in numbers, expansion of the seminary building, and a new four-year curriculum suggested gradual change, the remarkable fact about Mount Holyoke was its stability. Mary Lyon built more solidly than she knew, far more solidly than her innovative nature would have tolerated.

The world outside Mount Holyoke had changed markedly, including the opportunities for women's higher education. The creation of the women's colleges reverberated, to lower the seminary's status. Henry Fowle Durant, while believing that there could never be too many Mount Holyokes, understood this change and renamed Wellesley Female Seminary, Wellesley College. Daughter seminaries, such as Mills in Oakland, California, had already gained the power to grant the B.A. degree.[1]

Women's colleges meant competition for students and endowments. Once generous, Durant withdrew his financial support from Mount Holyoke after he created Wellesley. The founding of Smith College in Northampton, only nine miles away from Mount Holyoke, posed the most obvious threat. Smith's president and trustees came from the same Amherst intellectual and social milieu as Mount Holyoke, and in planning Smith they tried quite consciously to avoid Mount Holyoke's flaws. The seminary's position eroded to that of a preparatory school for the colleges, and an ineffective one at that, for it did not offer the classical training required for college admission.

While those within the seminary avoided confronting the situation, alumnae on the outside became painfully aware of the devaluation of their education. As graduates of an unrecognized school, they could not become members of the Association of Collegiate Alumnae. They felt unequal when they competed for teaching positions or when they met socially the more polished and worldly graduates of the women's colleges.[2] At the Fiftieth Anniversary celebration, the alumnae forced the issue. They resolved that Mount Holyoke call itself a college and "establish a curriculum befitting the name."[3] The trustees set up a study committee. The alumnae pressed the trustees to act quickly, and on November 30, 1887, the trustees petitioned the state legislature for the right to grant degrees and to call Mount Holyoke a "Seminary and College."[4]

Beyond the change of name, the alumnae disagreed on how to proceed. Logic forced those who wanted Mount Holyoke immediately to become a college to deny the need for further changes. They claimed that since Mount Holyoke was already an institution of collegiate grade, it required only the external recognition that would follow a simple substitution of the word *college* for *seminary*.

An articulate New York alumna disagreed. Pauline Woodford Halbert, of the class of 1882, representing the New York and Brooklyn Association, wrote a position paper in which she argued that Mount Holyoke was not a college and could not be one until it altered basic elements of its tradition.[5] She wanted the seminary to recognize its relative position and retain its name, but add a collegiate department. Acting "substantially in accordance with its [Halbert's paper] suggestions," the trustees petitioned for the dual name.[6] At the time, this seemed the conservative position, for it temporarily retained the seminary. But actually, it proved to be the more radical, for it recognized the need for basic change and initiated the process of transformation.[7]

Halbert identified two Mount Holyoke traditions that constrained its intellectual and social life: the practice, still maintained, of selecting new teachers from among the graduating class; and the self-reporting system. While Mary Lyon rightfully chose her teachers from within, this custom, continued a half-century later, "has become a restraint. It has driven the Seminary into ruts, given it narrow lines of development and an atmosphere intense and limited."[8] In contrast to the college-trained faculty "of breadth and attainments, who have moved among men, who have studied other methods," and who could bring to Mount Holyoke "a complete and developed womanhood," the seminary's teachers came "from country homes" with "few chances for social culture. . . . The Seminary walls have bounded their horizon."[9]

Perpetuation of Mary Lyon's disciplinary methods fostered these same tendencies. The self-reporting system that had once helped young women get control over their lives now narrowed them, making them morbid and introspective, rather than women with "ease of manner, self-respect and self-reliance."[10] A source of strength in 1837, Mount Holyoke's lack of worldliness became its weakness by 1887. Reflecting on her own experience, Halbert expressed her personal disappointment in Mount Holyoke and her hope for the future. If during her final years she and her classmates might have "stepped into a larger school room" and been treated as women "who no longer needed to be disciplined" and given "the inspiration and culture of a full college course under college professors[,] what a leap forward we should have made into broader thinking, more healthful feeling."[11]

Behind Halbert's critique is a clear conception of a women's college, quite different from Mount Holyoke's original mission. No longer a place for religious conversion or professional training, a college opened up the world of students, freeing them from the limits of their individual backgrounds. Worldly and experienced professors, not missionaries, composed its faculty. Living responsibly under a few rules, students grew intellectually and became confident and at ease in the world.

It took four steps to accomplish this. To become a college, Mount Holyoke had to establish a college curriculum and new standards for admission, change its teachers into professors, attract a different kind of student body, and build a college campus. By 1900, Mount Holyoke was well on its way to becoming a women's college; by World War I, it had attained equality with its six sisters.

The first step proved surprisingly easy. Treating the seminary as a preparatory school, the trustees added a collegiate department. With the aid of outsiders—including President Seelye of Smith—a committee proposed a classical and a scientific course and set entrance requirements equivalent to those of the New England colleges.[12] Eight students enrolled for college work the following year, added on to a seminary of almost three hundred. The principal resigned to leave the trustees free to seek a president to effect the broad changes to come. Circumstances forced the trustees to choose twice, as Mary Brigham, the initial choice, died en route. In her stead Elizabeth Storrs Mead brought Holyoke College into being.

Mead was an excellent choice. Trained at Ipswich and a veteran of many years of teaching, she had married Hiram Mead, who in the 1860s had been the pastor of South Hadley's Congregational Church and secretary to the seminary's board of trustees. Legend has it that the young minister's wife sympathized with Mount Holyoke students when they railed against seminary rules, and that she vowed to return to abolish them. Her silk dresses conveyed a new elegance, and, in the trio of faculty members that students tagged "The World, The Flesh, and the Devil," she stood for the world. Though hardly a representative of the Gilded Age, Mead understood life outside seminary walls. When her husband became a professor at Oberlin Theological Seminary, she served on the Women's Board of Managers and taught occasional courses. With her husband's death, she taught for two years at Oberlin and then became associate principal of Abbott Academy in Andover, Massachusetts. Her son, the philosopher George Herbert Mead, in Berlin after graduate work at Harvard, suggested the possibilities of contemporary intellectual life.[13]

Acting quickly, Mead created the popular literary course. By 1892, the collegiate department attracted all but eight of the students, thereby eliminating the need for the seminary. In 1893, a new charter changed the name to Mount Holyoke College. To raise the faculty to one of collegiate grade required more gradual steps: loyalty allowed no dismissals from the staff. Mead ended faculty responsibility for domestic work and encouraged existing staff to take graduate courses and to travel. She recruited women with graduate degrees and integrated the men, who theretofore had given only supplementary lecture courses, into the regular faculty. At her departure, out of a teaching staff of forty-three, eight had received the Ph.D.[14]

To attract college students meant more than just appealing to those with requisite standards for admission. By the 1890s, college life at Smith, Wellesley, and Vassar provided a standard for the new Mount Holyoke. The college had to loosen its ties with rural evangelical New England and encourage more prosperous and more worldly students to apply. While geographical distribution offers no clear measure of diversity, given the hold of New England ways in far-flung places, it is significant that Mount Holyoke attracted students from Missouri and the District of Columbia as well as from Massachusetts, Connecticut, Vermont, New Hampshire, and New York. Especially encouraging were the twenty-two transfers, in 1895–96, from other colleges, infusing Mount Holyoke with, as Mead put it, the "new life" of their "varied culture."[15]

Mead dispensed with the old rules, including both the intricate daily schedule and the self-reporting system, and instituted a form of self-government. Though she did not abolish domestic work completely, she released students from the more onerous tasks. Time once devoted to introspection, devotions, and manual labor could now be spent in the pleasurable pursuits of student organizations, publications, athletics, socializing, and rituals. Within a few years Mount Holyoke students created the entire panoply of college life: Students League (for self-government), yearbook, literary magazine, Christian Association, Ivy Day, Junior Promenade, banjo club, dramatics, and spreads. Mount Holyoke allowed Greek-letter secret societies, discouraged or forbidden on some campuses, and even gave them college rooms, because they suggested a clear break with the seminary past.[16]

The seminary building stood in the way of Mount Holyoke's progress. Once the fitting expression of a seminary organized as an asylum, the large plain structure became a barrier to collegiate status. With its founding in 1875, Smith College gave Mount Holyoke a new direction. When a science and art building became necessary, trustees and alumnae raised $50,000 from donations and college funds for A. Lyman Williston Hall, named for its chief donor, Mount Holyoke's treasurer and trustee.

A businessman from Northampton, Williston had become a member of Mount Holyoke's board in 1867. The nephew of Samuel Williston who signed the seminary's original articles of incorporation and endowed the Williston Academy for boys, Lyman Williston joined his uncle in supporting many evangelical organizations. He served on Smith College's board of trustees and its finance committee.[17] Though generous to Smith, Williston hardly accepted the view, common in Western Massachusetts, that the new college supplanted the seminary, as a daughter took the place of her mother. Quite the opposite: as treasurer, Williston encouraged Mount Holyoke to adopt the forms of Smith, with even some improvement on the Northampton model.

In Williston Hall, dedicated in 1876, Mount Holyoke followed Smith closely, choosing Smith's designers, Peabody & Stearns, as architects for the first Mount Holyoke building erected away from the seminary structure. For the South Hadley building, Peabody & Stearns created a smaller and more modest version of Smith's College Hall.[18]

While the new science and art building imitated its Northampton model, Mount Holyoke could not copy Smith's real breakthrough, the cottage system. Smith's plan had a profound impact on many American colleges, both coeducational and all-female. For example, as early as 1883, the Wooster Women's Educational Association hailed the Northampton experiment and began a campaign for cottages on the Wooster College campus in Ohio.[19] While Bryn Mawr's initial buildings imitated those of Smith, at Vassar and Wellesley seminary structures constrained both colleges. Mount Holyoke faced the same problem, made the more acute by its effort to shake its past. In 1889, the New York Association of alumnae launched a campaign for a cottage. President Mead endorsed the effort enthusiastically, as aiding "in the cultivation of the Aesthetic nature so essential in woman," hardly possible in the plain seminary structure.[20] Cottages also allowed the college to grow and created conditions of quiet, conducive to study. The trustees chose William C. Brocklesby, the Hartford architect then designing a series of cottages at Smith. Like his work in Northampton, Brocklesby planned a large dwelling house for students. He designed a rectangular block with a projecting ell, enlivened by Queen Anne gables. On to an essentially institutional façade he added an incongruous welcoming porch to suggest domesticity.[21]

Before Brocklesby's cottage could be built, an event changed completely the life and landscape of Mount Holyoke. On September 27, 1896, fire broke out in the main building. Quickly aroused, the college community evacuated the building and stood by helplessly as the building became completely consumed in the flames. Housed in South Hadley homes, students and faculty immediately resumed college work. The alumnae felt a terrible loss and urged the college to rebuild the seminary building. But to Mead and Williston the fire created an undreamt-of opportunity. The trustees voted to build Brocklesby's cottage immediately and to adopt "the cottage plan."[22] For the first time since Pauline Durant endowed the library, outsiders emerged to add to funds available through fire insurance: Dr. D. K. Pearsons of Chicago, who had known Mary Lyon, and John D. Rockefeller each contributed sums significant enough to have cottages named for them. Mount Holyoke now had the chance to look like the college it aspired to be.

The buildings that emerged suggest that, in 1897, Mount Holyoke continued to look to Smith as its model. The academic and administrative building awkwardly re-created Peabody and Stearns' College Hall. Seven cottages, a gymnasium, and separate buildings for music and art followed. By the early twentieth century, Mount Holyoke had all the building components of Smith of the 1880s. With one significant difference. Smith not only penetrated Northampton but let the campus itself take the feel of a town as it filled in all available space with buildings. Mount Holyoke protected its pastoral landscape, placing its buildings around circles of greensward among tall trees.[23]

Mary Lyon Hall rose along College Street, on the site of the burned seminary building. Designed as the central place of meeting, it held administrative offices, classrooms, an assembly hall, and a connecting chapel. While any number

Mary Lyon Hall; *Mount Holyoke College Library/Archives*

of forms might enclose such a space, Smith College's importance ordained that
Mary Lyon look like College Hall.

Mount Holyoke chose prominent Springfield architect Eugene C. Gardner
of Gardner, Pyne and Gardner to design Mary Lyon Hall.[24] Instead of Peabody
& Stearns' use of polychromy at Smith, Gardner employed at Mount Holyoke the more sombre, rough-cut local Longmeadow stone. A tall, thin clock
tower fronts College Street, conveying the power and importance of the institution. The administrative wing joins the tower on the south, with its important college offices and an assembly room. With the exception of the
cross-shaped finials, the hall bears little relation to Gothic form. It is a solid
box with largely rectangular windows, topped by a steeply sloping roof. A
Gothic chapel in a cruciform shape connects with the northern end of the
tower through a passageway. Of dimensions roughly equal to the south wing,
the chapel mirrors the other's form on College Street and creates an awkward
symmetrical composition. The chapel makes fine sense as a separate structure.
Two turrets frame a large tracery window above the street entrance. Perceived

Brigham Hall; *Mount Holyoke College Library/Archives*

in isolation, the chapel is a handsome church building; as part of a composition, it is a weighty afterthought.

Built on the site of the original seminary near the village church, Mary Lyon Hall fronted on College Street. Where should the cottages go? Beginning in the 1880s, gifts and purchases expanded the campus to about a hundred acres, and gave Mount Holyoke the lake that had become an expected feature of the landscape of the women's colleges. Rockefeller donated a skating rink. On the other side of the lake, a wooded tract offered a fine prospect; in 1882, E. A. Goodnow of Worcester gave forty acres of the land to the seminary. In addition to its wooded acres, Mount Holyoke purchased house lots across College Street and south of the seminary building. In 1881, Lyman Williston initiated building across the road. Because trees obstructed star-gazing near the seminary, the college placed the observatory, given by Williston in memory of his son, on the other side of College Street. A decade later, Lydia Shattuck Hall, a second science building, followed alongside Williston Hall. The fire left the college with Durant's library, Williston, Shattuck, the observatory, and the skating rink—in quite scattered locations.[25]

While President Mead favored placing the cottages in the woods on the other side of the lake, the sites of existing buildings and the decision to place Mary Lyon Hall on the ground of the original seminary favored a closer location, the house lots to the south. The cottages quickly rose on this land. As the campus filled out, academic buildings lined College Street. With two exceptions, the cottages took the land in back. They form an informal composition along a circular drive that surrounds a park-like green.[26]

Three architects designed the five cottages—Mary Brigham, Safford, Porter, Pearsons, and Rockefeller. Gardner designed one; Brocklesby, two; and C. Powell Karr of Newark, New Jersey, two more. Within four years Mount Holyoke authorized two more cottages: Mary Wilder, designed by Karr; and Elizabeth Mead, by George F. Newton of Boston. Solid buildings of red brick trimmed with local stone, the seven cottages comprise individual variations on a single theme: they are institutional buildings in freely interpreted historic modes that add incongruous embellishments to make them look home-like. Brocklesby's cottages at Smith and Addison Hutton's Merion at Bryn Mawr look like overgrown houses. Both architects employed a variety of domestic motifs—hipped gables, bay windows, dormers—to convey the message that the cottages were dwellings. At Mount Holyoke, the architects planned plainer, more box-like institutional buildings and used decorative schemes associated with public buildings, rather than with houses. Mary Brigham's steeped gable, a favorite Queen Anne motif, generally adorned schools and hospitals. The hold of the domestic tradition remained, however, in symbolic fragments. Mount Holyoke called these four-story buildings for fifty to a hundred "cottages" and tacked wooden porches on to their façades. The porches are curious reminders of the desire to preserve the threatened femininity of college women.

Each porch led to the single entrance which opened on to the public rooms. The reception room, drawing room, and dining room took a domestic scale. No clear separation divided student rooms from these communal areas, unlike at Smith where the living areas began on the second floor. The cottages accommodated faculty as well as students: the matrons and the teachers got more generous corner rooms connected to smaller chambers in two-room suites. Most students lived in single rooms, though the building had some rooms large enough for two as well as some suites in the Vassar manner, where two students had separate bedrooms and shared a study room.

The final structure completed during the Mead years rounded out the set of buildings necessary for a women's college. In 1899, Mount Holyoke erected a gymnasium, outfitted according to all the latest Swedish and American principles, and set it back from the street among the cottages. Designed by Brocklesby, the architect for Smith's gymnasium as well as its cottages, Mount Holyoke's gymnasium was an eclectic red brick structure ("a free treatment of French renaissance") with a tall window above the entrance, set under a semicircular gable. The large open space of the interior, well glazed by high windows, held not only apparatus, a raised running track, and a court suitable for basketball, but also a stage dignified by a proscenium arch.[27] Mount Holyoke clearly intended the gymnasium for the festivities of student life, as well as for its athletic events.

The cottages and the gymnasium fit perfectly the new collegiate order. Living in smaller units fostered comradeship among students, the development of house loyalty, and a large number of house traditions. The cottages allowed a more informal life without regulations: in their gracious parlors men now came to call not only on recreation days but on Sundays. The extra rooms of Mary Brigham housed campus organizations; the porches, college singers.[28] The gymnasium lent itself to team sports and to college theatricals. Within four years after the fire, Mount Holyoke had the appropriate settings for college life.

Mary Lyon's pioneer seminary for women successfully transformed itself into a women's college according to late-nineteenth-century conceptions. Not only did it offer a full college curriculum taught by professors to students attuned to college life, Mount Holyoke did so on a campus that looked right to its age. The nascent college was unaware, however, that by taking its cues from Smith, it was modeling itself along domestic lines soon to look out-of-date. In the early twentieth century the standard set by Bryn Mawr came to Mount Holyoke, bringing with it both new demands for a college faculty committed to scholarship and a vision of a campus heroically swathed in college Gothic.

I I

The beginning of the new century brought to Mount Holyoke a new standard. With an appropriate sense of symbolism, Mary Emma Woolley arrived to take up the presidency of the college on January 1, 1901. Among the first women to receive the B.A. from Brown, she served Wellesley as professor of the Department of Biblical History and Literature and the head of College Hall. Articulate, a capable manager, genuinely committed to women's concerns, Mary Woolley took the small and thriving seminary-reborn-as-a-college and turned it into a major force in the higher education of women.[29] In the Woolley years, Mount Holyoke eschewed domestic imagery and erected buildings in collegiate Gothic. As a row of academic buildings rose beside Mary Lyon Hall along College Avenue, Mount Holyoke acquired its twentieth-century façade.

Under Elizabeth Mead, the college expanded to take in what she regarded as the ideal number of students, slightly over 550. Coming from a larger college, Mary Woolley let the numbers rise, reaching 700 by 1902, over 800 by 1916. She oversaw the addition of two new residence halls. Elizabeth Mead

Hall, appropriately named, completed the cottage plan inaugurated under its namesake. The college built no new residence halls for more than a decade. In the intervening years Mount Holyoke acquired large houses adjacent to the campus and converted them into student dormitories. Like Wellesley, from which Mary Woolley came, Mount Holyoke allowed overflow students to live in village homes in their freshman year, enabling the expansion of the student body without the costs of erecting residence halls.[30]

To transform Mount Holyoke from a seminary into a college, Elizabeth Mead had attracted a new student body and housed it in appropriate cottages. Mary Woolley's work lay elsewhere: the recruitment and support of a college faculty. No Mount Holyoke daughter, Mary Woolley first visited South Hadley when the trustees asked her to become president. She brought to the office a clear vision of a professionally trained faculty committed to scholarship. She applied her considerable administrative talents to attract that faculty, give them adequate resources and support, and help them advance at the college. Mount Holyoke maintained during these years a faculty-student ratio of 1:7. As student enrollment increased, so did faculty positions. This enabled Mary Woolley to complete the task begun under Elizabeth Mead of upgrading the teaching staff while respecting those who had served the seminary of an earlier era. By 1911, the faculty had ninety members, thirty-four of whom held the Ph.D.[31]

Right before Mary Woolley took office Mount Holyoke ranked its faculty and gave them the more prestigious title of professor for department heads, assistant professor for permanent staff, and instructor or assistant for all others. Salaries were low, however: professors got only $1,000, while assistant professors lived on $800 and instructors $400 to $600.[32] These salaries required faculty to live in residence halls alongside students. While Mary Woolley herself seemed not to mind a life in "households of women," she knew those who did. At Wellesley she had come to love Jeannette Marks, a brilliant student. In one of her first acts as president, Mary Woolley appointed Jeannette Marks instructor in English literature. The two lived in separate quarters in Mary Brigham Hall, divided by three flights of stairs. What a contrast between this life and the gracious one led by Katharine Lee Bates and Katharine Coman at Wellesley! Marks pushed Woolley to think of the needs of women faculty who wanted to live independent lives according to their own private standards, away from students and official duties. Beginning in 1903–4, several faculty members moved off campus. With two friends, Jeannette Marks settled into a small house, which they named Green Pea. Marks found the change refreshing. Mount Holyoke faculty felt that sense of release from constraint that we have seen elsewhere. Mary Woolley understood and fostered this. Beginning in 1906, Mount Holyoke trustees gave the faculty an additional sum as a living allowance for residence outside dormitories. The scarcity of places to rent led the college to build a faculty house in 1917.[33]

Mary Woolley herself benefited: in 1909, she and Jeannette Marks moved into the President's House across College Avenue, donated by Joseph Skinner, after the Northwestern Alumnae Association inaugurated a campaign. Horace Frazer of Boston designed an ample stucco dwelling with public rooms suitable for entertaining. The Mount Holyoke President's House shared two elements with the houses built for Wellesley professors—ample studies, including a long oratory with low, raftered ceilings, where Jeannette Marks held her seminars, and a rear garden on to which the important windows of the house opened.[34] Much more modest than either the Deanery at Bryn Mawr or Oakwoods at Wellesley, both supported by private wealth, the Mount Holyoke President's House nonetheless gave the necessary privacy and status which the alumnae felt befitted the college's chief officer.

Mary Woolley waged a constant campaign to raise faculty salaries. They inched up slowly: by 1910, full professors who lived off campus took home $1,600 a year; by 1920, $3,000. In addition, junior faculty competed for fellowships to complete their graduate training; and, beginning in 1925, all ranks became eligible for sabbatical leave with pay. The college met with success. In these years Mount Holyoke attracted a faculty of high quality. Mary Woolley made a few stunning appointments, especially the Bryn Mawr–trained historians Bertha Haven Putnam and Nellie Neilson.[35]

It was not enough to raise salaries, enable faculty to live in their own dwellings, and support leaves. Mount Holyoke needed new academic buildings to house the work of the college. Classrooms, offices, laboratories, practice rooms, and library built for two hundred hardly served four times their number. Mary Woolley began her campaign for what she called "bricks," money to erect academic buildings. She became a highly successful builder. Proud of her accomplishments, she later reflected that "to those who have had a part in the building every stick and stone seems human."[36]

Beginning in 1901, with the Dwight Memorial Art Building, Mount Holyoke erected a succession of academic buildings along its public boundary, College Street. Each proclaimed more loudly than the last a variation on a single theme: the dignity of the college. Three Boston architectural firms, all trained at the Ecole des Beaux Arts in Paris—George F. Newton, Putnam and Cox, and Allen and Collens—gave these buildings increasingly elaborate Gothic or Jacobean dress. While no formal planning preceded the placement of buildings on the ground, Frederick Law Olmsted, Jr., helped to select sites, with an eye to preserving trees and areas of green lawn and to keeping buildings in an even line as they faced the street. The campus formed roughly two separate areas: the academic buildings centered on the north; the residential ones on the south. To keep the administration, library, and classrooms free from noise, the music building adjoined the residential cottages in a spot accessible by public road for concerts. Careful not to let Mount Holyoke crowd its structures as

Library interior before 1936 renovation; *Mount Holyoke College Library/Archives*

Bird's-eye view, 1907; *Mount Holyoke College Library/Archives*

had Smith, Treasurer Lyman Williston insisted that buildings surround green spaces, creating handsome, partially enclosed park land.[37]

At the conclusion of the campaign to raise one-half million dollars, inaugurated on Mount Holyoke's seventy-fifth anniversary, the college boasted, in addition to the art and music buildings, a library, a recitation hall, and a student-alumnae building. The library best illustrates Mount Holyoke's quest for dignified settings for collegiate work. In 1904, Andrew Carnegie promised $50,000 to the general funds of the college, on the condition that it be matched. The trustees authorized fund-raising for a library to cost $100,000. Unlike colleges whose alumnae represented wealth, Mount Holyoke depended upon large numbers giving small amounts. The class of 1853 presented a fiftieth reunion gift of $50 to begin a campaign that drew 100,000 givers in all.[38]

For the library, Mount Holyoke chose architect George F. Newton, who had designed one of the cottages after the fire. Trained at the Ecole des Beaux Arts, Newton began in the firm of Peabody and Stearns. In his independent practice he planned churches, public buildings, and residences.[39] Supplanting the library given by the Durants, Newton's building lay between Dwight Art Memorial and Mary Lyon Hall. Leaded windows richly adorned the library's low sweep of Kibbie stone. The broad Tudor Gothic entrance carried an arched tracery window under a central gable and two bay windows in the shape of battlemented turrets. Inside the Tudor Gothic façade, the interior copied Westminster Hall. Light flooded in from three great tracery windows and from the tall mullioned windows above the wooden book stacks. The leaded windows carried appropriate symbolism: the seals of the women's colleges later known as the Seven Sisters, Mount Holyoke's daughter colleges, and Brown, Mary Woolley's alma mater.

Mary Woolley's successful efforts to build a great college faculty brought Bryn Mawr graduates to Mount Holyoke. The look that she sought for the campus harmonized: to South Hadley came the dignity of Bryn Mawr's quadrangles. But just as the brown local stone of Western Massachusetts differed from the gray of Pennsylvania, so too did Newton's design for the Mount Holyoke library differ from that of Cope and Stewardson for the library at Bryn Mawr. Mount Holyoke looked to an ecclesiastical precedent, while Bryn Mawr linked itself to the secular collegiate tradition. Yet both appropriated monumental English forms as settings for American women, and neither sought any particular connection with structures associated with women. Bryn Mawr wanted its students to relive the Oxford experience. Mount Holyoke sought respectability. The buildings of the early years of the twentieth century created a campus façade to tell the surrounding world that Mount Holyoke was a place of academic seriousness and high purpose.

15

The Day of Small Things Is Over

RADCLIFFE, BARNARD

One of the clearest expressions of the power of the women's college in the early twentieth century came from two unlikely sources, the annexes of Harvard and Columbia. Radcliffe and Barnard never intended to be women's colleges. Their founders hoped only to open up the resources of two great male universities to women. Initially both annexes assumed that they bore no responsibility for students' lives outside college courses: students either lived at home or boarded locally. Neither school attached much importance to college buildings. While Barnard understood that buildings helped establish its clear presence in New York City, Radcliffe remained wary of alienating Harvard by assertive buildings and wanted to avoid any suggestion of the seminary past.

All this changed in the early twentieth century. To students in the women's colleges in the years around 1910, college life was the essence of the college experience. Bryn Mawr suggested to reluctant builders the possibilities of college buildings free of seminary and domestic associations. Consequently both Radcliffe and Barnard encouraged college life and built residence halls. However distinctive the origins of Radcliffe and Barnard, each annex turned to the women's colleges to learn what it ought to become.

I

In 1893, with its incorporation as Radcliffe College, Harvard's annex changed direction dramatically. The need for reticence that had once characterized its statements disappeared. College buildings no longer conjured up the image of the female seminary. College life, initially anathema to Boston society, became appealing. A once local endeavor vied for status on a national scale. The Radcliffe Yard and its residential quadrangle provide the texts that tell the tale.

In the years before its incorporation, Harvard's annex had suffered from its ambiguous position. Drawing on Harvard's faculty, but unrecognized by it, an institution for women, yet not a women's college, what was the Annex to be? Arthur Gilman and Elizabeth Cary Agassiz believed that tact and time might prove to Harvard that it could educate women as well as men with no strain upon its resources and no threat of coeducation. In 1883, hoping that money might convince where argument failed, the Society for the Collegiate Instruction of Women decided to raise $100,000 in endowment to induce Harvard to accept the Annex as a branch of the university. Yet Harvard proved remarkably resistant to the Annex's charms and substantial dowry. The university refused to accept the proposal as originally tendered.

Despite Harvard's rejection, by the early 1890s the Annex showed signs of increasing strength. Over two hundred students took courses from seventy Harvard instructors.[1] The Annex attracted a remarkable group of Harvard faculty, committed to teaching women and strengthening the society that provided that opportunity. Students became loyal alumnae. Yet fear of offending Harvard muted any expressions of the Annex's power: the Annex continued "as unnoticed as the daughters of any Cambridge residents."[2] Founders kept its material basis minimal and disguised.

Fay House provided classrooms, parlors for relaxation, and offices for Annex officials. In 1890, the Boston architectural firm of Longfellow, Alden & Harlow artfully redesigned Fay House to double its size while keeping the external appearance of a private house. The Annex acquired several small neighboring houses, already converted for educational purposes by the Gilman School and the Brown and Nichols School, and used them for laboratories, gymnasium, and music rooms.[3] Discretion characterized rhetoric as well as buildings. Publications made it clear that the Annex had no interest in "college life": it provided only a Harvard education and facilities to make life "as agreeable and rational as possible."[4] Annex literature portrayed the sponsors backing the Annex as cautious and safe: they were Cambridge ladies "not known as exponents of any particular set of views in regard to the education of their sex."[5] Despite obvious success, the Annex remained guarded and conservative in its public statements.

The Annex's advocates could not ignore the needs of students for degrees and the promise of continuity. After four years of study at a high level, students received, not a B.A. degree, but only a certificate. This put alumnae who sought teaching positions at a disadvantage. The Annex's framers hoped that, with time, Harvard would turn those certificates into Harvard degrees. Harvard had no such intention. Nor did the university wish to recognize the Annex in any official way. This left the future in doubt. Harvard was free, any time it chose, to forbid its faculty from teaching women on the side. The need to grant degrees and to guarantee the future of the Annex forced its backers to seek a clear, contractual relationship with Harvard.

With all the tact and persuasive power for which she was known, Elizabeth Cary Agassiz negotiated with President Charles William Eliot of Harvard an arrangement by which Harvard oversaw the Annex, countersigned its degrees, and described its offerings in the university catalogue. The president and Fellows of Harvard College became Visitors of the women's institution, responsible for appointing instructors and examiners. In 1893, the Society for the Collegiate Instruction of Women voted to become Radcliffe College, with full ability to grant degrees. The seventeenth-century gift of Anne Radcliffe to Harvard College, the first such by a woman, gave the Annex its new name.[6]

Having achieved such a victory, Elizabeth Agassiz hardly anticipated what followed. Alumnae of the Annex did not want half a loaf. They wanted to be part of Harvard or not at all. At issue was the B.A. degree: alumnae wanted a Harvard diploma, not a Radcliffe one countersigned by Harvard. A large majority of the sixty-six alumnae signed a petition of "disappointment and disapproval," addressed to the society. They had worked to raise money for a fund to give to Harvard in exchange for recognition of the Annex as a branch of the university, symbolized by the Harvard degree. Loyal to the original conception, they did not wish the Annex "to become either in fact or in name a separate college for women."[7] Using similar arguments, the New York Local Committee on Harvard Examinations for Women added their names to a petition to the Harvard Overseers to block the agreement. Here external forces added their weight. Eliza Theodora Minturn, whose description of Girton in the *Nation* provided Arthur Gilman with a model for the Annex, joined in the effort to block Radcliffe's incorporation, as did Barnard's dean, the Bryn Mawr alumna Emily James Putnam.[8] Minturn consulted with President M. Carey Thomas on her plan of action, enlisting her in a campaign to destroy Bryn Mawr's Cambridge competition. The Annex Fund Committee of the Woman's Education Association, responsible for raising $75,000 to offer to Harvard, reported that the Eliot-Agassiz agreement failed to meet its conditions.[9] The Association of Collegiate Alumnae fought Radcliffe's incorporation in the Massachusetts state legislature, using as supporting documents the alumnae petition, that of the New York committee, and the statement of the Annex Fund. Though normally avoiding the public forum, Elizabeth Agassiz went before the Committee on Education of the legislature to argue for Radcliffe's charter. Her brilliant testimony and that of President Eliot won over opposition. The legislature granted a charter to Radcliffe College, signed by the governor March 23, 1894.[10]

The transformation of the Annex into Radcliffe College inaugurated major changes. Alumnae fears that their alma mater would become a women's col-

lege were realized when the new college appointed Agnes Irwin as its first
dean. The elder of two sisters who presided over the Irwin School for Girls in
Philadelphia, Agnes Irwin brought neither college experience nor a Cambridge background to her demanding job. Students "viewed dubiously a dean
holding no degree" who believed in rules "more in harmony with the life in
the boarding school . . . than with the freedom of Harvard University."[11]
Shunning Irwin, they turned to Mary Coes, one of the Annex's early alumnae,
who served as the college's secretary. As a member of the class of 1897 recalled,
"the administration of 'the Annex' begins and ends with 'Coesy' ":

> How she made the center of our college life. . . . What a never-ending fountain
> of wisdom she was, and how her advice, gentle but firm, dispersed all that
> before seemed misty. How from behind that grave air her humor flashed out in
> a smile or a glance! How she understood![12]

Agnes Irwin did not understand. She had a different vision. As an outsider,
she did not recognize the boundaries that had hedged the Annex from the
beginning. She brought a new aspiration for Radcliffe: she wanted it to become
a national institution. "For Radcliffe, the day of small things is over," she proclaimed in Radcliffe's annual report.[13] She assumed neither the superiority of
young women from Boston nor the need for reticence. While not a college
woman, she wanted to transform an annex of a great male university into a
true women's college. Laura Gill fought the same battle at Barnard. At Radcliffe, as at Barnard, this meant a departure from the Annex's origins and
traditions.[14]

Harvard's annex began as an alternative to the women's colleges. Compared to them, Radcliffe portrayed itself as unabashedly academic. While women's
colleges concerned themselves with the social development of the female collegian, the Annex had no interest in any aspect beyond intellectual opportunity. As the alumnae petition suggests, students came for a Harvard education.
Their reminiscences, as a result, dwell on the characteristics of Harvard's male
faculty, not on the pranks of college girls. The memory of a freshman Latin
class with James Greenough is typical: "He amazed me by doing faun-like
dance steps while chanting lines from Latin poets."[15] A Radcliffe alumna who
transferred from Smith suggested that the "greatest difference" between Radcliffe and Smith was "the feeling at Radcliffe that you had somehow entered
into the great company of scholars. . . . You felt how infinitely much there
was to learn and how little you could ever attain to. It was humbling and
inspiring."[16] The diaries of Boston daughters attending Radcliffe raise a different possibility: that Radcliffe mattered less to students than did Smith. In contrast to the intense, transforming experiences of students in the women's colleges,
those of Radcliffe commuters living at home rested relatively lightly.[17] One

Students in study room, Agassiz House; *Radcliffe College Archives*

alumna recalled, "As I look back to my College Days, the life appears to me to have been rather monotonous with almost no time for college activities except study—study and a continual going back and forth from home to college, which task consumed almost two hours and a half each day."[18] Another, who lived a mile from college, "went home to lunch, so that I did not have so many opportunities for informal converse as others did."[19]

While such reminiscences fit the Annex's original intentions, they did not meet the new expectations of college women at the turn of the century who saw the value of college life. In addition, buildings which the founders saw only in negative terms now could be invested with positive value. Radcliffe's founders had eschewed building, not only because they had feared threatening Harvard, but also because they had wanted nothing to do with the seminary associations of the women's colleges. By the turn of the century, however, an important change had occurred. M. Carey Thomas had created in Bryn Mawr a women's college linked not to the seminary, but to the academic tradition of Oxford and Cambridge. Its emerging quadrangles symbolized new possibilities for the women's colleges. While Thomas' snobbery did not allow her to consort with a Philadelphia private school principal, Agnes Irwin nonetheless understood from Bryn Mawr that a women's college could confirm urbanity and intellectuality. Thus college life and buildings held no danger to Agnes Irwin: she could turn Radcliffe into a women's college.

Agnes Irwin succeeded in her larger purpose, but did not win the love of the community. As the years went by, she felt unappreciated. Those who brought her in as dean had led her to assume that she would become president of Radcliffe upon Elizabeth Agassiz's retirement. In 1901, when that time came, however, the society appointed Harvard's dean of the faculty, Le Baron Russell Briggs. Disappointed, Agnes Irwin remained as dean until 1909, continually advocating changes to make Radcliffe over in the image of the women's college.[20]

Quite unexpectedly, President Briggs proved to be a strong ally. His dual responsibilities meant that, as Radcliffe's advocate, his was a voice listened to at Harvard. He made Radcliffe "respectable" in the university.[21] And he helped provide the material means for the transformed Annex. He created the Radcliffe Auxiliary as the college's fund-raising arm to aid in realizing Agnes Irwin's hopes for Radcliffe.

To M. Carey Thomas' chagrin, Agnes Irwin's efforts at Radcliffe successfully countered Bryn Mawr's claim to be the most academically challenging of the women's colleges. Without altering a single element of its academic side, managed ably by Harvard professors who composed Radcliffe's Academic Board, Irwin campaigned successfully to change the material side of Radcliffe. In the years of her deanship, Radcliffe acquired land and built its academic quadrangle, the Radcliffe Yard. Insisting that Radcliffe cease to limit itself to local students and those mature enough to board in Cambridge, Dean Irwin urged the construction of dormitories. Responding to her leadership, in the early twentieth century Radcliffe planned its first residence hall and located its residential quadrangle.

Change began immediately. Within a year, major gifts made Radcliffe visible. In keeping with the transformation of the Annex into Radcliffe, the first two buildings of the academic quadrangle had nothing to do with the intellectual side of students' lives. In 1895, Mary Hemenway gave Radcliffe funds for a gymnasium, built in 1898; in 1902, the family of Elizabeth Cary Agassiz honored her eightieth birthday with the gift of a students' building, erected in 1904.

These new buildings confirmed Radcliffe's existence, its new commitment to college life, and its ties to the academic tradition. By the time that Radcliffe was ready to build, women's college structures could look like college buildings. In most settings this meant some form of Gothic; but in Cambridge, collegiate architecture took a different direction. During these same years, Harvard was undertaking a significant building program, filling up the Yard

Living room, Agassiz House; *Radcliffe College Archives*

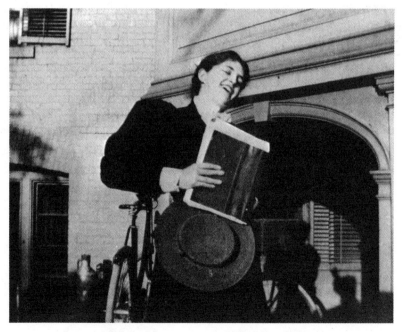

Radcliffe student, ca. 1900; *Radcliffe College Archives*

and the area between it and the Charles River with red brick Georgian structures. Thus when Radcliffe's turn came, its buildings followed the same form.
The 1890 reconstruction of Fay House had removed its mansard roof, added
in 1870, and restored it to its 1806 classical origins. In this spirit Radcliffe
turned to architects known for their work in Georgian Revival. The great New
York firm McKim, Mead & White designed the gymnasium, placed next to
Fay House in 1898, as a red brick Georgian rectangle with a white cornice,
cupola, and central porch. The second floor contained the great open space for
indoor athletics, complete with a running track. The basement held a swimming tank.[22] Next door, with its massive welcoming portico of tall white columns, Elizabeth Cary Agassiz House, the students' building, offered a lunch
room, an immense living room, an auditorium, and club rooms for college
activities.

In 1904, the Greenleaf property became available, allowing extension of
Radcliffe to Ash Street. The auxiliary raised almost two-thirds of the needed
$80,000 to purchase the land. President Briggs strongly supported the pur-
chase of the Greenleaf estate, but Agnes Irwin saw the extension of the grounds
in another direction.[23] Acquisition of the property led to questions about
placement of buildings and thus about the physical design of the college. Should
Radcliffe sprinkle its buildings in a variety of settings or should it concentrate
them? The issue was the old one of discretion versus power. To disperse its
buildings meant that Radcliffe softened its image, returning to its origins as an
annex; concentration suggested the strength of the women's college.

The critical moment came in 1906. With students' physical and social needs
partially met, it was now turn for a library. Radcliffe secured designs from
Henry Forbes Bigelow of the Boston architectural firm of Bigelow & Wins-
low. The Committee on the Location of Buildings called in the landscape architect Arthur A. Shurtleff to advise on the library's placement. He strongly
urged Radcliffe not to put the library on the Greenleaf property, separate from
Fay House, the gymnasium, and Agassiz. While isolation offered the advantage of retirement and quiet, it threatened to negate the creation of a unified
campus. The library should join the other buildings in a quadrangle composition. "The development of the Quadrangle would require buildings of the
type of the new Radcliffe Library, and the Library requires just that intimate
association with other collegiate buildings which the Quadrangle promises to
provide, not alone for convenience of access but for the best architectural setting." He recommended a building "of the general size and appearance of the
Gymnasium connected to Agassiz House by a colonnade." Both "the charm
of the English colleges" and "the success of the old Harvard Yard" depended
upon the close "nestling of buildings" and upon the coordination of their
design.[24]

Radcliffe took Shurtleff's advice and acquired, in 1906, a library that harmonized with the gymnasium and joined Agassiz in a colonnade. Though not completed until the 1930s, with the addition of Byerly and Longfellow halls, the Radcliffe Yard took its basic form. In 1906, Radcliffe decided unequivocally to look like a college.

Radcliffe's greatest break with the past came with the decision to build residence halls for its students, for the absence of dormitories had marked the Annex's distinctiveness. Thinking of their own daughters and neighbors, the founders intended the primary recipients of the Annex education to be local daughters or wealthy students able to pay for rooms in the best houses of Cambridge. For some, however, the reality was quite different. Students forced to board found themselves isolated from social life. A commentator asked rhetorically,

> Do the Annex girls enjoy the advantages of Cambridge society? . . . No; partly because the students are working women without leisure for frequent engagements; partly because Cambridge society is busy and absorbed and does not go out of its way to offer the Annex social culture.[25]

In contrast to images of graciousness, some students found themselves in "a tiny hall bedroom in a household of indifferent and unsympathetic persons."[26]

Dean Irwin's desire to transform Radcliffe into a national institution required dormitory rooms.[27] Surprisingly, given their loyalty to the original conception of the Annex, the alumnae agreed. By 1898, they felt that the lack of dormitories turned "many students against Radcliffe." As important, they perceived the absence of college life as a negative working against Radcliffe. They now recognized the positive value of life in residence halls. It developed in students "an *esprit de corps* and an active loyalty to the college" and brought to the fore "talents for leadership and executive work." For these reasons the Alumnae of Radcliffe and the Annex '95 Club mounted a campaign to raise $50,000 for a permanent house under college jurisdiction for twenty-five students. They hoped that it might be "the beginning . . . of a new system of halls of residence, carefully limited in size, healthful, tasteful, economical and bearing the prestige of College ownership and management . . . to offer to all her [Radcliffe's] students, rich or poor, the essentials, physical, aesthetic and social, as well as intellectual, of a true College education." In the past, Radcliffe had depended upon outside benefactors: the alumnae now called on graduates and past students to create the first dormitory.[28] It is intriguing that this first assumption of responsibility for fund-raising by the alumnae confirmed the transformation of the Annex into Radcliffe College. Even Annex alumnae, once committed to an alternative institution for the higher education of women, succumbed to the powerful example of the women's colleges.

The alumnae never had to raise money for the hall, for Mrs. David P. Kimball gave it to the college. Radcliffe's first residence hall, Bertram, opened in 1901. Designed by A. W. Longfellow for twenty-five students, its interior plan suggested Smith's cottages. Generous public rooms on the first floor led to student rooms on the upper floors, most of which formed bedroom-study combinations for several students.[29] On the exterior, however, Bertram never carried any cottage associations. Even though it was relatively small in scale

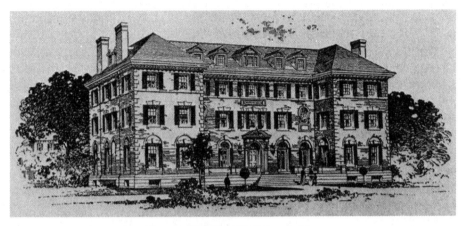

Bertram Hall; *Radcliffe College Archives*

and located on a residential Cambridge street, Bertram looked like a college structure, not a house. Its monumental Georgian red brick made its collegiate nature clear.

Bertram's location at the southwestern edge of the Homestead, a large tract of land—seven minutes' walk from the Radcliffe Yard—purchased by Radcliffe in 1900, made it possible to see the building as the first of a group of related residence halls. In 1907, Kimball gave an identical hall adjoining Bertram. Increasing demand for student rooms and the need for economy meant that forty-three single bedrooms took the place of the twenty-five bedroom-study combinations and part of the public space on the first floor of Bertram.[30] When Radcliffe went to build again, the Radcliffe Auxiliary appointed a special committee to examine the question of dormitories. Radcliffe wrote to all the prominent women's colleges for information to help guide its planning. Letters from the sister colleges advocated the hall of seventy-five students as the more economical, for it divided the cost of a matron and public rooms among a larger number of students and did not require a staff of servants proportionally as large as the small residence. According to college administrators, women students preferred modest single rooms to more costly suites, to fit their "more slender purses" and their sense of democracy. Because Radcliffe had already "severely taxed" the public interest in the college by earlier appeals, the committee recommended that the new residence hall be funded as an investment, selling shares of $1,000 to return 5 percent, a plan sounding very much like the "philanthropy and five per cent" of tenement house reformers.[31] Every element of the special committee's report met with favor, with the exception of this means of financing, and Radcliffe began a fund-raising campaign for a new and larger hall.

In keeping with the formality of the Georgian design of the residence halls, Radcliffe concentrated them in a symmetrical composition around an open green. Beaux Arts conceptions of college planning, the dominant tradition in the early twentieth century, emphasizing monumental masses and bilateral symmetry, came to Radcliffe with the building of this dormitory group. Sarah Whitman Hall took its place in the residential quadrangle. The addition of this sizeable Georgian brick dormitory assured Radcliffe's future direction. In time Barnard and Le Baron R. Briggs halls joined Whitman, giving Radcliffe the dormitory rooms of a women's college. Surrounding college land became Radcliffe's athletic grounds.

By Dean Irwin's retirement in 1909, Radcliffe was a curious hybrid. Academically, it remained an annex. The Academic Board of Harvard professors coordinated courses taught in the Radcliffe Yard exclusively by their university colleagues. Radcliffe had no separate faculty. Thus only men taught its women students.[32] But materially and socially, Radcliffe was a women's college. Women guided student choices and oversaw their living arrangements. Radcliffe students took courses, performed laboratory work, studied, practiced, met, rehearsed, had lunch, and relaxed in the academic quadrangle, the Radcliffe Yard. They slept, ate, and played sports in the residential quadrangle at a slight remove. In keeping with the breakthrough initially made at Bryn Mawr, these quadrangles took collegiate forms in formal compositions that gave no indication of the gender of the student body.

By the early years of the twentieth century, Radcliffe had changed direction. Breaking with its past, it chose to model elements of itself after the women's colleges. In these same years, Barnard was making the same decision. Like Radcliffe, Barnard chose to conceive of itself as a women's college and set about to create a campus to sustain that conception.

I I

While Radcliffe initially saw itself as an educational extension of Boston society, built firmly into Barnard's self-definition was its distinctive urbanity. Designed for New York students, Barnard initially emphasized its connection with the cosmopolitan culture of the city. A dominant image from the early years is the young commuter on the streetcar, rushing to get to class, trying to hold on to her obligatory hat.

By the turn of the century, Barnard had developed a unique blend of women's college and urban university. Barnard collegians enjoyed teas and dances with Columbia students, giving them a taste of coeducational university life. As seniors, they had classes with Columbia men. A Barnard senior reflected that in the classroom male and female collegians "have breathed the same erudite atmosphere; they have been subjected to the same soporific influence in lectures; they have taken sides with or against each other in class discussions." Unfortunately, knowing "the fiber of each other's mind" did not remove social barriers. The senior dreamed of a reception early in the term where the professor could introduce students properly and make it possible for polite men and women students to speak to each other outside class.[33] Students prided themselves that though they might have missed something of the intense college life of the women's colleges, they lived more normally and had fewer readjustments upon graduation.[34]

Unlike Harvard's annex, early in its history Barnard had developed significant elements of college life. Intense activity and discussion filled the college day. Class studies in the Milbank buildings provided central meeting places. Defying their name, the "studies" were places for gathering and chatting, not for serious work. "Before classes, between classes, and after classes, we retired to the jolly privacy of the study: there were our friends and there our books and hats and coats."[35] The senior study, with its great senior sofa, carried special honor as the location of great discussions: "woman suffrage, Pelleas and Melisande, Platonic philosophy, the cut of a professor's coat, or the intricacies of his character, the English budget and junior ball gowns."[36] The first class formed a sorority, which travelled north to Morningside Heights, where it and other sororities found rooms in college buildings.

While college life grew dramatically in the early twentieth century, as a day-campus connected with a large university in a great metropolis, Barnard had a special quality. It never lost this, but beginning at the turn of the century, the college began to reshape itself into the image of its country sisters. As it did so it acquired the one kind of building its founders assumed was unnecessary: the residence hall. Like Radcliffe, Barnard in the twentieth century decided to become a national institution. To do so in Barnard's case required it to downplay its distinctive history, attract Protestant students from outside New York City, build dormitories to house them, and identify firmly with the women's colleges. Each Barnard dean took a step in this direction. Virginia Crocheron Gildersleeve completed the process and confirmed it with the founding of the Seven College Conference.

In 1894, when Emily James Smith became dean, she brought Bryn Mawr's emphasis on intellectual discipline, high-quality instruction, and graduate op-

Undergraduate study, Milbank; *Barnard College Archives*

portunities to Barnard. She did not encourage Barnard's buildings to take the Jacobean Gothic forms of her alma mater. Only in naming her quarters in Fiske Hall "The Deanery" did Smith give any reference to her Bryn Mawr background, arousing M. Carey Thomas' ire for stealing the name ("Jim Smith's illness must have affected her mind. Did you know she had named her flat at Fiske 'The Deanery.' Just like her."[37]). In 1899, Emily Smith married publisher George Haven Putnam. In a move unprecedented in the women's colleges, the trustees allowed her to keep her position.

In the months that followed, Emily Smith Putnam and President Seth Low of Columbia negotiated an agreement that gave Barnard solid legal ground in the university. Under the university's federal system, Barnard took the same position as Columbia College. The university's president became the college's president and a member of its board of trustees. He appointed a dean for Barnard who sat on the University Council. Within this structure, Barnard's president, dean, and faculty shaped policy for the college. Gone was the compulsion that Barnard copy the requirements and programs of Columbia College. Barnard students had full access to the university library, and seniors took certain courses in selected graduate faculties. The 1900 agreement remains Emily James Smith Putnam's lasting achievement.[38]

Brooks Hall; *Barnard College Archives*

When the trustees learned of Putnam's pregnancy, they forced her to resign.[39] Barnard lost a wise and skilled, though frequently ailing, dean. By the agreement of 1900, the president of Columbia chose the next incumbent. Seth Low turned to Laura Drake Gill, a Smith graduate with a M.A. from the Sorbonne, who had administered Red Cross relief in the Spanish-American War.

Each Barnard dean faced a web of unresolved questions surrounding the college's relation to the university. Despite the firm footing that the 1900 agreement gave to Barnard, Laura Gill confronted knotty problems that her administrative experience outside the academy left her unprepared to resolve. She fumbled badly in her dealings with Low's successor, President Nicholas Murray Butler. In contrast to her growing national reputation in the Association of Collegiate Alumnae and in the College Equal Suffrage League, Laura Gill's Barnard years were a personal "nightmare."[40]

As Laura Gill faced Barnard's internal life, she felt on sure ground. Her Smith experience gave her a clear conception of what college ought to mean to young women. Barnard failed on two scores: its students were local and they came to campus only by day. What others had applauded as Barnard's cosmopolitanism, Laura Gill saw as "that most unlovely form of provincialism—the provincialism of a great city."[41] Even when Fiske was a dormitory, it largely served to house graduate students. In the years in which Barnard had no dormitory space, those students who needed rooms found them at Teachers College. To be a proper women's college, Barnard had to have a residence hall. The alumnae agreed and acquired a lease on an apartment building adjacent to the campus, which they fitted up as a temporary hall.

In 1902, Laura Gill outlined Barnard's most urgent needs. Land headed the list, followed by a dormitory "to give a nucleus for college social life."[42] Elizabeth Milbank Anderson, now Gill's loyal supporter, again provided the means to meet Barnard's physical needs. In 1903, she gave Barnard the 3.5 acres immediately to the south of Milbank Hall, all the way down to 116th Street. Small in comparison to the 300 suburban acres of Wellesley, the Anderson gift provided for New York City a large parcel of land, with an estimated value of a million dollars. This shrewd move gave the college room to expand.

Elizabeth Anderson met Laura Gill's second request and gave $150,000 for a dormitory named in honor of her pastor, Arthur Brooks. Designed as an urban residence by Lamb & Rich, the architects of Barnard's first buildings, Brooks Hall rose nine stories in brick and limestone to match the Milbank group some distance away. Built on a steel skeleton, it was a vertical rectangle. A handsome portico fitted with white limestone columns, an ornamental cornice, and bay windows kept Brooks from looking severe. Behind the façade, ninety-seven students lived in narrow singles or suites along corridors, while faculty women had larger rooms with private baths at the end of the building. As at Bryn Mawr, room prices varied greatly, depending upon location and amenities.[43]

Despite Brooks Hall's height, Barnard made efforts to minimize its scale. The dining hall on the first floor seated students around small tables of eight.[44] A floor held fewer than twenty dormitory rooms, of a size one contemporary called "small enough to be homelike."[45] While Smith drew on domestic imagery in cottages, Barnard took the New York apartment house as its primary reference, and added elements of the urban women's club. Elsie de Wolfe designed the interior public rooms, giving them "gilt appliqué like [the] parlor and tea room at [the] Colony Club."[46]

Brooks Hall began Barnard's partial transformation into a women's college along the lines of Vassar or Bryn Mawr. It did not change the composition of the student body as much as it affected those already enrolled. Laura Gill reported that while grades did not rise with residence in Brooks, students enjoyed a more pleasant life.[47] Barnard continued to draw its students from New York. But, with Brooks, a small portion of the more prosperous ceased riding the streetcars and moved to campus.

Beginning with the move to Morningside Heights, Barnard saw a flowering of student activities. Laura Gill encouraged college life, and her years saw
it pursued with a new intensity. The newspaper *Mortarboard*, class athletic ri-
valries, college dramatics, the Christian Association, and freshman hazing seized
hold of Barnard students as firmly as those of Smith. As at Bryn Mawr, observers recognized a new element at Barnard, "the girl who has come to college, not for the love of learning, but expecting to amuse herself."[48] Barnard's
songs encouraged these tendencies, urging students "to study hard and frolic
fast" in college days "of careless glee."[49] Barnard's special contribution to college life, which began with its classicist dean, was the use of Greek themes,
dramatizing women's new access to liberal learning. The Eleusinian Mysteries
initiated the freshmen, the dramatic club took the name Ai-Ai Hu, and freshmen and sophomores competed in the Greek games, an increasingly elaborate
pageant which became Barnard's equivalent of Wellesley's Tree Day or Bryn
Mawr's May Day.[50] Serious students found time to organize this life during
the college day. A contemporary described the frenzied existence of a "popular
junior or senior":

> After her morning classes, the girl tries to do everything at once. She goes
> upstairs to song-practice and wonders, as she joins in the vehement "*Rah*, rah
> for *dear* old *Barnard!*," why the dean wants to see her immediately. She hurries
> to the office, has a fifteen-minute interview, and dashes to a Y.W.C.A. com-
> mittee meeting. After despatching this business some one begs her to "come
> and Boston in the theater." Just as she is in the midst of a complicated dance,
> the business manager of the monthly pounces upon her, announces breathlessly
> that the printer has not sent the *Bear* yet; and the girl departs to reason with the
> printer. She returns to college in time for a two o'clock class; about three o'clock
> she makes for the basement lunchroom and implores the accommodating Mrs.
> Jameson to give her something to eat.[51]

To have even a small number of students on campus twenty-four hours a day
gave an important anchor to college life.

As at Radcliffe, the overwhelming majority of undergraduates continued
as day students. They needed a students' building for a lunch room, a reading
library, a gymnasium, club rooms, and living areas during the day between
classes and meetings. Barnard students campaigned actively for funds: one
entrepreneurial undergraduate even "sold" bricks on the streets, soliciting nickels
from passersby for bricks for the building.[52] In 1915, in honor of the fiftieth
anniversary of his arrival in America, Jacob Schiff gave over one-half million
dollars for a large building for all these purposes. Designed by Brunner &
Buckman & Fox, the four-story building of red brick trimmed in white stone
provided ample room. The vast gymnasium became the new scene of the Greek
games. The massive Roman columns and great arched doorway of Students'
Hall conveyed powerfully the solidity of Barnard's presence.[53]

Greek Games, 1920, Barnard College; the first with bobbed hair "horses"
Barnard College Archives

With the placement of Students' Hall, Barnard chose not to develop its campus, as had Columbia, in a Beaux Arts composition, governed by a central axis and the principle of symmetry. The design and site of the Milbank group and Brooks Hall had suggested that possibility. Symmetrical buildings by the same architect along the same axis, they faced each other at opposite ends of the piece of land—four blocks long and one deep—that constituted the Barnard campus. But the college rejected an internal Beaux Arts scheme for Barnard: it set Students' Hall squarely in front of Brooks, facing outward toward Columbia. One senses the desire at Barnard to make a small campus seem larger by separating its parts. The land between Students' Hall and Milbank became a picturesque park, known as the Jungle, whose trees blocked distant views of college buildings. This bit of overripe scenery was beloved by generations of students until it was removed for a library in the 1950s. The Jungle suggests Barnard's wish, in the midst of the city, to be a women's college. Like Olmsted's parks, it offered a symbolic refuge from sharp rectangular urban lines. It allowed the love of nature, so strongly cultivated at Wellesley and Mount Holyoke, to inform Barnard's life as well.

Tennis courts, the Jungle, and Barnard Hall; *Barnard College Archives*

Tension with President Butler and two operations to relieve a sinus condition forced Laura Gill's resignation, to no one's regret. In Virginia Crocheron
Gildersleeve, Barnard found the head it needed. To her classmates in Barnard's
class of 1899, Gildersleeve appeared destined from the beginning for the deanship. Her origins were in aristocratic New York. Studious and shy, she came
to Barnard to please her mother, but stayed to preside over her class and win
top scholastic honors. After graduate training in history, she taught English at
Barnard and, following a leave to get her Ph.D., was ready several years after
Laura Gill's retirement to assume her natural role.[54]

Virginia Gildersleeve entered her duties after a particularly trying period in
Barnard's relation to Columbia. In her conflict with President Butler, Dean
Gill had rallied the Barnard trustees, alienating them from the university's
president. With her resignation, one of the men on the faculty became acting
dean, a familiar and agreeable situation for President Butler. When Barnard
trustees insisted upon a woman dean, Butler attempted to protect himself from

gender conflict by creating the position of provost, which could be filled by a man. The provost was to hold academic power, reserving to the female dean external relations, building, and student supervision. Virginia Gildersleeve refused to become, as she put it, a mere chaperone to students, and the statutes were rewritten to provide her with authority over appointments and budget.[55] However, the signal from Butler was clear: Barnard was not to go its own way, but to coexist within the university. In 1922, Butler and Gildersleeve negotiated a new agreement between Barnard and Columbia which gave Barnard students greater access to the university and brought senior faculty greater prestige and opportunities. Faculty no longer exchanged teaching hours between parts of the institution: student fees served as the medium of trade, going into the treasury of the branch of the university from which the professor came. The appropriate graduate department voted on tenure appointments to Barnard and those holding Barnard professorships became part of the graduate faculty.[56]

Virginia Gildersleeve fought many other battles for Barnard, opening up graduate faculties to women, encouraging the international exchange of students and faculty, facing the mature woman's unsolved problem of reconciling home and work. Her view of Barnard was complex: she recognized and appreciated its urbanity and the strength it drew from the university; at the same time she worked to reshape Barnard and to bring it into closer relation with the other women's colleges. She patterned Barnard along the lines of Vassar and Smith. She encouraged college life, downplayed Barnard's distinctive past, promoted more national admissions, and oversaw the construction of a large residence hall.

In the 1910s, Barnard encouraged college life, as had Mount Holyoke in the 1890s, as part of a wider effort to attain status within the ranks of the women's colleges. Supported by alumnae, Laura Gill had promoted this in her brief administration, leaving in her wake the whole panoply of college organizations and Barnard's first residence hall. While Virginia Gildersleeve criticized Gill for trying to be a "mother" to students who valued their independence, she followed along her predecessor's path in encouraging college life.[57] A Barnard graduate who had been transformed by class spirit and intellectual stimulation, Virginia Gildersleeve sought to enrich college life at Barnard and make it more participatory.

Barnard never gave close oversight to students' morals. In the heady years of the early twentieth century it managed to avoid the entanglements that encumbered the other women's colleges. Students and faculty had the right to engage freely, not only in the fight for suffrage, but in the political movements of the day. In contrast to the illegal cemetery meeting for suffrage at Taylor's Vassar, Gildersleeve's Barnard had an active Socialist League. The Jungle boasted many a stump speaker for a controversial cause.

Two problems confronted Virginia Gildersleeve as she sought to pattern college life along the lines of the other women's colleges: sororities limited college life to a select minority; and students divided sharply along economic and ethnic lines. When the entire class of 1894 formed the first Barnard sorority, Kappa Kappa Gamma, little did they foresee 1912 when only one-quarter of the student body belonged to one of Barnard's eight Greek-letter societies. Students valued sorority membership "more highly . . . than any other college association." Forced out of college rooms in the Gill years, the sororities rented small apartments for their headquarters and held teas, receptions and plays, dances, meetings, and "spreads" there. They arranged country house-parties for members during vacations. On Barnard's day-campus sororities became the organizing principle of college life.[58]

Three-quarters of the student body remained outside. The sororities did not take Jewish members, even those who played a prominent part in college affairs. They left out those students too poor to pay the expensive sorority fees. Following college custom, it was taboo to mention sororities in college publications. In October 1912, Freda Kirchwey broke the silence to condemn sororities openly in the Barnard *Bear*. After listing the evils of Barnard's sororities, she responded to critics who proposed to reform, not abolish, fraternities for college women. The evils of fraternities were their "root and substance":

> Without secrecy and petty regulations, without exaggerated loyalty and artificial bonds, without social distinctions and the snobbery that inevitably accompanies them, without a certain unavoidable amount of politics—without all these, no fraternity can exist and be a fraternity.

Only the abolition of "useless and reactionary" Barnard sororities could return to the college its "birthright of Democracy."[59] Virginia Gildersleeve appointed a special committee of faculty, alumnae, and students, divided equally among members and nonmembers, to examine the question. The committee recommended that no new members be allowed to join sororities, thus effectively ending them within three years.[60]

As the controversy over sororities clarifies, Barnard's student body was not like that of the other women's colleges. By the turn of the century, commentators noted that Barnard had two types of students not found at Vassar or Smith: the young woman of modest means unable to afford the added expense of board at the "country college" and those from wealthy backgrounds unwilling to forgo the pleasures of New York society in their debutante years.[61] While significant, the extremes should not be exaggerated. Prerequisites barred daughters whose parents could not afford the special preparation, while the rigors of Barnard's academic schedule made it unlikely that truly fashionable young women would limit their time for consumption and entertainment. The

Barnard students in front of Milbank; Virginia Gildersleeve on bottom
Barnard College Archives

Alpha Phi, ca., 1912; *Barnard College Archives*

reaction of Mrs. Astor to Mrs. Duer's remark that her daughter Alice went to Barnard spoke for this group: "What! That sweet young thing!"[62]

Barnard also noted the cosmopolitan character of its students. Translated, this means that Barnard attracted and welcomed a significant number of Jewish students at a time when the other colleges reported only one or two. Initially these young women were German Jewish daughters who assimilated easily and enthusiastically: their presence formed part of Barnard's positive self-image as an urban college. By the Gildersleeve years, however, the numbers of poorer students increased, and Barnard attracted more ethnically conscious Eastern European Jews. Compared to the $425 fee for tuition and board at Mount Holyoke, the least expensive of the women's colleges, in 1914 Barnard charged only $150 tuition. State scholarships benefited seventy-one students, and this number greatly increased the next year when Joseph Pulitzer established scholarships covering tuition and other costs for thirty-nine students.[63]

The growing diversity of Barnard's student body can be read in the history of Barnard's Christian Association. As on other campuses the Christian Association presumed to speak for the whole college. As at Vassar, Smith, and Wellesley, it published the book given to freshmen giving college regulations and listing organizations. It welcomed the freshmen at a fall tea and gave weekly teas throughout the term. While active members of the Christian Association had to belong to an evangelical Protestant church, any Barnard student could become an associate member. Jewish students joined in the early years and served on important committees. None went to the encampment at Silver Bay, where women students from colleges and universities gathered each summer for fun and inspiration. The Catholics broke first from the Christian Association. The Craigie Club, founded in 1908, drew together those "who, because of their religion, are unable to participate in the comradeship that the Y.W.C.A. extends to the college." In 1912, the Barnard chapter of the Christian Association agreed to affiliate with the national Y.W.C.A., which required each member to pledge herself to the spirit of Jesus "as presented in the Gospels." This forced out the Jewish associate members. The college created the Religious and Social Organizations as an umbrella. Under it the Y.W.C.A., now frankly evangelical, took its place, along with the Newman Club for Catholics and ultimately the Menorah for Jews.[64]

Beginning in the 1920s, Barnard experienced what a later generation called "The Jewish Problem," the abundance of qualified Jewish applicants for admission.[65] Virginia Gildersleeve, like others of her age, made a sharp distinction between Sephardic and German Jews on the one hand and Eastern European Jews on the other. In one of her many campaigns to honor Jews associated with the American past, Barnard founder Annie Nathan Meyer had written to Gildersleeve asking for a donation. With her contribution, Virginia Gildersleeve commented, "I entirely understand and respect your desire to have an old New York Hebrew recognized as one of the fine citizens of the early days of New York. The immense influx during the years before the war of a particularly crude and uneducated variety of Jew from Russia and Central Europe gave rise, as you know better than I, to the strangest misconceptions of the nature of all Hebrews."[66] To Virginia Gildersleeve, this had a negative effect on Barnard. As a later letter to Meyer explained, "Many of our Jewish students have been charming and cultivated human beings. On the other hand, as you know, the intense ambition of the Jews for education has brought to college girls from a lower social level than that of most of the non-Jewish students. Such girls have compared unfavorably in many instances with the bulk of the undergraduates."[67]

To its credit, Barnard never established a Jewish quota, as did some other women's colleges in the period after World War I. But Virginia Gildersleeve committed the college to strategies to bring down the number of Eastern European Jewish students. She campaigned to make Barnard a national institution, drawing students from outside the city and region. The college strove to attain a "cross-section of the country geographically, economically, socially, and in other ways." As a Columbia observer noted, while this did not set up a formal quota system, it did rationalize "whatever policy the admissions office seems to pursue."[68]

The desire to transform Barnard into a women's college along the lines of its country sisters, appealing to elite daughters across the nation, led the college to downplay the distinctive role of New York City Jews in its history. The other women's colleges were firmly rooted in safe evangelical, Quaker, or Baptist hands. Radcliffe, while concerned about broadening its student base in much the same way as Barnard, relied on the prestige of its Unitarian founders. Tension had always characterized the relationship between the prominent Jews who gave early support to Barnard and the members of the New York elite attracted to the college. For example, a fragment from Ella Weed's hand commented to her correspondent, "You will see that the children of Israel have been ignored. The meeting should be a success."[69] Yet initially the two groups worked together effectively. As founder, Annie Nathan Meyer became an original trustee—unusual because she was both female and Jewish—and served until 1951. Jacob Schiff joined her on the board. But change pushed Barnard's Jewish leaders to the side. After Schiff's resignation in 1891, the trustees did not add another Jew to their number until the late 1930s. It is significant that in the 1920s, when the trustees renamed Students' Hall, they did not give it Schiff's name, but called it Barnard Hall, much to the anguish of Annie Nathan Meyer, who campaigned unceasingly to remove the impression that "the College is unwilling to place upon one of its buildings the name of a Jew."[70] Students, however, chose to remember Schiff: the plaque commemorating his gift became the favorite campus meeting place—"Jake."[71] Annie Nathan Meyer felt her role as founder underplayed in Barnard's collective memory and complained bitterly about being slighted in college histories and in twentieth-century anniversary celebrations.[72]

Under Virginia Gildersleeve, Barnard downplayed its distinctive history and urbanity to become identified as a women's college in the mold of Vassar or Wellesley. Initially all prestige had come from Barnard's association with Columbia. By the 1910s, the strength of the women's colleges brought Barnard into their orbit. Columbia's annex now perceived that it might gain in status if it were associated in the public mind with the women's colleges. To seal its connection to sister institutions, Barnard encouraged college life and attempted to attract Protestant young women from outside New York. As at Radcliffe, this required residence halls. Brooks was filled to capacity, and Barnard students were living in a number of different makeshift locations nearby. So strongly did the trustees feel the need to build that when no donor came forth, they authorized the building of a large dormitory from college funds. In 1925, Hewitt Hall opened with space for 250 students, making it possible for one-third of the Barnard student body to live on campus.

Designed by McKim, Mead & White, the architects of Columbia, Hewitt Hall formed a long arm of Brooks Hall up Claremont Avenue. Rising nine stories high on a steel frame skeleton, Hewitt's red brick and limestone matched Barnard's other buildings. A structure of elegant simplicity, described as Renaissance, it carried a cornice similar to Brooks, but with less ornamentation. Its flat wall surface contrasted with Brooks Hall's bays. The restrained use of limestone and terra-cotta trim provided the only ornamentation. Students entered the building through an elegant portico with columns. They adjourned to one of six small living rooms on the first floor which came to be known collectively as "mushrooms" or "manholes," a testament to Barnard's heterosexual social life.[73]

Virginia Gildersleeve had her own residence, which she called the Deanery, following Emily Smith Putnam's practice. Built into the north end of the first and second stories of Hewitt, with its own separate entrance, the Deanery made an elegant "townhouse." Furnished with gifts from college donors, its scale and detailing conveyed the interiors of Old New York in the middle of Barnard's Upper West Side campus. Persian rugs and old brass set an aristocratic tone for small-scale gatherings. A fitting backdrop for Barnard's refined—as well as energetic—dean.[74]

Hewitt signalled Barnard's full commitment to joining the ranks of the women's colleges. It is fitting that, in 1926, a year after Hewitt was built, Virginia Gildersleeve helped organize the Seven College Conference. Since 1915, Smith, Mount Holyoke, Wellesley, and Vassar had met informally to talk about common concerns. In 1925, Bryn Mawr joined with them for the first time.

Virginia Gildersleeve initiated a luncheon with the presidents of the five and of Radcliffe to talk about an association that might stimulate gifts. Out of this meeting the presidents formed the Seven College Conference, nicknamed almost immediately the Seven Sisters.[75] Through mutual association, Virginia Gildersleeve simultaneously solidified Barnard's image as one of the women's colleges—in the same league with Vassar and Bryn Mawr—and created a united appeal by the seven women's colleges to attract donors.

The landscapes of both Barnard and Radcliffe pay tribute to the power of the women's college in the early twentieth century. When Annie Nathan Meyer initiated the campaign for Barnard, she had no thought that opening Columbia University to women might re-create Vassar or Smith in New York City. Nor did Arthur Gilman envision Wellesley in Cambridge. The all-female world of the women's colleges had no appeal to either. By the twentieth century, however, both Barnard and Radcliffe saw the value of attracting young women beyond their metropolitan areas and offering to them the benefits of college life. Negative associations of women's college buildings with the restrictive world of the seminary had dissipated, and Radcliffe and Barnard now envisioned buildings whose exteriors harmonized with the universities in which they were a part. While Radcliffe and Barnard retained a distinctive urbanity and partook of the atmosphere of their universities, in the early twentieth century both looked to the women's colleges for guidance. They de-emphasized their distinctive local histories and traditions and attempted to strengthen college life and residence. Radcliffe and Barnard consciously adapted their images to fit that of their sister colleges and built students' buildings and residence halls to foster college life.

16

A Great Design

While, by the early twentieth century, Wellesley conformed comfortably to a common conception of the women's college, it shared with Mount Holyoke a distinctive characteristic. Although a man or two had joined each faculty, powerful women dominated the life of both institutions, as presidents and as professors. What this means is discernible most clearly on the land. Curriculum at Wellesley, as at Vassar, met the general requirements for liberal arts institutions, irrespective of gender, and thus was hardly distinctive. College life buffered students from the faculty's strong influence. It is the Wellesley campus that dramatizes the commitments of Wellesley's community of academic women.

On March 17, 1914, fire levelled Wellesley's College Hall. This cataclysmic event wiped out all tangible remains of Henry Fowle Durant's initial conception of the College Beautiful. Just as at Mount Holyoke, tragedy became opportunity. In the years that followed, Wellesley's female faculty successfully sought to create a college that fit their heroic self-conception. Wellesley today is their legacy.

Fire obliterated the seminary-influenced past in a night. Due to valiant efforts to rouse students and faculty, the college sustained no casualties. But all felt a deep sense of loss. In addition to destroying dormitory rooms, laboratories, classrooms, and administrative offices, the fire wiped out the great symbol of the college community, the beloved Centre. The college assembled for chapel the following morning. In a memorable service President Ellen Fitz Pendleton pledged the college to rebuild. The college launched a Restoration and Endowment Fund campaign headed by George Herbert Palmer to raise $2 million.[1] But 1914 was not 1875. However sentimental the alumnae, no one suggested rebuilding College Hall, a single building which combined residence, classrooms, offices, meeting rooms, and central gathering place. In 1914, what no one anticipated was that, in the rebuilding that followed the fire, Wellesley would obliterate its cottage past, as well. The college that emerged in the decades after 1914 expressed a compelling vision—an appreciation of the natural landscape linked to the Gothic quadrangle, expressive of a feminist commitment to scholarship. A complex of three dormitories rose on College Hill; on Norumbega Hill, the cottages gave way to an academic and administrative quadrangle which became the new heart of the college.

Planning for the new Wellesley was a long, complex process. It began with a donor who offered a large residence hall with vast ceremonial spaces. It continued with a plan commissioned by the trustees, which sited the donor's hall on College Hill and envisioned a Beaux Arts composition on the Great Meadow running from the library by the lake up to the observatory. At this point a new group entered in the planning: faculty women with a distinct vision of Wellesley fought openly against the trustees for a change of architects and a different design. They organized their campaign carefully and enlisted prominent alumnae on their side. They won. It is to them that Wellesley owes its present form. The plan that evolved sited the academic buildings on Norumbega Hill. With the hilltop building came a renewed understanding of the need to protect low ground from structures or formal landscape treatment. It took decades for Wellesley to complete what began in 1914. The campus today captures the vision of its women faculty of the early twentieth century.

Ironically, Wellesley's future came from its past. Louise McCoy North was an important alumna from Wellesley's early days. She exemplified the Mount Holyoke tradition: after graduating in 1879, she stayed to teach, and then married a minister. A close confidante of Pauline Durant during the agonizing years when the trustees took the college away from its evangelical commitments, Louise North served as the first alumna trustee and then as a regular life member of the board. Within three months after the fire, she convinced Ellen Stebbins Curtiss James, the donor of Hamilton College's library, to give generously to the rebuilding of Wellesley.[2] Under the pseudonym "Mr. Smith," Ellen James proposed to build for Wellesley a large residence hall. As a condition of the gift, she specified that the Boston architectural firm that had served her in the past, Coolidge & Carlson, design the building. This Beaux Arts–trained Boston firm was particularly experienced in college buildings, with commissions from Harvard, Hamilton, and Bates. Ellen James asked that before the college announce her donation, it establish a general plan.[3]

Since Caroline Hazard had authorized a plan in 1902, the college understood the value of long-term planning. Olmsted laid down certain principles of development in 1902: the special topography of the campus called for building on the plateaus of the hills in a style both "irregular and intricate." Within

a decade, however, the aesthetics of planning had changed. The early-twentieth-century belief in the need to conform to a site gave way to commitment
to formal composition. Colleges found the Beaux Arts planning of the 1893
World's Columbian Exposition especially attractive, for it promised to give
order to a large number of buildings with different uses. Campus after campus
took form according to Beaux Arts principles.[4] In 1912, President Pendleton
hired Shepley, Rutan & Coolidge to prepare a plan for the development of
the Wellesley grounds prior to erecting an additional dormitory. As the successor firm to H. H. Richardson, the Boston group were the pre-eminent architects of museums and libraries. Shepley, Rutan & Coolidge designed
Wellesley's library, erected in 1910, in proper Beaux Arts Renaissance form.
Following Richardson's death, they completed his plan for Stanford University. For Wellesley's master plan, Shepley, Rutan & Coolidge offered the pre-
dictable Beaux Arts composition, that fortunately never determined a single
building site.[5]

When the fire and Ellen James' gift required an immediate plan, the college
asked Coolidge & Carlson, in collaboration with landscape architect Arthur
A. Shurtleff, who had apprenticed in Olmsted's office, to prepare a design for
the whole campus. They completed their scheme quickly. The plan they outlined June 1, 1914, contained two parts. Most important for the donor, it reserved College Hill for student residence halls.[6]

College Hill provided the grand site for Ellen James' Coolidge & Carlson
building. The donor intended its vast public rooms to provide "suitable space
for the more formal and dignified social events and celebrations connected
with the College, in a measure, restoring a little of the old 'Centre' idea so
dear to the hearts of the alumnae." Later gifts furnished these rooms in a grand
manner. The donor also stipulated that the hall contain suites for "distinguished guests and visiting or exchange professors," including the visiting
minister.[7] Aware perhaps of the way that Vassar adapted Main in the twentieth
century, Ellen James suggested that the residence hall be reserved for Wellesley
seniors.

The trustees accepted the plan and the gift without thinking out its implications. It meant rooms for two hundred students, which the college desper-
ately needed, and assurance of Wellesley's future. On January 15, 1915, the
trustees laid the cornerstone.

The college named the new residence hall Tower Court. It rose as a massive
building of brick and composition stone. A seven-story tower dominates the
northern approach. From the motor entrance it rises as a wide, heavy square
surmounted by turrets and Gothic tracery. Except for the brick piers, the face
of the tower is stone, punctuated by large windows. Gothic decoration on
the lower levels gives external form to the great public spaces of the interior:

the arched windows of the foundation light the great double dining hall in the basement; the two-storied windows above, the reception rooms.

Tower Court's southern exposure explains its name. Extending south toward the lake are two residential wings, forming an inner courtyard. Due to the rise in the land, the tower appears a story shorter and becomes the center of a balanced composition. Polychromatic use of stone on the gables and dormers and above the doorways on the wings enlivens the view from the lake. The two additional dormitories that surround Tower Court form even longer arms to the lake, creating a vast courtyard at the center of which is the marker locating the once beloved Centre of College Hall.

Tower housed two hundred students, twice the number considered an appropriate residential unit by the college in 1915. Because of this, the college separated the two wings into two dormitories, Tower East and West, sharing a common dining hall and public rooms.[8] The double dormitory cost half a million dollars. The college treasurer regarded $1,500 per student as an appropriate cost for a residential building.[9] Tower almost doubled that sum, in considerable part because of the great public spaces. The donor's special interest in these led her to contribute an extra $20,000 for elaborate furnishings. A Gothic mood prevails in great fireplaces, stained-glass windows, and intricate wood paneling and carved furniture.[10] A monumental setting intended to replace the Centre, it provided an area for large gatherings but never became the object of sentiment. While students had passed to classes and appointments through the Centre, making it a natural crossroads, they entered the Tower Court living room deliberately, only for an occasion. Hammatt Billings had designed the Centre as a beauty spot: skylight, palms, statuary, and wrought-iron balconies embellished its vast open space. By contrast, the Tower Court living room is sombre, even severe, a room to engender awe, not affection.

As Tower Court took form, faculty and alumnae began to ask some hard and painful questions. Once the sole structure of Wellesley, College Hall remained until the fire the administrative, academic, and social center of the campus. Should academic buildings have taken its place on College Hill? If the building of Tower Court precluded this, might the long-dreamt-of students' building stand in a corner of that favored spot? The Coolidge & Carlson-Shurtleff plan also called for dormitories in five additional sites scattered around the campus: Norumbega Hill at the center and four locations along the perimeter. Like the Shepley, Rutan & Coolidge plan of 1912, the new scheme concentrated the academic buildings and placed them on the Great Meadow, a low stretch of land that ran from the lake to the Observatory. It offered the choice of a picturesque grouping around the meadow or a formal Beaux Arts composition.[11]

Twenty years before, when the siting of the chapel threatened the integrity of the natural wood, faculty and alumnae rallied behind Pauline Durant in protest. Now a much more serious incursion threatened. If realized, the 1914 plan would have destroyed the campus as four decades of students and faculty had known it. It would have transformed the center of Wellesley's pastoral landscape into a formal composition. In the twentieth century faculty and alumnae no longer needed indirect approaches. They sent no respectful petitions to the trustees or delegations to Lilian Horsford this time

Ellen Fitz Pendleton, who in 1897 had visited upon Lilian Horsford as a junior member of the faculty, was now Wellesley's president. The first alumna president, "Pres. Pen's" competent hands steered the college during the difficult years of rebuilding. She had complete mastery of detail. A mathematician who served as secretary and then as dean under Caroline Hazard, Ellen Pendleton engendered such clear respect that she allowed others to fight her battles.[12] She supported the women on the faculty in their struggle with trustees for control over landscape and building decisions. The art department took the lead for the faculty. Headed by Alice Van Vechten Brown, its distinguished and powerful creator, the department included Eliza J. Newkirk, an alumna and practicing architect; Agnes Abbot; and Myrtilla Avery, alumna and medieval scholar.[13] Confident that they understood the college's needs and its terrain, the women professors fought openly and hard. And they prevailed. While they began too late to stop the choice of College Hill for Tower Court, they won the major battle. The campus preserved its open spaces, even enhanced them. Wellesley sited its academic buildings on Norumbega Hill in a concentrated picturesque grouping of great power. And the college preserved the lowlands as an open park, edged with woods.[14]

The first sally came on October 27, 1914, when the art department wrote a comprehensive letter to the trustees stating confidently its special competence: "our familiarity with the ground and our study of its artistic possibilities in the light of our professional training." The letter set down certain guidelines to protect the picturesque quality and natural beauty of the campus. It insisted on the need for a "man of vision" to serve as supervising architect to create "a fully developed plan placing and massing future groups as well as the buildings now needed." The letter called for "a specialist in collegiate work," and specifically mentioned Princeton as the successful illustration of the effect of a master plan.[15] The art department not only had a job to be done: they had an architect. They based their letter on a belief that Wellesley needed Ralph Adams Cram. Remembered as a medievalist who wrested the Cathedral of St. John the Divine in New York from Heins & La Farge to return it to Gothic correctness, Cram enjoyed a large college and university practice. Not only Princeton, but West Point, Williams, Sweet Briar, and Rice felt his hand. In his academic work he showed a flexibility that belied his medieval polemics, and demonstrated an unusual sensitivity to siting and to campus building traditions.[16]

In the months that followed, the art faculty convinced powerful alumnae that Cram offered Wellesley's best hope; but the trustees held doubts. Treasurer Lewis Kennedy Morse spoke for them. In conversation, Alice Van Vechten Brown had repeated Bishop Lawrence's remark that the Cathedral of St. John the Divine selected Cram as architect because he was a "genius." Morse did not dispute Lawrence's judgment, but distinguished between the needs of a cathedral and Wellesley College: "A Cathedral demands architectural effects and does not have to consider an income on the investment"; it therefore can "take the large risks which the poverty of a Woman's College does not allow." Wellesley needed creative genius less than practicality, sense of economy, and adaptation to contemporary needs. Morse disapproved of Tower Court, for he believed that it set a bad precedent in creating expectations of grandeur too high for the future. Cram only made matters worse.[17]

Trustees, who expected to make decisions about college buildings alone, now faced a powerful department at their heels opposing the plan of a respectable architectural firm in collaboration with a well-connected landscape architect. Worse yet, the faculty were mobilizing alumnae support. Seeking some resolution, the trustees called a conference for January 29, 1915, with representatives of the faculty and alumnae. This gave official recognition to the two bodies, and they organized themselves into conference committees. The campaign of the art department now became a general faculty effort, and powerful professors from other departments joined Alice Van Vechten Brown and Eliza J. Newkirk: Alice V. Waite and Margaret P. Sherwood from English, Eliza H. Kendrick from Biblical history, and Elizabeth K. Fisher from geology.[18] Charlotte Conant, head of the Walnut School in Natick, and her co-worker and close friend, Florence Bigelow, led the alumnae committee, chaired by Candace Stimson.[19] After the initial conference, the executive committee of the board of trustees met regularly with the chairmen of the faculty and the alumnae committees.

On February 8, the faculty presented its full report. The faculty chose Ralph Adams Cram, making it clear that it did so free of alumnae pressure. The faculty came to its conclusion "deliberately by weighing all available evidence in the same manner that its members have been accustomed to decide other weighty College matters."[20]

The faculty report argued strongly for Cram on familiar grounds that the majority of trustees found unacceptable. But in doing so, the faculty gave full expression to their vision of Wellesley which lay behind their commitment to Cram. The women professors pointed out Cram's success in "great architectural compositions": his work has "the quality of the monumental, the feeling for mass, necessary in giving architectural expression to a great conception."

His imagination had "an heroic quality that would make him able to suggest visibly something of the splendid character of Wellesley as we see it—its faithfulness to duty, its justice, steadfastness and patience, its unselfishness in service, its aspiration, its high courage and heroism at need." While "residential parts of the grounds should be influenced by charming and intimate effects," when one approaches academic buildings one should be "raised to a higher plane of thought and emotion." West Point and Princeton gave just this elevation. Wellesley's faculty women wanted their college to convey the same aesthetic sensation as the two men's institutions.[21]

In fighting for an architect, the women of Wellesley's faculty revealed much about themselves and their conception of the college. Ordinary circumstances allowed them to run their own college under a president whom they regarded as one of their own. The faculty expected to exercise their professional competence and to dispute in reasoned arguments. In the 1890s, their concern about the campus began with the effort to preserve its natural features. By 1915, they linked their commitment to an English pastoral landscape to the hope for a symbolic expression of the college's inner life. While the Wellesley faculty constituted a community of women who shared their private lives as well as their work, it did not cast its self-conception in conventionally feminine terms. In 1915, American culture still distributed virtues and vices to the two sexes in traditional fashion. The Wellesley faculty included the typically female virtues of unselfishness and patience in its list; but added others associated with men—justice, steadfastness, and courage. The faculty cast itself in a distinctly heroic mold. It sought an architect to give monumental expression to this vision. For precedent it turned to male institutions, including the self-consciously masculine setting of the national military academy.

The fire reminded the Wellesley community of their vulnerability. Beyond the disaster itself, which threatened life and destroyed work, the rebuilding process made Wellesley's female community aware that its fate ultimately rested in the hands of a largely masculine board of trustees. Were the trustees, in their concern for economy and the resumption of business as usual, an alumna implicitly asked, "willing to let Wellesley have less than the best"?[22] The faculty wanted to insure that this did not happen. "A great design may be cut down and altered to meet limitations of price and so forth, and may still remain great, but a petty design can never afterwards be enlarged."[23]

Compromise gave both trustees and faculty what they wanted. The trustees picked the faculty and alumnae conference committees' second choice, Frank Miles Day of the Philadelphia firm Day & Klauder, as supervising architect, and in March 1915, commissioned him to create a master plan for the campus. Trained in London at the Royal Academy's School of Architecture, in his association with Charles Z. Klauder, Day had gained a strong reputation for his college work. He satisfied the trustees' need for practicality and economy. They then appointed Cram consulting architect to review Day's plan. By this process the faculty and alumnae got their genius and the artistic result.

Day immediately prepared his first plan. Responding to the constructive criticism of faculty and alumnae and to the brilliant analysis and judgment of Cram, Day ultimately made twenty-one plans. Two basic steps determined the academic center. Day contributed the first: the decision to build on Norumbega Hill. Day's plan followed Olmsted's design of 1902, only reversing, because of the siting of Tower Court, the location of residence halls and academic buildings.[24] While the college had long contemplated removing the wooden cottages—Norumbega, Wood, and Freeman—and replacing them with brick and stone, it assumed that the Farnsworth Art building and Wilder Hall would remain. Olmsted had criticized the symmetry of Wilder, a Georgian brick residence hall erected in 1900, but, because of its solid existence, had advocated a picturesque grouping of Georgian residence halls on Norumbega Hill. Day's plan kept Farnsworth, but required the moving of Wilder and no replacement of the cottages on that site. For a college which had just lost its major building to fire, to wreck consciously buildings on the ground was a bold move. But the college had no choice if it wanted to protect its natural setting. With the exception of the library and the chapel, major buildings had kept to hill sites, leaving low land free. Olmsted had applauded this and attempted to make it conscious college policy. On November 12, 1915, the trustees accepted Day's choice of Norumbega Hill.[25]

What happened on the hill required the intervention of Ralph Adams Cram. Day & Klauder worked in many different architectural styles, but held essentially Beaux Arts planning conceptions which balanced formal compositions of buildings along axes determined abstractly. Frank Day created a double tier of buildings on the southwest that climbed the hill. This Cram regarded as "a stroke of genius which demands the highest praise." At the top of the hill, however, the upper court violated the spirit of the land. Cram did "not endorse the formality and mathematical regularity of the upper court as indicated in the latest plan, being strongly of the opinion that the infinitely varied and strikingly picturesque contours" of the grounds should determine the siting of the buildings. Planning should avoid "exact right angles" and preserve the plateau on top of the hill "as it is, with all its trees."[26]

To the east the architects planned a formal composition that linked the quadrangle dormitories to the academic center. Cram also found this "inadmissible," for it violated "the picturesque site."[27] With Wilder removed, Cram urged Gothic forms, especially in its later, more feminine expressions, to harmonize with existing buildings and to allow the "irregular and spontaneous manner" required by the land.[28] "The unique topographical and landscape

Wellesley College, aerial view, between 1936 and 1958

qualities of the grounds must determine not only the general design but the disposition, alignment and composition of the buildings . . . buildings and groups should grow out of their sites and environment, not impose themselves on them, and . . . the great and beautiful features of hills, valleys, meadows, groves and winding roads should be preserved inviolate."[29]

Cram's report proved decisive. Day & Klauder reworked their plan to create the administrative and academic center on the ground today—Founders, Green, and Pendleton. The glory of the buildings is in their siting. From its eastern exposure, the liberal arts building, which took the name of Founders at the 1919 dedication, seems to come out of the earth itself. The walls below the crown of the hill are of rough-cut stone, as if they were made out of the very ground. The administrative building, Hetty H. R. Green Hall, built in 1931, joined the east wing of Founders. Pendleton, opened in 1936, completed the composition. The roofs of the three buildings form an irregular stepped outline which breaks out into a tall Gothic tower atop Green. The Galen L. Stone Tower, enclosing a thirty-bell carillon, dominates the composition and the campus. Rising ten stories on the edge of the top of the central hill, the tower's Gothic windows and turrets trimmed in stone became the emblem of the college.[30]

Contemporary architectural writers described Founders and Green as Continental Gothic, a Dutch interpretation from Spanish sources, creating an effect both "virile and scholarly."[31] Light stone trims brick walls at arched doorways, windows, and atop thin brick piers. The effect is crisp and dry. The projecting gables create a jagged, busy roofline. With its greater stretch of windows topped by horizontal lintels and minimal use of stone, Pendleton has a cleaner, more contemporary line. At a distance, however, distinctions diminish, and details are overwhelmed by the siting and by the powerful tower.

From the top of Norumbega Hill the long horizontal lines of the three academic buildings balance the upward thrust of the tower. Founders, Green, and Pendleton encircle the plateau, creating a handsome courtyard shaded by tall trees. A motor road winds up the hill from the east, protecting the courtyard from automobiles. A contemporary suggested that from the meadow the composition gives "an effect of massing on the top of the hill, comparable on a smaller scale to the effect of the hill towns of Italy."[32]

While the Wellesley campus saw many more buildings erected in the twentieth century, the construction of Tower Court and the academic quadrangle fixed the basic design of the campus. Out of a conflictual planning process came a fitting expression of the faculty's love of the natural landscape and their feminist commitment to scholarship. Olmsted and Cram had argued that buildings respect the land both in their placement and in their forms. The academic quadrangle and the Tower Court group did just that. Wellesley's academic quadrangle, in addition, boldly asserted the dignified calling and high hopes of Wellesley's community of academic women in the early twentieth century. In the rebuilding of Wellesley after the fire, the heroic vision of the women's college, which began at Bryn Mawr under M. Carey Thomas, found its most complete expression.

PART FOUR

The Post-war Women's College

World War I signalled the end of an era for the women's colleges. In the two decades that had preceded, the women's colleges had reached the high point of their influence and had moved toward a common design. In the years that followed the war, public criticism, new notions about female sexuality, and the changing nature of student life created an altered climate, less receptive to single-sex colleges for women.

The women's colleges differed in their responses to the new pressures. All of them were forced to accede to student demands for social "freedom." But some went even further. While Wellesley set its face to the wind and continued as it had been, Vassar designed a new curriculum intended for women students preparing to become homemakers and citizens. Mount Holyoke removed its female president and reoriented its campus. Even the colleges that refused to bend planned dormitories that reflected their concerns with students' sexuality. New colleges, without established commitments, sprang up, designed quite self-consciously for twentieth-century women. In their curriculum, governance, and buildings, Bennington, Sarah Lawrence, and Scripps most clearly illustrate the demands of the post-war world.

17

In Obedience to a Social Convention

COLLEGE LIFE AFTER 1920

The women's colleges had a remarkably good press in the early twentieth century. American magazines discovered the college girl. Article after article portrayed elements of college life: the traditions of the women's colleges; the pranks of college girls; the trials and joys of the freshman year; athletics, dramatics, and club life.[1] Undergraduates and young alumnae, such as Abbe Carter Goodloe, Jeannette Marks, and Alice Fallows, found a market for their observations and memories, and kept the magazines well supplied with articles.[2] Their reports surrounded the women colleges with a positive aura, contributing to their growing social acceptability. The glow suffused their women presidents and some of their faculty, as Jeannette Marks and other alumnae writers took them as their subjects.[3] In the Progressive years preceding World War I, the professional women who headed the women's colleges, taught there, or emerged from undergraduate ranks found a high degree of acceptance and respect in the society at large. As their nurseries, the women's colleges shared in the esteem.

A negative undertow existed from the beginning, however. As early as the founding of Mount Holyoke, critics of higher education for women had warned that liberal learning threatened femininity. In the early twentieth century, this criticism took a specific form: the women's colleges threatened the nation with race suicide. Racism flourished alongside Progressivism in the early twentieth century. While liberals looked to assimilation as a means of blunting the influence of alien cultures, conservatives decried the relative decline of Anglo-Saxon and Northern European stocks in the American melting pot. They placed the fault for this both in immigration policy and in the disinclination of the white Anglo-Saxon Protestant elite to breed. The most virulent racists aimed to close off immigration from Eastern and Southern Europe and Asia. As their second-

279

ary goal, they encouraged America's middle and upper classes to have more children.

To these eugenicists, the women's colleges posed a dangerous barrier to the continued dominance of Anglo-Saxons in America, for their graduates—of prime intelligence and racial stock—did not marry or bear children in adequate proportions. In the years around 1915, scholars came forward armed with statistics to prove that Mount Holyoke, Wellesley, Vassar, and Bryn Mawr graduates endangered the race. For Anglo-Saxons to survive, its women had to marry and produce three children. In contrast, these writers informed the public that only 50 percent of Mount Holyoke graduates of 1890–92 married, and those who did averaged fewer than two children. Wellesley and Bryn Mawr held the most dramatic statistics: only a third of the graduates of the last decades married and these bore only a child each. The women's colleges drew off "the best blood of the American stock and . . . [sank] it in a dry desert of sterile intellectuality and paralytic culture."[4]

What should the women's colleges do? Some critics put the issue outside the colleges' hands and urged parents to send their daughters to coeducational schools. As one writer put it, "Separate colleges for women . . . are from the viewpoint of the eugenist an historic blunder."[5] Others sought instead to reform the women's colleges. With little knowledge of the dynamics of college life, one professor urged that the solution lay in introducing "more strong men" and married persons of both sexes on the college faculties to serve as proper guides to youth. No staff of unmarried women could create a curriculum for young women to "idealize and prepare for the family and home life as the greatest work of the world and the highest goal of woman, and teach race survival as a patriotic duty."[6] With unreasoning faith in education as the solution to society's ills, critics agreed that the women's colleges needed to introduce domestic science into the curriculum to make women more appealing to men as "helpmeets and mothers of the new generation."[7]

While defenders of the women's colleges at the time argued that critics exaggerated the number of unmarried and childless graduates and mistook the causes of alumnae remaining single,[8] the basic thrust of the data remained unassailable. Alumnae of the women's colleges did not marry at the rate of their non-college sisters. In a society that forced women to make a choice between marriage and career, many college-educated women either explicitly chose careers or, in pursuing higher degrees or chosen work, cut themselves off unwittingly from opportunities to marry. Among the early Bryn Mawr classes, 53 percent remained single, in contrast to only 11 percent of American women in the same period who did not marry.[9]

These issues also troubled the Association of Collegiate Alumnae, but from a different perspective. Members of the ACA were not concerned about race suicide, but about the adult lives of college-educated women. The organization began in 1881, as a response to the need felt by alumnae to associate with other women who shared their interests and experience. Marion Talbot, a recent graduate of Boston University, found herself in the position of many alumnae, isolated from the world of her contemporaries by the serious purposes she had pursued in college. Prodded by her sympathetic mother, she called a meeting in her Boston parlor of other college graduates to discuss their common concerns. Talbot learned she was not alone in missing the serious friendships and intellectual discussions of college and, joined by those who attended the first gathering, issued a call for an association to link women graduates of the most demanding liberal arts institutions.

Undeniably, the pleasures of comradeship dominated the agenda of the ACA. Much of the energy of the organization went to defining its membership. The founding group circumscribed the colleges whose graduates were eligible to join. To prevent what they saw as the dilution of their degrees, leaders of the ACA fought against the incorporation of the Harvard annex as Radcliffe College and opposed the elevation of Mount Holyoke Seminary into a college. As colleges proliferated, graduates sought to certify the worth of their alma mater through ACA eligibility. Ultimately, however, leaders turned to questions of broader concern to college women. The first set of tasks that engaged the Association of Collegiate Alumnae involved proving that women could survive the rigors of college training without impairing their health. The ACA undertook a series of investigations to refute the statements of Edward H. Clarke in *Sex in Education* that scholarship caused women mental and physical damage. These studies addressed particularly the concerns of the early alumnae eager to defend the worth of their experience.[10]

At the turn of the century, the ACA began to take a more critical look at college education. It turned its attention to the lives of women after college, especially the minority of women who chose to marry rather than have careers. How could women with family responsibilities apply their knowledge both within and outside the domestic sphere? College had proven that they had brains but had left them unprepared for the challenges of household management and child care. In addition, their home responsibilities seemed to preclude participation in the world of work. Were there occupations, other than school teaching, compatible with women's traditional sphere? What responsibility did the women's colleges bear for preparing women for vocations both within and outside the home?[11]

After World War I, concern with the setting and content of women's higher education mounted. The conservative groundswell generated by wartime anxieties and dissatisfactions with the peace altered the public climate in which the women's colleges operated. In the generally liberal atmosphere before World War I, supportive to career and reform-minded unmarried women, only those concerned with race suicide openly questioned the women's colleges. With the conservative turn of the nation after the war, the women's colleges faced potential threats to their existence. Women reformers came under attack as pacifists and internationalists.[12] Opposition to policy turned personal, and conservatives mocked women reformers as spinsters.[13] As the training ground of these reformers, women's colleges came under scrutiny. In 1921, Vice President Calvin Coolidge openly attacked the seven women's colleges as "ministering to a new element which, sometimes, exhibits morbid tendencies" and as harboring "radicalism decidedly hostile to our American form of government" and to private property.[14] The larger public began to pay attention to the marriage rates of college women and wondered if the women's colleges inhibited healthy relations between the sexes.

They need not have worried. After the war, undergraduates of the women's colleges chose men of their own free will and accord. College life had consumed the energies of undergraduates at the turn of the century. In their all-female communities, collegians lived by their own rules, playing out dramas that transformed them. But while a fictional undergraduate of 1900 turned away from a male friend to "Vassar's all-sufficiency," her niece twenty-five years later would have found Vassar alone insufficient—indeed boring, perhaps even a bit threatening.

What separated the two generations of college women was the sexual revolution. As the writings of Havelock Ellis and then Sigmund Freud entered into the consciousness of educated Americans, their assumptions about the nature of women radically changed. In the nineteenth century, middle-class Americans had revised earlier notions about women to emphasize their purity and spirituality. The cult of domesticity had turned woman the temptress into woman the chaste, who had the task of creating a Christian home in which both husband and children grew in virtue. While more reasonable ministers and physicians did not deny that women had sexual natures, they assumed that women's sexuality remained latent until awakened properly by a man in the marital bed. Female friendship, however intimate, posed no threat, because it existed between two spiritually alive but sexually unawakened beings.[15] The all-female world of the women's college seemed an appropriate holding-ground for young women too young to choose a husband.

Sophisticated Americans learned in the early twentieth century that women had active sexual natures, not latent ones.[16] This had two important effects on attitudes toward college women and ultimately on female collegians' own consciousnesses. Sexuality which did not require male potency to bring it into being could turn to women as well as to men. This called into question female intimacy, which, as we have seen, was built into the original design of women's colleges. "Crushes" came under open scrutiny, and writers in the periodical press called on mothers to monitor closely their daughter's behavior in college.

Two Bennington students in open automobile, 1932–33; *Bennington College*

One anonymous writer warned mothers that while nine-tenths of such friendships were innocent, one-tenth involved "moral degenerates." She described a
"mutual crush": the young women involved felt guilt and profound unhappi-
ness because they knew that their relationship was "not legitimate." [17] The word
lesbian had not entered into common parlance, but young women and their
mothers clearly understood the concept.

Not only did female collegians begin to feel uncomfortable with the single-
sex world of the women's college, they began to feel deprived as well. If they
had sexual natures, then why did they waste themselves in a world without
men? Their contemporaries in coeducational universities were enjoying the
pleasures of casual dating. Not only did they see men in class or as they walked
across campus, they enjoyed movies, restaurant meals, and drinking and dancing with them in roadhouses. An elaborate set of rules governed the erotic
exchange between college men and women; but to the women confined
to single-sex colleges, the opportunities and behavior of coeds spoke of
freedom. [18]

Undergraduates at the women's colleges made no perceivable move to transfer
to coeducational institutions. To do so risked some loss of caste. As we have
seen, beginning at the turn of the century, daughters of the upper middle class

entered the women's colleges. For example, at Vassar, in the years between 1919 and 1922, over half the fathers of students were manufacturers, merchants, lawyers, bankers, brokers, or doctors. As at Bryn Mawr, the Episcopal Church, the fashionable denominational affiliation of America's Eastern elite, claimed the greatest number of adherents.[19] By the 1920s, prominent families expected their daughters, as well as their sons, to attend college.

When queried in the late 1930s about why they had chosen Vassar, alumnae from the classes before 1919 generally assumed that the question asked why had they gone to college at all. They most frequently answered that they had gone to Vassar with their family's encouragement to prepare themselves for professional work. For the classes beginning in 1920, the sense of the question shifted. Since they had always assumed that they would go to college, alumnae addressed themselves to the question of why they had chosen Vassar over other colleges. They answered most frequently that they had come to Vassar because "My friends were going" and because in their families Vassar had become a tradition. One member of the class of 1920 put it this way, "Six of my classmates were going to Vassar, so I drifted along with them. I doubt if I thought much about selecting a college or had any clear idea of why I was going." An alumna of the class of 1928 ended up at Vassar because "my family packed me off. I didn't object seriously."[20]

By the 1920s, going to college was the thing to do. President William Allan Neilson of Smith compared the students gathered to hear him to that "handful of eager souls, brought into this place because of their appetite for intellectual things," whom L. Clark Seelye had addressed in 1876. "Today we have here 2,000 students gathered—one must confess—largely in obedience to a social convention." To Neilson, once education became "the thing," Smith faced defeat "by its own success."[21] His students, however, hardly agreed with this assessment.

In this atmosphere of social respectability, the class barrier that had separated the men of Harvard, Yale, and Amherst from Wellesley, Vassar, and Smith vanished. Once their social equals made their way to the women's colleges, Ivy League men found the company of female collegians fully acceptable. The automobile made them accessible as well.

As men came on to campus to dances or took women away in their automobiles, the all-female world of the women's college dissolved. College life, as it had been known before World War I, began to ebb. Students turned the energy that had once gone inward into the college community—into college organizations, teas, and athletics—outward toward men. Female collegians did not cease to have friends or to run for student government, but their sense of the location of college's central drama shifted. Letters home, so recently filled with the calendar of college life, turned to dances, dates, and feelings about

Students awaiting transportation, Bennington, 1932–33; *Bennington College*

men. College women did not suddenly become hedonistic: they had been so for decades. What happened in the 1920s is that their hedonism turned to focus on men.

The women's colleges experienced these shifts in several ways. Students lost the "gang spirit" that had characterized college life before World War I. As a Vassar alumna from the class of 1908 looked back in 1930, she wondered, "How could we have wasted so much time in marching and cheering?" She saw meaningful change at all the Seven Sister colleges. The presence of men transformed students, who in her day had taken the part of the "hero," into feminine beings. As college students from the Ivy League visited the women's colleges on the weekend, the campuses assumed the appearance of coeducational colleges. Men took the male roles in college dramatics. In 1929, the last holdout—Bryn Mawr—held its first tea dance and had Princeton men act in plays.[22]

The entry of men into the formerly all-female domain of the women's college not only changed students' demeanor, it also altered the nature of communal life. College culture no longer revolved around team sports. While enthusiasm for athletics remained, students played more individualistic sports, such as tennis and golf, rather than basketball. They began to take up the

Mount Holyoke Hoover Club, 1928; *Mount Holyoke College Library/Archives*

games of the privileged: yachting, skiing, and fox-hunting.[23] Religious expression waned. The Christian Association had trouble getting members. As chapel became voluntary at Vassar and Barnard, it attracted only a minority to its services. Other colleges kept it mandatory in order to insure attendance.[24]

Students' political involvement declined markedly. The suffrage movement had generated considerable interest in the women's colleges. Each campus had its suffrage club, even if it required a graveyard meeting to evade a presidential ban. The seven colleges marched triumphantly in New York's great suffrage parade, each student group proudly carrying its college banner. The college settlement association had active chapters that introduced undergraduates to reform and served as a haven for young alumnae needing residence and meaningful work. World War I brought undergraduate idealism to a head. Mount Holyoke, Wellesley, and Vassar students staffed college farms as war work. Smith alumnae sent a Red Cross relief unit overseas, and the other colleges followed their lead. Students turned from dramatic productions to rolling bandages, from birthday feasts to meatless meals. As it mobilized for war, each women's college community was a microcosm of the larger society.[25] Each college also experienced intensely the letdown that followed. Students in the women's colleges helped initiate the reaction that engulfed the United States with the Armistice.

"We're not out to benefit society . . . or to make industry safe. We're not going to suffer over how the other half lives." This comment by one anonymous student summed up the political posture of most students in the women's colleges in the 1920s.[26] Mock elections, which generated less interest than their predecessors before the Nineteenth Amendment, confirmed the conservative cast of student bodies committed to the normalcy of the post-Progressive years.[27] Yet it was less conservatism than a retreat from the public world that characterized college life between the wars. Debating societies, once the object of keen competition and broad student interest, disbanded. Political clubs ceased to fight for particular causes and pooled members as informational forums. In the 1930s, a minority of college women in the Seven Sisters returned to political debate, but even during the Depression, private rather than public concerns shaped campus life.[28]

The traditions which formerly structured the college calendar lost their hold. "Even Wellesley, where the sentimental traditions are perhaps strongest, has difficulty in marshalling sufficient quota to make Senior 'step-singing' really affecting," reported an observer in 1930.[29] By then Vassar had lost its debating societies, its ride to Mohonk, and held on to step-singing only because "three of our classmates attended regularly."[30] As a writer in Wellesley's *News* lamented, "Debating has died out, I.C.S.A. has disbanded, College Government feels itself to be in such a poor condition that it has to make a radical change, Barnswallows made a mistake which has been enormously magnified, and the College *News* is dull. Nothing is in good condition but the acid critic."[31] A student writing in the *Vassar Alumnae Magazine* in 1936 conveyed the mood of the campus to its readers: "As this magazine goes to press, 30 per cent of the college is disturbed because the other 70 per cent is more interested in the bridge table and the movies than in trying to ascertain the proper function of a liberal arts college."[32]

In such an environment, little impelled campus traditions beyond inertia. While it had once been necessary to initiate freshmen into an all-female community whose culture differed in marked ways from that of the surrounding society, after 1920 no such need existed. College differed little from home. Tree Days remained but ceased to command the attention or genuine interest of many students.

What did engage women students in the years between the wars was the effort to knock down the restrictions that limited their "freedoms." At the Seven Sister colleges, as at other colleges and universities across the country, conflict raged over sex and its symbols. Students wanted the rights of access to the opposite sex, to privacy, and to pleasure. Two elements made the struggle on women's college campuses more intense than at other places. Heterosexuality required either bringing men on to campus or the right to leave it. Efforts to get proms and more informal dances, to have men act in plays, and to be able to ride in automobiles joined campaigns for the right to smoke and the liberalization of rules relating to chaperonage and curfews. And because the entry of young men into the immediate lives of undergraduates violated the traditional relationship between students and their female faculty, change meant a poignant loss not experienced elsewhere.

In the nineteenth century, men had come on to campus for occasional ceremonial occasions. Beginning in 1884, Wellesley students invited men to the Junior Promenade, where they had refreshments and enjoyed "a walk, en masse, to the music of a band along a prescribed route, decorated with lanterns."[33] As late as 1905, Mount Holyoke kept its Junior Prom a promenade, although it was rumored that brave couples took a waltz step or two in the bowling alley in the basement.[34] Wellesley also welcomed men to Float Night, an annual benefit for the college, where students performed in crew boats on Lake Waban. Vassar invited men to Founder's Day; Bryn Mawr to the May Day festival. Student pressure increased the number of these occasions and altered their nature. In 1894, Smith juniors added ballroom dancing to their prom; Vassar joined in 1897; Wellesley, in 1913; and Bryn Mawr held its first tea dance in 1929. The events themselves grew in scale. The Junior Prom for the Wellesley class of 1925, for example, took place over an entire weekend: the Williams College Dramatic Club performed on Thursday, and dancing followed; Friday night saw dancing in the society houses; on Saturday, there was tea dancing in the afternoon, a formal dinner, and a prom, by then a full evening of ballroom dancing. The 1920s differed from the 1960s, however, or even the 1940s. The college ordered a trolley car to take prom dates away at 12:10 a.m.[35]

In addition to these formal occasions, students at the women's colleges fought to bring men on campus for informal afternoons of picnicking or evenings of dancing. While Smith had always prided itself on its lack of rules, Wellesley students had to break through the regulations requiring chaperonage, even for dinners out. Wellesley's all-student House of Representatives took matters into its own hands and voted that students could go to the movies unchaperoned in the evening. This presumption led the faculty to resign from the joint faculty-student College Government. The House of Representatives then quickly moved to abolish the restrictions that most offended student freedom: students gave themselves the right to go on automobile drives on Sunday and in the evenings; to walk in the Harvard Yard without a chaperone; and to return on a train later than the evening 7:16. Bending to student will, the college confirmed the students' right to make their own rules, officially granting the House of Representatives the power that it had claimed *de facto* of legislation over chaperonage.[36]

Mount Holyoke faced issues quite similar to those of Wellesley and resolved them in similar fashion. Step-by-step, the faculty grudgingly acceded to student demands to liberalize chaperonage, allow students to return to their dormitories increasingly late in the evenings, and permit dances on campus with men. Mount Holyoke's governance system came under fire. Students now able to vote on such issues as the League of Nations resented their inability to determine the rules to govern their own lives. As restrictions became fewer and were enforced more tolerantly, the "ugly fact of the restriction" felt more insulting. Vocal students demanded "self-imposed discipline" rather than the "externally imposed discipline" of the *Students' Handbook of Faculty Legislation*. A student who titled her tirade "Rules, Regulations, and Revolution" declared, "Whenever I consider the 10 o'clock rule, I want to mount a soap box and wave a red flag."[37]

Smith had always emphasized its students' informal adherence to ladylike decorum, unlike the reliance of Mount Holyoke and Wellesley on rule books. But even Smith had to face the demands of the new era. The one rule that the college had enforced since its founding was the ten o'clock rule, which, as at Mount Holyoke, required students to assume a "horizontal position between the sheets" after they turned their lights out at ten. Students who needed to study later applied for light cuts. Their frequency weakened the rule, which became unenforceable. In 1921, to the displeasure of President Neilson, Student Government abolished the regulation.[38]

At all the women's colleges, smoking proved to be the most highly charged issue. This is curious, for unlike access to automobiles or extending curfews, it seems on its face to have the least relation to sexual freedom. Why was smoking such an issue? In the late 1910s and 1920s, the health hazards, while perhaps suspected, were largely unknown. A Bryn Mawr alumna of the class of 1927, the daughter of two Bryn Mawr faculty members, and a prominent anthropologist, uncleared the mists. In the early twentieth century, smoking was, in her words, "the gesture of the brothel."[39] It was the outward sign of acknowledged female sensuality. Its lure for the female collegian was that it announced her sexual maturity and her interest in men even when she remained in the weekday company of women. As they voted repeatedly against allowing students to‚smoke on campus, college administrators and faculty understood smoking's symbolic meaning.

At Wellesley the issue first surfaced in 1918, when a ban on smoking proved necessary for the first time. In the early 1920s, the college "campused" all the residents of one dormitory because they tolerated, without reporting, smoking by the thirty-two students who confessed to the deed. Students brought the issue before college government. President Ellen Pendleton spoke in vigorous defense of the faculty ban. Faculty almost unanimously opposed smoking and had defeated a move to allow it, on the grounds that "to sanction smoking is contrary to the spirit and traditions of the College." Students up-

1905 Junior Prom in Students' Building, Smith

held faculty will in the letter but not in spirit, forbidding smoking on campus or within the towns of Wellesley or Natick. "The result was the invention of a favorite pastime for that whole college generation—walking to the boundary lines of the town to sit on the old stone walls and smoke." Townspeople and faculty had to live with the unpleasant sight of "long rows of girls perched on their walls . . . puffing industriously." Finally, in the late 1920s, the college established smoking rooms in Alumnae Hall, Wellesley's version of a students' building.[40]

Mount Holyoke's students retreated to smoke "behind tombstones in the old cemetery," as faculty and students debated the issue throughout the 1920s, constrained by President Mary Woolley's repeated declaration that she would never give Mount Holyoke students the right to smoke.[41] Bryn Mawr ended almost a decade of debate when President Marion Park allowed smoking by executive decree. However faculty might regard the issue of smoking, to continue the rule in the face of widespread student disobedience seemed to threaten the standards of civility necessary for communal life: "No democracy can keep on its books a regulation . . . that no longer rests solidly on intelligent public opinion." President Park preferred to allow smoking than to continue conditions undermining trust.[42]

In the 1920s and 1930s, while the women's colleges could go far in responding to the demands of students for greater personal freedom and the right to access to men, those not coordinate with men's colleges faced a clear limit. Barnard and Radcliffe could bring men and women together during the work week, but the other five of the Seven Sisters kept the genders apart except for play. Vassar, Smith, Wellesley, Bryn Mawr, and Mount Holyoke retained a distinctive atmosphere, quite different from that of coeducational institutions. A critical Vassar alumna from 1928 recalled her reactions:

> I hated the noisy artificiality of the place: so many women at such close quarters, the lack of freedom to live where and as one chose, and what I called at the time "remoteness from real life." I had been brought up to be allowed to smoke, to motor with men, to stay out late in the evening. The restrictions at college were naturally very annoying. I had learned that men were not tin gods on wheels in yellow Packards with invitations to proms, but were congenial companions with whom one could live side by side in friendship and intellectual sympathy and love. All that seemed very remote from college and I hated the lack of it.[43]

While some students rankled at the colleges' special atmosphere, most women seeking the prestige of one of the Seven Sisters accepted ultimately the accommodations the colleges made to their heterosexual needs.

As a new generation of college women struggled to open their world to men and to the new freedoms possible after World War I, they experienced the mature women on the faculty and administration in a quite different manner from students who had preceded them. While distance had separated the "all-round girl" from her professors in 1900, the female collegian had generally admired her teachers from afar. After 1920, female faculty and administrators became Others. Conservatives had taken to calling unmarried women reformers "the third sex," suggesting that in their single state they were neither male nor female. College women started to look on the women who taught and guided them in the same derogatory light. The old intimate relationship persisted for a few talented students. A small minority continued to seek out and imitate their professors, as had the generations that had preceded them. The chain of teacher and student that began with Zilpah Grant and Mary Lyon, though thinned, continued unbroken. The dominant mood, however, changed. Students' respect for their faculty no longer extended automatically outside the classroom: few thought of modeling their futures after unmarried women professors.[44]

Women faculty and administrators felt betrayed. Only a few years earlier, they had been objects of student admiration. Now they were cast in the role of upholders of the Victorian moral order that had lost its hold over the young. Faculty and administrators, in turn, looked askance at students. A committed reformer, such as Wellesley's Vida Scudder, experienced the 1920s as the bleakest years of her life. Her autobiography ceases after the war to talk about teaching, other than to mention that "students came and went, seminars still met in my attic study." In reflecting on these "ten exhausted years" more generally, she wrote that "it was not easy to watch the surging flood of disillusion which threatened to submerge the idealism and drown the hopes of the world."[45] Barnard, in cosmopolitan New York, with its largely day-student body, had the fewest issues to trouble its president, Virginia Gildersleeve. Yet she shared her colleagues' dissatisfaction with students in the interwar years. She saw students in the 1920s as moved by "blasé indifference, self-indulgence, and irresponsibility."[46]

This changing relationship between faculty and students underlay the conflicts in the Seven Sister colleges that began after World War I. Students and faculty in women's colleges fought the same issues as those in male and coeducational institutions: they waged their battles, however, at a more intense pitch.

Each campus differed in the manner in which conflicts found resolution, reflecting the particular nature of its community. As each college searched to strengthen or redefine its mission in the years following the war, it responded both to the particular issues that students raised and to the concerns of the public. Wellesley's tradition of female faculty power perpetuated feminist imagery through the 1930s. Under the leadership of a male president, Vassar, however, embarked on a new course, designed to confront the new issues of the 1920s. Vassar built a great Gothic tower to house a college curriculum based on the needs of the home. The long tenure of Mary Woolley at Mount Holyoke—1901 to 1937—and her commitment to pre-war approaches insured that Mary Lyon's institution faced the conflicts most sharply. Ultimately the trustees forced Woolley's retirement and replacement by a man in the Smith mode; Mount Holyoke turned away from Gothic monumentality to build a new modern campus expressive of the college's adaptation to a new age. While the other Seven Sisters kept curriculum and campus intact, at least to the outside, as they built new dormitories, each corresponded to a new sense of the needs of heterosexual college women. Smith, for example, ultimately added to its complex, heterogeneous campus a controlled environment, outwardly designed as Georgian quadrangles, but inwardly planned to protect femininity.

As the Seven Sisters confronted the post-war world, they found themselves limited by tradition, faculty, and monumental buildings. Three new colleges launched in the 1920s faced no such constraints. Sarah Lawrence, Bennington, and Scripps quite consciously framed themselves as alternatives to the Seven Sisters. Their curricula, plans of governance, and building schemes clearly underscored their intention to create colleges for twentieth-century women. In the creation of Sarah Lawrence, Bennington, and Scripps, we can discern most clearly the pressures brought to bear on the women's colleges in the years after World War I.

18

In the Spirit of Our Times

VASSAR, MOUNT HOLYOKE

Virginia Gildersleeve disliked the changes in students that she saw in the 1920s. While she bent to student demands for greater personal freedom—allowing students to discard the hats they had worn by college regulation—she saw no reason to alter their education or adjust Barnard's campus to fit post–World War I notions about women's sexual nature or future prospects. Neither did Bryn Mawr, Wellesley, Radcliffe, Mount Holyoke under Mary Woolley, or Smith under the deanship of Ada Comstock. It is intriguing that these colleges were led by women who had committed themselves to academic careers at the turn of the century. In sharp contrast, Vassar and Mount Holyoke after Woolley's retirement, both headed by men, moved in a different direction. Vassar established a program to apply the liberal arts to the home and built a section of the campus to contain it. When a man took over the presidency of Mount Holyoke in 1937, he did not alter the curriculum, but he attempted to bring men to the faculty and to reorient the campus.

I

The creation of the Euthenics program at Vassar was a dramatic act. Vassar, the pioneer, had set out to give women the education of Harvard and Yale. While its system of discipline and buildings bowed to nineteenth-century conceptions of womanhood, female students took courses identical to their brothers in male liberal arts colleges. In 1924, Vassar departed from its past to establish a program which adapted the arts and sciences to homemaking.

In 1914, Vassar students sentimentally serenaded James Taylor upon announcement of his retirement, but the faculty expressed unabashed delight.

Lucy Salmon led the faculty in the interregnum year to reorganize its own body in a democratic fashion, to find direct ways to talk to the trustees, and to presume to set educational policy. Symbols of a new emancipated Vassar abounded: seniors donned cap and gown for graduation; a weekly news supplement to the *Miscellany* appeared; the students organized a Woman's Suffrage Club on campus, followed by a Socialist Club.[1] Henry Noble MacCracken's selection as president insured the liberalization so long delayed. A Chaucerian scholar who was neither Baptist nor a minister but who was a genuinely liberal and democratic leader, MacCracken encouraged the independence, cooperation, and political expression of faculty and students. They responded warmly to his presidency.

But not the trustees. In 1918, they tried to bring him down. The technical issue involved a new heating system's expenditures, which got out of hand during the war years when MacCracken went on partial leave for war service. The real issue was the correct perception on the part of the trustees of the man they had mistakenly chosen as president. MacCracken entered a presidency whose authority was blocked at every turn by fiefdoms reporting directly to trustees: gardener, director of halls, even dean. In trying to gain control over the budget and over personnel, MacCracken incurred the wrath of Charles M. Pratt, then chairman of the board of trustees. Pratt found him "difficult and uncooperative" and demanded his resignation. MacCracken determined to hold on and fight, without, however, hope of persuading the majority of trustees "that Vassar is anything more than the plaything of Mr. Charles Pratt."[2] MacCracken meant to change the way Vassar was governed. And he clearly meant to change it in a liberal direction. Pratt and other important trustees were deeply conservative. The unanswered question is why the trustees ever chose MacCracken in the first place.

Faculty and the women on the board of trustees fought to save Mac-Cracken. With the strong support of students, they won.[3] After the war, MacCracken returned to the full responsibilities of the Vassar presidency, with an agreement from the trustees that he could reorganize the administration and, with the faculty, determine new rules of college governance.[4] Mac-Cracken was firmly committed to liberalizing the college. He also felt grateful to the women on the board who supported him, and wanted to strengthen their hand.

Euthenics proved to be his strategy. Ellen Swallow Richards coined the word, defining it as the scientific study of the home. A generation of progressive reformers extended women's role as homemaker to include the sidewalks, streets, water, and sewage of their communities. In encouraging women's entrance into the public arena, a prominent suffrage leader urged them to become housekeepers to the nation. In 1917, the Smith-Hughes Act authorized federal funds for the teaching of home economics in land-grant colleges. One result of this was the New Jersey College for Women (renamed Douglass College in 1955), intended by the graduates of Barnard who initiated it as the annex of Rutgers. At N.J.C., home economics joined the liberal arts as legitimate college subjects.[5]

Julia Lathrop, a Vassar graduate of 1880, and a co-worker of Jane Addams in Hull-House in Chicago, brought this vision of reform to Vassar. At the fiftieth anniversary celebration she urged that Vassar become the center of research into family living. The war years promised just that. In 1918, Minnie Cumnock Blodgett, of the class of 1884, originated the idea that Vassar become the "female Plattsburgh," the training ground for women entering war service. Toward that end Professor Herbert Mills directed a Training Camp for Nurses designed for college graduates. In the summer of 1918, over two hundred students became Farmerettes, staffing the Vassar farm to replace the men called into the army or to war-related jobs.[6] When the war ended, the vision of young women scientifically trained for feminine service that transcended the boundary between home and polity became the basis of the largest single gift Vassar had yet received. In 1923, Minnie Blodgett offered $250,000 for a hall for Euthenics, a gift later enlarged to $550,000.

Prior to her gift, as chairman of the trustee committee on Household Management, Minnie Blodgett had recommended to the board that Vassar establish a Division of Euthenics to coordinate courses already being offered in the practical application of the arts and sciences to the home. The trustees agreed and sent the issue to the faculty. Here disagreements surfaced and the faculty decided to wait until MacCracken's return from abroad. Committed to the reform element of Euthenics and wanting to strengthen the women on the board, MacCracken announced to the faculty both the gift and his commitment to the creation of a Euthenics program. Some of the women faculty felt deeply stung. Margaret Washburn, Vassar's eminent psychologist, cried to MacCracken, "You are driving women back into the home, from the slavery of which education has helped us to escape."[7] Mabel Newcomer, the economist notable for her work on women and education, refused to associate with Euthenics in any way.[8] Prodded by professors committed to the idea, enough faculty reluctantly conceded to allow MacCracken to present a majority vote supporting Euthenics to the trustees.[9]

To ask, what was Euthenics? is to ask how the blind man saw the elephant. Perspective depends upon where one stood in the struggle. For MacCracken, Euthenics was a critical step in taking Vassar out of the hands of conservative trustees and delivering it to forward-looking women. Progressivism shaped his politics, and Euthenics was an extension of its female-dominated reform side, embodied by Julia Lathrop. Pedagogically, it promised to link the sciences and humanities, theory and practice, learning and life. As MacCracken put it, Euthenics was an expression of "the socialization of the curriculum."[10]

But Vassar adopted Euthenics in 1924, not 1914. By then reform ardor had cooled, and privatism and efficiency had taken its place. Much of the actual content of Euthenics centered on the application of science to the home, especially to child care, rather than to the broader community. Not all faculty who supported Euthenics felt committed to its principles. For some it was an opportunity to get a new building and to increase positions. Those who opposed it on principle clearly saw it as a threat to the meaning of education for women. With perspectives similar to M. Carey Thomas', they posed college in opposition to the home, a means of emancipation from its clutches. Euthenics threatened to return college education back to the home, tainting the disciplines with domestic usefulness.

That Euthenics was an important symbol, no participant doubted. To signal its significance, Vassar in the 1920s developed a whole section of land in the northeast corner of the campus. This area included the Euthenics building itself, the adjacent nursery school created by a second endowment, a new gymnasium, and a new dormitory, based on 1920s principles.

Annie Macleod, who became director of Euthenics, played a key role in planning the academic building. In 1924, she and MacCracken determined a set of fundamental principles to guide building. Both wanted the building to confirm the importance of the study of Euthenics. The requirements were thus clear: "It is essential that the building be fully the equal in beauty of any other academic building, and that it should not depart from the higher academic traditions as to architecture." While both viewed Euthenics as a new leap forward in education, neither wished to confirm this by architectural innovation. The design implications were conservative. They fancied Euthenics dressed in the "English Collegiate style of architecture . . . in the form of a quadrangle, like the Harkness Memorial." While Vassar's landscape offered no hills comparable to those of Wellesley, they agreed to place the Euthenics building on a plateau, thereby increasing its prominence.[11]

Designed by York & Sawyer at a cost of $500,000, Blodgett Hall of Euthenics caught just the note intended. College publicity shifted to fresh-faced collegians on bicycles framed by its arches. The building is in the shape of three sides of a quadrangle. One enters from the closed end under a handsome arch adjacent to a tower. Within the tower is the large auditorium, seating 328, and a smaller one for demonstrations. The three-story north wing coming out from the tower originally housed seminar rooms and classrooms, physiology laboratories, and nutrition laboratories. Parallel to these laboratories, the two-story south wing held laboratories devoted to the "study of applications of physics to household technology and of chemistry to problems connected with food," and an apartment as a "laboratory for the application of art to interior decoration and design." In the three-story center were administrative offices,

Blodgett Hall of Euthenics; *Vassar College Library*

research rooms for "mental hygiene," social science classrooms, library, and studios for art, mechanical drawing, and interior design.[12]

During the planning of Blodgett, a donor gave its small neighbor. The Mildred R. Wimpfheimer Nursery School, a laboratory school under the Department of Child Development, rose on the land to the north. In some ways the school grew logically out of Euthenics. Mothers who came to the Euthenics Institute for training needed child care, and a nursery school accommodated them. College students needed to experience little children at first hand, and the nursery school provided them with a ready group of subjects. The nursery school also gave MacCracken opportunity to build a link between Vassar and the surrounding community. By opening the school to townspeople's children, the college began to serve the town of Arlington and the city of Poughkeepsie. While MacCracken originally conceived of the nursery school within the Euthenics building, its separate endowment moved it outside. In keeping with the spirit of the Euthenics group, the nursery school took the form of "a sensible home," an English manor house.[13]

Allen and Collens originally designed the Helen Kenyon Hall of Physical Education, completed in 1933, as the companion of the Euthenics building and the nursery school. A fund-raising brochure described a "wide-spreading building" of "beauty and charm." With its many gables and broken roofline, it recalled "an English country house with farm outbuildings . . . suggestive of Matthew Vassar's birthplace in Norfolk."[14] One Vassar alumna found it not to her taste. Architect and critic Catherine Bauer unleashed her scorn for the plans in *Arts Weekly*. Lighting an indoor plunge with windows of leaded panes could give the student the experience of "swimming in a sort of Alice in Wonderland transformation of a don's private study." And what, she asked, was the function of the "Olde Halfe Timberede Englishe Inne" linked to a "forsaken abbey"? The answer that they were intended for offices and athletic rooms called her to declare the building "one of the all-round all-American worst buildings of this generation."[15] The gymnasium never took the form of the original plans. It emerged with the functional look Bauer appreciated, though without the imaginative form that she desired. Moderne styling with some Gothic touches gave a new look to a rather conventional brick building designed to house the sports which invigorated the 1930s college student: swimming, basketball, baseball, tennis, bowling, fencing, and archery.[16]

Beginning in the 1920s, Vassar built on its northeastern corner a model campus, devoted to Euthenics. Alumnae saw Cushing Hall, the dormitory named for Florence Cushing of the class of 1874 and Vassar's first woman trustee, as a major component of this new campus. With the completion of this hall in 1927, all freshmen, a third of whom lived in small frame houses outside the campus, came inside the hedge.[17] The college hoped initially that the students might live in a group of eight houses surrounded by a brick wall,

Cushing Hall; *Vassar College Library*

designed to "resemble a village enclosure in the Old English style." Euthenics claimed each of the eight buildings as a laboratory for Euthenics, "a home unit for purposes of observation and experiment within the departments of nutrition, hygiene, and home economics."[18]

This scheme did not prevail, but Cushing Hall carried with it both the hopes and the rhetoric of the Euthenics movement.[19] Allen & Collens did not get their way with the gymnasium, but they applied the same brush to the dormitory. They designed Cushing to resemble an English manor house, its half-timbering alternating with brick, built around three sides of a court. Steep gables and bay windows filled with leaded glass create an irregular outline. Divided into two units—each with elegant parlors, a dining hall softened by the light from the leaded windows, and single rooms coming off small wings rather than long corridors—Cushing gave its residents a sense of domestic enclosure reminiscent of Smith's cottages. In fact, though clothed in the language of the science of Euthenics, rather than in the patriarchal tones of Smith's founders, the impulse behind Cushing was much the same as that shaping the initial Smith student residences. In 1927, Vassar looked at its students and saw them as girls needing the influences of home. But while Smith never considered shaping a program of study around the gender of its students, in the 1920s Vassar did just that.

In the post-war years, Vassar combined the new with the old. Some elements remained constant: faculty continued to teach courses in traditional liberal arts disciplines; the campus, from Main to Taylor Hall, remained intact. Changes in college life altered the atmosphere significantly. Beginning in 1924, Euthenics added a new element to the curriculum and developed a new section of the college landscape. In building a Gothic tower to house a curriculum based on the needs of the home, an English manor house to train students to care for young children, a moderne gymnasium devoted to health, and a dormitory recalling English dwellings, Vassar expressed its partial accommodation to the new claims of the 1920s.

I I

Mount Holyoke illustrates more vividly than any of the Seven Sisters the reorientation that accompanied new notions about women after World War I. Because Mary Woolley stayed in the presidency until 1937, change was delayed. The results proved the more dramatic.

During the 1920s and 1930s, Mount Holyoke continued to build a campus to fit the classic design of the women's colleges in the early twentieth century. Modeling itself after Wellesley, Mount Holyoke's academic buildings took the monumental forms of collegiate Gothic. In the twentieth century, the college systematically acquired contiguous land, expanding its acreage to 267 by 1924.[20] There was talk in the air about greatly increasing the college's size. Mary Woolley favored the spawning of new affiliated colleges, along the lines of the Claremont Colleges in Southern California. To give form to the varied schemes, the trustees authorized a commission to make a comprehensive plan for development. At Wellesley, Green Hall's Galen Stone Tower rose triumphantly above Norumbega Hill, a symbol of rebirth after the fire which destroyed College Hall. Mount Holyoke chose Wellesley's consulting architect, Ralph Adams Cram, and Arthur A. Shurtleff, who, while supplanted as Wellesley's planner, was serving as the working landscape architect to put Day & Klauder's scheme on the ground.

The plan Shurtleff and Cram devised for Mount Holyoke is intriguing in the way it took existing buildings, already in collegiate Gothic, and redressed them in grander, more monumental form. In addition, Shurtleff dusted off his symmetrical Beaux Arts composition, rejected for Wellesley's academic buildings, and applied it to the college in South Hadley. Up until this point, Mount Holyoke had placed its academic buildings somewhat stiffly in two rows.

Shurtleff turned these rows into two stretches of buildings fronting a green parterre. The northern end of the campus, which opened rather unpretentiously on to the small country town, received a monumental entry. The plan called for enlarging Dwight Memorial and pairing it with a new physical-chemical laboratory. A monumental gateway, topped by a tower, joined the two.[21] While new buildings and refitted old ones had monumental masses, they also shaped enclosed courtyards, quadrangles similar, as the college put it, to "the older English colleges." On land across the brook between the two small lakes, Cram designed a monumental chapel in line with the Field Gateway on College Street. Its light stone tower of 180 feet "would lift above the surrounding trees and the crown of Prospect. . . . white and delicate among the trees and against the hill behind."[22]

The stock market crash in 1929 and the depression which followed turned a plan for future development into a paper scheme never realized. Perhaps it is just as well. Despite the monumental dignity that the Shurtleff and Cram plan promised, its formality and scale jarred with Mount Holyoke's setting in a country town. Bryn Mawr's gray stone matches that of the great houses that surround it in an affluent suburb; Wellesley's site within a large country estate fittingly shelters Gothic towers. But Mount Holyoke must coexist with the white clapboard houses, a small Victorian church, and the modest commercial structures of South Hadley, of which the Shurtleff plan gave only faint suggestion.

While Mount Holyoke abandoned the larger plan, its 1930s buildings—the physics and chemistry laboratory, the library extension, and Abbey Memorial Chapel—express the college's commitment to collegiate Gothic on a monumental scale. After years of reworking designs for the addition to the library in line with the Shurtleff plan, George Newton lost the commission. His successors, Vassar's architects Allen, Collens & Willis, created an imaginative solution within the limits of collegiate Gothic. In 1931, Wellesley dedicated Green Hall, with its ten-story tower. Mary Woolley admired it as "the last word in attractiveness and suitability."[23] What Wellesley had, Mount Holyoke wanted. Williston Memorial Library provided the place for Mount Holyoke's tower. The original building in the shape of a T became an H, as a long eastern wing fronted the college green. Along the south end, the architects enclosed the courtyard by joining the two great wings. A bold square castellated tower with four turrets rose at the center of the new wing.[24] Architect's plans put book stacks in the tower, but this proved impractical. Williston's tower has no functional purpose, only a symbolic one. The dominant feature of the campus, the great Gothic tower of Mount Holyoke expressed Mary Woolley's heroic vision, borrowed from Wellesley, of a women's community dedicated to scholarship.

In the eyes of the trustees Mary Woolley stayed too long in the Mount

Holyoke presidency. In her early administration, they had lauded her as the
"second founder" of the college. By the 1930s, they eagerly awaited her retirement. As Smith and Vassar had experienced in the last years of Seelye and
Taylor, there can be a certain defensiveness and rigidity at the end of a long
tenure. Change challenges the president's personal history, as well as that of
the college. In Mary Woolley's case, the last years became embittered by the
process of succession and the selection of a man to follow her.[25]

What trustees assumed in 1901 no longer held true in 1937, that Mount
Holyoke's president be a woman. Powerful members of the board of trustees,
including the son of the oldest living graduate, wanted the head of the college
to represent power in its expected male form, supported by a wife who set the
proper "social tone" for the community. The world outside Mount Holyoke
had changed: the generation of college-educated, progressive women who gave
leadership to reform were dying off, not to be replaced. The unmarried woman
head of a college seemed old-fashioned, a link with an earlier, more independent generation of women. The college returned to the concern of the Mead
years that it broaden its student body to attract daughters of affluence. Roswell
Ham, a Yale professor with an attractive wife from a prominent family, fit
perfectly the trustees' image of what a Mount Holyoke president ought to be.
In the spring of 1936, they offered the position to him.

What followed proved a great embarrassment. The trustees anticipated that,
despite Mary Woolley's strongly expressed preference for a woman, she would
graciously accept her male successor when they actually chose him. Instead
she lent her support to alumnae protests, stirred up by Jeannette Marks. From
the beginning Marks had been the more radical and feminist of the "twosome." She understood both the political and the personal meaning of the
trustee decision. Alumnae lodged protests, the most dramatic of which was a
flyer put out by Woolley supporters, *The Case of Mount Holyoke Versus the
Committee of Nine*, a pastiche of articles unfavorable to Ham with suggestions
about forms of alumnae protest. The trustees held firm; so did Mary Woolley.
She never recognized her successor in any form. After Mary Woolley moved
out of the President's House, she never returned to Mount Holyoke, even
when ceremonially honored.[26]

The tension of the final years made Roswell Ham's actual installation as
president a great relief. Mount Holyoke embarked on a campaign to strengthen
the geographical distribution of its student body and enhance its competitive
position among the elite colleges for women. One element of Mount Holyoke's effort involved changing the gender ratio of the faculty. Ham was eager
to attract and retain male professors. Along with favoring men outright, he
promoted a housing plan that enabled married faculty to build their own homes.[27]

Another key element was altering the look of the college. The final years
of the Depression, World War II, and the construction stringencies of the mid-

Torrey Hall, originally Lakeside; *Mount Holyoke College Library/Archives*

Ampitheater/Eliot; *Mount Holyoke College Library/Archives*

1940s delayed building on the campus. During these years of waiting, Mount Holyoke evolved a clear plan of development that changed both the orientation and the image of the college. When building resumed, the break with the past was unmistakable.

In 1948–49, Mount Holyoke erected Lakeside. Renamed Louise Torrey Hall for the alumna wife of William Howard Taft, the original name "Lakeside" revealed its location along the upper lake. This signalled a new direction for the campus, away from the Gothic-inspired buildings of the previous half-century. Designed by Douglas Orr of New Haven, who, in 1939, had been responsible for the stylized Georgian dormitory Emily Abbey Hall, Lakeside was a frankly modern building, "functional by necessity and desire." Ham defended the decision to break with collegiate Gothic. In the post-war world, Gothic cost too much to build and maintain. More significant was the break with the college of Mary Woolley. Ham intended that Mount Holyoke's shift to modern buildings demonstrate that the college had "moved forward in the spirit of our times."[28] While collegiate Gothic suggested embattled feminists, modern structures fit the more comfortable and socially acceptable hetero-sexuality of post–World War II America.

Lakeside presaged a major building program. Mount Holyoke expanded its student body by 75 percent and moved its students from scattered frame dwellings into modern, functional brick residence halls, placed along the two lakes. It took over three decades and three male presidents to complete the rebuilding of Mount Holyoke. Unlike the process at Wellesley, no fire consumed buildings, no plan called for major demolition. Mount Holyoke just moved over. The buildings of the Mead and Woolley years remained on College Street. Mount Holyoke added to them a whole new set of structures, placed along the lakes, and then reoriented the entrance to the campus to emphasize them.[29]

In deciding to concentrate modern structures by the lake, Mount Holyoke symbolically broke with its past. Mary Lyon's seminary had traversed a long, winding path. In the twentieth century, Mary Woolley transformed a lesser Smith into a strong college committed to scholarship. She chose Gothic towers to express Mount Holyoke's strength. In the years that followed her presidency, Mount Holyoke accommodated itself to the demands of the mid-twentieth century. It presented a clean, polished surface to the new age, suggestive of the college's post-feminist approach to women. In a paradoxical way, the modern Mount Holyoke buildings of the years after World War II join the Gothic and traditional English Euthenics group at Vassar as emblems of the adaptation of the two women's colleges to new concerns about women in the years following World War I.

19

The Training Which a College Can Give in Character and in the Art of Living

1920S DORMITORIES

The efforts to bend to the spirit of the times at Vassar and Mount Holyoke found no followers among the other Seven Sisters. In the face of changing public opinion and the new demands of student life, the other women's colleges maintained their traditional commitments. Academic women, nurtured in the colleges in the late nineteenth century, served as their presidents or deans. As a result, no other college established a Euthenics Institute or sought to reorient its campus to reconstruct its image. College buildings generally followed along lines laid down before World War I. There is, however, an important, but hidden, exception to this: college dormitories built during the 1920s or 1930s. While on the outside their monumentality suggested the strength of the women's college, their interior planning sprang from the new concerns about women's nature that surfaced after the war.

While each campus has a 1920s or 1930s dormitory that might serve as illustration, Smith and Wellesley provide the most interesting cases. Smith had to build on a large scale. Because it had relied on private dormitories and boarding houses, when the college decided to house all its students on campus, Smith required an immense building program. Under Dean Ada Comstock and later President William Allan Neilson, Smith built two residential quadrangles, totalling ten dormitories. Wellesley, on the other hand, provides an intriguing contrast between its commitment to heroic conceptions in the academic quadrangle on Norumbega Hill and its quite different approach to dormitory planning.

I

In 1910, Smith witnessed its first changing of the guard: after thirty-five years, President L. Clark Seelye retired. In his stead, the trustees turned to Marion LeRoy Burton, an engaging Midwesterner whose experience at the University of Minnesota suggested to him the model of the public university for a women's college. In his brief tenure, Burton shook Smith from top to bottom. Had he remained, he would have transformed Smith into a women's university, a Northampton version of Henry Fowle Durant's unrealized dream for Wellesley. But in 1917, the University of Minnesota pulled him back to the Midwest to become its president.

Burton did have time to initiate major changes at Smith. He immediately launched a successful endowment drive to raise funds to improve faculty salaries. He encouraged faculty efforts to revamp the curriculum, increasing electives but directing them into groups and majors. Along with the administrators of Mount Holyoke, Wellesley, and Vassar, he overturned admissions procedures to end the certificate system—which had favored private schools—and thereby opened Smith to more students from public high schools. In 1912, in keeping with the modern spirit of his administration, Burton brought back to Smith as dean its able alumna Ada Louise Comstock, who had been dean of women at the University of Minnesota since 1907.[1]

Working first with Burton, then as chief administrator during an extended interregnum, and finally with Smith's third president William Allan Neilson, Ada Comstock re-created the residential life of the college.[2] She believed strongly in the ideal of Smith democracy. In 1919, she bluntly contrasted Smith's reality with its rhetoric: of 1,993 undergraduate students, only 870, or 43 percent, lived in campus houses. Thirty-nine lived at home, but 1,084 lived in private dormitories. Some students who needed to economize found accommodations less expensive than the dormitories, while others paid as much as $650 a year, significantly more than for college housing. Smith set minimum health standards for private student housing, but it failed to foster the right kind of communal life. Comstock saw two extremes as threatening the off-campus student: if she is popular and wealthy, she is menaced by the "complacency" arising from "segregation with her own type"; "if her purse is small . . . her horizon is likely to be equally limited and she suffers from a sense of inferiority."[3]

Ada Comstock understood that parents sent their daughters to a college rather than to a university because of "the training which a college can give in character and in the art of living." Unable to control the living conditions of the majority of its students, Smith lacked "the means for fulfilling this trust." Students needed common provision for social development, such as meeting and recreation rooms, kitchenettes for preparing treats, and proper receiving rooms for callers. At a more fundamental level, undergraduates needed to live in settings that put each on an equal footing: "Of all the disguises which the human spirit assumes none is so complete as that embodied in circumstances of living." Inhibitions springing from economic differences existed in the outside world, but "in college . . . we have our chance to see what the human spirit can do when unhampered either by deprivation or by excess."[4]

Ada Comstock began her campaign within Burton's university scheme. He intended the existing Smith campus to become one unit of a larger institution composed of colleges either of social science, art, music, and drama or of a nonspecialized nature, following the English model. To build such a complex, Smith sought to acquire the grounds of the Massachusetts State Hospital, contiguous to the campus.[5] As Burton was working out this scheme, he engaged the city planner and landscape architect John Nolen of Cambridge, Massachusetts, to evaluate the existing campus and to suggest ways of improving its design.

Trained at the Ecole des Beaux Arts and experienced in urban and campus planning, Nolen predictably criticized the small scale, rich variety, and organic growth of Smith. No principle of orderly composition determined the site of buildings. While College Hall and the library held some possibilities as focal points, each failed to relate to the other buildings. In sum, Nolen judged Smith to have "very few good vistas. General feeling of disorderly crowding. No breadth of scheme." Nolen proposed ways to clean out the campus and to connect structures. He called for the removal of the smaller cottages from the campus, reserving the central area for academic buildings. He found two sites for groups of dormitories: one south of the existing campus on the opposite side of Green Street; the other northwest along Elm.[6] By 1915, the dormitory group's location changed to Allen Field, Smith's athletic area farther to the northwest between Paradise Road and Kensington Avenue.

Nolen's planning heritage remained after Burton's departure. When the trustees courted William Allan Neilson, a professor of English at Harvard, as Burton's successor, they faced his implacable opposition to Burton's university plan. Neilson wanted nothing to do with the fund-raising that acquisition of the hospital property required. He cared about intellectual quality, not institutional expansion. Neilson accepted the presidency only when the trustees agreed to table plans for the women's university. The trustees promised Neilson that he could remain a scholar in office, free from the job of raising money.

This promise they did not keep. Neilson saw the need to build student residence halls. Ada Comstock kept alive this concern of the Burton years. Neilson's own Scottish commitment to the principles of equality meant that he supported Comstock fully. In addition, as a scholar, Neilson found convincing college studies of undergraduates which pointed out that those housed

off campus tended to become absorbed in social life to the exclusion of intellectual commitments. As a man of integrity, he refused to tolerate the lie in
calling Smith a residential college, when the college gave only a minority of
students rooms. Neilson threw himself wholeheartedly into the effort to buy
and build residence halls.[7] Against his intentions, Neilson became a fund-raiser:
in 1920, the college launched a $4 million drive, and, in 1925, a Golden An-
niversary campaign. In 1934, Neilson reported that "for the first time in more
than fifty years, the College has been able to house on campus all its resident
members."[8]

The first addition to the Smith campus was the President's House. When
Elizabeth Muser Neilson, the president's gracious and domestic German-born
wife, saw the house built for the Seelyes in its noisy public location along Elm
next to College Hall, she judged that it served neither as an appropriate dwelling in which to raise children nor as an adequate setting for presidential hospitality. Mrs. Neilson was a skilled hostess: the honorary Doctor of Humane
Letters, conferred on her by the trustees in 1939, she insisted on calling "My
sandwich degree."[9] The trustees agreed to build a fitting President's House for
the Neilsons in a more secluded spot, permitting the flower gardens Mrs. Neilson
so enjoyed. One of the Neilsons' close Cambridge friends was John W. Ames,
the Boston architect. Built in 1920, the President's House was Ames' first Smith
commission. A graceful and generous Georgian house with a hall large enough
for great receptions, it combined well the needs of the college and of a family.

As well as adding a touch of elegance to the campus, the President's House
fundamentally changed the orientation of Smith's landscape. Paradise Pond,
Smith's lake, had never been part of the campus. On its shores were the ruins
of a stocking factory, a laundry, and some frame buildings. When Ames selected a site off Paradise Road on the hill overlooking Paradise Pond toward
Mt. Tom, he not only gave the President's House a handsome setting, accessible yet secluded, he also provided a new impetus to claim the lake for the
college. In 1922, the college cleared the lake shores of utility buildings and
brush, opening up beautiful vistas.[10]

Ames began his design career at Smith with the President's House. Its success, visible before completion, led the trustees to hire Ames for larger tasks.
The great building achievement of the Neilson years was the construction of
the Quadrangles on Allen Field. Six residence halls compose the great Quadrangle. Two others form the smaller Mandelle Quadrangle below it. Two final
dormitories present a semicircular façade to Elm Street. To design them John
Ames entered into a collaboration with Edwin Sherrill Dodge, a Boston architect known for his work in educational buildings, and Karl S. Putnam, a
Northampton architect who later joined the Smith faculty.[11] The plans developed quickly. By April 1919, Ames wrote to Neilson: "I have written out the
program given me by the Dean and we have worked up a very good scheme."[12]

Paradise Pond; *Smith College Archives*

Dean Ada Comstock's program for Smith's dormitories is an intriguing one, ascertainable only by the buildings' internal plans. Smith's Quadrangles present an extreme contrast between the upper floors of study-bedrooms and the first floor devoted to living room, dining room, parlors, and suites for the head of house and the member of the faculty. The planners clearly intended all socializing to take place in the public areas downstairs. These generous and elegant spaces invited both formal and casual gatherings. Smith alumnae who were professional interior decorators took charge. They created light and elegant rooms, finished in painted woods and delicate moldings and traditionally furnished with wing chairs and fine oriental rugs. In contrast to this first-floor elegance are the Spartan upper floors where two long rows of study-bedrooms, small identical cubicles, line each side of a corridor.[13]

Ada Comstock's plan broke both with patterns of men's residence halls and with earlier traditions at the women's colleges. From the beginning, men's college buildings, such as those at Amherst, had multiple entries which allowed rooms to open off stairways. Harvard's twentieth-century quadrangles avoid completely the connecting corridor by having many entries leading directly to undergraduate suites. While women's college residences channelled entrance through a main front door, nineteenth-century college women had frequently lived in suites: at Wellesley and Vassar several bedrooms adjoined a common parlor; an individual student at Bryn Mawr could have connecting

Aerial view, the Quadrangles; inset, a view into the Quadrangles—Wilder House from Comstock

to her bedroom a study with a fireplace. Harvard built just such suites for twentieth-century college men, adding the luxury of fireplaces, bay windows, and elegant moldings to the shared living room.

In contrast, Smith built the Quadrangles with single identical rooms lining a long corridor. Neilson liked single rooms because he felt that Smith sociability needed to be counteracted by solitude. In addition, given the college's undemocratic past, he felt it important to create uniform conditions, where possible. Yet, more was at issue. Smith built the Quadrangles in the 1920s. College planning manuals considered the single room of identical size the best arrangement in women's residence halls. While men's colleges set out consciously to foster male friendship in their living arrangements, female friendship was what the women's colleges, under attack for race suicide, feared the most. Thus in planning dormitories, the women's colleges created forms to constrain expressions of female friendship which could not be monitored. Small, cell-like rooms hardly invited intimacy. In addition, college students themselves wanted handsome rooms to receive male guests. In the 1920s, planning aimed to move socializing from the upstairs bedrooms and parlors downstairs into the public rooms.

Ames' scheme gave Georgian exteriors to Smith's 1920s dormitories. In 1920, the firm of McKim, Mead & White assessed both the Allen Field site and the initial plan put forward by Ames, Putnam, and Dodge. The prestigious New York firm looked realistically at the existing campus. They complimented the college on the "distant charm" of "the rolling nature of the ground, the beautiful shade trees and planting, the views of the river, pond and distant hills." They, too, found unfortunate the irregular locations of the buildings and their range of styles. Certain of the older buildings might be removed in time. But McKim, Mead & White did not see, as had John Nolen, any fundamental reworking of the central campus to obtain the "regular formal grouping of buildings" that corresponded with their Beaux Arts design principles. Thus the importance of the scheme before them. The Quadrangle offered to Smith its unique opportunity to plan "a large group of College buildings . . . at one time in proper relationship to each other."[14]

The original plan called for fifteen dormitories, each to house 60 students, thus bringing to the campus 900 students. Ultimately, because of the bequest of five buildings of the Capen School and the purchase of private dormitories, the college built only ten. The first three, Ellen Emerson, Cushing, and Jordan, completed in 1922, composed half of the great Quadrangle, to be matched in 1926 by Morrow, Martha Wilson, and Gardiner. Wilder and Comstock made up the Mandelle Quadrangle; Laura Scales and Franklin King the crescent on Elm Street.[15] Neilson departed from the tradition of naming buildings for donors and trustees to honor Smith faculty and distinguished alumnae.

The Quadrangles brought to the Smith campus the red brick Georgian of the Harvard Yard. Initially the trustees reacted unfavorably. Georgian to them looked industrial. In response to objections to the "long factory-like building in the center of Paradise Road," Ames modified his design to "introduce plenty of variety."[16] Generous use of white trim for windows, stringcourses, and cupolas enlivened the regularity and symmetry of the four-story structures. Dormer windows, allowing the use of the top floor for student rooms, broke up the roofline, as did the tall red brick chimneys. Round arched loggias and white service buildings of terra cotta covered in stucco, attached to the brick structures, introduced variety. The monumental form of Martha Wilson opened into the Quadrangle through an arched entry marked by a bay forming a central pavilion topped by a tall white cupola.

On the outside Smith's Quadrangles look very much like the houses Harvard built along the Charles River during this same period. At one level, they achieve for Smith what Harvard was seeking. Both schools' quadrangles assert the dignity of collegiate life and put their students in a different world from that of the town. Brick walls front the street, while courtyards create an inner enclosed space. The large scale and use of brick present a sharp contrast to the houses of the town. With its Quadrangles, Smith set half of its students off from Northampton, as the Houses do Harvard students from Cambridge. This signalled the final end of Smith's dream of cottage life integrated into the life of the town. As the college had grown, practical concerns eroded the initial scheme; but elements had remained to keep Smith's college life distinctive. The building of the Quadrangles changed that. While the cottages were interspersed throughout the campus, the Quadrangles sharply separated residential life from academic buildings and library. The scale of each unit remained small; but concentrating hundreds of students in a single area changed the atmosphere for half of the student body and separated town from gown. A half-century after its founding, Smith no longer looked to the town to protect its women students' femininity.

Protection remained the issue, however. While to the outside Smith proclaimed in its Georgian Quadrangles that the college dared house its women as Harvard did its men, on the inside Smith kept its concern with the special risks that college women faced. The Quadrangles attempted to separate women in private, breaking up the intimate life women created with each other to move them into public areas under supervision. These halls used space as Mary Lyon had used the rigorous schedule of Mount Holyoke, to control intimacy among students. Smith had always been afraid of female friendship. Initially it rejected the seminary system of rules and its building form to create cottages to keep college women within the patriarchal world. Ironically, the cottages fostered female intimacy. The Quadrangles tried another approach to control.

While Smith failed in the 1870s, it succeeded in the 1920s, but for an external reason. College women after World War I turned away from each other.

This did not happen because of the constraints posed by dormitory form, however, but because college women turned toward college men. College authorities had no need to control the behavior of female collegians with each other in their private rooms and little need to oversee them in the common rooms. The living room became a waiting room for men, taking women away to the privacy of the unsupervisable automobile. With the Flapper, heterosexuality won. The ghost of L. Clark Seelye must have regarded it as a dubious victory.

II

Smith was not alone in planning its dormitories to fit new notions of the needs of college women. Each of the other Seven Sister colleges has at least one dormitory built after World War I that shares Smith's contrast in the Quadrangles between elegant public space and Spartan private space. Mandelle and Rockefeller halls at Mount Holyoke, Rhoads at Bryn Mawr, Hewitt at Barnard, Le Baron R. Briggs and Barnard at Radcliffe, Cushing at Vassar provide similar settings for their female collegians. Even Wellesley, where heroic conceptions determined the academic quadrangle on Norumbega Hill, followed the 1920s dormitory form when it built Severance Hall on College Hill.

Wellesley's faculty had made a distinction between academic buildings with monumental masses and residential ones "influenced by charming and intimate effects."[17] This hardly characterized Tower Court, a particular source of dissatisfaction to the Alumnae Conference Committee. In June 1915, the committee reported to the trustees on living conditions. Almost every recommendation that they made stood in opposition to the residence hall taking form on College Hill.

The report argued for small residence halls, ideally for sixty students, two-and-a-half stories high, grouped as "country dwellings in an open park," not "crowded together," in a "city environment." It opposed dormitories for separate classes: "older and younger girls and Faculty [should] be together in the same house" to help mold the young student in the image of the older. Wellesley needed "no elaborate buildings." Rather fine proportions, adaptation to the site, and simplicity "in finish and furnishings" served as guiding principles. Tower Court violated them all.[18]

The committee got the donor of Tower Court to withdraw her stipulation that Tower Court be reserved for seniors, but nothing could alter the forms of the great hall. Different planning conceptions, however, could govern succeeding dormitories. Claflin Hall followed Tower Court immediately. Planned as a western wing of the great residence complex, it formed a long arm extending toward the lake. Its lower lines, repeating Tower Court's architectural detail,

Severance Hall; *Wellesley College Archives*

helped anchor the tall building to the hill. Claflin's smaller size and less monumental public rooms fit the alumnae judgment about scale and simplicity.

The architects of Tower Court and Claflin, the Boston firm of Coolidge &
Carlson, intended that an identical dormitory match Claflin on the east. By
the time funds became available, the Philadelphia firm of Day & Klauder, the
designers of the academic quadrangle, were firmly installed as campus architects and set about devising plans. The change caused Coolidge & Carlson
professional embarrassment and artistic pain. As Harry J. Carlson wrote to
Charles Z. Klauder, "I feel a good deal like a sculptor who has been allowed
to finish the head and torso and right arm, but was required to leave the left
arm for some one else to do." [19]

Despite Carlson's protest, Wellesley kept Klauder and Frank Day as the
designers of the wing, named Severance Hall. Faced with the tall tower "much
too large in mass . . . perched on top of a hill," the architects conceived of
Severance as they had the eastern wing of Founders, as a base growing out of
the hill to anchor a tower. Consulting architect Ralph Adams Cram commended it with glowing enthusiasm. While he judged Tower Court a mistake,

the Day & Klauder plan "will not only correct its defects in mass and placing, but will actually develop a composition that will be of the most extraordinary impressiveness and beauty." The design built "up against the existing dormitories a varied and mounting mass of buildings," which tied "the whole thing into the landscape." It achieved a "Mont St. Michel effect, though collegiate and domesticated."[20]

Cram recognized that it was expensive to plan Severance in this way. The architects estimated a cost of $400,000 for 113 students, over $3,500 per student.[21] The college agreed to build because the dormitory offered such a brilliant resolution to a troubling mistake. The exterior of Severance unquestionably succeeds. It respects the sweep of College Hill, the scene of college festivals, to crown it with a long low picturesque building of varying heights. The architect "let his fancy play freely." The building abounds with decorative Gothic detail, especially on the exterior. The irregular plan allowed "courtyards and sheltered nooks and angles."[22] At the primary entrance near the junction with Tower Court on the north, a short wing, shaped like a medieval manor house, juts out, creating a lovely small courtyard and breaking the formal approach to Tower Court.

The alumnae wanted "no 'Gold Coast.'" Despite the building's costliness, Severance gave only plain living along its corridors. The alumnae had requested common rooms on each floor to inhibit the kind of social life in student rooms that they had enjoyed: "There should be no need of using beds as lounges, and wash bowls as dishpans, and the lazy, untidy, and profitless habit of loafing about in each other's bedrooms would be discouraged."[23] Severance did not get common rooms on each floor, but it did get grim cells as bedrooms designed to force students into public areas for socializing.[24] The Conference Committee had urged that the public rooms suggest informal uses—"dancing after dinner, house frolics on Hallowe'en, the Sunday 'sing,' family prayers Sunday morning."[25] Severance's common rooms turned out to be grand, rather than domestic. The living room, 20 feet by 75 feet, "reminiscent of the medieval hall with its open roof construction, supported by hewn and carved oaken trusses and a huge stone fireplace at each end," was more appropriate for formal teas and receptions than for home-like gatherings.[26]

Severance Hall looks entirely different from the Georgian Quadrangles of Smith, and the living rooms of the two residential areas create unlike atmospheres, but the internal planning shares a basic characteristic. In the 1920s, Smith and Wellesley—as well as the other Seven Sisters—separated sharply public and private space. Public areas took a grand treatment; private ones, Spartan modesty. Even those women's colleges which sustained their traditional commitments and retained their basic forms altered their conceptions of student living spaces. Hidden behind Georgian or Gothic façades are quiet accommodations to the changing times.

20

Without Reference to the Analogy of Colleges for Men

SARAH LAWRENCE, BENNINGTON, SCRIPPS

Sarah Lawrence, Bennington, and Scripps captured the spirit of the times. While existing women's colleges resisted or adapted to the pressures of the 1920s, according to the commitments of their presidents and faculty, these three new colleges—free of tradition, faculty, and buildings—offered a clean canvas on which to sketch an educational plan for twentieth-century women.

Even those in the Seven Sisters most enthusiastically attuned to the demands of the age found themselves constrained by the traditions maintained by alumnae and faculty loyal to the turn of the century's classic design. At Vassar, for example, President Henry Noble MacCracken created the Euthenics Institute, a highly important symbol in its effort to reshape a curriculum to the needs of the home. But Euthenics was added on to a women's college with a half-century commitment to the liberal arts, whose faculty chose largely to ignore or oppose its existence. Its buildings at the edge of the Vassar campus expressed appropriately Euthenics' marginality.

The new women's colleges of the 1920s faced none of these constraints. Sarah Lawrence, Bennington, and Scripps started afresh. Founders created each as a college for the new woman of the new age. In Vermont, New York, and California those interested in women's education linked local interests to national debates. In all three cases, ties to the Seven Sisters created a special angle of vision. Founders knew well the strengths of the existing women's colleges, especially the newly prestigious Seven Sisters. But they were aware of the weaknesses as well. The claims of heterosexuality were as apparent as the need for a less rigid curriculum. Sarah Lawrence, Bennington, and Scripps each saw itself as a new departure, an effort to reform women's education so that it served the needs of the new women of the post-war world. In doing so, each rejected the collegiate Gothic quadrangles of the classic design to build a campus based on domestic imagery, recalling Smith's initial conception in 1875.

I

Sarah Lawrence sprang from the curious alliance between Vassar's progressive president and a conservative builder. As Helen Lynd, Sarah Lawrence's distinguished philosopher, recalled, "Some people used to say that Sarah Lawrence represented what Mildred Thompson [Vassar's powerful dean] wouldn't let President MacCracken do at Vassar."[1] MacCracken knew Vassar's history well enough to see himself as a latter-day Milo Jewett guiding a new man of wealth to found an appropriate monument to immortality. William Van Duzer Lawrence came to MacCracken's attention as the rich father and grandfather of Vassar alumnae, ripe for cultivation. Lawrence had known Vassar throughout the Taylor era, recalling in his diary of 1913, on the occasion of a visit to Vassar, the time when "over twenty-five years before this, in Dr. Taylor's first year, I called first at Vassar to introduce Louise, then about to enter college."[2] Early in his presidency of the college, MacCracken entertained Lawrence and began to court him as a potential donor to Vassar.

Lawrence clearly had other ideas about how to distribute his wealth. He was a builder. After a successful career as a drug manufacturer, he had retired only to begin his most satisfying work as the developer of Lawrence Park in Bronxville, a planned artistic and restricted suburb of New York City.[3] There, beginning in 1914, he built Westlands, his own estate on twelve hilly acres. Entrepreneur, social planner, country gentleman, and philanthropist, Lawrence built and owned Bronxville's Gramatan Hotel and founded the Lawrence Hospital. As he neared the end of his life, he turned over to his four children the control of his business affairs and contemplated creating on his estate an institution to the service of his society. He first thought of Westlands as an improved site for the Lawrence Hospital.[4]

It is here that MacCracken intervened to guide Lawrence to found New York State's first junior college for women. Over the course of several years, MacCracken convinced Lawrence of the needs of higher education and of women.[5] Lawrence harbored serious doubts about the value of college. As a self-made businessman, he had often observed the spoiled college boy, unwilling to begin in business at the bottom, who became "floating debris in the business world." The usual college course wrecked boys, providing them with a place for "losing time and forming bad and selfish habits which ruin their future."[6] Furthermore, though proud of his wife's philanthropic accomplishments, Lawrence clearly did not like the new breed of educated women headed for the professions. He opposed "the existing idea that women should be trained for a career, as men are trained, for law, politics and religion, thereby becoming prominent in public places, filling such positions in the world which lower their standard and put them in competition with men."[7] Lawrence believed that "there is a woman's sphere of activities and a man's sphere . . . the border line between these is more or less chaotic and undefined and ought to be more clearly divided and set apart."[8] Women need to become "leaders of their own sex and to inspire them with the great secret of woman's power over the coming race . . . character and happiness obtained only by earliest training and accomplished only by a mother's love."[9] MacCracken suggested to Lawrence an alternative goal of higher education for women: a training to prepare them to "appreciate the value of leisure."[10] A junior college provided opportunities for cultivation, but none for professional training. In the beautiful setting of Bronxville, with the combined advantages of "real country life" and the "great metropolis," a student could gain that education that comes not "from a diligent study of books given her in her college course," but from "cultivation of grace and manners, of diplomacy and the fine arts and the creation of character. . . . not necessarily acquired in school or college," but rather from "her surroundings."[11] With his wife's sudden death in 1926, Lawrence decided to act immediately to found in her honor Sarah Lawrence, a junior college for women.

From the beginning Lawrence centered his plan on his estate in Bronxville. Like the pleasures of his gracious community of homes, Lawrence intended the opportunity of his junior college to be limited to the few. "According to the traditions of the village itself . . . it should be restricted and confined to the education and finish of our best American girls."[12] Parents need the "satisfaction of knowing with whom their daughters are associating during the most impressionable years of their lives" and they should be assured that they come from "homes which are genuinely American."[13] Just as his college would imitate his suburb by barring students of foreign parents and Jews, so, too, would it house students in Bronxville Tudor homes, designed by his favorite architects, the New York firm of Bates & How.

In the true spirit of noblesse oblige, Lawrence assumed that he was acting for the good of Bronxville. He did not consult his neighbors, who opposed the establishment of a college. Bronxville residents feared an intrusion that might disrupt the tranquility of suburban life and lower property values. Opposition to the college prompted a letter from Lawrence's physician testifying that senility had not impaired his judgment, thus cutting off medical grounds for a court fight to bar establishment of the college.[14]

MacCracken effectively dissuaded Lawrence from restricting the college's student body ethnically, helped him gain a charter from the conservative Regents of the State of New York, and suggested, as the first president of Sarah Lawrence, Vassar alumna Marion Coats, the principal of Bradford Academy.

At this point MacCracken intended to withdraw from Sarah Lawrence affairs, but a major hurdle unexpectedly forced him to remain engaged.[15] While William Lawrence wanted to found a college, he did not have the wealth to endow it adequately. Lawrence thought that he had solved the problem of support in a manner compatible with his wish that students come from the wealthier strata: the college would be "self-supporting."[16] Sarah Lawrence set its fees high enough to cover all operational costs—$1,600. But this solution assumed that the college attracted a full complement of students. Lawrence's children feared the college might founder and opposed their father's scheme. None of the Lawrence heirs wanted the potential financial responsibility that involvement in their father's college suggested, and they dreaded being sucked into an unorganized institution.[17] Lawrence's daughter, Louisa Lawrence Meigs, declined to serve on the college's board of trustees, but may have suggested a solution: formal affiliation with her alma mater, Vassar. Nicholas Murray Butler's precipitate overture to Lawrence to affiliate with Columbia as a second Barnard prompted an immediate response.[18] Without earlier intention on MacCracken's part, Sarah Lawrence entered the world as Vassar's child. Vassar agreed to a partnership in which the majority of the first board of trustees of the new college consisted of Vassar trustees and Vassar's president served as its chairman. Vassar lent its consulting engineer to advise on the physical plant and its comptroller to oversee the books. Vassar faculty formed a board of examiners, and several of them taught at Sarah Lawrence part-time. By signed agreement, Vassar promised to sponsor the fledgling school for an initial five-year period, after which Sarah Lawrence would become independent or accede its property to Vassar.[19] William Lawrence was ecstatic and proposed to MacCracken that Vassar affiliate with junior colleges "from the Atlantic to the Pacific," following the model of American industry.[20] Lawrence's analogy was apt: financial considerations, not questions of educational policy, had prompted the alliance.

When the Regents granted Sarah Lawrence's charter, December 9, 1926, the new college got some unexpected publicity. Reporters eager for a story pounced on Lawrence's conventional notions of femininity, even quoting him to the effect that he intended his college to prepare young women for marriage.[21] MacCracken and Marion Coats were mortified, though Coats reassured Lawrence that the new college was really lucky: "The reporters might have featured your anti-Jewish feeling or the size of the tuition fee."[22] The result was unexpected. Applications poured in steadily, insuring a full class of entering students whose tuition could support the college. Marion Coats realized that Lawrence's rhetoric "struck squarely at the great need in the field of education for women of the present day."[23] The current publicity connected with the New York production of *The Captive* and "the consequent discussion of 'crushes,' particularly in college, lent a somewhat wholesome atmosphere"

Dudley Lawrence, a Sarah Lawrence dormitory; *Archives of Sarah Lawrence College*

Westlands; *Archives of Sarah Lawrence College*

to Lawrence's statements.[24] They clearly reassured young college-bound women and their parents that Sarah Lawrence could safely protect students' heterosexuality.

Chartered and announced, the new college required buildings, a faculty, and an educational plan. While Marion Coats tried to wean Lawrence from his architects and get the commission for Allen & Collens, the designers of Vassar's Gothic façade, Lawrence held on to Kenneth G. How, who had served him well for decades. While Lawrence professed himself ignorant of college building needs and called on MacCracken and Coats for guidance, he had a clear image of Sarah Lawrence from the beginning. Lawrence had no desire for monumental buildings that suggested the repellant women's college. He wanted his students to live "in small homes" similar to those of his beloved Bronxville.[25] As Lawrence put it, he wanted the buildings to look "more like an English village than one of our great institutions of learning."[26] He gave his own house Westlands as the central building; outlined an overall scheme that included a music hall, an art building, a gymnasium, a hospital, a central heating plant, and a service building; and then, experienced builder that he was, commissioned Bates & How to design a prototype cottage that could be replicated ten times.[27] As a developer, Lawrence understood that the clientele that he wished to attract required certain amenities; thus, over objections about added cost, he instructed his architect to connect two student rooms by a bathroom, because "up-to-date" rooms would attract to his college "high class girls . . . belonging to wealthy families mostly."[28]

Unwittingly, both in rhetoric and in design Lawrence re-created Smith College's initial plan on his Bronxville land. He envisioned picturesque cottages offering home-like environments grouped around Westlands, which served as the original College Hall. To this he intended to add a number of other buildings, which, if built, would have made Sarah Lawrence resemble the Smith of 1890.

At the time he died, May 16, 1927, Lawrence was employing his own work crews to grade the land in preparation for construction. His death threatened the enterprise. The most pressing immediate need was financial: Lawrence's endowment was too small to build the necessary buildings. The college required a half-million-dollar loan to complete construction even on a modest scale. Here the value of Vassar's aegis proved itself. MacCracken journeyed to Wall Street with Lawrence's son Dudley and with Vassar trustee Ray Morris, and, on the basis of Vassar backing, secured for the new venture a loan. MacCracken persuaded Dudley Lawrence to become a trustee and to supervise the building process,[29] and MacCracken himself assumed an important role in physical planning.

Economic pressures forced retrenchment and dictated the order of construction. To open, the college required rooms for enough students to support faculty salaries. Thus building went ahead on the residence halls and a common dining room. To cut costs, planners put into the basements of the residence hall classrooms, as well as a theater and, later, the college library. As MacCracken put it, "everything was highly concentrated in an extremely economical way and yet it didn't look parsimonious because the buildings were dignified inside and you just didn't ask a question." The college survived without a gymnasium or athletic fields.[30] In addition, the college adapted Westlands' servant quarters on the third floor for student rooms.

In his opposition to professional women and the blurring of gender distinctions, Lawrence knew from the beginning that he wanted his college to "be administered without reference to the analogy of colleges for men."[31] This anti-feminist commitment had an unanticipated effect. It allowed the new college to serve as a fertile ground in which progressive ideas of education might take root.[32] MacCracken convinced William Lawrence not only of the need for women's education designed for domestic futures but also of the value of the tutorial and seminar systems that engaged students actively in their own education. Prodded by MacCracken, Lawrence forswore professional training, requirements, and examinations as inappropriate to women's experience and future destiny. Before Lawrence died, Marion Coats had drafted for him a "Letter of Instruction" to the Sarah Lawrence trustees, an amalgam of Lawrence's words with those of MacCracken, embellished by Coats' own interpretations. This first public statement of intention spelled out Sarah Lawrence's commitment to small-scale, informal instruction, to the liberal and fine arts, and to leadership in creative methods of teaching twentieth-century women. It also dedicated the college to search for an education appropriate for young women freed from "the craze for financial independence" and from the misplaced notion of the sex "as the ornament of a man-made society."[33]

It took several years for the college to slough off Lawrence's conventional notions of femininity and to develop these guidelines into their unique form in the don system and governance structure by which Sarah Lawrence is best known. Guided by Constance Warren, the president who replaced Marion Coats after the initial year, the faculty—whose ethnicity and political philosophy Lawrence would have abhorred—seized the freedom that Lawrence's legacy offered as a special opportunity to rethink the nature of higher education.[34] Each student worked out her individual program with a "don," her faculty advisor, with whom she met each week. The don sought to take into account the "total development of the student," in consultation with the staff psychiatrist. Students had no requirements. Normally each student had "one experience" in the four fields of the Sarah Lawrence curriculum: the social sciences, the natural sciences, the arts, and languages and literature. Through a difficult and conflictual process, teachers opened up their course outlines to allow subjects to develop through the students' questions and growth. Faculty at-

Maxwell Geismer, a Sarah Lawrence "don," with student
Archives of Sarah Lawrence College

Art class, ca. 1934; *Archives of Sarah Lawrence College*

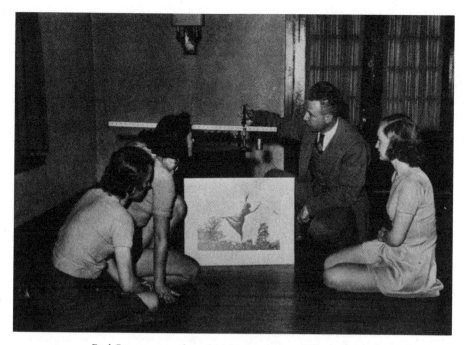

Paul Garrett, a member of the Mathematics and Physics faculty,
with dance students; *Archives of Sarah Lawrence College*

Student Council, Sarah Lawrence, ca. 1936; *Archives of Sarah Lawrence College*

tempted to shape courses defined by problem, rather than by discipline. In addition to regular class meetings, the professor met weekly with each student in each course. Students received reports of their individual development, not grades. Group divisions took the place of departments. Faculty served without hope of tenure or promotion. The college encouraged field work and attempted to incorporate group activity into the curriculum, including the usually extra-curricular college government and student publications. Members of the community forced themselves to break through the normal hierarchical relationship that characterized faculty and student interchange. They reached out to nonacademic employees to offer courses and to encourage the college to grant fair employment conditions. Faculty and administrators learned to trust students outside the classroom, as well as in. The college eased up on social restrictions and allowed smoking and unlimited weekends away. It offered to students a full measure of self-governance.[35]

As students pressed to stay to complete the full college course, Sarah Lawrence gradually became a four-year college.[36] In 1933, it awarded its first B.A. degree and, in 1934, graduated its first class.[37] At the end of its first decade, Sarah Lawrence had emerged as a women's college committed to experimental learning. By this time its buildings were set on the ground. Structurally, their unique feature is that they all combine residence and offices, classrooms, assembly hall, or library. While arising not out of educational philosophy, but out of William Lawrence's re-creation of Smith scaled down by straitened economic circumstances, Sarah Lawrence's landscape has proved fortuitously apt for the college's special educational philosophy. Classrooms, theater, and library in residence halls suggested informality and the link between learning and life that the faculty sought to foster.

This is curiously emblematic of the college as a whole. Ironically, William Lawrence's very conventionality about women allowed the college to develop an unconventional approach to education. While the early buildings and their placement were pure Lawrence, like the college which they enclose, they were adapted to express progressive approaches to the education of women. In its odd blend of anti-feminism and progressivism, the Sarah Lawrence campus captures perfectly the contradictory impulses of the 1920s.

I I

Bennington arrived at Sarah Lawrence's conclusions by a very different logic. By the time that the college opened in 1932, almost a decade of discussion had shaped its plan of organization, curriculum, and campus. Its origins lay in the hopes of a Congregational minister in Old Bennington, Vermont, to enrich the life of his adopted community by re-creating within its boundaries Mary

Lyon's Mount Holyoke. As at Sarah Lawrence, advocates of progressive education saw an opportunity to create a college along new lines. Bennington became a self-conscious experiment. It set out to prove that young women could live and study without rules.[38] Bennington's campus, like that of Sarah Lawrence, is a curious adaptation that appropriately symbolizes the college's ethos.

After several years in Old Bennington, Vincent Ravi Booth began casting about for a way to enliven the historic but declining town, especially in the winters after the summer residents had departed. While Booth appeared the epitome of the proper gentleman of an earlier genteel age, he sprang from unconventional origins. He was born in Naples of an Italian father, Vincenzo Ravi, who had once studied for the priesthood but had converted to Methodism and become a minister. Ravi sent his children to Ohio Wesleyan, and his son followed him in the Methodist ministry. In 1916, the son, Vincent Ravi, now the pastor of the North Congregational Church in Cambridge, Massachusetts, and an American citizen, added to the name of his father that of his Scottish mother, becoming the Reverend Mr. Booth. In 1919, he withdrew to the First Church in Old Bennington in the hope of restoring his health. As his two-year furlough in the mountains stretched into a permanent living, he began to look for diversions. Because he had daughters of high school age, he considered founding a private school for girls. Competition from fine preparatory schools in the region turned his thoughts to those of a college. He had been lecturing on Italian literature at Russell Sage College, and he initially encouraged the miserably located women's college to move from Troy, New York, but state boundaries complicated the change. Encouraged by President Paul V. Moody of Middlebury College, Booth began to discuss with some of Bennington's prosperous summer residents the founding of a women's college. Edith and Hall Park McCullough and James Colby Colgate caught Booth's enthusiasm. President William Allan Neilson of Smith, once Booth's parishioner in Cambridge, proved another important ally. Booth united the growing support in Old Bennington into a Committee of Twenty-One and encouraged Edith McCullough to organize a meeting in New York to bring the plan of a women's college in Bennington to a wider public.[39]

In these initial discussions, Booth not only generated support, he defined the nature of the early college. His conceptions were grand. He proposed that Bennington begin with an endowment of $4 million. To promote the college, Booth encouraged supporters to enlist an architect to prepare presentation sketches. Guided by Neilson and his former dean, Ada Comstock, now president of Radcliffe, the Architectural Committee of the future college chose John W. Ames and Edwin S. Dodge of Boston, the architects of Smith's new Georgian Quadrangles.[40]

Ames & Dodge created for the future Bennington a design that linked

Smith's past and present. Like the Northampton college's 1875 plan, the scheme for Bennington surrounded a college hall with cottages. But in keeping with the taste of the 1920s, Beaux Arts principles determined the form, and Georgian motifs the façade. At the center, the central college building in brick harked back to the elegant late-eighteenth-century civic designs of Charles Bulfinch. Extending as two arms, the brick residence halls, in the small scale deemed appropriate for the necessary "home-like" environments for college women, adapted Smith's new residential halls to the composition.[41]

During the long years of fund-raising, this plan gave visual expression to Booth's hopes for Bennington College. Booth wanted a women's college for Old Bennington that followed the classic design. As he prepared a brochure to publicize the college, his initial draft called on the tradition springing from Mary Lyon and included her portrait.

Booth began his efforts in 1923, however, not 1903. Unbeknown to him, educators and the broader public were questioning the value of the women's colleges. Edith McCullough had been deeply disappointed when, on presenting to Vassar her daughter—the first female member of her family to enter college—the dean had countered her excitement with the warning: "This is nothing to be excited about. It is just sheer grind."[42] Rather than upholding the old order, William Neilson advocated that Bennington "pioneer and blaze a new path in higher education." He wanted Booth's new college to design an education based not on the masculine subjects of mathematics and the classics but rather designed to meet the needs of contemporary women: "art, music, literature, the social sciences, and the consideration of problems arising out of the industrial conditions of the modern world."[43] Edith McCullough enlisted William Heard Kilpatrick of Columbia Teachers College. He brought to the debate an intense commitment to "a fresh start in a new college." Involved deeply in efforts to extend progressive education to the academy, Kilpatrick had repeatedly seen reform lost to the entrenched interests of college faculties. "Bennington College with a slate clean of hampering traditions can introduce from the start the best that the modern world has to show."[44]

To publicize the scheme for Bennington College, Booth encouraged the Committee of Twenty-One to hold a public meeting in New York. Efficient organizing and the full use of social contacts generated an enthusiastic gathering, April 28, 1924, at the Colony Club, where an overflow crowd heard Comstock, Neilson, Kilpatrick, and Booth state the need for a new college for women, the importance of educational innovation, and the charms of Old Bennington. While the potential conflict among Bennington's supporters was masked, that from the audience erupted openly. Barnard's redoubtable dean, Virginia Gildersleeve, rose to defend "some of the old things still existing" in good women's colleges, and another critic harked back to the achievement for women inherent in their mastering the "same curriculum" as that of men. Undaunted, Bennington supporters moved and passed a statement of endorsement for the new college.[45]

The Colony Club meeting ended Booth's dominance in planning the new college, as Edith McCullough, William Kilpatrick, and their supporters in New York joined with Booth's forces to compose a board of trustees. To give an adequate power base from which to seek a charter, the early backers added regional notables and Morton D. Hull, the prominent Chicago lawyer with a summer place in Bennington. At their initial meeting, the trustees chose Edith McCullough as their head and committed themselves to raising money for the enterprise. Booth proved immediately successful in Old Bennington: within ten days he got one-half million dollars in pledges, contingent on the college raising two-and-a-half million by 1928.[46]

As the board attempted to develop the educational scheme for Bennington, the collaboration between traditional collegiate conceptions and new progressive notions proved unworkable. Booth continued to try to influence educational policy. He enlisted Amy Kelley, a former Wellesley faculty member who headed the Bryn Mawr School. The trustees sent her on a fact-finding investigation of existing colleges, where she tried out her conception of six required orientation courses for entering students. Her report confirmed her idea's wisdom, but did not find trustee acceptance. Booth wrote his ill-fated brochure which supported Kelley's plan, rapturously described Old Bennington, and placed Bennington College firmly in the tradition of the existing women's colleges. One influential critic suggested that Booth omit Mary Lyon's portrait as suggesting "an old-fashionedness."[47] Edith McCullough's threat to resign and to take with her influential board members ultimately prevented Booth from pressing acceptance of his text. The board authorized a new brochure and asked Kilpatrick to write it. Such internal conflict over the essential purpose and direction of the college made it impossible for the trustees to get the necessary backing, even in the flush times of the 1920s.[48]

In the next four years, as the trustees sifted through prevailing educational currents to chart Bennington's course and tried ineffectively to raise money, they more successfully snared a president. The board only considered men. Edith McCullough felt that none of the women in education had the qualities of an effective Bennington president and that they lacked "the feminine attributes which would be one of the chief reasons for having a woman." Later she had to respond to over a hundred letters from "angry feminists. . . . the same crowd" who "attacked" Roswell Ham of Mount Holyoke when he assumed the presidency. After uncounted refusals, in January 1928 Robert Devore Leigh, a young government professor at Williams College, accepted. Commitment to experimental education learned while at Reed College, a clear mind, and

ambition characterized the new Bennington president. Leigh gave the necessary leadership to the conflict-ridden board, and in the next five years guided
it to solve systematically the major problems of creating a college.[49]

Leigh ended the debate over curriculum by publishing in December 1929
his prospectus, "The Educational Plan for Bennington College." As did Sarah
Lawrence, Bennington proposed admitting students based on their "entire school
record and history," rather than on specific requirements or examinations. Expediency as well as progressive tenets dictated this policy, for conversations
with private school headmistresses had identified a pool of prospective students unable to pass the necessary mathematics courses for admission to the
Seven Sisters. Bennington divided the curriculum into junior and senior divisions. To pass into the senior division, a student did not have any general
requirements, but rather "individually prescribed work." Only those in certain
majors had to take "tool courses, such as mathematics and foreign languages."
Senior division students concentrated in a major from one of four fields: science, fine arts, literature, and social studies. Bennington intended to choose
its faculty on the basis of "teaching ability," with every effort "to avoid 'dead
wood' and to maintain flexibility." Consistent with its concern for change,
Bennington also limited its trustees to single terms and suggested that its president tender his resignation at seven-year intervals to free the board not to
renew his appointment.[50] All of this sounds remarkably like Sarah Lawrence.

Bennington differed from the new junior college in its postponement of
individualized and small group instruction until the senior division, normally
the last two years of the college course. A Bennington student usually began
with a two-year sequence of introductory courses. Only in the trial major
conference group did "informal, individualized methods" prevail.[51] In contrast
to Sarah Lawrence, Bennington had a positive commitment to careers. Leigh
had "no sympathy with the false antithesis between vocational and liberal studies." The college planned majors for "future adult activity," paid as well as
volunteer.[52] Bennington also took a more questioning attitude toward college
life. Leigh wanted it limited to the "main intellectual and artistic program
sponsored by the faculty," discouraging those "trivial, imitative student organizations" which have hitherto created a "gulf now lying between student and
faculty purposes."[53] To compensate for Bennington's isolated location, Leigh
advocated a long winter recess, allowing students and faculty time for "travel,
field work and educational advantages of metropolitan life" and suggested
nonresident work in the last year or two. And while tuition had "to pay for
full cost of instruction"—$1,675 in Bennington's case—the college committed
itself to "selective regional and special scholarships" for those who could not
afford the high fees.[54]

Bennington's timing could not have been worse. By the time that Leigh
clarified the college's educational mission, the stock market had crashed. Leigh

Bennington dormitory: Kilpatrick; *Bennington College*

The Commons and a row of dormitories; *Bennington College*

realized that while educational leaders understood the need for an experimental college for women, the idea lacked "a wide popular appeal." Rather than attempting to encourage "a large number of small contributors," he decided to try to reach "a few persons of great wealth who can be convinced of the wisdom of endowing" Bennington.[55] The Crash and the Depression made this task exceedingly difficult. Some of the trustees despaired: Morton Hull remarked to McCullough, "Maybe we best let the old cat die."[56] James Colgate resigned as treasurer and withdrew his offer of forty-five acres in Old Bennington. Fearing failure, Leigh sounded out the possibility of merging with an existing institution, of which the most promising seemed Sarah Lawrence.[57]

On September 3, 1930, Leigh presented a set of alternatives to the board: either give up or scale down expectations. The trustees had the choice of limiting their goal or of disappointing parents, thwarting secondary schools, and making its "efforts and expenditures of money . . . come to naught." He asked the trustees to think small and to authorize a modest, "semi-permanent" campus. Leigh had investigated the New Jersey College for Women connected with Rutgers. While he privately reported that the interiors of the N.J.C. dormitories gave "horrible examples of what not to do," he admired their economy. He suggested to the trustees that if Bennington went ahead and then proved its value, foundations would come to its aid.[58]

Elizabeth Jennings Franklin, a firm supporter of Bennington, offered the Frederic B. Jennings estate, 140 acres in North Bennington, as the site of the college. A working farm, it included cultivated fields, a large, rambling barn, and orchards, set on a plateau framed by the Vermont hills. Leigh went back to Ames & Dodge to request that they adapt their original plan to modest, wood structures.[59]

Leigh never advocated single-sex education. He agreed with one of the friendly critics of his "Educational Plan" that a college for women only was "certainly one of the most debatable points in the Bennington program." Booth's initiating efforts had assumed separate education, and this set the course for the immediate future. With a women's college a given, Leigh wanted Bennington to encourage "normal social contacts between the sexes."[60] When he advised Ames & Dodge about dormitories, he reduced their size and included apartments for faculty members.

The college ultimately built twelve students' houses in wood, each with single rooms for twenty students and a faculty apartment. The college renovated the barn—a large structure built as three sides of a square—for offices, a faculty assembly room, a library, science laboratories and lecture room, and small classrooms. The Commons, which included the five dining halls, kitchen, college store, post office, infirmary, art studios, and theater, stood at the head of student houses.[61] Ames & Dodge's original scheme survived only in the

Two students in front of dormitories,
1932–33; *Bennington College*

Faculty-student group, 1932–33
Bennington College

Professor Kurt Schindler and student; college buildings in background
Bennington College

Aerial view, 1933; *Bennington College*

Beaux Arts composition and the conception of this central building. The Commons carried the white columns and cupola of a Bulfinch state capitol. The student houses extended out in two long, straight white rows, framing a green. This plan and the student houses' small scale and white clapboard simplicity suggested the democratic spirit of the New England town.

Bennington's governance structure seemed to follow naturally from its form. Bennington stressed community participation by all of its members and recognized students as full partners with faculty in governance. Not only did students have the majority of members of the Community Council, which set standards and disciplined students and faculty, students advised on educational policy and buildings and grounds. Students and staff turned the college store in the Commons into a consumer cooperative.[62]

In the public mind, the social freedom that Bennington gave to students distinguished the college from the outset. No arbitrary rules governed behavior. "A series of 'thou shalt nots,' while they might protect us from unsympathetic outside criticism, would probably be evaded, leading perhaps to hypocrisy or childish rebellion against imposed authority."[63] Just as a student's academic program developed from the "logic implicit in learning rather than blind submission to requirements," so too did the standards of communal living.[64] While the established women's colleges agonized over smoking regulations, Bennington sought to gradually build up a "growing body of common law, integrating the results of our experience in community living."[65]

Bennington attracted a compelling faculty which set its stamp on the new college. Unlike the "grand group of old war-horses" of the women's colleges, who had repelled Edith McCullough, Bennington's teachers came from the modern world of artistic experimentation and sexual freedom.[66] The intense intellectual atmosphere they created shaped undergraduate experience. Bennington alumnae tend to remember their college less as alma mater than as Ben Belitt, Genevieve Taggard, Catharine Osgood Foster, or Martha Hill.[67] College photographs suggest that to early faculty and students, Bennington's New England village became Blithedale, the utopian community of intellectual adventure and intense personal relationships.

Educational experimentation had overpowered Booth's original conception of a women's college in the classic mold. The needs for economy had turned a design originally intended to fit Booth's conception into an unorthodox departure. Leigh delighted in the result. Unlike the 1920s, when "huge castles, cathedrals and towers built by irresponsible donors for vulgar, personal satisfactions and with difficulty adapted to the purposes of learning, almost suffocated some of the universities," Bennington in the 1930s had "honest structures fitted to the serious purpose of education." The Bennington campus symbolized "simplicity, directness, and relation to function."[68] Economic constraints had unwittingly created out of necessity a fitting emblem. A campus of white houses around a green, facing a town hall, with a barn to the side, suggested a new departure—a women's college in the form of a democratic New England village.

III

By the 1920s, debates about women's education reverberated far beyond their points of origin. In Southern California, transplanted Americans confronted the twin challenges of population growth and cultural change. A munificent benefactor offered new opportunities to an established coeducational institution. As had that of Sarah Lawrence and Bennington, Scripps College's planning focused discussion on the educational needs of post-war women and the kind of environment for their proper development.

In the early years of the twentieth century, population growth in Southern California and the expansion of the public high school created an increasing pool of applicants for Pomona College in Claremont. Founded by Congregationalists at the end of the railroad boom of the 1880s, Pomona had been coeducational from its beginning. In the 1920s, pressure to take in more women threatened to upset the 60:40 male-female ratio of entering students necessary to graduate a class in which the men equalled the women. The question on President James Blaisdell's mind was, should Pomona College grow? In his address at the Commencement of 1925, "The College at the Crossroads," William Bennett Munro suggested a different future: that rather than simply swelling in size, Pomona might spawn other separate, but coordinate, colleges along the lines of Oxford and Cambridge.[69]

A Canadian trained in Scotland, Munro had just arrived at the California Institute of Technology from Harvard and he brought to the West the questions that President A. Lawrence Lowell was raising about the scale and purpose of undergraduate education—and Lowell's answers. Reacting against Harvard's unstructured curriculum, Lowell introduced sequential courses and concentrations; to make college life more personal and fraternal, he gathered students into small residential units based on the Oxbridge colleges. At Pomona College, Munro saw the chance to apply Lowell's ideas more fully, combining "the personal nature" of college instruction with the "creative scholarship" of the university.[70]

Coincidentally, Pomona was beginning to receive the benefactions of a remarkable philanthropist, Ellen Browning Scripps. Advanced in years, unmarried, very rich by Southern California standards, and generous to a variety of institutions, Ellen Browning Scripps offered a unique opportunity. Stimulated by Munro's urgings and the Scripps fortune, Blaisdell developed his scheme for the Claremont Colleges group.[71] He persuaded Ellen Browning Scripps to

Organization meeting of board of trustees, June 18, 1926; William Bennett Munro on left;
Ethel Richardson Allen second from right; *Scripps College Archives*

endow a college for women as the first element in a coordinated system of
affiliated colleges and graduate schools surrounding Pomona. The dean of the
Pomona faculty, Ernest Jaqua, became the acting director of the new enterprise. To persuade the Pomona College board of trustees that the infant wom-
en's college would not draw its strength at the expense of its parent, Blaisdell
promised to turn to untapped sources of support. Scripps College's initial board
of trustees was the unusual result: talented women, composing one-half of the
board, joined William Munro and male Southern California civic leaders.[72]
Two women had attained professional distinction—Susan Dorsey, the superintendent of schools for Los Angeles, and Ethel Richardson Allen, the head of
California's Division of Adult Education. They brought experience from the
women's colleges. Dorsey graduated from Vassar; Allen, from Bryn Mawr.
Jaqua quite consciously recruited other women to represent the Seven Sister
colleges on the Scripps board, women such as Mary Routt from Wellesley and
Mary Kimberly Shirk from Smith.[73]

Ellen Browning Scripps believed in women being clear-thinking and high-minded, but beyond these broad guidelines, she left decisions of educational policy up to the board. The women of the Scripps board brought to their service the concerns of the Association of Collegiate Alumnae in the twentieth century. They were all married women with strong interests outside the home. Scripps became their experiment. As the report of the board's special subcommittee of the Education Committee put it, women's education in the past "precisely" copied "the education given her brother in the effort to prove her emancipation and equality." Scripps College would be a departure. They intended it to offer to women an education designed to "train her for the fullest and richest life that she herself may have, as well as the chance to give to society her greatest contribution."[74] In other words, women might combine work ("contribution") with marriage and children ("fullest and richest life").

In examining women's special needs and concerns, the education committee determined that women had a special interest "in individuals, in personalities, in what men are, rather than in objects or in what men do," that they cared about growth, human relationships, and beauty. These particular qualities of women suggested a curriculum featuring psychology, botany, sociology, and art. Women's special weaknesses called for methods to counter their lack of "objectivity and the capacity for critical judgment and independent thinking." The subcommittee suggested that women's distinctive attributes set the first two years of required courses. They further recommended that the final two years concentrate on prevocational training to give women the groundwork for those areas in which "marriage and the rearing of children" will be "the least possible interruption and the greatest asset": public health; child training; social research; business; and art.[75] Caught in the marriage-career dilemma of their own time, the women trustees, hoping to enable women to enjoy families and make contributions to society, sought a curricular solution that accepted the reality of discrimination—women's work—rather than one that gave women the intellectual ammunition to fight it.

As part of their concern about female education, the women trustees insisted that one-half of the faculty be female and argued for a woman president, much to the discomfort of Blaisdell, who supported Jaqua as one "intimately interwoven with Pomona," experience that Blaisdell felt necessary for the success of the Claremont group system.[76] Jaqua became president and recruited an initial faculty dominated by men. While he reported to the board that he was making every effort to locate women, in fact he relied on male faculty ties and inquired in his letters about "the best men" available.[77] He later explained that he wanted to get distinguished men in place at the outset, fearing that they would be harder to draw, once surrounded by women. Susan Dorsey fought him, saying that she wanted to bring to Scripps Laura Wylie, Vassar's brilliant teacher and literary critic; but silence met her words. Jaqua promised to equalize the ratio in future appointments.[78] He did, but with younger women brought

First faculty-student dinner, fall 1928; President Ernest Jaqua seated at far left;
standing at right, Professor Hartley Burr Alexander; *Scripps College Archives*

in at lower levels and smaller salaries—as assistant professor of biology, instructor in physical education, and director of residence.

The men who ventured west to become the founding faculty at Scripps
brought with them not the progressive approaches of their counterparts at
Sarah Lawrence and Bennington but the questions that World War I raised
among conservative intellectuals. Could a nation seemingly committed to
pragmatism fight? Did a society composed of immigrants share a culture that
commanded loyalty? These questions had profound implications for curriculum, especially in universities which had adopted an elective system allowing students free rein. If basic values lay at the center of a common culture,
the academy held a responsibility to teach them to all students. Recognizing
this, in 1919 Columbia had initiated a freshman course in contemporary
civilization.

Hartley Burr Alexander, who came to Scripps from the University of Nebraska, had joined this debate. A versatile philosopher and anthropologist, he
had written about questions of liberty and democracy in wartime.[79] At the

University of Nebraska, he had been active in curricular reform. Alexander believed that the liberal arts college had a mission "to initiate the generations into the traditions of civilization, preserving what men have clung to as their highest in days past, and rendering this as a charge to the young who come to us."[80] Like the Columbia faculty, he wanted to break through the disciplinary organization of knowledge. In the small setting of a women's college, where each faculty member came from a different field and held no prior loyalties, Alexander organized, as part of the freshman-sophomore required program, a course on the history of Western Civilization. Within a few years, nine members of the faculty collaborated on a sequence of courses entitled "The Humanities: History of Occidental Culture," a required double course for freshmen and sophomores and an elective offered for juniors (later to become required).[81] This intensive survey of the cultural contributions of Western Civilization provided a reassuring antidote to American commercial culture, right at its Southern California source. Scripps' Humanities program became the symbolic center of the college's curriculum. Its male professors set the tone of serious high-mindedness that influenced generations of undergraduates.

What of the program of the women trustees to offer Scripps students an education suited to feminine needs? It survived in the elective work of the third and fourth years, grouped according to the "predominant interest of the student." Each student selected a field of major interest for concentration. As at Sarah Lawrence and Bennington, Scripps broke with conventional academic departments. "Interests" differed from customary majors in that they were "in no case confined to any one department."[82] They grouped fields related intellectually. The women trustees' selection of courses—based on women's reputed strengths and weaknesses and designed for careers compatible with family life—led to an emphasis on art, psychology, literature, and the social sciences and an initial disregard of mathematics, the theoretical sciences, and political science.

Scripps trustees knew at first hand the importance of the college campus. As they confronted the task of building a new college, they acted much like their counterparts at Bennington and Sarah Lawrence. Their deliberations assumed that neither collegiate Gothic nor the large residence hall fit the needs of contemporary college women. In considering a possible architect, the trustees appointed an art commission which drew up a list that included the distinguished names working in the "Colonial Spanish or California style" that the trustees favored. As they discussed nominee Wallace Neff, they questioned his ability to create "very simple and homelike" buildings. They agreed unanimously that the architect of Scripps should be selected to "give to the dormitories the appearance and atmosphere of a beautiful home."[83] The trustees ruled out Julia Morgan for unknown reasons.[84] Gordon Kaufmann, recognized for his fine domestic work and for the desert resort La Quinta, won the commis-

Toll Hall; *Scripps College Archives*

Scripps campus, mid-1930s; *Scripps College Archives*

Two seniors from the first graduating class, at Commencement party, 1931
Scripps College Archives

Dinner party, Star Court, Toll Hall, 1931; *Scripps College Archives*

sion. The building committee sent him on a fact-finding visit to the East, suggesting that he view Rockefeller Hall at Mount Holyoke, Tower Court at Wellesley, the Radcliffe residence halls, and the new dormitories at Smith, among others.[85]

Kaufmann created an elegant design for Scripps College. On a gently sloping stretch of land, he planned a campus built as a great courtyard, facing inward. The major buildings establish the outer borders, lining the perimeters with great stucco walls entered through archways, doors, and wrought-iron

Gordon Kaufmann's plan, ca. 1926; *Scripps College Archives*

gates. Separate Mediterranean-inspired gardens form the interior, offering varied spaces and vistas. Each individual building is itself composed of small courtyards, which offer intimate, sheltered outdoor spaces, appropriate to the climate.

Kaufmann's presentation watercolors of the initial dormitories created a vision of grand San Marino, California, houses, with all they promised of class and protection. The board had explicitly directed that the dormitories be only two stories in height.[86] Kaufmann artfully hid the third story. Courtyards, balconies, and setbacks give the dormitories the appearance of a generous house, disguising its scale.

The first dormitory, Eleanor Toll Hall, linked California design to the women's college dormitory plan. Just as at Smith or Mount Holyoke, the organization of the residence hall reflected the house plan. An elegant and generous living room opens to the right of the reception area and leads to two smaller alcoves, the "dating rooms," at the north end. The dining hall, to the left of the entrance, attempts in its small scale and cork floor to lessen the

Mt. Baldy between Toll and Browning halls, ca. 1930; *Scripps College Archives*

clatter of dishes. Students' living quarters lie beyond the receiving desk and up a short flight of stairs. As in Smith's Georgian Quadrangles, the individual student rooms provide a Spartan contrast with the carefully appointed, and supervisable, public rooms. Departing from the precedents in the Eastern schools, student rooms stretch around courtyards on three stories, each room looks out on a court, and the second floor opens on to balconies.

In presenting the college to the public, Scripps emphasized the distinctiveness of its plan. The college had rejected the "early Republican style" of Pomona's library as "too masculine." The atmosphere of the new women's college formed "one chord with a world of vast bright spaces, where the air is flooded with latent color, where the background is a near wall of shining mountains, and the atmosphere most of the time is a brooding silence. . . . A strange blend of dreaminess and alertness, of brilliancy with repose." Scripps had chosen a style to fit "an essentially American conception of how the members of a woman's college, in their most plastic years, should be housed."[87] Scripps quite consciously attempted to build a campus appropriate to women's nature. More profoundly than in its adaptation to a moody landscape, the college sought feminine structures. Unlike Kaufmann's courtyard dormitories at the California Institute of Technology a few miles away, planned for men, his Scripps dormitories followed the pattern of the women's colleges in adapting the house form to a residence hall for college women. While Kaufmann employed the entry system at the Institute, giving the future engineers access to their rooms from the four corners, the Scripps buildings had only the single entrance. While the Institute intended the entry to promote fellowship among men perceived as needing male companionship, Scripps separated each female into her modest private space, forcing her into the public rooms for socializing. Moreover, while Scripps chose its dormitories as the first buildings on the new campus, erected before classrooms and library, the Institute turned to housing for men only as an afterthought, once it had built the essential laboratories and classrooms.[88]

Scripps tried to reinforce the domestic lesson of the dormitory's form by setting up a practice house. Dorothy A. Kuebler, the first dormitory's director, with a major in home economics, established a small bungalow off campus where students coped with household budgets and attempted dinner parties.[89] It proved a short-lived experiment. Scripps students had little interest in directly preparing for their domestic futures. The faculty-student tea, held each day after Humanities lectures, provided a more lasting form of social training. Scripps collegians combined a remarkable academic seriousness with a desire for private pleasures. While the college upheld the quite conservative social standards of a Congregational college town, Scripps students learned forms of quiet rebellion away from supervision. Dormitory balconies and roofs became

Freshmen in the first class, fall 1927, on balcony of Toll Hall
Scripps College Archives

the centers of social life, places where the young women gathered for cigarette breaks.[90]

While Sarah Lawrence and Bennington represented progressive departures from the established women's colleges, Scripps stood for a conservative alternative. Male professors committed to upholding Western Civilization under siege joined the faculty of a college formed by Southern California alumnae of the Seven Sisters who hoped for an education for twentieth-century women seeking careers compatible with marriage. A Mediterranean-inspired campus linked the college with one of the great traditions. Yet, underneath these apparent differences, much ties Scripps to the experimental women's colleges of the East Coast. All took advantage of a new beginning to devise curricula free of traditional disciplinary and departmental boundaries to address the needs of women in the post-war world. And whether dressed in Tudor suburban, New England farmhouse, or California Mediterranean, all three women's colleges consciously broke with collegiate Gothic to offer students the small scale and informality of the house as a proper preparation for their domestic and heterosexual futures.

Epilogue

Almost one hundred years separates the foundings of Sarah Lawrence, Bennington, and Scripps from Mount Holyoke. The century witnessed critical changes in conceptions of women and their education. As founders created colleges to offer women the higher learning, their hopes and fears took form in organizational schemes and buildings designed to seclude, protect, or inspire young female collegians. The special landscapes of the women's colleges are the direct result.

So, too, are the students and faculty whose lives changed within the female communities of the women's colleges. Their individual and collective experience rewrote the texts founders had provided.

As alumnae became faculty, trustees, and college presidents, they not only confronted men but new generations of women students, with different conceptions of themselves and their futures. By the end of the first century after Mount Holyoke's founding, the women's colleges responded to the claims of heterosexuality, as well as to those of female friendship, to the demands for an education relevant to twentieth-century women as well as to the traditions of the liberal arts. In each college the array of forces differed. The classic era of the women's college weighed more heavily at Wellesley than at Vassar and hardly at all at Sarah Lawrence. But each college faced the same pressures.

Since World War II, the women's colleges have confronted new challenges. In the 1960s, sexual mores changed dramatically, forcing each college to meet the demand for privacy and for the entry of men into formerly forbidden reaches of the dormitories. Faced with fewer women students willing to enter into an all-female community for four years, the women's colleges negotiated cooperative arrangements with neighboring men's institutions, and Vassar, Sarah Lawrence, and Bennington became coeducational.

351

Smith class of 1882 in 1917; official Smith photographer Katherine McClellan at far right
Smith College Archives

Feminism brought new opportunities and new demands. The women's colleges reclaimed their historic task to develop women's minds free of the gender stereotypes of American society. The colleges faced the needs of a new generation of young women eager for service and ambitious for personal success. The women's colleges addressed the question of women's intellectual choices and asserted women's strength in the sciences. Lesbianism stopped being a whispered secret, and homosexual women began openly expressing their sexuality. Athletics assumed a political posture, creating a new interest in women's strength and prowess. Women's Studies programs unmasked the heritage of sexism and the strength of women's separate culture.

Each of these issues challenged the women's colleges in profound ways. Yet, unlike an earlier period, the colleges largely responded in academic and extra-curricular programs, rather than in new buildings. With only a few exceptions, the landscape of earlier eras remains intact.

The exceptions are suggestive. Committed to expand as it accepted men, Vassar went outside its hedge to build a variety of coeducational student residences in the form of garden apartments. These do not, however, affect the central campus, and they blend with the private housing of the surrounding neighborhood. Wellesley and Smith each added an emblem of contemporary feminism. Wellesley's new Science Center claims instant attention because its post-Beaubourg façade in glass and primary colors breaks sharply with its Gothic neighbors. Smith's athletic facility more subtly suggests that the college supports richly the physical development of its students.

Smith recast Scott Gymnasium, using the existing structure designed by Ames, Putnam and Dodge in the mid-1920s, but greatly expanding its space. The building plays delightfully on the contrast between old and new. Similarly, Wellesley adapted the Music building and Billings, its early-twentieth-century addition, as a students' center. Vassar reconstructed the rear of Main, creating a vast atrium lit by skylights. These structures imaginatively confront present-day needs within the basic contours of the past.

While contemporary colleges have adapted old buildings for new purposes because of economic constraints inhibiting building, they also have responded to a new interest in preserving college buildings and recovering campus traditions. Threatened with the demolition of the 1890 Brocklesby gymnasium, Smith students and alumnae successfully campaigned to preserve it: restored, it houses the Smith College Archives and Sophia Smith Collection. Student interest in the history and architecture of the women's colleges has generated fine undergraduate papers and senior theses, which have greatly aided my exploration. A reawakened sense of the importance of tradition has led Bryn Mawr students, after a lapse of decades, to revive the May Day fête. Students at the women's colleges are seeing their customs and their landscapes as part of the rich heritage of women's collective past.

In 1915, Lucy Salmon, Vassar's distinguished professor of history, tried to get students to locate themselves within the American past by discovering history in their own backyards. She wrote *Is This Vassar College?*, a pamphlet demonstrating how the Vassar campus served as a complex text about American life since 1865. She imagined an older woman coming to Vassar with the words of James Russell Lowell in her head: " 'The divine faculty is to see what everybody else can look at.' " As she toured the campus, the visitor asked herself, "Was there something more to see at Vassar College than what was indicated on the plan?" After her day of looking and reflecting, "Vassar College . . . shaped itself in her mind into an innumerable number of records that form the raw material from which all history is written, and it was with these records that her mind busied itself and from which she reconstructed the life of the college."[1]

I found this little-known source while engaged in research at the Vassar College Library. Its words struck me keenly: without knowing it, undergraduates at the women's colleges and I had pursued Lucy Salmon's quest, across the generations.

My own study extends her effort to make the material forms remaining on the Vassar campus and other women's colleges intelligible to this age. In the Progressive era Lucy Salmon focused on how the Vassar campus demonstrated changing educational methods and evolving notions of democracy. Three-quarters of a century later, I have explored what organizational schemes, buildings and landscapes, and—in the twentieth century—curricula tell about American conceptions of women, especially those exposed to the danger of higher education. I have tried to understand not only the initial meanings ascribed by college founders but also the ways that those who dealt with the rules, lived in the buildings, and taught the courses transformed these meanings. Contemporary questions about gender, as well as the contextual concerns of cultural history, informed my study.

Offering the liberal arts to women began as—and remains—a bold experiment. Throughout their complicated histories, the women's colleges have accepted the challenges this posed with a mixture of fear and hope. Mount Holyoke, Vassar, Wellesley, Smith, Radcliffe, Bryn Mawr, Barnard, Sarah Lawrence, Bennington, and Scripps serve as vivid emblems of how Americans once perceived college women and how women students, alumnae, and faculty came to perceive themselves.

Notes & Index

Notes

1. I do not argue in this study that the issue of gender in founders' minds led them to erect unique structures for the early women's colleges, but rather that they turned to existing building forms—especially the female seminary modeled after the asylum—not considered appropriate for male collegians. An asylum enclosed men as well as women, and thus carried no associations with feminine space as such. Its link was with dependency more generally, and thus was considered appropriate for hospitals, orphanages, and academies of either sex. Its significance for understanding gender comes only as it is used by colleges for women, but not for men. As far as I can determine, those male or coeducational colleges that had "asylum" structures began as academies that took in male students as young as twelve. The larger question of college and university architecture awaits the important study by Paul Turner of Stanford.

CHAPTER I *Plain, Though Very Neat*

1. Laurel Thatcher Ulrich, "Vertuous Women Found: New England Ministerial Literature, 1668–1735," *American Quarterly* 28 (1976): 20–40; Lyle Koehler, *A Search for Power: The "Weaker Sex" in Seventeenth-Century New England* (Urbana: University of Illinois Press, 1980), offers a quite different reading of the same sources, but even he recognized that Puritan women listened to sermons and that three published transcriptions of their ministers' sermons.

2. Most works on the history of education, such as Lawrence A. Cremin, *American Education: The Colonial Experience, 1607–1783* (New York: Harper & Row, Publishers, 1970), virtually ignore women. Kenneth A. Lockridge, *Literacy in Colonial New England* (New York: W. W. Norton & Co., 1979), is an exception. He has calculated that one-third of the initial female settlers and 45 percent of women born in the New England colonies could write in the colonial period (p. 38); however, significantly more may have been able to read. The history of women's education must still rely on the monumental but outdated study of Thomas Woody, *A History of Women's Education in the United States*, 2 vols. (New York: The Science Press, 1929).

3. Robert Middlekauff, *Ancients and Axioms: Secondary Education in Eighteenth Century New England* (New Haven: Yale University Press, 1963): *The Age of the Academies*, ed. with intro. Theo-

dore R. Sizer, Classics in Education no. 22 (New York: Teachers College Bureau of Publications, 1964); Harriet Webster Marr, *The Old New England Academies Founded before 1826* (New York: Comet Press Books, 1959), esp. pp. 97–106.

4. Linda K. Kerber first pointed to the important link between changes in women's education and Republican ideology in "Daughters of Columbia: Educating Women for the Republic, 1787–1803," in *The Hofstadter Aegis: A Memorial*, ed. Stanley Elkins and Eric McKitrick (New York: Alfred A. Knopf, 1974), pp. 36–59. Two new books highlight the importance of the changes: Linda K. Kerber, *Women of the Republic: Intellect and Ideology in Revolutionary America* (Chapel Hill: University of North Carolina Press for the Institute of Early American History and Culture, 1980), and Mary Beth Norton, *Liberty's Daughters: The Revolutionary Experience of American Women, 1750–1800* (Boston: Little, Brown, 1980).

5. Sherry B. Ortner, "Is Female to Male as Nature Is to Culture?" in *Women, Culture, and Society*, ed. Michelle Zimbalist Rosaldo and Louise Lamphere (Stanford: Stanford University Press, 1974), pp. 67–87; Michelle Zimbalist Rosaldo, "Women, Culture, and Society: a Theoretical Overview," *ibid.*, pp. 17–42.

6. Michael B. Katz, *The Irony of Early School Reforms: Educational Innovation in Mid Nineteenth Century Massachusetts* (Cambridge, Mass.: Harvard University Press, 1968); Stanley K. Schultz, *The Culture Factory: Boston Public Schools, 1789–1860* (New York: Oxford University Press, 1973). Kathryn Kish Sklar has documented the opening of town reading and writing schools to girls in Massachusetts between 1750 and 1800, underlying the rise in their literacy to 90 percent by 1850 ("Public Expenditures for Schooling Girls in Massachusetts Towns, 1750–1800" [unpublished, 1976]).

7. Woody, *History of Women's Education*, 1: 329–459.

8. On Beecher, see Kathryn Kish Sklar, *Catharine Beecher: A Study in American Domesticity* (New Haven: Yale University Press, 1973), and Barbara M. Cross, *The Educated Woman in America: Selected Writings of Catharine Beecher, Margaret Fuller, and M. Carey Thomas*, Teachers College Classics in Education no. 25 (New York: Teachers College Press, 1965), pp. 3–13, 51–101.

9. Anne Firor Scott, "The Ever Widening Circle: The Diffusion of Feminist Values from the Troy Female Seminary, 1822–1872," *History of Education Quarterly* 19 (1979): 3–25.

10. David F. Allmendinger, Jr., "Mt. Holyoke Students Encounter the Need for Life Planning, 1837–1850," *History of Education Quarterly* 19 (1979): 27–46, discussed the need for planning in a more narrow frame, intriguingly linked to demographic statistics.

11. The following discussion of Mary Lyon's life and the founding of Mount Holyoke draws heavily on the material in Elizabeth Alden Green, *Mary Lyon and Mount Holyoke: Opening the Gates* (Hanover, New Hampshire: University Press of New England, 1979). The interpretation of this material, however, is my own. Also useful are Sydney R. MacLean, "Mary Lyon," *Notable American Women*, ed. Edward T. James (Cambridge, Mass.: Belknap Press of Harvard University Press, 1971), 2:443–47; Arthur C. Cole, *A Hundred Years of Mount Holyoke College: The Evolution of an Educational Ideal* (New Haven: Yale University Press, 1940), pp. 12–29; and Sarah D. Stow, *History of Mount Holyoke Seminary, South Hadley, Mass. during Its First Half Century, 1837–1887* (Springfield, Mass.: Springfield Printing Company, 1887), pp. 12–77.

12. Edward Hitchcock, *The Power of Christian Benevolence Illustrated in the Life and Labors of Mary Lyon* (Northampton: Hopkins, Bridgman, and Company, 1852). Hitchcock was actually the editor and a contributor; Eunice Caldwell Cowles wrote Part Two, from which this quote is taken (p. 37). This is the major source for Mary Lyon's letters. While the letters were unfortunately altered by her biographers, the changes are largely matters of grammatical form, not substance. The volume also reprints Lyon's major public statements.

13. Mary Lyon to Miss C., Feb. 21, 1825, *ibid.*, p. 41.

14. Joseph Emerson, "Society for Instruction," Byfield, Nov. 24, 1818, quoted in Ralph

Emerson, *Life of Rev. Joseph Emerson* (Boston: Crocker and Brewster, 1834), p. 249; Mary Lyon, "On His Estimate and Treatment of Females," April 12, 1834, quoted *ibid.*, p. 421; Green, *Mary Lyon*, p. 25.

15. Sydney R. MacLean, "Zilpah Polly Grant," *Notable American Women*, 2:73–75; Linda Thayer Guilford, *The Use of a Life: Memorials of Mrs. Z. P. Grant Banister* (New York: American Tract Society, 1885).

16. Carroll Smith-Rosenberg, "The Female World of Love and Ritual: Relations Between Women in Nineteenth-Century America," *Signs* 1 (1975): 1–29.

17. Mary Lyon to her sister F., Aug. 22, 1827, quoted in Hitchcock, *Mary Lyon*, pp. 53–54.

18. Guilford, *Mrs. Z. P. Grant Banister*, p. 69.

19. Green, *Mary Lyon*, pp. 54–55.

20. Mary Lyon to Zilpah Grant, Feb. 2, 1829, quoted in Hitchcock, *Mary Lyon*, p. 68.

21. David J. Rothman, *The Discovery of the Asylum: Social Order and Disorder in the New Republic* (Boston: Little, Brown, 1971), pp. 109–54. I am grateful to Nancy Tomes for letting me read "A Generous Confidence: Thomas Story Kirkbride and the Art of Asylum-Keeping, 1840–1883" (forthcoming, Cambridge University Press). This balanced presentation, while de-emphasizing reformers' concerns with social order, nonetheless supports the view of the asylum as a separate place, ruled by a superintendent, capable of restoring the insane to health through reason.

22. Hitchcock, *Mary Lyon*, pp. 141–43.

23. *Ibid.*, p. 134.

24. *Ibid.*, pp. 139–40.

25. [Zilpah Grant,] "The Ipswich Female Seminary," *American Quarterly Register* 11 (1839): 372.

26. Green dates Lyon's faith much earlier, in 1816; however, she experienced too much religious anguish in the years that followed to place her conviction of faith that early.

27. Hitchcock, *Mary Lyon*, pp. 148–49.

28. Hitchcock, *Mary Lyon*, is filled with Lyon's reports of her religious work among students. For example, see Mary Lyon's letter to her sister F., July 4, 1826, pp. 48–49.

29. *Ibid.*, pp. 37–39.

30. *Ibid.*, p. 248; Stow, *Mount Holyoke*, p. 76.

31. Michel Foucault, *Madness and Civilization: A History of Insanity in the Age of Reason*, trans. Richard Howard (New York: Pantheon Books, 1965), esp. pp. 241–78. Nancy F. Cott, *The Bonds of Womanhood: "Woman's Sphere" in New England, 1780–1835* (New Haven: Yale University Press, 1977), and Ann Douglas, *The Feminization of American Culture* (New York: Alfred A. Knopf, 1977), have clarified the ideology of separate spheres. The classic statement of the change to modern rhythms is E. P. Thompson, "Time, Work-Discipline, and Industrial Capitalism," *Past and Present* no. 38 (1967): 56–97. Fidelia Fisk, *Recollections of Mary Lyon, with Selections from Her Instructions to the Pupils in Mt. Holyoke Female Seminary* (Boston: American Tract Society, 1866), pp. 317–33. Keith Melder, "Mask of Oppression: The Female Seminary Movement in the United States," *New York History* 55 (1974): 261–79, offered a quite different interpretation.

32. Nancy Chodorow, *The Reproduction of Mothering: Psychoanalysis and the Sociology of Gender* (Berkeley and Los Angeles: The University of California Press, 1978). Boys and young men experienced similarly intense, affectionate, transforming relationships with their teachers (David Newsome, *Godliness & Good Learning* [London: John Murray, 1961], pp. 84–89).

33. [Grant,] "Ipswich Female Seminary," 371.

34. Hitchcock, *Mary Lyon*, pp. 41–43, 136–37; Guilford, *Mrs. Z. P. Grant Banister*, pp. 98–99.

35. [Grant,] "Ipswich Female Seminary," 373.

36. Cole, *Hundred Years*, p. 9.

37. Quoted in Hitchcock, *Mary Lyon*, p. 158.

38. Mary Lyon to Edward Hitchcock, February 4, 1832, quoted *ibid.*, pp. 160–64; quote from p. 162.

39. Mary Lyon to Zilpah Grant, February 4, 1833, quoted *ibid.*, p, 176.

40. Lyon made this explicit in a letter to Grant, May 6, 1834, quoted in Hitchcock, *Mary Lyon*, pp. 193–95. Grant opposed both the domestic system and the missionary pay for teachers.

41. Prospectus, May 1837, quoted in Stow, *Mt. Holyoke*, pp. 72–73.

42. Mary Lyon to Zilpah Grant, March 1, 1833, quoted in Green, *Mary Lyon*, p. 93.

43. Circular to ladies, quoted in Hitchcock, *Mary Lyon*, p. 235.

44. *Ibid.*

45. M.L., *Mount Holyoke Female Seminary*, South Hadley, Sept. 1835, p. 2. Copy in The Huntington Library, San Marino, California.

46. Quoted in Green, *Mary Lyon*, p. 160.

47. *Ibid.*, pp. 130–34; 363, note 29.

48. Porter supervised the building process; Safford laid the original floor covering (Stow, *Mt. Holyoke*, pp. 62–63; Green, *Mary Lyon*, pp. 128–30).

49. A clear description is found in Laura A. Alaimo, "Mount Holyoke Female Seminary: A Setting," student paper, May 2, 1980, Mount Holyoke College Library/Archives, South Hadley, Mass.

50. Plates III and IV by Lucinda J. Goodale, 1888, in Mount Holyoke College Library/ Archives.

51. Guilford, *Mrs. Z. P. Grant Banister*, p. 117.

52. Plate VI by Elizabeth Landfear, Mount Holyoke College Library/Archives.

53. Conversation with Clifford Clark, January 1980, Carleton College, Northfield, Minnesota.

54. Richard P. Dober, *Campus Planning* (New York: Reinhold Publishing Corp., 1963), p. 14; Bryant Franklin Tolles, Jr., "College Architecture in New England before 1860 in Printed and Sketched Views," *Antiques* 103 (March 1973): 502–9.

55. Claude Moore Fuess, *Amherst: The Story of a New England College* (Boston: Little, Brown, 1935), pp. 40, 50, 56, 90–91; illustrations opposite pp. 39, 52, 69.

56. [George Rugg Cutting,] *Student Life at Amherst College: Its Organization, Their Membership and History* (Amherst: Hatch & Williams, 1871), esp. pp. 19, 96, 97–98, 132. Walter Pilkington, *Hamilton College, 1812/1962* (Clinton, New York: Hamilton College, 1962), pp. 89–113. On student culture more generally, see Frederick Rudolph, *The American College and University* (New York: Alfred A. Knopf. 1962), pp. 136–55.

57. Cole, *Hundred Years*, pp. 72–101, has the best discussion of discipline.

58. Louisa Maria Torrey to mother, April 1844, quoted *Ibid.*, p. 78.

59. *Foreshadowing of Smith College: Selections from the Letters of Louisa Dickinson to John Morton Green, 1856–1857*, ed. Helen French Greene (Portland, Maine: Southworth Press, 1928), p. 44.

60. Cole, *Hundred Years*, pp. 128–51.

61. *Ibid.*, pp. 57–58, 136–39.

62. *Ibid.*, pp. 54–55, 132–33.

63. *Foreshadowings of Smith College*, pp. 20–23; quote from p. 20.

64. David F. Allmendinger, Jr., "Mt. Holyoke Students Encounter the Need for Life Planning, 1837–1850," *History of Education Quarterly* 19 (1979): 40.

65. Frances Juliette Hosford, *Father Shipherd's Magna Charta: A Century of Coeducation in Oberlin College* (Boston: Marshall Jones Company, 1937), pp. 21–23.

CHAPTER 2　*More Lasting Than the Pyramids*

1. Arthur C. Cole, *A Hundred Years of Mount Holyoke College: The Evolution of an Educational Ideal* (New Haven: Yale University Press, 1940), pp. 9–10.

2. Frederick Rudolph, *Curriculum: A History of the Undergraduate Course of Study since 1636* (San Francisco: Jossey-Bass Publishers, 1977), pp. 54–98.

3. Henry Clyde Hubbart, *Ohio Wesleyan's First Hundred Years* (Delaware, Ohio: Ohio Wesleyan University, 1943), p. 18.

4. *Ibid.*, pp. 50–52.

5. Thomas Woody, *A History of Women's Education in the United States* (New York: The Science Press, 1929), 2: 160–67.

6. Gilbert Meltzer, *The Beginnings of Elmira College, 1851–68* (Elmira, New York: The Commercial Press, 1941).

7. Milo P. Jewett, "Origin of Vassar College," March 1879, typed copy, p. 5, Vassar College Library, Poughkeepsie, New York. The underlinings in the original have been deleted.

8. I have used extensively the excellent source, James Monroe Taylor, *Before Vassar Opened* (Boston and New York: Houghton Mifflin Co., 1914).

9. *Survey of London*, vol. 22, Bankside (London: London County Council, 1950), pp. 36–40; inscription on monument, quoted p. 40.

10. Edmund Platt, *The Eagle's History of Poughkeepsie from the Earliest Settlements, 1683–1905* (Poughkeepsie: Platt & Platt, 1905), pp. 104, 107, 108, 139, 140–42, 146, 148.

11. Christopher Tunnard, *The City of Man*, 2nd ed. (New York: Charles Scribner's Sons, 1970), pp. 179, 182.

12. Jewett, "Origin of Vassar College," pp. 5, 6.

13. *Ibid.*, p. 1; "Milo Parker Jewett," *Dictionary of American Biography* (New York: Charles Scribner's Sons, 1933), 10: 69–70.

14. Jewett, "Origin," p. 1.

15. Milo P. Jewett to Mary Lyon, Dec. 3, 1838, Mount Holyoke College Library/Archives, South Hadley, Mass.

16. *Alabama: A Documentary History to 1900*, ed. Lucille Griffith (University, Alabama: The University of Alabama Press, [1972]), p. 282; Louise Manly, *History of Judson College* (Atlanta, Ga.: Foote & Davies Company, 1913), photograph opposite p. 78.

17. *Alabama*, ed. Griffith, pp. 282–83.

18. Matthew Vassar to Angelina Grimké Weld, July 8, 1862, quoted in *The Autobiography and Letters of Matthew Vassar*, ed. Elizabeth Hazelton Haight (New York: Oxford University Press, 1916), p. 92.

19. John Howard Raymond to his wife, June 7, 1864, quoted in *Life and Letters of John Howard Raymond*, ed. Harriet Raymond Lloyd (New York: Fords, Howard, Huelbert, 1881), p. 513.

20. Letter from Matthew Vassar, July 1862, quoted in *Autobiography and Letters*, ed. Haight, p. 131.

21. Jewett, "Origin," p. 6. I have corrected Jewett's misspelling.

22. *Ibid..*, pp. 28–29.

23. I have relied heavily on Rosalie Thorne McKenna, "A Study of the Architecture of the Main Building and the Landscaping of Vassar College, 1860–70" (M.A. diss., New York University, 1949). This was summarized in two articles: "Mr. Vassar's Consecrated Bricks," *Vassar Alumnae Magazine* 35 (June 1950): 5–9; and "James Renwick, Jr. and the Second Empire Style in the United States," *Magazine of Art* 44 (1951): 97–101; "James Renwick," *Dictionary of American Biog-*

raphy (New York, Charles Scribner's Sons, 1927), 15: 507–8. Blackwells was renamed Roosevelt Island in 1973.

24. Nikolaus Pevsner, *A History of Building Types* (Princeton, N.J.: Princeton University Press, 1976), pp. 139–58; David J. Rothman, *The Discovery of the Asylum: Social Order and Disorder in the New Republic* (Boston and Toronto: Little, Brown, 1971), esp. pp. 109–54.

25. McKenna, "James Renwick, Jr.," 100.

26. Richard P. Dober, *Campus Planning* (New York: Reinhold Publishing Corp., 1963), pp. 19–23; quote from p. 19.

27. Bucknell University's Academy Building (1849) and Swarthmore College's Parrish Hall (1869) depart from collegiate planning for their coeducational student bodies, in their provision for all functions within a single monumental building. The religious emphasis and academy beginnings of both colleges suggest possible links to the asylum tradition, here deemed appropriate for younger and less worldly students, male as well as female.

28. Jewett, "Origin," p. 39.

29. *Ibid.*, p. 29. This may have been in imitation of Christopher Wren's Chelsea Hospital (1682–92), a great hospital structure which had just such an internal corridor (Kerry Downes, *The Architecture of Wren* [New York: Universe Books, 1982], pp. 83–87, plate 112).

30. *Autobiography and Letters*, ed. Haight, p. 68.

31. Jewett, "Origin," p. 29.

32. Taylor, *Before Vassar Opened*, p. 120.

33. *Autobiography and Letters*, ed. Haight, pp. 110, 175.

34. Milo P. Jewett to Matthew Vassar, ca. 1855–56, quoted in Jewett, "Origin," p. 8.

35. Quoted in McKenna, "Architecture of Main Building," p. 7.

36. The best source for the original internal plan of Vassar's Main is the detailed description, plans, illustrations in Benson J. Lossing, *Vassar College and Its Founder* (New York: C. A. Alford Printer, 1867); details here are from pp. 121–28.

37. *Ibid.*, pp. 126–28.

38. *Ibid.*, pp. 131–41; see also *Autobiography and Letters*, ed. Haight, pp. 126–28, 152–55.

39. Lossing, *Vassar College*, pp. 143–46.

40. *Ibid.*, p. 128.

41. McKenna, "Architecture of Main Building," pp. 55–63.

42. Matthew Vassar to Rufus Babcock, Oct. 23, 1861, quoted in *Autobiography and Letters*, ed. Haight, p. 65; underlinings in the original, misspelling corrected.

43. Ruth E. Finley, *The Lady of Godey's: Sarah Josepha Hale* (Philadelphia and London: J. B. Lippincott Company, 1931), pp. 205–21. Hale is chiefly remembered at Vassar as the one who urged the "Female" be removed from the original title "Vassar Female College."

44. In a letter to Rufus Babcock, Oct. 23, 1861, Vassar expressed his pleasure in the manner in which his college "meets with the highest encomium among the Literati" (quoted in *Autobiography and Letters*, ed. Haight, p. 65).

45. [Horatio Hale,] "Vassar College," *Godey's Lady's Book* 68 (1864): 199–200; quoted, 199.

46. Quoted in Finley, *Lady of Godey's*, p. 216.

47. The conflicts around Jewett are the subject of much of both his "Origin" and of Taylor, *Before Vassar Opened*, pp. 129–201.

48. Matthew Vassar, address to board of trustees, Feb. 23, 1864, *Communications to the Board of Trustees of Vassar College by Its Founder* (New York: Standard Printing and Publishing Company, 1886), p. 22.

49. *Ibid.*, p. 23.

50. "Vassar College To Be Opened This Year!" *Godey's Lady's Book* 68 (1864): 93–94; quote, 94.

51. See, for example, John Howard Raymond, "Mission of Educated Women," 1871, in *Life and Letters of John Howard Raymond*, pp. 725–38.

52. "Vassar College—And Its Organization," *Godey's Lady's Book* 68 (1864): 488.

53. *Life and Letters of John Howard Raymond*, pp. 533–56.

54. The former Zilpah Grant not only recommended Hannah Lyman, but visited Vassar on several occasions to review her work (Linda Thayer Guilford, *The Use of a Life: Memorials of Mrs. Z. P. Grant Banister* [New York: American Tract Society, 1885], pp. 331–50).

55. Elizabeth Alden Green, *Mary Lyon and Mount Holyoke: Opening the Gates* (Hanover, N.H.: University Press of New England, 1979), p. 141; Guilford, *Mrs. Z. P. Grant Banister*, p. 254; James Monroe Taylor and Elizabeth Hazelton Haight, *Vassar* (New York: Oxford University Press, 1915), p. 94.

56. Jewett, "Origin," pp. 29–30.

57. Lossing, *Vassar College*, plan, p. 122.

58. The conservatism of the board of trustees, especially of Matthew Vassar's nephews, is most clearly treated in Benson J. Lossing, "Secret History of the Founding of Vassar College," Autograph file, Vassar College Library. See Chapter 6 below.

59. Helen Wright, *Sweeper in the Sky: The Life of Maria Mitchell, First Woman Astronomer in America* (New York: Macmillan Co., 1949), pp. 153–56.

60. Matthew Vassar to M. B. Anderson, Jan. 28, 1864, in *Autobiography and Letters*, ed. Haight, p. 137. In discussing whether the college ought to furnish the apartments, Vassar wrote "some of them (if we have men) may have furniture & familys, and if Widows Ladies Teachers some may be thus situated also they may not all be single Women."

61. Frances A. Wood, *Earliest Years at Vassar* (Poughkeepsie: The Vassar College Press, 1909), p. 27.

62. *Historical Sketch of Vassar College, Founded at Poughkeepsie, N.Y., January 18, 1861* (New York: S. W. Green, Printer, 1876), p. 49.

63. Taylor, *Before Vassar Opened*, pp. 137–40.

64. *Life and Letters of John Howard Raymond*, p. 519; italics in the second quote deleted.

65. President's Report, 1866, manuscript, Vassar College, Vassar College Library.

66. *Historical Sketch*, p. 49.

67. John Howard Raymond to his wife, Sept. 23, 1865, quoted in *Life and Letters of John Howard Raymond*, p. 559.

68. John Howard Raymond to Matthew Vassar, May 13, 1864, quoted *ibid.*, p. 511; original italics removed.

69. John Howard Raymond to Lewis Henry Morgan, Feb. 20, 1873, Lewis Henry Morgan Papers, University of Rochester Library, Rochester, New York.

CHAPTER 3 *That Beauty Which Is Truth*

1. Sarah D. Stow, *History of Mount Holyoke Seminary, South Hadley, Mass. during Its First Half Century, 1837–1887* (Springfield, Mass.: Springfield Printing Company, 1887), p. 239.

2. The most candid source of biographical information about Durant is Florence Converse, *Wellesley College: A Chronicle of the Years, 1875–1938* (Wellesley: Hathaway House Bookshop, 1939), pp. 3–35. Though marred by extreme filiopietism, a full-length biography of Durant is useful: Florence Morse Kingsley, *The Life of Henry Fowle Durant* (New York: The Century Co., 1924). A balanced summary is given by Alice Payne Hackett, *Wellesley: Part of the American Story* (New York: E. P. Dutton, 1949), pp. 17–27.

3. Thomas Wentworth Higginson, "The Founder of Wellesley College," *The Woman's Journal* 12 (Oct. 15, 1881): 329.

4. Converse, *Wellesley College*, p. 8.

5. Higginson, "Founder of Wellesley College," 329.

6. Converse, *Wellesley College*, p. 9.

7. Higginson, "Founder of Wellesley College," 329.

8. Kingsley, *Henry Fowle Durant*, pp. 175–76; Mount Holyoke Journal letter, July 27, 1866, pp. 13–14, Mount Holyoke College Library/Archives, South Hadley, Mass.

9. Mount Holyoke Journal letter, p. 35, Mount Holyoke College Library/Archives.

10. Ann Douglas, *The Feminization of American Culture* (New York: Alfred A. Knopf, 1977), especially Chapter 2.

11. Henry Fowle Durant to Mr. Buttrick, Dec. 1, 1871, ALS file, Wellesley College Archives, Wellesley, Mass.

12. In contrast to the record of Mary Lyon and Matthew Vassar, there are few documents recording the vision of Durant. The fullest is Henry Fowle Durant, "The Spirit of the College," notes from a sermon, Founders File, Wellesley College Archives. Quote here is from p. 3.

13. *Ibid.*, pp. 4–5.

14. *Ibid.*, p. 5.

15. Mount Holyoke Journal letter, p. 34; Arthur C. Cole, *A Hundred Years of Mount Holyoke College: The Evolution of an Educational Ideal* (New Haven: Yale University Press, 1940), p. 142.

16. Quoted in Converse, *Wellesley College*, p. 16.

17. Converse, *Wellesley College*, p. 17; "Wellesley and Mount Holyoke: Some Early Connections of Mount Holyoke with Mr. Durant and Wellesley College," Mount Holyoke College Library/Archives.

18. Dorothy Scovil Vickery, *Hollins College, 1842–1942* (Hollins College, Va.: Hollins College, 1942), pp. 19–41; Frances J. Niederer, *Hollins College: An Illustrated History* (Charlottesville: The University Press of Virginia, 1973), p. 11.

19. Circular of Wellesley College, 1876, copy in Wellesley College Archives. The women trustees with husbands on the board were, in addition to Mrs. Durant, Mrs. William Claflin and Mrs. M. H. Simpson. Mrs. Arthur Wilkinson had no husband on the board.

20. Cole, *Hundred Years*, pp. 182–83.

21. James Monroe Taylor and Elizabeth Hazelton Haight, *Vassar* (New York: Oxford University Press, 1915), pp. 149–50.

22. Richard Stoddard, "Hammatt Billings: Artist and Architect," *Old-Time New England* 62 (1972): 57–65, 76–79. College Hall was lost in the fire of 1914.

23. *Gems from Tennyson*, with illustrations by Hammatt Billings (Philadelphia: Porter & Coates, 1888).

24. Hackett, *Wellesley*, pp. 32–33.

25. "Possibly visits to Vassar had had something to do with the change, for Mr. and Mrs. Durant studied Vassar when they were making their own plans" (Converse, *Wellesley College*, p. 17).

26. Three important descriptions of the college are Edward Abbott, "Wellesley College," *Harper's New Monthly Magazine* 53 (1876): 321–32, the best contemporary account; Margaret Shackford, "College Hall," copy in Wellesley College Archives; and Lee Ann Clements, "Tower and Roof and Pinnacle: A Study of College Hall and Its Architects," student paper, May 5, 1978, Wellesley College Archives.

27. Hammatt Billings, "Sketch Plan of Principal Story of Wellesley Female Seminary," Wellesley College Archives.

28. Abbott, "Wellesley College," 323, 324.

29. Montgomery Schuyler, "Three Women's Colleges—Vassar, Wellesley & Smith," *Architectural Record* 31 (1912): 535.

30. Abbott, "Wellesley College," 324.

31. Quoted in Kingsley, *Henry Fowle Durant*, p. 199. This quotation has wrongly been considered not as an observer's reaction but as indicative of Durant's intention: see, for example, Margaret Shackford, "College Hall" [p. 1].

32. Abbott, "Wellesley College," 325.

33. Kingsley writes of the Durants' disillusionment with college students in their first year, giving the breaking of the Wedgwood as her example (*Henry Fowle Durant*, pp. 233–34).

34. Shackford, "College Hall," [p. 7].

35. *Ibid.*

36. The best description of student rooms is Shackford, "College Hall," [p. 2].

37. Speech at the laying of the cornerstone of Stone Hall, quoted in Kingsley, *Henry Fowle Durant*, p. 256.

38. Minutes of the Board of Trustees, Wellesley College, June 18, 1872, vol. 1, p. xxii, Wellesley College Archives.

39. Henry Fowle Durant to [Dr. Azel Ames?], Nov. 11, 1874, ALS file, Wellesley College Archives. The position was Professor of Physiology.

40. Hackett, *Wellesley*, pp. 48–49.

41. *Ibid.*, quoted, p. 31.

42. Thomas Wentworth Higginson, "Wellesley College," *The Woman's Journal* 11 (June 5, 1880): 177.

43. Converse, *Wellesley College*, pp. 24–26; Shackford, "College Hall," [p. 4].

CHAPTER 4 *Acting a* Manly *Part*

1. Mabel Newcomer, *A Century of Higher Education for American Women* (New York: Harper, 1959), p. 19.

2. Thomas Woody, *A History of Women's Education in the United States* (New York: The Science Press, 1929), 2: 185.

3. [E. A. Andrews,] "General View of the Principles and Design of the Mount Holyoke Female Seminary," *The Religious Magazine*, n.s., 1 (1887): 188.

4. *Ibid.*, 186.

5. *Ibid.*, 188.

6. Elizabeth Alden Green, *Mary Lyon and Mount Holyoke: Opening the Gates* (Hanover, N.H.: University Press of New England, 1979), p. 335.

7. President's Report, 1869, Vassar College, manuscript, Vassar College Library, Poughkeepsie, New York.

8. Diary entry, Dec. 19, 1869, quoted in C. L. Hunt, *The Life of Ellen H. Richards* (Boston: Whilcomb & Barrons, 1912), p. 67.

9. John Howard Raymond to his wife, Feb. 16, 1872, Autograph file, Vassar College Library.

10. Sarah Glazier to Isabel Treadwell, March 7, 1865, printed in "Some Vassar Letters, 1865–1870," ed. with intro. by Constance Mayfield Rourke, *Vassar Quarterly* 7 (May 1922): 161–62.

11. Diary entry, Dec. 19, 1869, quoted in Hunt, *Ellen H. Richards*, p. 67.

12. *Maria Mitchell, Life, Letters, and Journals*, compiled by Phebe Mitchell Kendall (Boston: Lee and Shepard, 1896), pp. 178–80; Mary King Babbitt, *Maria Mitchell as Her Students Knew Her* (Poughkeepsie: n. pub., 1912), pp. 20–21.

13. Quoted in *Maria Mitchell, Life, Letters, and Journals*, p. 185. Original in italics.

14. Helen Wright, *Sweeper in the Sky: The Life of Maria Mitchell, First Woman Astronomer in America* (New York: Macmillan Co., 1940), pp. 146–204.

15. Diary entry, quoted in Hunt, *Ellen H. Richards*, p. 78.

16. *Ibid.*, p. 53.

17. *Letters from Old-Time Vassar, Written by a Student in 1869–70* (Poughkeepsie: Vassar College, 1915), p. 66.

18. President's Report, 1870, Vassar College, manuscript, Vassar College Library.

19. *Ibid.*

20. John Howard Raymond to O. C. Gardiner, Jan. 25, 1871, Autograph file, Vassar College Library.

21. Mary Harriott Norris, *The Golden Age of Vassar* (Poughkeepsie: Vassar College, 1915), p. 102.

22. *Ibid.*, p. 111.

23. *Historical Sketch of Vassar College Founded at Poughkeepsie, New York, Jan. 18, 1861* (New York: S. W. Green, Printer, 1876), p. 39.

24. Vivian Gurney, "Philaletheis," *The Vassar Miscellany*, Fiftieth Anniversary number (Oct. 1915): 93–99.

25. *Letters from Old-Time Vassar*, pp. 71, 74.

26. Norris, *Golden Age of Vassar*, p. 160.

27. *Letters from Old-Time Vassar*, p. 147.

28. *Ibid.*, p. 23.

29. *Ibid.*, p. 102.

30. Norris, *Golden Age of Vassar*, pp. 18–19.

31. *Ibid.*, p. 21.

32. I am struck by the similarities between the emergence of college life and the adaptations of inmates to total institutions that Erving Goffman describes in *Asylums: Essays on the Social Situation of Mental Patients and Other Inmates* (Garden City, New York: Doubleday & Co., 1961). See, for example, pp. 54–60.

33. Diary entry, March 20, 1870, quoted in Hunt, *Ellen H. Richards*, p. 74.

34. *Ibid.*, April 26, 1869, p. 54.

35. Quoted in Nancy Sahli, "Smashing: Women's Relationships Before the Fall," *Chrysalis* 8 (1979): 22.

36. *Ibid.*

37. *Letters from Old-Time Vassar*, p. 43.

38. Norris, *Golden Age of Vassar*, p. 76.

39. President's Report, 1872, Vassar College, manuscript, Vassar College Library.

40. *Letters from Old-Time Vassar*, pp. 136–37.

41. Quoted in Sahli, "Smashing," 21.

CHAPTER 5   *To Preserve Her Womanliness*

1. The following narrative is based on Elizabeth Deering Hanscom and Helen French Greene, *Sophia Smith and the Beginnings of Smith College* (Northampton: Smith College, 1926). The book is a complex work: early documents and correspondence are interspersed with John Morton Greene's narrative, dating from 1910 to 1919, and the author's own commentary.

2. Copy of will, *ibid.*, pp. 60–62.

3. John M. Greene to Sophia Smith, April 28, 1869, quoted *Ibid.*, pp. 70–71.

4. L. Clark Seelye, *The Early History of Smith College, 1871–1910* (Boston: Houghton Mifflin Co., 1923), pp. 7–10.

5. Claude Moore Fuess, *Amherst: The Story of a New England College* (Boston: Little, Brown, 1935), pp. 192–94.

6. This is best seen in L. Clark Seelye, "The Need of a Collegiate Education for Women," paper read before the American Institute of Instruction, July 28, 1874 (n.p.: American Institute of Instruction, 1874), pp. 27–31.

7. Hanscom and Greene, *Sophia Smith*, pp. 80–81.

8. Quoted *ibid.*, p. 96.

9. Harriet Seelye Rhees, "Laurenus Clark Seelye, a Biographical Sketch," *Smith Alumnae Quarterly* 16 (May 1925): 267–70.

10. Thomas Le Duc, *Piety and Intellect at Amherst College, 1865–1912* (New York: Columbia University Press, 1946). Reference to Seelye, p. 14.

11. Le Duc, *Amherst College*, p. 14.

12. Hanscom and Greene, *Sophia Smith*, p. 84.

13. Seelye, "Need of a Collegiate Education for Women," p. 16.

14. *Ibid.*, pp. 15–16.

15. *Ibid.*, p. 13.

16. *Ibid.*, p. 14.

17. *Ibid.*, p. 28.

18. *Ibid.*, p. 31.

19. *Ibid.*, p. 24.

20. *Ibid.*, p. 25.

21. *Celebration of the Quarter-Century of Smith College*, Oct. 2, 3, 1900 (Cambridge, Mass.: Riverside Press, 1900), p. 91, footnote 1.

22. Homer Folks, *The Care of Destitute, Neglected and Delinquent Children* (New York: Macmillan Co., 1911), pp. 14–15, 220–21.

23. Gerald N. Grob, *Mental Institutions in America: Social Policy to 1875* (New York: The Free Press, 1973), pp. 325–38.

24. [J. G Holland,] "A New Woman's College," *Scribner's Monthly* 6 (Oct. 1873): 748.

25. L. Clark Seelye, *Addresses at the Inauguration of Rev. L. Clark Seelye as President of Smith College, July 14, 1875* (Springfield, Mass.: Clark W. Bryan and Co., 1877), p. 27.

26. Wheaton A. Holden, "The Peabody Touch: Peabody and Stearns of Boston, 1870–1917," *Journal of the Society of Architectural Historians* 32 (May 1973): 130–31. The firm submitted the winning entry in a competition.

27. I profited from the undergraduate paper of Ann Gilkerson, "The High Victorian Style: College Hall (Peabody & Stearns, 1875)," April 1976, Smith College Archives, Northampton, Mass.

28. Material on Social Hall, Smith College Archives; floor plans, Seelye, *Early History*, illustration between pp. 36 and 37.

29. Richard C. Cote, "Rethinking the Early Greek Revival: The Success of Influences and the Failure of a Builder," *Old-Time New England* 64 (Jan.–June 1974): 61–74.

30. Plans of Smith College Buildings, Registrar's Office, Smith College Archives.

31. Smith College President's Report, typescript copy, 1876–77, p. 4; 1877–78, p. 4, Smith College Archives.

32. Montgomery Schuyler, "Three Women's Colleges—Vassar, Wellesley & Smith," *Architectural Record* 31 (1912): 529.

33. Plans of Smith College Buildings, Registrar's Office, Smith College Archives.

34. Quoted in Hanscom and Greene, *Sophia Smith*, p. 63.

35. Seelye, *Early History*, Appendix I, p. 226.

36. *Ibid.*, pp. 36–37.

37. Kate Morris Cone, "Dewey House Rounds Out a Century," *The Smith Alumnae Quarterly* 18 (May 1927): 257.

38. *Addresses at the Inauguration of Rev. L. Clark Seelye*, p. 26.

39. [Holland,] "A New Woman's College," 749; italics in original.

40. Seelye, *Early History*, p. 36.

41. Smith College President's Report, typescript copy, 1875–76, pp. 1–2, Smith College Archives.

42. Kate Sanborn, "Social Life at Smith College," *Demorest's Monthly Magazine* 19 (July 1883): 539.

43. Smith College President's Report, typescript copy, 1875–76, pp. 4–5, Smith College Archives.

44. *Ibid.*, 1877–78, p. 4.

45. *Ibid.*, p. 3.

CHAPTER 6   *The Advantages of the So-called "Cottage System"*

1. Nancy Sahli, "Smashing: Women's Relationships Before the Fall," *Chrysalis* 8 (1979): 19–20; letters from Francis Robinson Johnson to her mother, June 11, 1876 and June 14, 1876, quoted p. 20.

2. Florence Morse Kingsley, *The Life of Henry Fowle Durant* (New York: Century Co., 1924), pp. 233–34.

3. "Wellesley College," *Barnard's American Journal of Education*, International Series 5 (March 15, 1880): 169.

4. Louise Manning Hodgkins, "Wellesley College," *New England Magazine*, n.s., 7 (1892): 367–68.

5. Circular, Wellesley College, 1877–78, p. 24, copy in Wellesley College Archives, Wellesley, Mass.

6. Alice Payne Hackett, *Wellesley: Part of the American Story* (New York: E. P. Dutton, 1949), p. 72.

7. "A Woman's Work for Woman," *Journal of Education* 14 (June 30, 1881), Clippings Scrapbook, Wellesley College Archives.

8. William R. Ware had organized the School of Architecture at the Massachusetts Institute of Technology, after the scientific school had sent him to study at the Ecole des Beaux Arts. Working in an eclectic mode in partnership with Henry Van Brunt, Ware designed important educational buildings. (Henry F. Withey and Elsie Rathburn Withey, *Biographical Dictionary of American Architects [Deceased]* [originally published 1956, facsimile edition Los Angeles: Hennessy & Ingalls, 1970], pp. 632–33.)

9. "Stone Hall, Wellesley," *American Architect and Building News* 7 (Feb. 7, 1880): 46, illustration no. 215.

10. Mary Watters, *The History of Mary Baldwin College, 1842–1942* (Staunton, Va.: Mary Baldwin College, 1942), pp. 101–4.

11. Circular, Wellesley College, 1880–81, pp. 35–37, copy in Wellesley College Archives.

12. This was pointed out when the new music building was dedicated (*Address at the Opening of Billings Hall, Oct. 15, 1904*, copy in Wellesley College Archives).

13. "Wellesley College" and "Reception at Wellesley" (Sept. 24, 1888), Clippings Scrapbook,

Wellesley College Archives; *Wellesley: The College Beautiful*, ed. Mary Brigham Hill and Helen Gertrude Eager (Boston: Frank Wood, Printer, 1894), pp. 28–29. Montgomery Schuyler pointed to the discordant effect of buildings in such varied styles in "Three Women's Colleges—Vassar, Wellesley and Smith," *Architectural Record* 31 (1912): 535.

14. Minutes of the Board of Trustees, Wellesley College, June 7, 1888, vol. 2, p. 3, copy in Wellesley College Archives.

15. Kingsley, *Henry Fowle Durant*, pp. 336–37.

16. Thomas Wentworth Higginson, "Wellesley College," *The Woman's Journal* 11 (June 5, 1880): 177.

17. Kingsley, *Henry Fowle Durant*, p. 328.

18. Minutes of the Board of Trustees, Wellesley College, June 5, 1884, vol. 1, p. 130, copy in Wellesley College Archives.

19. Barbara Miller Solomon, "Alice Elvira Freeman Palmer," *Notable American Women*, ed. Edward T. James (Cambridge, Mass.: Belknap Press of Harvard University Press, 1971), 3:4–8; Hackett, *Wellesley*, pp. 71, 77–78, 88; see, for example, *The President's Report to the Board of Trustees for the Year Ending June 19, 1883* (Boston: Frank Wood, Printer, 1883).

20. Roberta Frankfort, *Collegiate Women: Domesticity and Career in Turn-of-the-Century America* (New York: New York University Press, 1977), pp. 60–69.

21. Letters from Alice Freeman to Sophonisba Preston Breckinridge, Breckinridge Family Collection, Library of Congress, Washington, D.C.

22. "Wellesley College," *Boston Journal*, June 9, 1881, copy in Clippings Scrapbook, Wellesley College Archives.

23. *Wellesley: The College Beautiful*, p. 29.

24. Winifred Augsbury Cook, "Norumbega History," manuscript in Wellesley College Archives; quote from Margaret Sherwood's recollections included in the manuscript history. Letter to Mrs. Samuel C. Cook, Jan. 17, 1938, copy in Unprocessed Residence files, Wellesley College Archives.

25. Benson J. Lossing did everything within his power to keep Vassar College from accepting the brothers' bequests (Lossing letters in Autograph file, Vassar College Library, Poughkeepsie, New York). His "Secret History of the Founding of Vassar College," undated, Autograph file, Vassar College Library, outlines the case against the Vassar brothers. Milo Jewett's "Origin of Vassar College," March 1879, Vassar College Library, gives much detail.

26. President's Report, 1884, Vassar College, Vassar College Library.

27. M. Carey Thomas, Notebook I, April 22, 1884, M. Carey Thomas Professional Papers, Bryn Mawr Organization, Bryn Mawr College Archives, Bryn Mawr, Pa.

28. A trustee, J. Ryland Kendrick, served as "provisional president" for a year, during which the trustees looked for someone to become Vassar's president (James Monroe Taylor and Elizabeth Hazelton Height, *Vassar* [New York: Oxford University Press, 1915], p. 145).

29. Debra Herman, "College and After: The Vassar Experiment in Women's Education, 1861–1924," Ph.D. dissertation, Stanford University (University Microfilms, 1979).

30. President's Report, 1889, Vassar College, Vassar College Library.

31. James Monroe Taylor, "The Future of the Woman's College," in *Addresses at the Celebration of the Completion of the Twenty-fifth Academic Year of Vassar College, June, 1890*, pp. 92–93, quote from p. 93, copy in The Huntington Library, San Marino, California; President's Report, Vassar College, 1897, manuscript, Vassar College Library.

32. The president's house was designed after the manner of an English house by Ellsworth Rossiter of the New York firm Rossiter and Wright. (James M. Taylor to Mr. Elsworth, July 2, 1895, Taylor letters, Vassar College Library)

33. James Monroe Taylor, "The Vassar Campus: A History, 1886–1914," *Vassar Quarterly* 1 (July 1916): 161.

34. Henry Noble MacCracken, "Uncle Fred and Aunt Mary," *Vassar Alumnae Magazine*, May 15, 1936, pp. 3–5. Quote from p. 3; Henry Noble MacCracken, *The Hickory Limb* (New York: Charles Scribner's Sons, 1950), p. 31.

35. Taylor, "Vassar Campus," 162.

36. MacCracken, "Uncle Fred and Aunt Mary," p. 4.

37. Taylor, "Vassar Campus," 162–63; Sarah Stage has graciously furnished me with this information from her research on Ellen Richards.

38. Allan Nevins, *John D. Rockefeller: The Heroic Age of American Enterprise* (New York: Charles Scribner's Sons, 1940) 1:456; *The Magnificent Enterprise: A Chronicle of Vassar College*, compiled by Dorothy A. Plum and George B. Dowell (Poughkeepsie: Vassar College, 1961), pp. 26–32.

39. "Strong Hall, Vassar," *American Architect and Building News* 42 (Dec. 16, 1893): illustration no. 938, following p. 140.

40. Taylor, "Vassar Campus," 164.

CHAPTER 7   *As Unnoticed as the Daughters of Any Cambridge Residents*

1. Arthur Gilman to Charles W. Eliot, Dec. 23, 1878, copy in Arthur Gilman diary, pp. 4–7, Radcliffe College Archives, Cambridge, Mass.

2. "Society for Collegiate Instruction of Women in Cambridge," p. 8.

3. Thomas Wentworth Higginson, "Which College?" *The Woman's Journal* 7 (Feb. 26, 1876): 65.

4. Thomas Wentworth Higginson, "The Wellesley College for Women," *The Woman's Journal* 5 (Nov. 28, 1874): 379.

5. Higginson, "Which College?" 65.

6. For example, "The Atlantic Monthly on Scientific Education for Women," *The Woman's Journal* 5 (May 30, 1874): 169; "Harvard Courses for Both Sexes," *The Woman's Journal* 7 (June 17, 1876): 193.

7. Ronald Story, *The Forging of an Aristocracy: Harvard and the Boston Upper Class, 1800–1870* (Middletown, Conn.: Wesleyan University Press, 1980).

8. Hugh Hawkins, *Between Harvard and America: The Educational Leadership of Charles W. Eliot* (New York: Oxford University Press, 1972).

9. Thomas Wentworth Higginson, "President Eliot at Smith College," *The Woman's Journal* 10 (June 28, 1879): 201; italics deleted.

10. See M. Carey Thomas' famous rejoinder, "The Bryn Mawr Woman," reprinted in Barbara M. Cross, *The Educated Woman in America*, Classics in Education no. 25 (New York: Teachers College Press, 1965), pp. 139–44. This quite provocative selection of documents first pricked my scholarly interest in the subject of women's higher education.

11. Charlotte Williams Conable, *Women at Cornell: The Myth of Equal Education* (Ithaca, N.Y.: Cornell University Press, 1977), pp. 115–26.

12. "The Society for the Collegiate Instruction of Women in Cambridge, Mass.: Report of the Ladies of the Executive Committee" (Cambridge, Mass.: William H. Wheeler, 1884), p. 7.

13. Arthur Gilman diary, Nov. 25, 1878, p. 1.

14. Barbara Stephen, *Girton College, 1869–1932* (Cambridge: University Press, 1933), pp. 1–69, esp. pp. 57–60 for the building.

15. [E. T. Minturn,] "Girton College," *The Nation* 22 (1876): 58. This article was read at a meeting of the Ladies' Committee and Prof. Greenough, Feb. 4, 1879 (Arthur Gilman diary, p. 11).

16. Arthur Gilman to Charles W. Eliot, Oct. 23, 1879, copy in Arthur Gilman diary, p. 34.

17. *Ibid.*, p. 36.

18. Arthur Gilman diary, Nov. 26, 1878, pp. 2–3.

19. Arthur Gilman, "Elizabeth Cary Agassiz," *Harvard Graduates Magazine* 16 (1907–8): 39.

20. Lucy Allen Paton, *Elizabeth Cary Agassiz: A Biography* (Boston and New York: Houghton Mifflin Co., 1919), pp. 192–274 passim.

21. W. E. Byerly, "Arthur Gilman and the Harvard Annex," *Harvard Graduates Magazine* 18 (1909–10): 586–87.

22. "Private Collegiate Instruction for Women, Cambridge, Mass., Feb. 22, 1879," copy in Radcliffe College Archives.

23. Arthur Gilman diary, Feb. 13, 1879, p. 13.

24. "Private Collegiate Instruction for Women."

25. Arthur Gilman letter, Feb. 17, 1879, copy in diary, p. 16.

26. Arthur Gilman to Charles W. Eliot, Dec. 23, 1878, copy in Arthur Gilman diary, p. 6.

27. Arthur Gilman diary, Sept. 27, 1879, pp. 30–31.

28. "Society for Collegiate Instruction of Women in Cambridge," p. 6.

29. Ladies of the Executive Committee, "The Harvard 'Annex,'" flyer, June 15, 1885, p. 2, copy in Radcliffe College Archives.

30. Elizabeth Cary Agassiz to Arthur Gilman, March 24, 1882, quoted in Paton, *Elizabeth Cary Agassiz*, p. 206.

CHAPTER 8 *A Certain Style of "Quaker Lady" Dress*

1. Data on Taylor's life and on the founding of Bryn Mawr are from Cornelia Meigs, *What Makes a College? A History of Bryn Mawr* (New York: Macmillan Co., 1956) and Margaret Taylor MacIntosh, *Joseph Wright Taylor, Founder of Bryn Mawr College* (Haverford, Pa.: C. S. Taylor, 1936).

2. Meigs, *History of Bryn Mawr*, p. 19.

3. Francis King to Joseph W. Taylor, April 13, 1877, quoted in MacIntosh, *Joseph Wright Taylor*, p. 184.

4. James E. Rhoads to Joseph W. Taylor, June 30, 1877, quoted *ibid.*, pp. 186–87.

5. Quoted *Ibid.*, p. 188.

6. Quoted in Michelle Osborne, "The Making of the Early Bryn Mawr Campus," part 1, *Bryn Mawr NOW*, Bryn Mawr College Archives, Bryn Mawr, Pa.; misspelling corrected.

7. MacIntosh, *Joseph Wright Taylor*, p. 192.

8. Francis T. King to Joseph W. Taylor, Aug. 28, 1878, quoted *ibid.*, p. 192.

9. L. Clark Seelye to J. W. Taylor, Nov. 27, 1878, draft copy, Seelye correspondence, box S-T, Taylor file, Smith College Archives, Northampton, Mass. The final version is given unless indicated. This was a commissioned letter, as were those from President Gilman of Johns Hopkins and Annie E. Johnson, principal of Bradford Academy.

10. *Ibid.*, pp. 2–13, quote from p. 4.

11. *Ibid.*, p. 4.

12. *Ibid.*, p. 5.

13. *Ibid.*, p. 15.

14. *Ibid.*, pp. 15–16.

15. *Ibid.*, p. 18.

16. *Ibid.*, pp. 18–19.

17. The first quote was crossed out in the original. *Ibid.*, p. 13.

18. *Ibid.*, p. 19.

19. MacIntosh, *Joseph Wright Taylor*, p. 188.

20. King to Taylor, March 11, 1879, quoted *Ibid.*, p. 194.

21. *Bryn Mawr College: Academic Buildings and Halls of Residence: Plans and Descriptions* (n. p.: n. pub., 1907), n.p.

22. *A History of Haverford College for the First Sixty Years of Its Existence* (Philadelphia: Porter & Coates, 1892), pp. 419–20.

23. *Bryn Mawr College: Academic Buildings.*

24. *Ibid.*

25. Addison Hutton, record and letterbook, M. Carey Thomas Papers, Incoming Correspondence, Bryn Mawr College Archives.

26. Quoted in Meigs, *History of Bryn Mawr*, p. 28.

27. Anna Heubeck Knipp and Thaddeus P. Thomas, *The History of Goucher College* (Baltimore: Goucher College, 1938), pp. 4–20, 262.

28. Martha Carey Thomas to Dr. J. E. Rhoads, Aug. 14, 1883, quoted in *The Making of a Feminist: Early Journals and Letters of M. Carey Thomas*, ed. Marjorie Houspian Dobkin (Kent, Ohio: The Kent State University Press, 1979), p. 278.

29. Journal entry, March 14, 1872, reproduced *ibid.*, pp. 69–70.

30. Biographical material on Thomas is found *ibid.*, 1–27; Edith Finch, *Carey Thomas of Bryn Mawr* (New York: Harper & Brothers Publishers, 1947); Lawrence R. Veysey, "Martha Carey Thomas," *Notable American Women*, ed. Edward T. James (Cambridge, Mass.: Belknap Press of Harvard University Press, 1971), 3:446–50.

31. Charlotte Williams Conable, *Women at Cornell: The Myth of Equal Education* (Ithaca: Cornell University Press, 1977), pp. 84–97.

32. M. Carey Thomas to Mary Whitall Thomas, Nov. 30, 1882, quoted in *Early Journals and Letters of M. Carey Thomas*, ed. Dobkin, p. 265.

33. M. Carey Thomas to Mary Whitall Thomas, Jan. 30, 1883, quoted *ibid.*, p. 272.

34. *Ibid.*, p. 271.

35. M. Carey Thomas to Mary Garrett, April 26, 1884, M. Carey Thomas Papers, Bryn Mawr College Archives.

36. M. Carey Thomas Notebook I, April 22, 1884, M. Carey Thomas Professional Papers, Bryn Mawr Organization, Bryn Mawr College Archives.

37. M. Carey Thomas, Report to the President and Trustees, Bryn Mawr College, June 7, 1884, p. 19, M. Carey Thomas Professional Papers, Bryn Mawr Organization, Bryn Mawr College Archives.

38. M. Carey Thomas to Mary Garrett, July 21, 1884, M. Carey Thomas Papers, Bryn Mawr College Archives.

39. Thomas, Report to President and Trustees, pp. 9–11; quotes from p. 9 and p. 11.

40. M. Carey Thomas Notebook I, M. Carey Thomas Professional Papers, Bryn Mawr Organization, Bryn Mawr College Archives.

41. *Ibid.*, April 22, 1884.

42. M. Carey Thomas to Mary Garrett, April 26, 1884, M. Carey Thomas Papers, Bryn Mawr College Archives.

43. M. Carey Thomas to Mary Garrett, May 3, 1884, M. Carey Thomas Papers, Bryn Mawr College Archives.

44. Thomas, Report to President and Trustees, p. 29.

45. *Ibid.*, p. 24.

46. M. Carey Thomas to Mary Garrett, May 28, 1884, M. Carey Thomas Papers, Bryn Mawr College Archives.

47. M. Carey Thomas to Mary Garrett, July 21, 1884, M. Carey Thomas Papers, Bryn Mawr College Archives.

CHAPTER 9   Behold They Are Women!

1. M. Carey Thomas to Mary Garrett, March 24, 1893, M. Carey Thomas Papers, Bryn Mawr College Archives, Bryn Mawr, Pa.

2. Cornelia Meigs, *What Makes a College? A History of Bryn Mawr* (New York: Macmillan Co., 1956) only gives the barest hint of these controversies, pp. 66–67. They are apparent from M. Carey Thomas' personal correspondence, Bryn Mawr College Archives, especially her letters to Mary Garrett. Lucy Fisher West's careful preparation of the M. Carey Thomas Papers for microfilming includes useful summaries at the beginning of each reel, which point directly to Thomas' conflicts with the board.

3. Michelle Osborne, "The Making of the Early Bryn Mawr Campus," part 2, *Bryn Mawr NOW*, Bryn Mawr College Archives. Thomas invited Peabody and Stearns, architects of early Smith College, to enter a competition, but they did not make an entry.

4. Buford Pickens and Margaretta J. Darnall, *Washington University in St. Louis: Its Design and Architecture* (St. Louis: School of Architecture, Washington University, 1978), provides an excellent summary of the work of Cope and Stewardson and an introduction to college planning. They make it clear that Cope was the principal designer, p. 21. For information on Walter Cope and John Stewardson, see Henry F. Withey and Elsie Rathburn Withey, *Biographical Dictionary of American Architects (Deceased)* (originally published 1956, facsimile edition Los Angeles: Hennessy & Ingalls, 1970), pp. 139–40, 574. M. Carey Thomas, "Memorial Address on Walter Cope, Architect," *The Lantern* 14 (Feb. 1905): 10–14, establishes Thomas' relation to Cope's aesthetic.

5. M. Carey Thomas made assertions that she was fully responsible for the plan and for many design elements of buildings in her correspondence, such as in her letter to John G. Johnson, Jan. 4, 1908, M. Carey Thomas Professional Papers, Bryn Mawr College Archives. While this may have exaggerated her role, it is clear that she set internal plans prior to discussion with the architect. See Monthly Reports of the President to the Trustees, Jan. 10, 1890, Bryn Mawr College Archives.

6. Journal entry, March 14, 1874, reproduced in *The Making of a Feminist: Early Journals and Letters of M. Carey Thomas*, ed. Marjorie Housepian Dobkin (Kent, Ohio: The Kent State University Press, 1979), p. 70.

7. M. Carey Thomas, "Education for Women and for Men," reprinted in Barbara M. Cross, *The Educated Woman in America*, Classics in Education no. 25 (New York: Teachers College Press, 1965), p. 151.

8. *Ibid.*, pp. 147–48.

9. Barbara Cross, "Introduction," *ibid.*, pp. 32–45; Academic Dress file, Bryn Mawr History, M. Carey Thomas Professional Papers, Bryn Mawr College Archives.

10. The first non-Quaker is discussed in Monthly Reports of the President to the Trustees, Oct. 10, 1887, Bryn Mawr College Archives.

11. *Ibid.*, Feb. 15, 1901.

12. Meigs, *History of Bryn Mawr*, pp. 54–58.

13. M. Carey Thomas to Mary Garrett, May 10, 1895, M. Carey Thomas Papers, Bryn Mawr College Archives.

14. The clearest statement comes in Gertrude Stein, *Fernhurst* in *Fernhurst, Q.E.D., and Other Early Writings* (New York: Liveright, 1971), pp. 5–6, where Thomas appears in fictional guise as Helen Thornton.

15. "In all these years I have grown Ruskinian. In a sense I believe every word of our modern Chrysostomos" (M. Carey Thomas to Mary Garrett, July 31, 1884, M. Carey Thomas Papers, Bryn Mawr College Archives).

16. M. Carey Thomas to Mary Garrett, May 10, 1897, M. Carey Thomas Papers, Bryn Mawr College Archives.

17. Lawrence R. Veysey, "Martha Carey Thomas," *Notable American Women*, ed. Edward T. James (Cambridge, Mass.: Belknap Press of Harvard University Press, 1971) 3: 446–50.

18. M. Carey Thomas to Mary Garrett, March 8, 1891, M. Carey Thomas Papers, Bryn Mawr College Archives.

19. Trustees tended to question the propriety of May Day festivities, for the frolics looked much like dancing. See Opal Thornburg, *Earlham: the Story of the College, 1847–1962* (Richmond, Indiana: The Earlham College Press, 1963), pp. 223–24.

20. For example, M. Carey Thomas to Mary Garrett, Jan. 11, 1897, M. Carey Thomas Papers, Bryn Mawr College Archives.

21. Edith Finch, *Carey Thomas of Bryn Mawr* (New York: Harper & Brothers Publishers, 1947), pp. 244–45.

22. Veysey, "Martha Carey Thomas," assumes her homosexuality, while Dobkin, Introduction to "Boarding School and College," *Making of a Feminist*, pp. 78–87, asserts her heterosexuality. Dobkin printed the letters from the years before 1885, which include Thomas' affectionate relationship with her cousin Frank Smith, her involvement with Francis Gummere, and her decision to have a career and not marry. Throughout her letters to Mary Garrett, Thomas expresses her attraction for individual men and women (for example, April 10, 1884), but always within the context of her faithfulness to Garrett.

23. Osborne, "Making of the Early Bryn Mawr Campus," Part 2.

24. *Ibid.*, this brief but able summary of planning decisions was very useful; as was George Thomas, "The Architecture of the Bryn Mawr Campus," *Bryn Mawr NOW*, Bryn Mawr College Archives, and Pickens and Darnall, *Washington University*, pp. 8–10. Of greatest benefit was Kennedy Smith, "History of the Architecture and Planning of the Bryn Mawr Campus," B.A. thesis, Bryn Mawr College, 1979. I am grateful to Kennedy Smith not only for making available to me her fine study, but also for her generous guidance through the Bryn Mawr College Archives and the M. Carey Thomas Papers, which included lending me her own transcripts of archival material unavailable due to microfilming. Denbigh predates both Cope and Stewardson's reshaping of the University of Pennsylvania and Henry Ives Cobb's plan for the University of Chicago, normally seen as the critical breakthroughs in quadrangle design (Richard P. Dober, *Campus Planning* [New York: Reinhold Publishing Corp., 1963], p. 32).

25. Osborne, "Making of the Early Bryn Mawr Campus," Part 2; M. Carey Thomas to F. L. and John C. Olmsted, Dec. 27, 1897, M. Carey Thomas Professional Papers, Bryn Mawr College Archives.

26. *Bryn Mawr College: Academic Buildings and Halls of Residence: Plans and Descriptions* (n.p.: n. pub., 1907). Room prices were stable in the late nineteenth and early twentieth centuries.

27. M. Carey Thomas, Report to the President and Trustees, Bryn Mawr College, June 7, 1884, p. 11, M. Carey Thomas Professional Papers, Bryn Mawr Organization, Bryn Mawr College Archives.

28. *Bryn Mawr College: Academic Buildings.*

29. Quoted in Meigs, *History of Bryn Mawr*, p. 28.

30. Monthly Reports of the President to the Trustees, Oct. 26, 1897, Bryn Mawr College Archives.

31. See M. Carey Thomas to John Garnett, Dec. 22, 1892, M. Carey Thomas Professional

Papers, Bryn Mawr College Archives, copy furnished by Kennedy Smith; Monthly Reports of the President to the Trustees, Feb. 10, 1888, Bryn Mawr College Archives.

32. Thomas had fund-raising success unusual for a women's college president: Rockefeller gave $250,000 and friends of the college another $250,000; see article June 6, 1902, Library file, Bryn Mawr History, M. Carey Thomas Professional Papers, Bryn Mawr College Archives.

33. M. Carey Thomas to Cope and Stewardson, April 14, 1903, and to John G. Johnson, Jan. 4, 1908, M. Carey Thomas Professional Papers, Bryn Mawr College Archives, copy furnished by Kennedy Smith.

34. Isabel Ely to M. Carey Thomas, Dec. 5, 1900, Incoming Correspondence, M. Carey Thomas Professional Papers, Bryn Mawr College Archives, copy furnished by Kennedy Smith.

35. M. Carey Thomas to Henry Tatnall, Aug. 25, 1903, Aug. 14, 1903, M. Carey Thomas Professional Papers, Bryn Mawr College Archives, copy furnished by Kennedy Smith.

36. Document, Dec. 5, 1907, Cope and Stewardson file, Bryn Mawr History, M. Carey Thomas Professional Papers, Bryn Mawr College Archives, outlines the dispute.

37. Floor plan of library and rules for seminary libraries, May 3, 1906, Library file, Bryn Mawr History, M. Carey Thomas Professional Papers, Bryn Mawr College Archives.

38. Meigs, *History of Bryn Mawr*, pp. 101–8.

39. Lockwood de Forest, "Illustration of Design Based on Notes of Line as Used by the Craftsmen of India," p. 3, in Lockwood de Forest file, Bryn Mawr History, M. Carey Thomas Professional Papers, Bryn Mawr College Archives.

40. Finch, *Carey Thomas*, p. 238 for quote; description of Deanery, pp. 237–40.

41. Pamphlet on Deanery, Deanery file, Bryn Mawr History, M. Carey Thomas Professional Papers, Bryn Mawr College Archives.

42. Running Expenses of the Deanery, Deanery file, Bryn Mawr History, M. Carey Thomas Professional Papers, Bryn Mawr College Archives.

43. Finch, *Carey Thomas*, p. 239.

44. Note on Deanery Garden, Oct. 18, 1933, Deanery file, Bryn Mawr History, M. Carey Thomas Professional Papers, Bryn Mawr College Archives.

CHAPTER 10 *The Stately Columned Way*

1. The full story of Barnard's origins has been told by Marian Churchill White, *A History of Barnard College* (New York: Columbia University Press, 1954); Annie Nathan Meyer, *Barnard Beginnings* (Boston and New York: Houghton Mifflin Co., 1935); and Alice Duer Miller and Susan Myers, *Barnard College: The First Fifty Years* (New York: Columbia University Press, 1939).

2. Quoted in Meyer, *Barnard Beginnings*, p. 72.

3. Miller and Myers, *Barnard College*, pp. 21–22.

4. As Virginia Gildersleeve put it, "the college in those days took no interest in 'guidance' and cared little about our health, our social life, and our student activities" (Virginia Gildersleeve, *Many a Good Crusade* [New York: Macmillan Co., 1954], p. 45).

5. Meyer, *Barnard Beginnings*, pp. 155–58.

6. Annie Nathan Meyer to Ella Weed, Oct. 1, 1890, Barnard College Archives, New York, N.Y.

7. Jacob Schiff to Ella Weed, Feb. 11, 1891, quoted in Meyer, *Barnard Beginnings*, Appendix E, p. 176.

8. George A. Plimpton to Frederick S. Wait, Feb. 7, 1894, Barnard College Archives.

9. Annette Baxter, "Emily James Smith Putnam," *Notable American Women,* ed. Edward T. James (Cambridge, Mass.: Belknap Press of Harvard University Press, 1971) 3:106–8; and White, *History of Barnard College,* pp. 27–29.

10. White, *History of Barnard College,* p. 30.

11. Meyer, *Barnard Beginnings,* p. 118.

12. George A. Plimpton to Frederick S. Wait, May 14, 1896 and June 7, 1898, Barnard College Archives.

13. "Barnard College, New York, Plan of the New Building on the Boulevard at One Hundred-and-Nineteenth Street," copy in Barnard College Archives.

14. "Barnard College, West One Hundred and Nineteenth Street and the Boulevard, New York, N.Y.," *American Architect and Building News* 58 (Sept. 18, 1897), plate no. 1134.

15. Harriet Ruth Fox, "Student Life at Barnard," *Columbia University Quarterly* 12 (1910): 186; "Fair Barnard," *Barnard College Song Book* (New York: Undergraduate Association of Barnard College, 1911), p. 5.

16. Margaret Hamilton Welch, "Life at Barnard College," *Harper's Bazar* 34 (April 27, 1901): 1130.

17. For one example, see Helen L. Horowitz, "Animal and Man in the New York Zoological Park," *New York History* 56 (1975): 426–55.

18. Francesco Passanti, "The Design of Columbia in the 1890s, McKim and His Client," *Journal of the Society of Architectural Historians,* 36 (1977): 69–84.

19. Buford Pickens and Margaretta J. Darnall, *Washington University in St. Louis: Its Design and Architecture* (St. Louis: School of Architecture, Washington University, 1978), pp. 18–21.

20. For example, Herbert M. Richards, "The Curriculum and the Equipment of Barnard College," *Columbia University Quarterly* 12 (1910): 176.

CHAPTER 11   *The Life*

1. Mary Atwater Mason, "An Institution Report," *Vassar Miscellany,* Feb. 1903, p. 223.

2. Editorial, *The Lantern,* 1910, pp. 8–9.

3. Editorial, *The Lantern,* 1895, p. 8.

4. Smith College President's Report, typescript copy, 1892–93, Smith College Archives, Northampton, Mass.

5. Smith College President's Report, typescript copy, 1895–96, Smith College Archives.

6. Grace Margaret Gallaher, "In the Matter of Roommates," *Vassar Stories* (Boston: Richard G. Badger & Co., 1900), p. 13.

7. Edith Rickert to parents, March 3, 1888, Edith Rickert Papers, Special Collections, The Joseph Regenstein Library, University of Chicago, Chicago, Ill.

8. *Ibid.*

9. Alice K. Fallows, "Self-Government for College Girls," *Harper's Bazar* 38 (July 1904): 698–705.

10. An example of the use of the phrase is in the *Students' Handbook,* Vassar College, 1909–10, p. 26, Vassar College Library.

11. Edith Rickert to parents, Sept. 21, 1890, Edith Rickert Papers, Regenstein Library.

12. Edith Rickert to parents, Nov. 2, 1890, Edith Rickert Papers, Regenstein Library.

13. For example, Edith Rickert, March 15, 1891, Edith Rickert Papers, Regenstein Library.

14. See, for example, Evangeline Walker scrapbook, Bryn Mawr College Archives, Bryn Mawr, Pa.

15. Gallaher, "The Clan," *Vassar Stories*, p. 185.

16. *Ibid.*, pp. 180–81.

17. *Ibid.*

18. *Ibid.*, p. 190.

19. *Ibid.*, p. 196.

20. Described by Ruth Adams in letters to her parents, Spring 1903, Vassar Student Letters, Vassar College Library.

21. Interview with Frederica de Laguna, June 1980.

22. Memorandum on The Eliot, Notes on College History, A78–61, Wellesley College Archives, Wellesley, Mass.

23. Grace Louise Cook, "Submerged," *Wellesley Stories* (Boston: E. H. Bacon & Co., 1907), p. 161.

24. Zeta Alpha to Board of Trustees, April 26, 1893, and Memorandum, May 1896, Society House packet, Unprocessed Treasurers' Files, Wellesley College Archives; "Report of the Committee on Society Houses," *Wellesley College, President's Reports*, 1895–96, pp. 30–31.

25. Jeannette A. Marks, "College and Home Life," *Good Housekeeping* 35 (July 1902): 9–11; *American Architect and Building News* 73 (Aug. 3, 1901): no. 1336.

26. Cook, "Submerged," p. 148.

27. Society House packet, Unprocessed Treasurers' Files, Wellesley College Archives.

28. Kate Keith to mother and family, Oct. 7, 1906, Smith Alumnae Collection 1910, Smith College Archives.

29. Ruth Huntington Sessions, *Sixty Odd: A Personal History* (Brattleboro, Vt.: Stephen Daye Press, 1936), p. 385.

30. White Lodge Memorandum and The Early Days of Delta Sigma Invitation House, typed manuscripts, 22 White Lodge and Delta Sigma, Smith College Archives.

31. "Luxury for College Girls," clipping, and "Plymouth Hall," pamphlet, 22 Plymouth, Smith College Archives.

32. M. Carey Thomas to Mrs. Seth, copy in M. Carey Thomas letterbook 15, Oct. 11, 1898, M. Carey Thomas Professional Papers, Bryn Mawr College Archives.

33. Bonita Grubbs, "Case Study: NAACP vis-à-vis Smith College, in 1913," Smith student paper with documents, Spring 1977, copy in Smith College Archives. I am grateful to Ms. Grubbs for locating these important letters.

34. Grace Louise Cook, "Clorinda," *Wellesley Stories*, p. 111.

35. Cook, "Submerged," p. 161.

36. Gallaher, "Roommates," p. 34.

37. *Ibid.*, p. 37.

38. *Ibid.*; Henry Seidel Canby makes a similar typology for Yale students of the early twentieth century in his evocative *Alma Mater: The Gothic Age of the American College* (New York: Farrar & Rinehart, 1936), pp. 125–31.

39. Jeannette Marks, "The Crowded Hours of the College Girl," *New England Magazine* 42 (March 1910): 204–207.

40. Hester Gunning, "The Point System," *The Smith Alumnae Quarterly* 6 (Feb. 1915): 79–83, quote from 79.

41. Gallaher, "The Clan," p. 205.

42. *Ibid.*, p. 203.

43. Grace Louise Cook, "President Jefferson," *Wellesley Stories*, pp. 6, 11, 38.

44. *Ibid.*, p. 35.

45. *Ibid.*, p. 37.

46. *Ibid.*

47. *Ibid.*, p. 34.

48. Julia Augusta Schwartz, "For the Honor of the Class," *Vassar Studies* (New York: G. P. Putnam's Sons, 1899), pp. 152–74.

49. M. Carey Thomas to Mary Garrett, May 3, 1899, M. Carey Thomas Papers, Bryn Mawr College Archives.

50. Vivian Gurney, "Philaletheis," *The Vassar Miscellany*, Fiftieth Anniversary Number (Oct. 1915): 93–99.

51. L. Clark Seelye, *The Early History of Smith College, 1871–1910* (Boston: Little, Brown, 1935), pp. 196–204.

52. Lavinia Hart, "A Girl's College Life," *The Cosmopolitan* 31 (June 1901): 192.

53. *Ibid.*

54. Schwartz, "Heroic Treatment," *Vassar Studies*, p. 82.

55. "Official Circular of Information, 1910–11," Wellesley College, pp. 36–37, Wellesley College Archives.

56. Bryn Mawr Self-Government Association, Extracts from Minutes, Dec. 8, 1897, Feb. 17, 1898, March 17, 1898, M. Carey Thomas Professional Papers: History, Bryn Mawr College Archives.

57. Jeanette Eaton, "The College Girl of 1930," *The Woman's Journal* 15 (May 1930): 5, 6.

58. Schwartz, "Heroic Treatment," p. 83.

59. Josephine Dodge Daskam, "The Evolution of Evangeline," *Smith College Stories* (New York: Charles Scribner's Sons, 1900), p. 264.

60. *Wellesley Lyrics*, ed. Cornelia C. Nevers (Boston: Frank Wood, Printer, 1896), esp. Alice Welch Kellogg, "My Sophomore," p. 132.

61. "Slang of College Girls," newspaper clipping, no reference, no date, 10.9 ASC, 1893–94, Smith College Archives.

62. "Free Press," *Wellesley News*, Feb. 18, 1893, pp. 253–54.

63. Edith Rickert to parents, Jan. 23, 1890, Edith Rickert Collection, Regenstein Library.

64. C.P., "The Relations between Faculty and Students at Wellesley College," *Wellesley Magazine* 2 (Dec. 23, 1893): 156.

65. "College Comparisons," *The Radcliffe Magazine* 11 (Feb. 1909): 53.

66. M. Carey Thomas to X (name withheld by Bryn Mawr to protect privacy), Nov. 4, 1893, copy in letterbook, M. Carey Thomas Professional Papers, Bryn Mawr College Archives.

67. Kate Keith, Oct. 10, 1906, Smith College Alumnae 1910, Smith College Archives.

68. This is best understood through letters home and college fiction. See also Content York, "The College Girl's Room," *House Beautiful* 40 (Oct. 1916): 278–80, 308–10; Martha Culter, "How to Furnish a College Room," *Harper's Bazar* 43 (1909): 792–94.

69. Daskam, "The Evolution of Evangeline," p. 248.

70. Smith tore down its Students' Building; Vassar adapted its to new uses; Radcliffe has renovated Agassiz; Wellesley and Bryn Mawr built their buildings in the 1920s and emphasized formal uses; the buildings which best recall the initial intentions are Barnard Hall at Barnard and Mary Woolley Hall at Mount Holyoke.

71. Alice K. Fallows, "The Girl Freshman," *Munsey's Magazine* 25 (Sept. 1901): 818–28.

72. *Ibid.*, 828.

73. Florence Converse, *Wellesley College: A Chronicle of the Years, 1875–1938* (Wellesley: Hathaway House Bookshop, 1939), pp. 148–49.

74. "College Comparisons," 55.

CHAPTER 12   *Households of Women*

1. Grace Louise Cook, "Sir Toby's Career," *Wellesley Stories* (Boston: E. H. Bacon & Co., 1907), p. 281.

2. Helen Wright, *Sweeper in the Sky: The Life of Maria Mitchell, First Woman Astronomer in America* (New York: Macmillan Co., 1949), pp. 181–82; Maria Mitchell to Benson Lossing, June 8, 1871, Maria Mitchell Papers, Vassar College Library, Poughkeepsie, N.Y.

3. Louise Fargo Brown, *Apostle of Democracy: The Life of Lucy Maynard Salmon* (New York: Harper & Brothers, 1943), p. 143.

4. Smith College catalogues, Smith College Archives, Northampton, Mass.

5. Brown, *Lucy Maynard Salmon*, pp. 114–15, 222.

6. [Eben Norton Horsford, ed.] *Souvenir of Wellesley College, Wellesley, Massachusetts, 1888* (Cambridge, Mass.: n. pub., 1889).

7. Lee Chambers-Schiller, "The Single Woman: Family and Vocation among Nineteenth Century Reformers," in *Woman's Being, Woman's Place: Female Identity and Vocation in Ameican History*, ed. Mary Kelly (Boston: G. K. Hall & Co., 1979), pp. 334–50.

8. Quoted in George Herbert Palmer, *The Life of Alice Freeman Palmer* (Boston and New York: Houghton Mifflin Co., 1908), p. 103.

9. Emily F. Wheeler, "Households of Women," *The Critic* 15 (Aug. 24, 1889): 89–90.

10. Quoted in Dorothy Burgess, *Dream and Deed: The Story of Katharine Lee Bates* (Norman, Oklahoma: University of Oklahoma Press, 1952), pp. 91, 84.

11. Lucy Salmon to Adelaide Underhill, Aug. 5, 1900, quoted in Brown, *Lucy Salmon*, p. 176.

12. Lucy Salmon to Adelaide Underhill, Aug. 23, 1900, *ibid.*, p. 180.

13. Quoted in Burgess, *Katharine Lee Bates*, pp. 84–85.

14. Conversation with Isabel Fothergill Smith, Florence Bascom's student and biographer; Florence Bascom letters, Sophia Smith Collection, Smith College, Northampton, Mass.

15. M. Carey Thomas to Mary Garrett, March 8, 1899, M. Carey Thomas Papers; Monthly Reports of the President to the Trustees, 1899–1900 volume, March 17, 1899, Bryn Mawr College Archives, Bryn Mawr, Pa.

16. M. Carey Thomas to Mary Garrett, Jan. 25, 1898, M. Carey Thomas Papers, Bryn Mawr College Archives.

17. "Low Building," pamphlet and Constitution, typescript, "Low Building" file, Bryn Mawr History, M. Carey Thomas Professional Papers, Bryn Mawr College Archives.

18. Brown, *Lucy Maynard Salmon*, pp. 138, 141, 144, 194, 212–15, 220–24.

19. James Monroe Taylor, "Vassar's President on Households of Women," *The Critic* 15 (Nov. 23, 1889): 257.

20. President's Report, 1897, Vassar College, Vassar College Library. See Chapter 6. In 1904, Vassar alumnae built a house for Frances A. Wood, to go after her death to women professors (Poughkeepsie *Daily Eagle*, June 9, 1904, clipping in Vassar College scrapbook, vol. 3, Vassar College Library).

21. President's Report, 1903 and 1900, Vassar College, Vassar College Library.

22. Typescript report of the Committee on Faculty Housing, President's Office Papers (IDB/1899–1966), faculty housing folder, 1918–66, Wellesley College Archives, Wellesley, Mass.

23. Burgess, *Katharine Lee Bates*, pp. 162–63.

24. Vida Dutton Scudder, *On Journey* (New York: E. P. Dutton & Co., 1937), p. 272.

25. I am grateful to the current occupants of the houses of Katharine Lee Bates, Vida Scudder, and Ellen Hayes for allowing me to tour their houses and gardens. It was particularly moving to see the wildflower garden of Vida Scudder, growing as she had planted it.

26. Nan Bauer Maglin, "Vida to Florence: 'Comrade and Companion,'" *Frontiers* 4 (1979): 13–18; Judith Schwarz, "*Yellow Clover*: Katharine Lee Bates and Katharine Coman," *Frontiers* 4 (1979): 57–67; Blanche Wiesen Cook, "Female Support Networks and Political Activism: Lillian Wald, Crystal Eastman, Emma Goldman," *Chrysalis* 3 (1977): 43–61; Blanche Wiesen Cook, "'Women Alone Stir My Imagination': Lesbianism and the Cultural Tradition," *Signs* 4 (1979): 718–39, quote from 738.

27. I wrote this section before reading Lillian Faderman's provocative work. However, her understanding of women's love for each other prior to twentieth-century understandings of lesbianism largely confirms my own (Lillian Faderman, *Surpassing the Love of Men: Romantic Friendship and Love between Women from the Renaissance to the Present* [New York: Morrow, 1981]).

28. Katharine Lee Bates, *Yellow Clover: A Book of Remembrance* (New York: E. P. Dutton, 1922).

29. Burgess, *Katharine Lee Bates*, p. 209.

30. I am grateful to Patricia A. Palmieri for her insightful work on Wellesley faculty women, "A Social and Cultural Portrait of Academic Women at Wellesley College, 1890–1910," qualifying paper, Harvard School of Education, copy in Wellesley College Archives. These real communities of women pose intriguing contrasts to the images in imaginative literature that Nina Auerbach explored in *Communities of Women: An Idea in Fiction* (Cambridge: Harvard University Press, 1978).

31. Mary Woolley to Jeannette Marks, March 23, 1900, April 8, 10, 12, 1900, Mary Woolley Papers, Mount Holyoke Library/Archives, South Hadley, Mass.

32. Lucy Salmon to Adelaide Underhill, Oct. 1, 1899, Lucy Salmon Papers, Vassar College Library. President Taylor did not understand the nature of Salmon's relationship, however. On March 1, 1903, Salmon wrote to Underhill that she had "hinted gently to Dr. Taylor that you needed me to go South with you. He asked if you couldn't get somebody else! It is quite impossible to show to any one how indispensable you are to me" (Salmon Papers, Vassar College Library, spelling corrected).

33. Edith Rickert to Lucy Salmon, Dec. 13, 1906, Lucy Salmon Papers, Vassar College Library.

34. M. Carey Thomas to Mary Garrett, Nov. 11, 1887, M. Carey Thomas Papers, Bryn Mawr College Archives.

35. M. Carey Thomas to Mary Garrett, April 10, 1884, M. Carey Thomas Papers, Bryn Mawr College Archives.

36. Anna Mary Wells, *Miss Marks and Miss Woolley* (Boston: Houghton Mifflin Co., 1978), pp. 46–47.

37. For example, Lucy Salmon wrote to Adelaide Underhill a "Daily Report" in June 1904: "Pulse—normal, Temperature—98, Heart—active, state of [unreadable word] for A.U., Lungs—vigorous, Appetite—ditto, Diet—eggs by the dozen." (Lucy Salmon Papers, Vassar College Library; punctuation regularized.)

38. Annie Nathan Meyer, critical in the founding of Barnard also joined the anti-suffrage association and wrote in its behalf, but her position was a thoroughly eccentric one that hardly fits the pattern of the movement: she argued that the suffragists' arguments that women were purer and more moral than men had no validity; and thus she opposed suffrage.

39. Mary A. Jordan, "Noblesse Oblige," pamphlet no. 36 of Massachusetts Association Opposed to the Further Extension of Suffrage to Women, p. 7, copy in Huntington Library, San Marino, Calif.

40. Interview with Evalyn A. Clark, June 1981.

41. Alice Payne Hackett, *Wellesley: Part of the American Story* (New York: E. P. Dutton, 1949), pp. 184–87.

42. Mercedes M. Randall, *Improper Bostonian: Emily Greene Balch, Nobel Peace Laureate, 1946* (New York: Twayne Publishers, 1964), pp. 246–57; Katharine Lee Bates to Emily Greene Balch, Sept. 28, 1919, Emily Greene Balch Papers, Swarthmore Peace Collection, Swarthmore College, Swarthmore, Pa.

43. See especially Katharine Lee Bates to Emily Greene Balch, Aug. 26, 1920, Emily Greene Balch Papers, Swarthmore Peace Collection.

44. Lucy Salmon to Adelaide Underhill, quoted in Brown, *Lucy Maynard Salmon*, p. 159.

45. Burgess, *Katharine Lee Bates*, p. 164. Dogs seem to have served faculty twosomes as surrogate children.

46. See Chapters 16 and 17 below.

CHAPTER 13   *The Necessities Peculiar to Women of Today*

1. Pauline A. Durant's letters to trustee Louise McCoy North, often written before board meetings, convey her anguish at changes being proposed. Letter, Feb. 8, 1899, about proposed art historian, considers her religious belief and character, Autograph file, Wellesley College Archives, Wellesley, Mass.

2. Ronald Story, *The Forging of an Aristocracy: Harvard and the Boston Upper Class, 1800–1870* (Middletown, Conn.: Wesleyan University Press, 1980), provides the network of Boston cultural institutions identified with Proper Boston that Wellesley joined at the turn of the century.

3. Pauline A. Durant to Dr. Warren, 1894, copy in Wellesley College Archives, original at Boston University Library.

4. George Herbert Palmer to Caroline Hazard, July 22, 1921, Wellesley College Archives.

5. Florence Converse, *Wellesley College: A Chronicle of the Years, 1875–1938* (Wellesley: Hathaway House Bookshop, 1939), pp. 161–63; Alice Payne Hackett, *Wellesley: Part of the American Story* (New York: E. P. Dutton, 1949), pp. 122–27; George Herbert Palmer, *The Life of Alice Freeman Palmer* (Boston: Houghton Mifflin, the Riverside Press, 1908), pp. 230–32, considers his wife's role in these changes.

6. See Chapter 7.

7. James F. O'Gorman, "Unbuilt Wellesley I: A Fragment from the Great Debate," *Wellesley Wragtime* 2 (May 1979): 8–9.

8. Edward L. Clark to Horace E. Scudder, Nov. 9, 1896, Treasurer's office, unprocessed files, Wellesley College Archives.

9. *Ibid.*

10. Edward L. Clark to Horace E. Scudder, Oct. 13, 1896, Treasurer's office, unprocessed files, Wellesley College Archives.

11. Edward L. Clark to Horace E. Scudder, Oct. 16, 1896, Treasurer's office, unprocessed files, Wellesley College Archives.

12. Edward L. Clark to Horace E. Scudder, April 9, 1897, Treasurer's office, unprocessed files, Wellesley College Archives.

13. Horace E. Scudder and Edward L. Clark, report of committee to consider a scheme for the decorative windows of the Houghton Memorial Chapel, May 3, 1897, Treasurer's office, unprocessed files, Wellesley College Archives.

14. Pauline A. Durant to Horace E. Scudder, Jan. 16, 1897, Treasurer's office, unprocessed files, Wellesley College Archives.

15. Minutes of the Board of Trustees, Wellesley College, special meeting, April 17, 1897, Wellesley College Archives.

16. Lilian Horsford to Horace E. Scudder, April 2 [1897], Treasurer's office, unprocessed files, Wellesley College Archives.

17. Edward L. Clark to Horace E. Scudder, April 6, 1897, Treasurer's office, unprocessed files, Wellesley College Archives.

18. E.A.S., "Wellesley's New Chapel," *The Congregationalist* 84 (June 8, 1899): 829.

19. Montgomery Schuyler, "Three Women's Colleges—Vassar, Wellesley & Smith," *Architectural Record* 31 (1912): 537.

20. Quoted in Jean Glasscock, "The Selection of Wellesley's Presidents," *Wellesley College 1875–1975: A Century of Women*, ed. Jean Glasscock (Wellesley: Wellesley College, 1975), p. 62.

21. Wellesley College announcement, March 7, 1899, copy in Wellesley College Archives.

22. Caroline Hazard's letters to Katharine Lee Bates, Wellesley College Archives, give a sense of Hazard's involvement in the lives of the faculty.

23. Minutes of the Board of Trustees, Wellesley College, Feb. 6, 1902, Wellesley College Archives.

24. This provided Charles William Eliot with a platform to state his concerns about higher education. His suggestion that the great traditions of learning from the time of the Egyptians were the creation by and for men, serving as no guide for the education of women, aroused the ire of M. Carey Thomas and prompted one of her most pointed statements arguing that the life of the mind was neuter (see Chapter 9).

25. Harriet B. Creighton, "The Grounds," in *Wellesley College 1875–1975*, p. 275. I am indebted to this excellent summary of Wellesley planning history.

26. Frederick Law Olmsted, Jr., to Caroline Hazard, March 24, 1902, Wellesley College Archives. Specific reference is from p. 2.

27. *Ibid.*, p. 3.

28. *Ibid.*, p. 5.

29. *Ibid.*, pp. 6–8; quotes from pp. 7, 8.

30. Quoted in Creighton, "The Grounds," p. 276.

31. One of four architect sons of a German engineer who immigrated to America after 1848, Julius Adolph Schweinfurth served as a draftsman for Peabody and Stearns before establishing his own office in Boston. Along with a brisk residential practice, J. A. Schweinfurth received many commissions to design schools. He was also responsible for the Wellesley gymnasium, 1909. (Stephen J. Neitz, *Julius A. Schweinfurth, Master Designer, 1858–1931*, ed. Wheaton A. Holden [Boston: Northeastern University, 1975].)

32. "Dormitories, Wellesley College," *The American Architect and Building News* 84 (June 25, 1904), plate no. 1487.

33. L. Clark Seelye, *The Early History of Smith College, 1871–1910* (Boston: Houghton Mifflin Co., 1923), pp. 53–57.

34. Hillyer fronted Elm with a tall, thin façade of brick and Longmeadow stone in the shape of a Gothic tower. It stretched its main bulk toward the campus, a rather heavy rectangle with a tall peaked roof providing skylights. The interior held statuary and painting exhibition rooms where, following typical art instruction of the day, the students copied the works of art. The $50,000 bequest that Hillyer added in his will underwrote Smith's fine collection of American art. Growth in the School of Art and changing methods of instruction called for an expansion of the building, and in 1887, Smith built an addition to the northwest. The new wing gave Hillyer a heavier, more rounded appearance. Students now had studios for painting and drawing classes using live models. (Mary P. Spivy, "The Hillyer Art Gallery of 1881: A Peabody and Stearns

Masterpiece," unpublished student paper, May 4, 1976, Smith College Archives, Northampton, Mass.)

35. Peabody & Stearns designed another variation on the theme of the Gothic Revival for Pierce. In contrast to College Hall, Pierce is a solid, calm building. Composed of red brick, trimmed in red stone, its façade presents straightforward, rectangular windows. Only at the roofline is there any drama: a high-pitched roof, gables, smokestacks, and finials relate Pierce to its more richly decorated neighbor. Designed to house a large lecture hall, classrooms, and practice rooms, the School of Music has two entrances, one to the campus and one to the street, suggesting Smith's involvement in the life of Northampton. ("Dedication of a Music Building at Smith College," news clipping, Record Group 22: Pierce, Smith College Archives.)

36. "Smith College Hall of Science," news clipping, Record Group 22: Lilly, Smith College Archives.

37. National Register of Historic Places, Inventory-Nomination Form, Record Group 22: Gymnasium Alumnae, Smith College Archives.

38. Agnes CoraRuth Stillman, "Senda Berenson Abbott: Her Life and Contributions to Smith College and to the Physical Education Profession," p. 27, unpublished M.A. dissertation, 1971, Smith College Archives.

39. Helen C. Bragdon, "Students' Building Looks Back," *Smith Alumnae Quarterly* 56 (Nov. 1964): 11–13.

40. Margaret Grierson, "The History and Development of the Smith College Library," unpublished student paper, Smith College Archives.

41. Massachusetts Historical Commission, Survey Record, March 25, 1977; "The Smith College Auditorium," news clipping, Record Group 22: John M. Greene, Smith College Archives.

42. Henry Noble MacCracken, *The Hickory Limb* (New York: Charles Scribner's Sons, 1950), pp. 29–30.

43. James M. Taylor to Rev. Alvah Hovey, March 1, 1899, Taylor Papers, Vassar College Library, Poughkeepsie, New York.

44. "Charles Pratt," *Dictionary of American Biography* (New York: Charles Scribner's Sons, 1933), 14: 168–70; obituary, Charles M. Pratt, New York *Times*, Nov. 27, 1935; Allan Nevins, *John D. Rockefeller: The Heroic Age of American Enterprise* (New York: Charles Scribner's Sons, 1940) 1:677 (quote); 2:188–89, 443–44.

45. Frequently a donor chose an architect because of personal connections. In some cases family relationships played their part. A nephew of the donor of Sanders Laboratory received its commission; Edward York of York & Sawyer, responsible for Rockefeller Hall and other Vassar buildings, was the cousin of a Vassar administrator. In some cases, the choice of an architect was sentimental. Vassar's Students' Building went to a nephew of Maria Mitchell in the firm of McKim, Mead & White. (Poughkeepsie *Eagle News*, Jan. 3, 1928, copy in Vassar College Buildings file [General], Vassar College Library; MacCracken, *Hickory Limb*, pp. 115–16.)

46. Mary Seymour Pratt to Mary Thaw Thompson, May 26, 1901, April 21, 1902, May 14, 1902, Feb. 10, 1904, Pratt Papers, Vassar College Library.

47. New York *Daily Tribune*, Nov. 5, 1904, typescript copy in Vassar College Buildings file (Chapel), Vassar College Library.

48. Montgomery Schuyler, "The Three Women's Colleges—Vassar, Wellesley & Smith," *Architectural Record* 31 (1912): 520, 525.

49. Beaux Arts symmetry dominated planning. The tower enclosed Memorial Hall, a tall room with a sixty-foot ceiling, decorated with carved friezes, Gobelin tapestries, marble floor, and fireplace. In this rarefied setting, the reference librarian had a desk, as did the circulation department. Radiating from the tower, three wings carried study alcoves and seminar rooms.

Mullioned windows on the sides and large end windows of stained glass lit the study areas where, surrounded by symbols of dignity and spirituality, Vassar students read ("The Frederick Ferris Thompson Memorial College Building, Vassar College," *Library Journal* 31 [Nov. 1906]: 769–70).

50. Elizabeth Hazelton Haight, "Taylor Hall: The New Art Building at Vassar College," *Art and Archeology* 2 (Sept. 1915): 54–57.

51. MacCracken, *Hickory Limb*, p. 24.

52. *Ibid.*, p. 200.

53. Nevins, *John D. Rockefeller* 2:568, 676–84.

54. James M. Taylor to Laura Wylie, March 24, 1909, Taylor Papers, Vassar College Library.

55. MacCracken, *Hickory Limb*, pp. 25–28, 33–34.

CHAPTER 14   *A Larger School Room*

1. Rosalind A. Keep, *Fourscore Years: A History of Mills College* (Oakland, California: Mills College, 1931), pp. 83–84.

2. Pauline Woodford Halbert, "Mount Holyoke Seminary in the Light of Today," Nov. 12, 1887, copy in Mount Holyoke College Library/Archives, South Hadley, Mass.

3. Resolutions presented by Mrs. Moses Smith, quoted in *Mount Holyoke Seminary Semi-Centennial Celebration, 1837–1887*, ed. Sarah Locke Howe ([South Hadley:] The Seminary, 1888), p. 106.

4. At the hearing George Herbert Palmer, husband of Wellesley's former president, and two leaders of the Association for Collegiate Alumnae—Marion Talbot and Florence Cushing (an active Vassar alumna)—spoke against the change (Arthur C. Cole, *A Hundred Years of Mount Holyoke College: The Evolution of an Educational Ideal* [New Haven: Yale University Press, 1940], pp. 192–93).

5. Halbert, "Mount Holyoke Seminary."

6. N. G. Clark to Mary Holbrook, Jan. 28, 1888, Mount Holyoke College Library/Archives.

7. This interpretation differs from that found in Cole, *A Hundred Years of Mount Holyoke College*, pp. 188–94.

8. Halbert, "Mount Holyoke Seminary," p. 6.

9. *Ibid.*, p. 7.

10. *Ibid.*, p. 9.

11. *Ibid.*

12. Cole, *A Hundred Years of Mount Holyoke College*, pp. 195–96.

13. *Ibid.*, p. 205; Mary Sumner Benson, "Elizabeth Storrs Billings Mead," *Notable American Women*, ed. Edward T. James (Cambridge, Mass.: Belknap Press of Harvard University Press, 1971) 2: 519–20.

14. Cole, *A Hundred Years of Mount Holyoke College*, pp. 205–9.

15. Mount Holyoke College, Annual Report of the President, 1895–96, typescript copy, p. 7, Mount Holyoke College Library/Archives.

16. Cole, *A Hundred Years of Mount Holyoke College*, pp. 209–21.

17. H.A.B., "A Layman's Work for Mt. Holyoke," *The Congregationalist and Christian World*, July 31, 1913, clipping in Mount Holyoke College Library/Archives.

18. Williston Hall Folder, Building file, Mount Holyoke College Library/Archives.

19. Lucy Lilian Notestein, *Wooster of the Middle West*, 2 vols. (Cleveland: The Kent State University Press, 1971) 1: 82–83. Because of financial constraints Hoover Cottage was not built until 1895–96.

20. Mount Holyoke College, Annual Report of the President, 1890–91, typescript copy, p. 18, Mount Holyoke College Library/Archives. See also the reports for 1894–95 and 1895–96.

21. I am indebted to the carefully researched study, Laura Ann Alaimo, "Building Mount Holyoke College, 1896–1900," honors thesis in history, Mount Holyoke College, May 1981, copy in Mount Holyoke College Library/Archives.

22. Mount Holyoke College, Annual Report of the President, 1896–97, typescript copy, p. 5, Mount Holyoke College Library/Archives. Mead met directly the alumnae wish for the "old home" by suggesting that "a gracious providence" made possible the new cottage (pp. 27, 25).

23. Williston quite consciously avoided filling up the campus (Alaimo, "Building Mount Holyoke College," p. 29).

24. Henry F. Withey and Elsie Rathburn Withey, *Biographical Dictionary of American Architects (Deceased)* (originally published 1956, facsimile edition Los Angeles: Hennessy & Ingalls, 1970), pp. 229–30. Eugene C. Gardner gave the architect's sense of the building in "Housing Mt. Holyoke College," clipping Mount Holyoke College Library/Archives.

25. Henrietta Hooker, "Mount Holyoke College," *New England Magazine* 15 (1897): 16–17.

26. Alaimo, "Building Mount Holyoke College," pp. 28–30.

27. "Mount Holyoke's Gymnasium," bound clipping scrapbook, vol. 3, p. 59, Mount Holyoke College Library/Archives.

28. Alaimo, "Building Mount Holyoke College," pp. 38–48, discusses college life within the new cottages.

29. Though a full-scale biography of Mary Emma Woolley is still needed, Anna Wells' excellent, though controversial, study of the relationship between Woolley and Jeannette Marks contains invaluable information and insights (*Miss Marks and Miss Woolley* [Boston: Houghton Mifflin Co., 1978]).

30. Cole, *A Hundred Years of Mount Holyoke College*, pp. 243, 246–47.

31. *Ibid.*, pp. 252–53; Mary Woolley's annual reports read like reports in progress in the campaign to recruit and encourage faculty. For example, Report of the President, 1908–9, p. 7, lists the institutions granting Ph.D.'s to Mount Holyoke faculty. Bryn Mawr led with five.

32. Cole, *A Hundred Years of Mount Holyoke College*, p. 252.

33. Wells, *Miss Marks and Miss Woolley*, pp. 79–88; Mount Holyoke College, Annual Report of the President, 1903–4, pp. 10–11.

34. Wells, *Miss Marks and Miss Woolley*, pp. 101–3.

35. Cole, *A Hundred Years of Mount Holyoke College*, pp. 252–53.

36. Mary E. Woolley, "Mount Holyoke College from 1901–1924," *Mount Holyoke Alumnae Quarterly* 8 (1925): 187.

37. See correspondence between John C. Olmsted and A. Lyman Williston, 1910, Olmsted Papers, Library of Congress, copy in Mount Holyoke College Library/Archives.

38. Cole, *A Hundred Years of Mount Holyoke College*, p. 244; Mount Holyoke College, Annual Report of the President, 1903–4, p. 13.

39. Withey and Withey, *American Architects*, p. 440.

CHAPTER 15 *The Day of Small Things Is Over*

1. *The Society for the Collegiate Instruction of Women, Annual Reports*, 1891, p. 7.

2. "The Society for the Collegiate Instruction of Women in Cambridge, Mass.: Report of the Ladies of the Executive Committee" (Cambridge, Mass.: William H. Wheeler, 1884), p. 6.

3. *Radcliffe College, Annual Reports*, 1896–97, pp. 21–22.

4. *The Society for the Collegiate Instruction of Women, Annual Reports*, 1890, p. 17.

5. *Ibid.*, 1891, p. 5.

6. Lucy Allen Paton, *Elizabeth Cary Agassiz: A Biography* (Boston: Houghton Mifflin Co., 1919), pp. 232–42.

7. "The Petition of the Alumnae of the Harvard Annex to the President and the Members of the Society for the Collegiate Instruction of Women," Appendix B of Association of Collegiate Alumnae, "Petition of the Committee on Endowment of Colleges," pp. 12–13, copy in Radcliffe College Archives, Cambridge, Mass.

8. "The Petition of New York Citizens and Alumni of Harvard University to the Board of Overseers of Harvard University," *Ibid.*, pp. 6–11.

9. "The Report of the Annex Fund Committee of the Woman's Education Association," in Association of Collegiate Alumnae, "Petition," pp. 13–16.

10. Hugh Hawkins, *Between Harvard and America: The Educational Leadership of Charles W. Eliot* (New York: Oxford University Press, 1972), pp. 193–95.

11. [Jennie Watts?] Reminiscences of Student Life, 1893–97, typescript, 1922, pp. 2–3, Radcliffe College Archives.

12. Quote from Emily Lovett, in Reminiscences of Student Life, p. 4, Radcliffe College Archives.

13. *Radcliffe College, Annual Reports*, 1897–98, p. 23.

14. Agnes Repplier, *Agnes Irwin: A Biography* (Garden City, N.Y.: Doubleday, Doran & Co., 1935), pp. 57–99 passim.

15. Quote from Beulah Dix, in Reminiscences of Student Life, p. 5, Radcliffe College Archives.

16. Quote from Bertha Scripture, *ibid.*, p. 6, Radcliffe Archives.

17. Sampling of Radcliffe letters, Schlesinger Library, Radcliffe College, Cambridge, Mass.

18. Quote from Marion Lincoln Cain, in Reminiscences of Student Life, p. 11, Radcliffe College Archives.

19. Quote from Edith Claflin, in *ibid.*, p. 12, Radcliffe College Archives.

20. Repplier, *Agnes Irwin*, pp. 51, 75, 99.

21. Rollo Walter Brown, *Dean Briggs* (New York: Harper & Brothers, 1926), pp. 208–49; quote from p. 208.

22. Description of the Radcliffe Gymnasium, one-page typescript, Radcliffe College Archives.

23. L. B. R. Briggs to John F. Moors, Dec. 6, 1904, Radcliffe College Archives.

24. Arthur A. Shurtleff to L. B. R. Briggs, June 4, 1906, Radcliffe College Archives.

25. Helen D. Brown, "The Harvard Annex," *Woman's Journal* 13 (Dec. 2, 1882): 383.

26. "Report of the Committee on a Hall of Residence for Radcliffe College," April 9, 1898, pamphlet, copy in Radcliffe College Archives.

27. Irwin made this explicit in a 1895 letter quoted in Paton, *Elizabeth Cary Agassiz*, p. 301.

28. "Report of the Committee on a Hall of Residence for Radcliffe College."

29. Description of Bertram Hall with floor plans, copy in Radcliffe College Archives.

30. Description of Grace Eliot Hall with floor plans, copy in Radcliffe College Archives.

31. Report of the Special Committee Appointed by the Radcliffe Auxiliary to Look into the Question of Building a New Dormitory for Radcliffe College, typescript copy in Radcliffe College Archives.

32. This remained a concern of Dean Irwin, who saw it as "a disadvantage, and sometimes a very serious one, in its effect on character and conduct, and on what is now known as personality" (*Radcliffe College, Annual Reports*, 1906–7, p. 28).

33. "A Suggestion," *Barnard Mortarboard*, 1901, p. 82.

34. Harriet Ruth Fox, "Student Life at Barnard," *Columbia University Quarterly* 12 (1910): 183.

35. [Charlotte E. Morgan,] "A Glimpse into the Future," *Barnard Alumnae Bulletin* 13 (1924): 11.

36. Fox, "Student Life at Barnard," 186–87.

37. M. Carey Thomas to Mary Garrett, Feb. 27, 1899, M. Carey Thomas Papers, Bryn Mawr College Archives, Bryn Mawr, Pa.

38. *The Rise of a University II. From the Annual Reports of Nicholas Murray Butler,* ed. Edward C. Elliott (New York: Columbia University Press, 1937), pp. 387–90; Marian Churchill White, *A History of Barnard College* (New York: Columbia University Press, 1954), p. 46.

39. Fragment written by Annie Nathan Meyer, 1929, recalled Emily Putnam's initial effort to conceal her pregnancy and her pleading, when pregnant, to remain as dean. Also Emily James Putnam to Silas B. Brownell, Jan. 13, 1900, both in Barnard College Archives, New York, N.Y.

40. Laura Drake Gill to Silas B. Brownell, Dec. 10, 1911, Barnard College Archives; White, *A History of Barnard College,* pp. 49–59, discusses the Gill years.

41. *The Dean's Annual Report, Barnard College,* 1902, p. 183, copy in Barnard College Archives.

42. *Ibid.,* p. 186.

43. In 1927–28, Brooks Hall rooms went for $160 to $575 a year; the suites originally designed for faculty went as high as $935. "Barnard College Announcement Regarding Residence, 1927–28," Barnard College Archives; "We Are Responsible for Dormitory Life," *The Bulletin of the Associate Alumnae* 16 (May 1927): 3–6.

44. White, *A History of Barnard College,* p. 53; Herbert M. Richards, "The Curriculum and the Equipment of Barnard College," *Columbia University Quarterly* 12 (1910): 180.

45. Fox, "Student Life at Barnard," 186.

46. Elsie de Wolfe to Mrs. Fairfield Osborne, May 29, 1907, Buildings and Grounds Committee file, Barnard College Archives.

47. *The Dean's Annual Report, Barnard College,* 1909, pp. 98–99.

48. Alice Duer Miller, "Social Life at Barnard," *Columbia University Quarterly* 2 (1900): 219.

49. From "There is a College on Broadway," and "Rah Rah for dear old Barnard," *Barnard College Song Book* (New York: Undergraduate Association of Barnard College, 1911), pp. 10–11, 14.

50. Alice Duer Miller and Susan Myers, *Barnard College: The First Fifty Years* (New York: Columbia University Press, 1939), pp. 37–39.

51. Fox, "Student Life at Barnard," 183; punctuation corrected.

52. "Barnard Girl Sells Bricks," New York *Herald,* Oct. 31, 1911, clipping in Barnard College Archives.

53. Barbara Rouse Hatcher, "Barnard's Buildings—A Short History," typescript, Barnard College Archives.

54. White, *A History of Barnard College,* pp. 68–69; Annette K. Baxter, "Virginia Crocheron Gildersleeve," *Notable American Women,* vol. 4 (Harvard University Press, 1980): 273–75.

55. Virginia Crocheron Gildersleeve, *Many a Good Crusade* (New York: Macmillan Co., 1954), pp. 62–66.

56. White, *A History of Barnard College,* pp. 100–101.

57. Gildersleeve, *Many a Good Crusade,* p. 52.

58. *The Dean's Annual Report, Barnard College,* 1913, p. 5.

59. Freda Kirchwey, "Observation and Discussion: Fraternities *versus* Democracy," The *Barnard Bear* 8 (1912–13): 3–6, quote from p. 6. The word *sorority* did not come into general use until the 1920s.

60. White, *A History of Barnard College,* pp. 89–91.

61. For example, Florence Lucas Sanville, speech on behalf of the undergraduates at the

installation of Laura D. Gill, May 9, 1901, date questioned on typescript in Barnard College Archives.

62. Annie Nathan Meyer, *Barnard Beginnings* (Boston and New York: Houghton Mifflin Co., 1935), p. 115.

63. *The Dean's Report, Barnard College,* 1915, p. 2; Arthur C. Cole, *A Hundred Years of Mount Holyoke College: The Evolution of an Educational Ideal* (New Haven: Yale University Press, 1940), pp. 243, 315.

64. Barnard College, Y.W.C.A. Scrapbook of Activities and Silver Bay, Barnard College Archives, chronicles through its newspaper clippings these changes in the Christian Association.

65. Wellesley's President's Office Papers contain a file labelled "Jewish Problems (1938–54)," Wellesley College Archives, Wellesley, Mass. Radcliffe undertook a study of Jews, Catholics, and Protestants in its concern about its student body, copy in Radcliffe College Archives.

66. Virginia C. Gildersleeve to Mrs. Alfred Meyer, January 12, 1932, Annie Nathan Meyer Papers, box 7, folder 1, American Jewish Archives, Hebrew Union College-Jewish Institute of Religion, Cincinnati, Ohio.

67. Virginia C. Gildersleeve to Mrs. Alfred Meyer, March 30, 1933, Annie Nathan Meyer Papers, box 7, folder 1, American Jewish Archives.

68. Horace Coon, *Columbia: Colossus on the Hudson* (New York: E. P. Dutton, 1947), pp. 208–209. The cross-section statement comes from a Barnard College announcement. The establishment of a formal quota system at three prestigious men's colleges has been studied: see Marcia Graham Synnott, *The Half-Opened Door: Discrimination and Admissions at Harvard, Yale, and Princeton, 1900–1970* (Westport, Conn.: Greenwood Press, 1979).

69. Ella Weed fragment to unknown, undated, Barnard College Archives.

70. Form letter, Annie Nathan Meyer to ———, Feb. 14, 1934, Annie Nathan Meyer Papers, box 4, folder 8, American Jewish Archives.

71. Hatcher, "Barnard's Buildings."

72. Annie Nathan Meyer to Virginia C. Gildersleeve, Feb. 12, 1944, Annie Nathan Meyer papers, box 7, folder 2, American Jewish Archives. Linda Kerber, "Annie Nathan Meyer," *Notable American Women,* 4: 473–74. This may be one of the reasons why Meyer's own history of the college is filled with such boasting. I have also benefited from my talks with Linda Kerber about Barnard.

73. The basement on a level with Claremont Avenue contained two large dining rooms. Students lived in thirty-five single rooms on both sides of a corridor running the length of the building that almost doubled that of Brooks. Without the bays of Brooks, Hewitt had narrow, regular rooms, with the end rooms enjoying an open fireplace. Room prices varied from $160 to $575: the more expensive rooms were located on the upper floors or on the ends with the fireplace. Such prices certainly kept New York scholarship students living at home. "Barnard College, Announcement Regarding Residence, 1927–28"; "Hewitt Hall, Barnard College, New York City," *Architecture and Building* 58 (Jan. 1926): 1; White, *A History of Barnard College,* pp. 119–20.

74. Jean T. Palmer, "The Deanery: Legend and Landmark," *Barnard Alumnae Magazine* 61 (Winter 1972): 37.

75. Elaine Kendall, *"Peculiar Institutions": An Informal History of the Seven Sister Colleges* (New York: G. P. Putnam's Sons, 1975), pp. 29–30; Gildersleeve, *Many a Good Crusade,* pp. 89–91.

CHAPTER 16   *A Great Design*

1. Katharine C. Balderston, "The Great Fire," *Wellesley College 1875–1975: A Century of Women,* ed. Jean Glasscock (Wellesley: Wellesley College, 1975), p. 339–50.

2. William Warren Carman, who served as Ellen James' representative, was a friend of Mrs. North and her husband. (See Lisa Mausolf, "Tower Court: The Phoenix of College Hill," undergraduate thesis, May 5, 1980, p. 11, copy in Wellesley College Archives, Wellesley, Mass. This is a valuable compendium of information about Tower Court.)

3. "Three New College Buildings," *The Brickbuilder* 25 (1916): 39–41; [Ellen James,] to Bishop Lawrence, Aug. 17, 1914, "Mr. Smith" packet, Treasurer's office, unprocessed files, Wellesley College Archives.

4. For the Olmsted plan, see Chapter 13. Alfred Morton Githens, "Recent American Group Plans III: Colleges and Universities: Development of Existing Plans," *The Brickbuilder* 21 (1912): 313–16 and Githens, "Recent American Group Plans IV: Colleges and Universities: Development of New Plans," *The Brickbuilder* 22 (1913): 11–14.

5. Frances Gotkowitz, "The Development of a Master Plan for Wellesley College," undergraduate thesis, May 1980, pp. 43–48, copy in Wellesley College Archives. I am greatly indebted to this fine honors thesis.

6. *Ibid.*, pp. 50–51; Gotkowitz did not understand the sequence of events, however.

7. [Ellen James] to Bishop Lawrence, Aug. 17, 1914, copy in "Mr. Smith" packet, Treasurer's office, unprocessed files, Wellesley College Archives.

8. The entrances to the side of the tower led to entrance halls, off which came two small reception rooms, the suite for the head of house, and the great common living room. Students lived in single rooms, 10 feet by 17 feet, along a long corridor on the four stories of the wings and on the top floors of the tower. Tower projections facing north held the larger suites for faculty and guests. ("Three New College Buildings," *The Brickbuilder* 25 [1916], plates 8 and 9; Mausolf, "Tower Court," pp. 43, 46.)

9. Lewis Kennedy Morse to Charles Z. Klauder, Dec. 9, 1918, Day & Klauder packet, Treasurer's office, unprocessed files, Wellesley College Archives.

10. Mausolf, "Tower Court," pp. 43–75, has carefully described the craftsmanship of the interior.

11. Gotkowitz, "Development of a Master Plan for Wellesley College," pp. 59–64; [Coolidge and Carlson, A. A. Shurtleff,] "Report of Advisory Committee," June 1, 1914, copy in Wellesley College Archives.

12. William Allan Neilson, "President Pendleton as an Educator," *The Wellesley Magazine*, Ellen Fitz Pendleton Anniversary Number, 20 (1936): 7–50.

13. Creighton, "The Grounds," in *Wellesley College 1875–1975*, p. 280.

14. Two helpful discussions of the planning process are *ibid.*, pp. 279–83, and Gotkowitz, "Development of a Master Plan for Wellesley College," pp. 50–56.

15. Alice Van Vechten Brown, Edith R. Abbot, Alice Walton, Eliza J. Newkirk, and Myrtilla Avery to the President of the College and the Executive Committee of the Board of Trustees, Oct. 27, 1914, Architecture packet, Treasurer's office, unprocessed files, Wellesley College Archives.

16. "Statement of the Conference Committee of the Faculty," Wellesley College, Board of Trustees Minutes, Feb. 1915, in Wellesley College Archives.

17. Lewis Kennedy Morse to Alice Van Vechten Brown, Nov. 27, 1914, copy, "Buildings packet," Treasurer's office, unprocessed files, Wellesley College Archives.

18. Creighton, "The Grounds," p. 280.

19. Their leadership is derived from their active correspondence. See Treasurer's office, unprocessed files, Wellesley College Archives.

20. "Statement of the Conference Committee of the Faculty"; misspelling corrected.

21. *Ibid.*

22. Charlotte H. Conant to Bishop Lawrence, March 10, 1915, Architecture packet, Treasurer's office, unprocessed files, Wellesley College Archives.

23. "Statement of the Conference Committee of the Faculty."

24. Ellen F. Pendleton to Caroline Hazard, July 27, 1915, ALS file, Pendleton to Hazard, Wellesley College Archives, points out the parallels.

25. Day & Klauder to the Executive Committee of the Board of Trustees of Wellesley College, June 15, 1916, Day and Klauder packet, Treasurer's office, unprocessed files, Wellesley College Archives.

26. Ralph Adams Cram, "Report upon a General Plan for the Architectural Development of Wellesley College, made by Messrs. Day & Klauder, Architects," undated, pp. 1–2, Day and Klauder packet, Treasurer's office, unprocessed files, Wellesley College Archives.

27. *Ibid.*, p. 5.

28. *Ibid.*, p. 8.

29. *Ibid.*, p. 9.

30. Green's width required a roof far too high for the lines of the building. To prevent this, the architects invented a "parallel ridge type" construction for the roof which centers two gables over the outside rooms. On the inside Green Hall offered ample classrooms, faculty and administrative offices, a great reception hall, and ceremonial rooms devoted to the governing bodies. Barnard's treasurer, George A. Plimpton, gave the Trustees Room, paneled in oak from an English church. Many years before, he had given the Plimpton Collection of Italian Books in memory of his wife, an alumna. Caroline Hazard made the last of her many gifts to the college in donating the murals at both ends of the reception hall representing scenes from Katharine Lee Bates' "America the Beautiful." ("Buildings for Wellesley College, Wellesley, Massachusetts," *The Architectural Review* 12 [1921]: 129–33; discussion of "parallel ridge type" construction, 130.)

31. "Buildings for Wellesley College," 133.

32. Faculty Conference Committee, "The New College Plan and Problems," *Wellesley Alumnae Quarterly* 1 (1917): 225.

CHAPTER 17   *In Obedience to a Social Convention*

1. See, for example, "The Girls of Wellesley and Bryn Mawr," *The Ladies' Home Journal* 18 (June 1901): 1; Carolyn Halsted, "What A Girl Does At College," *Ladies' Home Journal* 19 (Jan. 1902): 24–25.

2. See, for example, Abbe Carter Goodloe, "Undergraduate Life at Wellesley," *Scribner's* 23 (May 1898): 515–38; Jeannette Marks, "Outdoor Life at Wellesley College," *Outing* 32 (May 1898): 117–24; Alice K. Fallows, "Self-Government for College Girls," *Harper's Bazar* 38 (July 1904): 698–705; "The Girl Freshman," *Munsey's Magazine* 25 (Sept. 1901): 818–28.

3. Jeannette Marks, "What It Means to be President of a Woman's College," *Harper's Bazar* 47 (June 1913): 264–67; Mary A. Jordan, "The Heads of Some Women's Colleges," *New Outlook* 71 (Aug. 12, 1902): 828–33; Lavinia Hart, "Women as College Presidents," *Cosmopolitan* 33 (May 1902): 72–79.

4. Robert J. Sprague, "Education and Race Suicide," *Journal of Heredity* 6 (May 1915): 158–62, quote from 160.

5. Roswell H. Johnson and Bertha Stutzmann, "Wellesley's Birth-rate," *Journal of Heredity* 6 (May 1915): 231–32.

6. Sprague, "Education and Race Suicide," 162.

7. *Ibid.*

8. Laura E. Lockwood, "College Women As Wives and Mothers," *School and Society* 3 (March 4, 1916): 332–38. Lockwood was a professor at Wellesley.

9. Roberta Frankfort, *Collegiate Women: Domesticity and Career in Turn-of-the-Century America* (New York: New York University Press, 1977), p. 73.

10. Rosalind Rosenberg, *Beyond Separate Spheres: Intellectual Roots of Modern Feminism* (New Haven: Yale University Press, 1982), pp. 1–12, 18–27.

11. Frankfort, *Collegiate Women*, pp. 85–103.

12. J. Stanley Lemons, *The Woman Citizen: Social Feminism in the 1920s* (Urbana, Illinois: University of Illinois Press, 1973), esp. pp. 209–27.

13. See, for example, the speech by James A. Reed and the surrounding debate in the Senate, June 20, 21, 22, 1921, against the Maternity Bill, Senate bill 1039, *Congressional Record* 61, part 9, pp. 8759–69.

14. Calvin Coolidge, "Enemies of the Republic: Are the Reds Stalking Our College Women?" *The Delineator*, June 1921, p. 4.

15. Lillian Faderman, *Surpassing the Love of Men: Romantic Friendship and Love between Women from the Renaissance to the Present* (New York: William Morrow, 1981), discusses both this belief in the innocence of women's romantic friendship and the changing understandings after World War I that informed the public about lesbianism.

16. While there is a spate of new literature chronicling changing attitudes toward sexuality in the early twentieth century, there is yet to be the needed study of the meaning of this for American women. Some works have helpful suggestions, however: Paul Robinson, *The Modernization of Sex* (New York: Harper & Row, 1976); David M. Kennedy, *Birth Control in America; The Career of Margaret Sanger* (New Haven: Yale University Press, 1970); Nathan Hale, *Freud and the Americans: The Beginnings of Psychoanalysis in the United States, 1876–1917* (New York: Oxford University Press, 1971); Linda Gordon, *Woman's Body, Woman's Right: A Social History of Birth Control in America* (New York: Grossman, 1976).

17. "Your Daughter: What Are Her Friendships?" by a College Graduate, *Harper's Bazar* (Oct. 1913): 16, 78.

18. Paula S. Fass, *The Damned and the Beautiful: American Youth in the 1920s* (New York: Oxford University Press, 1977), pp. 262–70.

19. Agnes Rogers, *Vassar Women: An Informal Study* (Poughkeepsie: Vassar College, 1940), pp. 31, 191.

20. *Ibid.*, pp. 42–43.

21. Margaret Farrand Thorp, *Neilson of Smith* (New York: Oxford University Press, 1956), pp. 253–54.

22. Jeanette Eaton, "The College Girl of 1930," *The Woman's Journal* 15 (May 1930): 5–7, 42–44.

23. Rogers, *Vassar Women*, pp. 61–62, 86.

24. Rogers, *Vassar Women*, p. 68; Elaine Kendall, *"Peculiar Institutions": An Informal History of the Seven Sister Colleges* (New York: G. P. Putnam's Sons, 1975), pp. 178–79.

25. Hackett, *Wellesley*, pp. 199–204; Arthur C. Cole, *A Hundred Years of Mount Holyoke College: The Evolution of an Educational Ideal* (New Haven: Yale University Press, 1940), pp. 258–64.

26. Quoted in William Chafe, *The American Woman: Her Changing Social, Economic and Political Roles, 1920–1970* (New York: Oxford University Press, 1972), p. 92.

27. Hackett, *Wellesley*, p. 221.

28. Hackett, *Wellesley*, pp. 209–10; Rogers, *Vassar Women*, pp. 67, 188–90; Cole, *Hundred Years*, pp. 268–70.

29. Eaton, "The College Girl of 1930," 7.

30. Quoted in Rogers, *Vassar Women*, p. 85.

31. Quoted in Hackett, *Wellesley*, p. 244. I.C.S.A. was probably the Intercollegiate College

Settlement Association; Barnswallows had turned itself from an open social club for the whole college into a competitive theatrical organization.

32. Quoted in Rogers, *Vassar Women*, pp. 97–98.

33. Hackett, *Wellesley*, p. 97.

34. Cole, *Hundred Years*, p. 287.

35. Hackett, *Wellesley*, p. 218.

36. *Ibid.*, pp. 219–20.

37. Cole, *Hundred Years*, p. 281.

38. Thorp, *Neilson of Smith*, pp. 251–52.

39. Interview with Frederica de Laguna, June 1980.

40. Hackett, *Wellesley*, pp. 241–43.

41. Cole, *Hundred Years*, pp. 284–88, quote from p. 285.

42. Cornelia Meigs, *What Makes a College? A History of Bryn Mawr* (New York: Macmillan Co., 1956), pp. 126–27, quote from p. 127.

43. Quoted in Rogers, *Vassar Women*, p. 82.

44. Chafe, *American Women*, pp. 92–94.

45. Vida Dutton Scudder, *On Journey* (New York: E. P. Dutton, 1937), pp. 298, 300.

46. Quoted in Chafe, *American Women*, p. 93.

CHAPTER 18   *In the Spirit of Our Times*

1. *The Magnificent Enterprise: A Chronicle of Vassar College*, compiled by Dorothy A. Plum and George B. Dowell (Poughkeepsie: Vassar College, 1961), pp. 47–48.

2. Henry N. MacCracken to Lucy Salmon, Sept. 29, 1918, Lucy Salmon Papers, Vassar College Library, Poughkeepsie, N.Y.

3. Lucy Salmon wrote a letter summarizing events intended to be shown to alumnae, Oct. 23, 1918, Lucy Salmon Papers, Vassar College Library.

4. Henry Noble MacCracken gives his side in *The Hickory Limb* (New York: Charles Scribner's Sons, 1950), pp. 51–53.

5. George P. Schmidt, *Douglass College: A History* (New Brunswick, N.J.: Rutgers University Press, 1968), pp. 17–20, 25–27.

6. *The Magnificent Enterprise*, pp. 51–53.

7. MacCracken, *Hickory Limb*, p. 59.

8. Mabel Newcomer to Henry N. MacCracken, Nov. 26, 1927, MacCracken Papers, Vassar College Library.

9. Typescript memorandum written by C. W. Moulton, E. B. Thelberg, A. L. Macleod, n.d., re: Euthenics program, MacCracken Papers, Vassar College Library.

10. Henry N. MacCracken to Marion Coats, Nov. 30, 1925, Archives of Sarah Lawrence College, Bronxville, N.Y.

11. Henry N. MacCracken, Memorandum of Interview with Prof. Macleod Concerning the Euthenics Building, Oct. 1, 1924, MacCracken Papers, Vassar College Library.

12. "Blodgett Hall of Euthenics, Vassar College," pamphlet in Vassar College Library.

13. Henry N. MacCracken to Minnie C. Blodgett, Feb. 22, 1926, MacCracken Papers, Vassar College Library.

14. "The New Gymnasium of Vassar College," Poughkeepsie, New York, 1929, pamphlet in Vassar College Library.

15. Catherine Bauer, "New Calisthenium for Vassar Female College," *Arts Weekly* 1 (May 4, 1932): 192–93.

16. "Helen Kenyon Hall of Physical Education," Vassar College, Poughkeepsie [1934], pamphlet in Vassar College Library.

17. "Cushing Hall," Vassar College, 1927, pamphlet in Vassar College Library.

18. [Henry N. MacCracken,] Report to the Committee on Buildings on a Plan for a Dormitory Group, Oct. 4, 1924, MacCracken Papers, Vassar College Library.

19. Information about Cushing Hall, Vassar College Buildings file (Cushing), Vassar College Library.

20. Mary E. Woolley, "Mount Holyoke College from 1901–1924," *Mount Holyoke Alumnae Quarterly* 8 (1925): 187.

21. Arthur A. Shurtleff in consultation with Ralph Adams Cram, "Mount Holyoke College General Plan," revised to Jan. 13, 1929, copy in Mount Holyoke College Library/Archives, South Hadley, Mass. Shurtleff changed his name to Shurcliff shortly after this report.

22. "Program for Campus Development, Mount Holyoke College," brochure, ca. 1929, Mount Holyoke College Library/Archives.

23. Bertha Blakely to George F. Newton, June 12, 1931, Blakely Correspondence, Mount Holyoke College Library/Archives.

24. Jytte Muus notes on Williston Memorial Library, Mount Holyoke College Library/Archives.

25. Anna Wells, *Miss Marks and Miss Woolley* (Boston: Houghton Mifflin Co., 1978), pp. 211–22; Sydney R. McLean, oral history interview, 1972, copy in Mount Holyoke College Library/Archives.

26. Wells, *Miss Marks and Miss Woolley*, pp. 223–39.

27. McLean discussed in her 1972 oral history interview presidential policy favoring men in the administrations after Woolley, copy in Mount Holyoke College Library/Archives.

28. *Mount Holyoke College, Annual Report of the President*, 1948–49, p. 24.

29. Beginning in the 1960s under President Richard Glenn Gettell, the college made stunning architectural choices. The architectural firms of Hugh Stubbins and Carl Koch & Associates turned Mount Holyoke away from the cold institutional functionalism of Douglas Orr to a warmer, more lyrical modernism. Architectural periodicals have given good press to the recent buildings of Mount Holyoke. For example, Eliot House was described and pictured in "Lighting that Complements Architecture," *Architectural Record* 131, part 1 (1962): 156–59, and in "Shrine Set on a Slope," *Architectural Forum* 116 (1962): 62–63.

CHAPTER 19   *The Training Which a College Can Give
in Character and in the Art of Living*

1. In the absence of a history of Smith during this period, the story is best followed in *The Smith Alumnae Quarterly* articles by Marion LeRoy Burton: "To the Alumnae," 2 (Jan. 1911): 65–68; "The Present Status of the Campaign," 3 (April 1912): 117–22; "The New Curriculum," 7 (Nov. 1915): 1–8; and "The New Method of Admissions," 7 (April 1916): 169–74.

2. Barbara Miller Solomon, "Ada Louise Comstock," *Notable American Women: The Modern Period* (Cambridge, Mass.: The Belknap Press of Harvard University Press, 1980), pp. 157–58. Comstock was deeply stung by the trustees' refusal to give her the title "Acting President."

3. Ada Comstock, "Why Smith College Should House Its Students," *The Smith Alumnae Quarterly* 11 (Nov. 1919): 14–17; quote from p. 16.

4. *Ibid.*, 17.

5. Ada Comstock to Marion Burton, Nov. 27, 1916, and Charles H. Allen to Samuel W.

McCall, Nov. 28, 1916, copy to Burton, Record Group 32: Burton, General, Unit College, Smith College Archives, Northampton, Mass.

6. John Nolen to Marion Burton, Feb. 18, 1914, Record Group 32: Burton, Correspondence, Nolen, Smith College Archives.

7. The lack of an adequate history of Smith College is partially remedied by the fine biography of its important twentieth-century president, Margaret Farrand Thorp, *Neilson of Smith* (New York: Oxford University Press, 1956), pp. 148–62, 254–55.

8. *Ibid.*, p. 255.

9. *Ibid.*, pp. 157, 313, 316–17.

10. *Ibid.*, p. 306–7, 313.

11. Putnam practiced in Northampton beginning in 1913. He joined the Smith faculty after beginning the collaboration with Ames and Dodge. He developed a connection between Smith and the Cambridge School of Architecture for the training of women, which ultimately moved to Smith College.

12. John Ames to William Neilson, April 1, 1919, Record Group 32: Neilson, Smith College Archives.

13. "Plans of Smith College Buildings, Registrar's Office," Record Group 20: Buildings and Grounds, Smith College Archives.

14. "Smith College Report—Proposed Dormitory Group, April 30, 1920," Record Group 32: Neilson, buildings, Smith College Archives.

15. "Recent Dormitories at Smith College," *Architectural Forum* 38 (April 1923): 183–86 and plate 35.

16. William Neilson to John Ames, Jan. 18, 1921, and Ames to Neilson, Jan. 20, 1921, Record Group 32: Neilson, Smith College Archives.

17. "Statement of the Conference Committee of the Faculty," Wellesley College, Board of Trustees, minutes, Feb. 8, 1915, Wellesley College Archives, Wellesley, Mass.

18. "Report on Living Conditions by the Alumnae Conference Committee, June 25, 1925," submitted by Charlotte H. Conant, Wellesley College, Board of Trustees minutes, June 28, 1915, Wellesley College Archives.

19. Harry J. Carlson to Charles Z. Klauder, Feb. 4, 1922, Severance Hall file, President's office, Wellesley College Archives.

20. Ralph Adams Cram to President Pendleton, April 17, 1923, Severance Hall file, President's office, Wellesley College Archives.

21. Charles Z. Klauder to Ellen F. Pendleton, June 24, 1922, Severance Hall file, President's office, Wellesley College Archives.

22. Architects' notes on East Dormitory, Sept. 19, 1925, Severance Hall file, President's office, Wellesley College Archives.

23. "Report on Living Conditions."

24. Author's three years in Severance, 1960–63.

25. "Report on Living Conditions."

26. Architects' notes on East Dormitory.

CHAPTER 20   *Without Reference to the Analogy of Colleges for Men*

1. Helen Merrell Lynd, *Possibilities*, with the collaboration of Staughton Lynd (Youngstown, Ohio: Ink Well Press, 1978), p. 41.

2. William Van Duzer Lawrence, *A Diary and Reminiscences Portraying the Life and Times of the Author* (Poughkeepsie, New York: A. V. Haight Co., 1922), p. 100.

3. Lawrence, *Diary and Reminiscences*, pp. 64–69; "William Van Duzer Lawrence," *Sarah Lawrence College, First Year, 1927–1928, Bronxville, New York*, pp. 43–47.

4. Early Recollections by Dudley B. Lawrence, July 1958, typescript, p. 2, copy in Archives of Sarah Lawrence College, Bronxville, N.Y.

5. Letters between William Lawrence and H. N. MacCracken, beginning Aug. 14, 1924, in Archives of Sarah Lawrence College.

6. William Van Duzer Lawrence, autobiographical fragment, typescript, pp. 2, 4, "Early History" file, Archives of Sarah Lawrence College.

7. *Ibid.*, p. 6.

8. William Lawrence, outline, enclosed in letter to H. N. MacCracken, June 8, 1925, Lawrence-MacCracken letters, 1925 file, Archives of Sarah Lawrence College.

9. William Lawrence, autobiographical fragment, p. 6.

10. William Lawrence, Letter of Instruction, p. 6, typescript copy in "Early College Documents" notebook, Archives of Sarah Lawrence College.

11. William Lawrence, autobiographical fragment, unpaged following p. 6.

12. *Ibid.*

13. Lawrence, Letter of Instruction, p. 4; typographical error corrected.

14. Dr. Henry E. McGarvey to William J. Wallin, October 4, 1926, Lawrence-MacCracken-Coats, October–December 1926 file, Archives of Sarah Lawrence College.

15. Lawrence-MacCracken correspondence, 1925–27, Archives of Sarah Lawrence College.

16. William Lawrence to Marion Coats, July 15, 1926, Lawrence-MacCracken-Coats, January–September 1926 file, Archives of Sarah Lawrence College. Lawrence underlined "self-supporting" in the original.

17. Early Recollections by Dudley B. Lawrence, p. 4.

18. H. N. MacCracken to William Lawrence, Nov. 17, 1926, with attached note by Louisa Lawrence Meigs; Lawrence to MacCracken, Nov. 17, 1926, describes Butler's overture; H. N. MacCracken to Marion Coats, undated, suggests that the idea of the Vassar affiliation may have come from Louisa Meigs, Lawrence-MacCracken-Coats, October–December 1926 file; Louisa Meigs to H. N. MacCracken, July 11, 1926, inquired if Vassar or Barnard could receive as a gift Westlands to be conducted as a junior college for girls (Lawrence-MacCracken-Coats, January–September 1926 file, Archives of Sarah Lawrence College).

19. A Statement of the Board of Trustees of Sarah Lawrence College for Women to the Board of Trustees of Vassar College, Archives of Sarah Lawrence College; [Constance Warren,] President's Report on the First Ten Years of Sarah Lawrence College, Dec. 9, 1936, pp. 3–4, Archives of Sarah Lawrence College.

20. William Lawrence to H. N. MacCracken, Dec. 16, 1926, Lawrence-MacCracken-Coats, October–December 1926 file, Archives of Sarah Lawrence College.

21. "Lawrence College to Fit Girls to Wed," New York *Times*, Dec. 17, 1926, was the initial article.

22. Marion Coats to William Lawrence, Dec. 22, 1926, Lawrence-MacCracken-Coats, October–December 1926 file, Archives of Sarah Lawrence College.

23. *Ibid.*

24. Marion Coats to H. N. MacCracken, Dec. 22, 1926, Lawrence-MacCracken-Coats, October–December 1926 file, Archives of Sarah Lawrence College; punctuation corrected. Edouard Bourdet's *The Captive*, one of the several plays in the winter of 1926–27 closed by New York censors, openly dealt with lesbianism.

25. William Lawrence, outline, enclosed in letter to H. N. MacCracken, June 8, 1925, Lawrence-MacCracken letters, 1925 file, Archives of Sarah Lawrence College.

26. William Lawrence, Proposed Scheme of Buildings for the Sarah Lawrence College,

in Lawrence-MacCracken-Coats, October–December 1926 file, Archives of Sarah Lawrence College.

27. William Lawrence, Proposed Scheme of Buildings; Lawrence to Charles Collens, Jan. 13, 1926, Lawrence-Bates & How, 1926 file, Archives of Sarah Lawrence College.

28. William Lawrence to Kenneth G. How, Feb. 4, 1927, Lawrence-Bates & How, January–March, 1917 file, Archives of Sarah Lawrence College.

29. Early Recollections by Dudley B. Lawrence, pp. 8–9; Conversation between Constance Warren and H. N. MacCracken, Oct. 13, 1961, pp. 9–11, typescript, copy in Archives of Sarah Lawrence College.

30. Conversation between Warren and MacCracken, 1961, pp. 14–15, quote from p. 15.

31. Lawrence, Letter of Instruction, p. 6.

32. I am grateful to Amy Swerdlow, a member of the Sarah Lawrence faculty, for this insight.

33. Lawrence, Letter of Instruction, quote from p. 8; Marion Coats described the process of composing the Letter of Instruction to H. N. MacCracken, Aug. 20, 1926, Lawrence-Coats-MacCracken, January–September 1926 file, Archives of Sarah Lawrence College.

34. Helen Lynd wrote movingly of this process in *Possibilities*, pp. 41–45.

35. President's Report on the First Ten Years of Sarah Lawrence College, pp. 19–37; conversation between Warren and MacCracken, 1961, pp. 20–21.

36. Conversation between Warren and MacCracken, 1961, p. 18.

37. President's Report on the First Ten Years of Sarah Lawrence College, p. 32.

38. I am grateful to the excellent study by Thomas P. Brockway, *Bennington College: In the Beginning* (Bennington, Vermont: Bennington College Press, 1981). I have used this source extensively in the following discussion. In writing this account, I examined many of the same sources as Brockway, and invariably found that he had understood and used them appropriately. My own interests and emphasis differ from his. Anyone with an interest in the larger Bennington story should consult his fine account.

39. Brockway, *Bennington College*, pp. 1–7; "Preface," from a speech by the Reverend Vincent Ravi Booth given at Old Bennington in August 1928, *Bennington College Bulletin* 25 (June 1957): 7–11. In keeping with Booth's signature on Bennington documents, I have not hyphenated his name.

40. Minutes of the Board of Trustees of Bennington College, April 12, 1928, Bennington College, Bennington, Vt.

41. Ames and Dodge plan, Bennington College. Notes of first conference between architects and Bennington representatives, April 29, 1928, contain the decision that "for the present, the Architects are to proceed on the Dwelling and Dining Halls on much the same basis as at Smith College" (Building Construction, General, Buildings and Grounds, 1925–28 file, Bennington College Archives, Bennington, Vt.).

42. Edith van Benthuysen McCullough, "Recollections," *Bennington College Bulletin* 25 (June 1957): 17.

43. Quoted in Brockway, *Bennington College*, p. 4.

44. William H. Kilpatrick, letter, March 23, 1926, copied in *Bennington College Bulletin* 25 (June 1957): 71–78. Quotes from p. 72.

45. Brockway, *Bennington College*, pp. 7–10. Quotes from p. 9.

46. *Ibid.*, pp. 11–16.

47. Ernest H. Wilkins to Dr. Booth, July 11, 1927, copy appended to Minutes of the Board of Trustees of Bennington College, July 28, 1927, Bennington College.

48. Brockway, *Bennington College*, pp. 16–22.

49. *Ibid.*, pp. 23–31. McCullough quotes from p. 23 and from "Recollections," 33.

50. [Robert D. Leigh,] "The Educational Plan for Bennington College," (New York: Office of Bennington College, 1929), unpaged 18-point "Essential Features of the Bennington Program," copy in Bennington College Archives. I have eliminated headings in capital letters. Notes of Meeting of Heads of Schools, Dec. 8, 1930, in Schools Admissions 1930–33 file, Bennington College Archives.

51. [Leigh,] "Educational Plan," 18-point plan.

52. *Ibid.*, p. 11.

53. *Ibid.*, p. 13.

54. *Ibid.*, "Essential Features."

55. Report of the President, appended to Minutes of the Board of Trustees of Bennington College, April 12, 1928, Bennington College.

56. Hull quote, Brockway, *Bennington College*, p. 45.

57. The interest in merger continued well into 1931.

58. Robert D. Leigh to Members of the Board of Trustees, Aug. 25, 1930, attached to Minutes, Sept. 3, 1930, Bennington College; Report of visitation, Nov. 4, 1928, New Jersey College for Women, Bennington College Archives.

59. Brockway, *Bennington College*, pp. 42–48.

60. Leigh's handwritten notes under the comment by T. V. Smith of the University of Chicago, accompanying letter to Members of Executive Committee, May 16, 1930, in Critical Comments on Educational Plan file, Bennington College Archives.

61. "Building Bennington College," *Bennington College Bulletin* 2 (Nov. 1933): entire, unpaged.

62. Robert D. Leigh, "The College Organization," *Bennington College Bulletin* 3 (Nov. 1934): 1–4.

63. "Community Standards and Rules," adopted Nov. 14, 1932, in *Bennington College Bulletin* 3 (Nov. 1934): 15. An early memo, Robert D. Leigh to Mrs. Lee, May 14, 1932, informed her that the college wanted "as little regulation of the students' life as possible." Students wanting to leave campus informed the registrar, who had discretion to grant or refuse such absences on the basis of information about the student's "reliability and ability to carry on her work." This would be done by an "honor system" (Bennington College Archives).

64. "Partial Answers to Persistent Questions about Bennington," *Bennington College Alumnae Quarterly* 1 (Spring 1949): 9.

65. "Community Standards and Rules," 16.

66. McCulloch, "Recollections," 15.

67. Conversation with Rebecca B. Stickney, April 25, 1983. I am grateful to Ms. Stickney for her generous help in locating materials. Of course, she bears no responsibility for my interpretation of the data.

68. Robert D. Leigh, "The College and the World About Us," extract from remarks of the First Community Meeting of the Second Year, Sept. 6, 1933, printed in *Bennington College Bulletin* 2 (Aug. 1933): 6.

69. William Bennett Munro, "The College at the Crossroads," Pomona College Commencement, June 15, 1925; E. Wilson Lyon, *The History of Pomona College, 1887–1969* (Claremont: Pomona College, 1977), pp. 232–56, discusses the founding of Scripps and the Group Plan.

70. Munro, "College at the Crossroads."

71. The usual discussion centers on Blaisdell's admiration for the English university system, rather than on practical concerns, the influence of others, or opportunities. My reconstruction is based on a reading of all available printed material and archival materials in the Scripps College Archives, Claremont, Calif.

72. "I am surprised at the richness of material among women. We certainly ought to be able to corrall . . . a group of exceptionally experienced women" (Ernest Jaqua to James Blaisdell, Oct. 26, 1925, Scripps College Archives).

73. In 1975, Mary Routt related to the author that when Jaqua asked her to join the initial board, he specifically said that she was the "Wellesley representative."

74. Ethel R. Allen, "Report of the Special Committee on Vocational Training at Scripps College," typescript, p. 4, Scripps College Archives.

75. *Ibid.*, p. 2.

76. James Blaisdell to Jacob C. Harper, June 15, 1926, typed copy in Scripps College Archives.

77. For example, Jaqua sent a telegram to Blaisdell, June 29, 1925, about the position in French: "Man instructor preferred." Jaqua wrote to Blaisdell, Nov. 24, 1925: "Of all the men I have met anywhere I think Morey [C. R. Morey of Princeton] would be the best man to head up a great department of art and archeology here" (Scripps College Archives).

78. Minutes of the Board of Trustees of Scripps College, May 27, 1927, President's Office, Scripps College.

79. Hartley Burr Alexander, *Liberty and Democracy and Other Essays in War-Time* (Boston: Marshall Jones Company, 1918).

80. "A Philosophy for the Liberal Arts College in the Modern World," Address at the Proceedings of the Association of Colleges and Universities of the Pacific Southwest, 1936, p. 9, copy in Scripps College Archives.

81. "Scripps College and Its Needs, Note II. The Humanities: History of Occidental Culture," copy in Scripps College Archives.

82. *Scripps College Bulletin*, 1931–32, p. 33.

83. Memorandum for Members of the Building Committee for Scripps College, reporting on May 12, 1926, meeting, Scripps College.

84. Only this elliptical comment survives in a letter from Ernest Jaqua to Bernhard Hoffman, June 25, 1916: "Mrs. Moses asked for more deliberate consideration and after a discussion with Mr. Allison and others is inclined to think that it would be unwise to select Miss Morgan" (Scripps College Archives).

85. Notes made at the meeting of the Building Committee of Scripps College, July 30, 1926, Scripps College.

86. Memoranda dictated by Mr. Judy for Dean Jaqua, May 13, 1926, reporting on May 12, 1926, meeting, Scripps College.

87. *Scripps College, Claremont*, pamphlet, ca. 1929, copy in Scripps College Archives.

88. William Munro was on the special committee to study undergraduate life at California Institute of Technology, and he helped draft the report to the board of trustees that established undergraduate housing, making the goals of fellowship explicit (report of the special committee to study the problem of undergraduate life at the Institute, March 21, 1928, California Institute of Technology Archives, Pasadena, Calif.).

89. *Scripps College News*, Feb. 17, 1936.

90. Ada Elizabeth Watkins (Hatch) Scrapbook, Scripps College Archives.

EPILOGUE

1. Lucy M. Salmon, *Is This Vassar College?* (Poughkeepsie: n. pub., 1915), p. 4.

Index

Abbot, Agnes, 266
Abbott, Edwin Hale, 205
"academical village," 3, 32
academic dress (Bryn Mawr), 120 and *illus.*,
   172
academic freedom, 193–94
academy and academy curriculum, 10
adaptations of buildings:
  Barnard: Fiske Hall, 138
  Bryn Mawr: Deanery, 131–32
  Mount Holyoke: Seminary Building, 26 and
    illus.
  Radcliffe: Fay House, 238
  Vassar: Main, 90, 91–92, 353
  Wellesley: Music building, 353
admissions policy, and ethnic heritage of
    students, 155
  Barnard, 258, 259
  Jews, 155
  quotas, 259
  Sarah Lawrence, 321
admission standards and requirements:
  Barnard, 136
  Bennington, 332
  Bryn Mawr, 107, 115
  Ipswich Seminary, 17
  Mount Holyoke, 25, 225, 226
  Smith, 78, 213, 308
  Vassar, 41
  Wellesley, 85

affluent students, *see* wealthy students
Agassiz, Elizabeth Carey, 100, 104, 238, 239,
   242
Alexander, Hartley Burr, 342 and *illus.*, 343
"all-around girls," 156, 159, 163, 179
Allen, Ethel Richardson, 340 and *illus.*
Allen, Francis R., 93–94, 219, 221
Allen & Collens, architects:
  Mount Holyoke, 234, 303
  Sarah Lawrence, 324
  Vassar, 219, 221, 301
alumnae:
  and campus planning: Wellesley, 265–69
    passim, 316, 353
  careers of: Mount Holyoke, 27
  clubs of: Wellesley, 86
  as critical of alma mater:
    Mount Holyoke, 224–25
    Vassar, 292, 300
  fund-raising by:
    for Mount Holyoke, 228, 236
    for Radcliffe, 245
  marriage rates of, 280, 281, 282
    Bryn Mawr, 280
    Mount Holyoke, 27
  as trustees:
    Vassar, 46, 222, 300
    Wellesley, 263
  see also alumnae *under individual colleges*
Ames, John W., 310, 329–30, 334

399

Amherst College:
 buildings, 22
  contrasted to women's college buildings,
   22, 24, 311
 classics at, 72
 faculty and president's residences, 24
 founding of, 72
 influence on Smith, 70, 71, 72–73
 societies and fraternities, 22, 24, 71
Anderson, Elizabeth Milbank, 138, 139, 251
Andrews, E. A., 57–58
Andrews, Evangeline Walker, 122
annexes:
 Bryn Mawr rejects status of, 106, 115
 Columbia's, *see* Barnard College
 Harvard's, *see* Radcliffe College
anti-Semitism, 155
 Barnard, 256, 258–59
 and faculty, 184
 Sarah Lawrence, 321
architectural styles, *see* Georgian; Gothic;
  Tudor
art buildings:
 Mount Holyoke, 234
 Smith, 214
 Vassar, 221
 Wellesley, 84
art course:
 Smith: School of Art, 213–14
 Vassar, 35, 221
 Wellesley, 84
 see also fine arts
art gallery:
 Smith, 214, 382 *n.* 34
 Vassar, 35
assembly rooms and buildings:
 Mount Holyoke, 21, 228
 Smith, 76, 77, 217
 Vassar, 219
 Wellesley, 265
 see also chapel (building)
Association of College Alumnae (ACA),
  280–81
 and Mount Holyoke, 224
 and Radcliffe, 239
 and Scripps, 341
asylum planning, 14
 "congregate system" in, 74
 and gender, 357 *n.* 1

and Mount Holyoke Seminary, 21
and Renwick's Vassar plan, 31–32
athletic fields:
 Bryn Mawr, 126, *illus.* 160
 emphasis on individual sports (post–World
  War I), 285
 Radcliffe, 247
 see also exercise and physical training;
  gymnasium
athletics, competitive, 159, *illus.* 160–61, *illus.*
  215, 352
autonomy of students, 145, 148–49, 196
 inhibited by seminary system and building,
  24
 Vassar, 38, 63–64, 68
 viewed as dangerous for Smith, 75
Avery, Myrtilla, 266

Balch, Emily Greene, 194, 196
Barnard, Frederick A. P., 134
Barnard College, 134–42, 247–61
 benefactors of, 135, 137–39, 251, 252
 buildings, 138–42, *illus.* 138–40, 248–60
  Brinckerhoff Theater, 138, 139, 141
  Brooks Hall, *illus.* 250, 251
  Fiske Hall, 138, 139, 141
  Hewitt Hall, 260, 388 *n.* 73; Deanery, 260
  Milbank Hall, 138, 139, *illus.* 140; studies,
   248, *illus.* 249
  original (343 Madison Ave.), 135
  Students' Hall, 252; renamed Barnard
   Hall, *illus.* 254, 259
 campus, 138–42, *illus.* 138–40, *illus.* 254
  Jungle, 253, *illus.* 254
  land as Anderson gift (1903), 251
  planning of, 141, 253
 and Columbia, 6, 134–42, 248–50, 254–55
  agreements: (1900), 249; (1922), 255
 faculty, 134, 135, 136, 137
 fund-raising, 136, 252
 Greek themes at, 252, *illus.* 253
 influenced by Radcliffe, 134
 intentions of founders, 6, 134
 "Jewish Problem," 256, 258–59
 sororities, 248, 256
 students:
  admission standards for, 136
  economic circumstances of, 256, 258
  ethnic backgrounds of, 256

fund-raising of, 252
geographic distribution of, 250–51, 259
residences for, 141, 248, 251, 260
trustees, 134–35, 259
urbanity of, 247–48
basketball, 159, *illus.* 160, *illus.* 215, 216
Bates, Katharine Lee, 174, 182, 184, 188, 196
Yellow Clover, 196
Bates & How, architects, 321
Bauer, Catherine, 300
Beaux Arts planning:
Barnard, 141–42, 253
Bennington, 330, 338
Bryn Mawr, 118
Mount Holyoke, 234, 302
Radcliffe, 247
Smith, 309, 338
Vassar, 219, 383–84 *n.* 49
Wellesley, 263, 264, 269
bedrooms, *see* rooms, students'
Beecher, Catharine, 11
Beecher, Henry Ward, 38, 71
benefactors, *see* men, as benefactors; women, as benefactors
Bennington College, 319–20, 328–39
admission standards, 332
aerial view (1933), 336–37
buildings:
Commons, *illus.* 333, 334
dormitories, *illus.* 333, 334
faculty, 332, 338
financial support for, 331, 332, 334
influenced by:
Mount Holyoke, 328–29
Smith, 329–30
opening of (1932), 328
planning of, 329–34
president, *see* Leigh, R. D.
trustees, 331, 332
Bigelow, Henry Forbes, 244
Billings, Hammatt, 44–45, 46, 48
black students, 155–56
Blackwell, Alice Stone, 65
Blaisdell, James, 339, 340
Blodgett, Minnie Cumnock, 297
boarding houses, *see* student residences: off campus
boards of trustees, *see* women, as trustees; *and* trustees *under specific colleges*

Booth, Vincent Ravi, 329–31
Boston, Mass., attitudes toward:
Harvard, 96, 97
Wellesley, 203–04, 205
Breckinridge, Sophonisba, 87 and *illus.*, 205
Briggs, Le Baron Russell, 242
Brigham, Mary, 226
Brinckerhoff, Mrs. Van Wyck, 138
Brocklesby, William C., 214, 216, 228, 231
Brooks, Arthur, 135
Brooks, Phillips, 204–05
Brown, Alice Van Vechten, 266, 267
Brown University, 218
Brunner & Buckman & Fox, architects, 252
Bryn Mawr College, 105–33
buildings, 116, 118
Deanery, 130–33, *illus.* 131–32; garden, 132, *illus.* 133
Denbigh Hall, 124 and *illus.*
early planning for, 106–07, 110
gymnasium, 111
Low Buildings, 185, 186 and *illus.*
Merion Hall, *illus.* 108, 110–11, 116
Pembroke Hall, 124, *illus.* 125
Radnor Hall, 122
Rockefeller Hall, 126 and *illus.*, 127
Taylor Hall, *illus.* 109, 110, 116, *illus.* 125; library in, *illus.* 120
Thomas library, 127, *illus.* 128, 129 and *illus.*, 130; cloister, 127, *illus.* 129, 130; reading room, *illus.* 128, 130; site selected, 129
campus, *illus.* 108–09
location selected, 106
planning of, 122, 126, 374 *n.* 24
playing fields, 126, *illus.* 160
siting of buildings, 129
Thomas's influence on, 118, 373 *n.* 5
curriculum, 107
faculty, 107, 180–81
rebel against Thomas (1916), 130
recruitment of, 115, 116
religious affiliations of, 184
residences of, 180, 185, 186 and *illus.*
fees, 127, 152
founding of, 105–16
graduate school, 115
and Haverford, 105–06
influenced by:

Bryn Mawr College (*continued*)
    English universities, 6, 127
    Radcliffe, 115
    Smith, 6, 105, 107, 114
    Wellesley, 114, 115
  influence on:
    Barnard, 237
    Mount Holyoke, 236
    Radcliffe, 104, 237, 241–42
  president, *see* Park, M.; Rhoads, J. E.;
    Thomas, M. C.
  rituals, 175–76
    Lantern Night, 172, 174–75
    May Day, 122, *illus.* 123, 353
  rooming policy of, 155
  students:
    admission requirements for, 107, 115
    religious background of, 127
    residences of, 110–11, 122, 124 and *illus.*,
      illus. 125, 126 and *illus.*, 127
    self-governance, 119–20, 130
    smoking by, 184, 289, 292
    wealthy, 127
  trustees, 106, 111
    and Thomas, 113, 116, 117–18, 127,
      129–30
Burton, Marion LeRoy, 308, 309
Butler, Nicholas Murray, 136, 250, 255

Caldwell, Eunice, 18, 19, 24
Caldwell, Samuel L., 91
Carnegie, Andrew, 217, 236
chapel (building):
  Amherst, 22
  Mount Holyoke, 228, 229
  Smith, 75, 217
  Vassar, 35, 219, *illus.* 220
  Wellesley, 51, 204, 205–08, *illus.* 207
chapel (services):
  compulsory:
    repudiated by Wellesley, 205
    retained in 20th century, 286
    seminary system, 15
  decline of, 286
  Smith, 77, 217
  as social/communal event, 150, 170, 172
chaperonage, 288–89
Chase, Thomas, 106
Choate, Mrs. Joseph H., 135

Christian influence on colleges:
  Amherst, 22
  Mount Holyoke, 19
  and secularization, 150
  Wellesley, 43–44, 54, 86, 205
Claremont Colleges group, 339–40
Clark, Edward L., 206
Clark, John B., 137
Clarke, Edward H.: *Sex in Education*, 281
classical languages:
  Bryn Mawr, 107
  lacking at female seminaries, 11
    Mount Holyoke, 25, 224
  for males only, 9, 28, 72
Coats, Marion, 321, 322, 324, 325
coeducational institutions, women's education
  in, 56, 73
coeducation *vs.* single-sex education, *see*
  separate education for women
Coes, Mary, 240
Cole, Frank N., 137
Colgate, James Colby, 329, 334
college curriculum, 28–29
  fine arts, 35, 73, 84; *see also* art course;
    music course
  Vassar, 40–41
college life, 5, 56–68, 147–78, 277–92
  Amherst, 24, 71
  Barnard, 252, 255–56
  buildings for, *see* students' building
  decline of, after 1920s, 277–92
  effect on, of having men on campus (post–
    World War I), 284–85
  Mount Holyoke, 227
    inhibited at (Seminary), 24, 58–59
  Radcliffe, 238, 245
  Smith, 213, 216
  Vassar, 63–68
    feared as model for Smith, 75
  Wellesley, 68, 89
  see also athletics, competitive; autonomy
    of students; "crush"; dramatics;
    organizations; rituals; "smash"
colleges for men, *see* men's colleges
colleges for women, *see* women's colleges
Collens, Charles, *illus.* 220, 221; *see also* Allen
    & Collens, architects
Columbia University, and Barnard, 6, 134–42,
    248–50, 254–55

Coman, Katharine, *illus.* 164, *illus.* 183, 188, 190, 196
common school, 11, 16
Comstock, Ada Louise, 307, 308–09, 311, 329
confession, public, 15, 24
"congregate system," 74, 75, 78
Converse, Florence, 174, *illus.* 176, 188
Coolidge, Calvin, 282
Coolidge & Carlson, architects, 212, 263, 264, 317
Cope & Stewardson, architects, 118, 120, 122, 124, 126, 127
Cornell University, 56, 97, 105, 112
cottage system:
  Bennington, 330
  Bryn Mawr, 107, 110–11, 114
  Mount Holyoke, 228, 230–31, 232, 233
  Sarah Lawrence, 324
  Smith, 71, 75, 78, *illus.* 79, 80, 153, 214, 216
    contrasted to dormitories, 315
    impact of, 227–28
    removal recommended by Nolen, 309
  Vassar, 91, 92
  Wellesley, 87–90
    replacement of, 210, 211
Cram, Ralph Adams, 266–67, 268, 269, 272, 302–03, 315–16
"crush," 166–67, 191, 193, 282
curriculum:
  classical, 28
  college, 28–29
  English, 10, 11, 17, 28
  liberal arts, *see* liberal arts curriculum
  see also curriculum *under specific colleges*
Cushing, Florence, 300, 384 *n.* 4

dame school, 9
Dana Hall School, 83, 86
dances:
  all-female:
    male roles and attire for, 162
    Smith, 216
  proms, 216, 288
    Smith (1905), *illus.* 290–91
daughter-mother bond, 4, 17, 25, 58
Davies, Emily, 98
Davison, Eliza, 93
Day, Frank Miles, 268–69

Day & Klauder, architects, 268, 269, 272, 317
day students, 36
De Forest, Lockwood, 131–32
devotions, private, 15
  Mount Holyoke, 21
  Wellesley, 54, 55, 205
Dewey, Melville, 135, 136
De Wolfe, Elsie, 251
Dickinson, Louisa, *see* Greene, Louisa Dickinson
"digs" (or "grinds"), 150, 156
dining room:
  Bryn Mawr, *illus.* 126
  college life in, 172
  Mount Holyoke, 21, *illus.* 23
  Smith, *illus.* 154
  supervision in, 64
  Vassar, 35
  Wellesley, 51, 83
discipline:
  in common schools, 11, 16
  system devised by Grant and Lyon, 13–15
    Mount Holyoke Seminary, 24
  see also self-reporting system; supervision of students
Dodge, Edwin Sherrill, 310, 329–30, 334
domestic science:
  Scripps (practice house), 348
  Vassar (Euthenics), 280, 295–302
domestic work, done by students:
  in Lyon's seminary system, 18
  Mount Holyoke, *illus.* 23, 25, 227
  Wellesley, 55; terminated (1896), 205
Donnelly, Lucy, 186
donors, *see* men, as benefactors; women, as benefactors
dormitories, *see* student residences
Dorsey, Susan, 340, 341
Douglass College (*formerly:* New Jersey College for Women), 297, 334
Downing, Andrew Jackson, 30, 32
dramatics, 162–63, *illus.* 165
  Wellesley, *illus.* 176
  see also rituals
dress:
  academic, 120 and *illus.,* 172
  men's (worn by women), 162, 163, *illus.* 165
  unconventional, 162
  Vassar, 36, 37, 39

Durant, Henry Fowle, 42–48, 52–55, 81–85
  dominance of Wellesley trustees, 45
  early life of, 42–43
  feminism of, 43–44
  intentions of, for Wellesley, 4–5, 54
  as Mount Holyoke trustee, 42, 44
Durant, Pauline, 45, 46, 82, 85, 204–05
  as benefactor:
    to Mount Holyoke, 44
    to Wellesley, 87, 88
  and siting of Houghton Memorial Chapel,
    206

economic strata of students, 147–48
  Bryn Mawr, 152
  poor, sought by seminary, 17–18
  Smith, 308–09
  wealthy, 127, 226, 245, 256, 258
  Wellesley, 152
education, women's:
  colonial period, 9
  common schools, 11
  conservatively experimental: Scripps, 341,
    350
  Durant's views on, 44
  progressive:
    Bennington, 329, 330, 332, 334, 338
    Sarah Lawrence, 325, 328
  revolutionary period, 10
  separate (*vs.* coeducation), *see* separate
    education for women
Eliot, Charles William, 95, 97, 209, 239, 382
  n. 24
Elmira (N.Y.) College, 29
Emerson, Joseph, 13, 15
endowment(s):
  Lyon's efforts, for Ipswich and Mount
    Holyoke, 18
  Sarah Lawrence, 322
  Smith, 308
  Vassar, 90, 91
  Wellesley, 85
English curriculum, 10, 11, 17, 28
English universities, influence on:
  Byrn Mawr, 6, 127
  Harvard, 22
  Radcliffe, 241–42
  Smith, 309

entrance requirements, *see* admission standards
    and requirements
epidemics, danger and fear of, 25
ethnic heritage of students, 155–56
  Barnard, 256
  Sarah Lawrence, 321
Euthenics (Vassar), 295–302, 319
evangelical Christianity:
  and Amherst, 22
  and Mount Holyoke Seminary, 19
  and seminary model for women's education,
    4
  and Wellesley, 43–44, 54, 205
  see also missionaries
exercise and physical training:
  Mount Holyoke, 26
  Vassar, 32, 33, 36, 39
  see also athletic fields; athletics, competitive;
    gymnasium

faculty:
  distinction and relation between male and
    female, 180
    rent allowances, 187
    salaries, 180, 185
    Scripps, 341–42
    Vassar, 40, 187
  ranks and distinctions among, 180
    Mount Holyoke, 233
    Vassar, 40, 62
  sabbatical leave, 81, 234
  see also male faculty; teacher-student
    relationship; women faculty; *and*
    faculty *under specific colleges*
faculty, female, *see* women faculty
faculty, male, *see* male faculty
faculty residences, *see* male faculty: residences;
    women faculty: residences
"family government":
  in asylum, 21
  Mount Holyoke Seminary, 21
  rejected at Bryn Mawr, 119
  Smith, 75
  Vassar, 38
Farnsworth, Isaac D., 84
Farrar, Charles, 39, 61
fees (including tuition):
  Barnard, 258

Bennington, 332
Bryn Mawr, 127
Ipswich, 17
minimized in seminary system, 18, 25
Radcliffe, 102
Sarah Lawrence, 322
Smith, 114
Wellesley, 85, 86
fees for room and board:
Barnard, 388 *n.* 73
Bryn Mawr, 127, 152
Smith, 114
Wellesley, 152
female friendship:
among faculty, 188, 190–91, 193
Grant's and Lyon's, 13, 17, 58
19th century acceptance of, 13
among students:
erotic, 166–67, 191, 193, 282
fears about, 65, 66, 75
and heterosexuality, 282, 315–16
inhibited: Mount Holyoke, 58–59; Smith,
75, 314, 315; Wellesley, 318
"smash," 65–68
Vassar, 65–68
teacher-student bonds, 17, 25, 58–59, 167,
179, 191
Thomas's, 112, 113, 114, 117, 122, 130,
131, 193
Woolley's and Marks's, 191, 233, 304
female sexuality, *see* sexuality
femininity, protection of:
Mount Holyoke: with porches on cottages,
231
and racism, 279–80
Smith, 68, 69, 75, 80, 315
and "unsexing" of students, 167, 169
Vassar, 29, 59
see also masculinity, fears of
feminism:
feared at Vassar, 59
and women's colleges (post–World War I),
352
financial support, *see* fund-raising; men, as
benefactors; women, as benefactors
fine arts:
Smith, 73
Vassar, 35

Wellesley, 84
see also art course; music course
fires on campus:
Mount Holyoke (1896), 228, 230
Wellesley (1914), 84, 213, 262, 268
Fiske, Mrs. Josiah M., 138
Forbes Library, Northampton, Mass., 216–17
Franklin, Elizabeth Jennings, 334
"freaks," 150, 156
Freeman, Alice, *see* Palmer, Alice Freeman
friendship, female, *see* female friendship
fund-raising:
by alumnae, 228, 236, 245
Barnard, 136, 252
Bennington, 331
Bryn Mawr, 127, 375 *n.* 32
cooperative, by Seven College Conference,
261
Mount Holyoke, 19, 224, 234
Radcliffe, 102, 242, 245
Sarah Lawrence, 324
Smith, 308, 309–10
Vassar, 218
Wellesley, 262
see also men, as benefactors; women, as
benefactors

gardens:
Alexandra Garden, Wellesley, 212
Deanery, Bryn Mawr, 132, *illus.* 133, 188
of faculty homes, 188
President's House, Mount Holyoke, 234
Scripps, 346
Gardner, Eugene C., 229, 231
Garrett, Mary, 112, 113, 114, 117, 122, 130,
131 and *illus.*, 193
Garrett, Paul, *illus.* 327
Gates, Frederick T., 218–19
Geismer, Maxwell, *illus.* 326
geographic distribution of students:
Barnard, 250–51, 259
Mount Holyoke, 25, 226–27, 304
Radcliffe, 104
Vassar, 62
Georgian architectural style:
Mount Holyoke: Seminary building, 20 and
illus.
Radcliffe:

Georgian Architectural Style (*continued*)
    Fay House reconstruction (1890), 244
    residence halls, 246, 247
  Smith:
    President's House, 310
    Quadrangles, 314–15
  Wellesley: Wilder, 210–11
Gettell, Richard Glenn, 393 *n.* 29
Gildersleeve, Virginia Crocheron, 248,
    254–56, *illus.* 257, 258–61 *passim*
  defends women's colleges (1924), 330
  on students in 1920s, 293
Gill, Laura Drake, 240, 250–52, 254
Gilman, Arthur, 95, 98, 100, 102, 238
Gilman, Daniel Coit, 106
Gilman, Stella Scott, 98, 100
Girton College, Cambridge, England, 98
Glazier, Sarah, 82
Goodnow, E. A., 230
Gothic architectural style, 201, 242
  Bryn Mawr, 118, 121
  Mount Holyoke, 302
    chapel, Mary Lyon Hall, 229
    (Tudor:) library, 236
    Williston Memorial Library, 303
  Smith:
    College Hall, 76 and *illus.,* 77
    Hillyer Art Gallery, 214
  Wellesley, 269
    College Hall, 49
    Founders and Green, 272
    Tower Court, 264–65
Goucher College, 111
governance systems:
  Mount Holyoke, 21, 24
  of seminary system, 15
  by students, *see* self-governance; self-
    reporting
  Vassar, 33–34, 38
  see also president; self-governance; trustees
graduates, *see* alumnae
Grant, Zilpah:
  influence and importance of, 11–12, 27
  and Lyon, 13–14, 17, 58
  opposes single rooms for students, 21, 39
  Vassar influenced by, 39
Greek and Latin, *see* classical languages
Greek themes (Barnard), 252, *illus.* 253
Greene, John Morton, 69–71, 74

Greene, Louisa Dickinson, 26–27, 70, 71, 74
Greenough, James B., 100, 240
Greenwood, Grace, 60
Gregory, Emily L., 136
"grinds" (or "digs"), 150, 156
Gwinn, Mamie, 112, 113, 130
gymnasium:
  Barnard, 252
  Bryn Mawr, 111
  college life in, 169, 232, 252
  Mount Holyoke, 26, 231–32
  Radcliffe, 242, 244
  Smith, *illus.* 160–61, 169, 216, 353
  Vassar, 36 and *illus.,* 169, 300
  see also athletic fields; athletics, competitive;
    exercise and physical training

Halbert, Pauline Woodford, 224–25
Hale, Horatio, 37
Hale, Sarah, 37, 38
Hallowell, Susan Maria, 54
Ham, Roswell, 304, 306
Harvard College:
  Boston and, 96, 97
  influenced by Cambridge University, 22
  and Radcliffe, 5–6, 95–104, 238–40
  student residences at, 22, 311, 314
Haverford College, 105–06
Hawks, Roswell, 19
Hazard, Caroline, 204, 208–10, 390 *n.* 30
health, concern for:
  and education of women, 281
  Mount Holyoke, 25–26
  Vassar, 33
  see also exercise and physical training
Heins & La Farge, architects, 205, 208, 210,
    266
Hemenway, Mary, 242
heterosexuality:
  and dormitory design, 74–75, 315–16
  ensured by involvement in village life, 80
  and female friendship, 282, 315–16
  "protected" at Sarah Lawrence, 324
  stressed at Bennington, 334
  see also femininity, protection of
Higginson, Thomas Wentworth, 96–97, 205
Hillyer, Winthrop, 214, 382 *n.* 34
Hitchcock, Edward, 13, 18, 19
Holland, J. G., 59, 60, 74–75

home life, imitated:
  Bennington, 330
  Bryn Mawr, 110
  Radcliffe, 104
  Sarah Lawrence, 324
  Vassar, 38
  see also cottage system; domestic work,
    done by students
homemaking program:
  Scripps (practice house), 348
  Vassar, 295–98, 319
    building for (Blodgett), 298, 299, 300–01
homosexuality, *see* lesbianism
Horsford, Eben, 51–52, 54, *illus.* 86, 181, 205
Houghton, Elizabeth G. and Clement S., 205
house plan for student residences:
  Mount Holyoke Seminary, 20, 22
  Scripps, 346, 348
housing policy, *see* rooming policy
How, Kenneth G., 324; *see also* Bates & How
Howard, Ada, 53, 85
Howe, Samuel Gridley, 74
Hubbard, George W., 70
Hull, Morton D., 331
Humphrey, Heman, 19
Humphrey, Sarah W., 78
Hutton, Addison, 106, 110

independence of students, *see* autonomy of
    students
intimate friendship between women, *see*
    female friendship
invitation houses (Smith), 154
Ipswich (Mass.) Seminary (*formerly:*
    Academy), 11, 14, 15, 17, 59
Irvine, Julia, 209
Irwin, Agnes, 240, 242
Ivy Day, Smith, *illus.* 174, 175 and *illus.*

James, Ellen Stebbins Curtiss, 263, 264
Jaqua, Ernest, 340, 341, *illus.* 342
Jefferson, Thomas, 3, 32
Jewett, Milo P., 27, 30–33, 37–38, 40, 90
Jewett, Sophie, 89
Jewish students:
  Barnard, 256, 258–59
  quotas for, 259
  Sarah Lawrence, 321
Johns Hopkins University, 105, 115, 116

Jordan, Mary Augusta, 193–94, *illus.* 195, 217
Judson Institute, Marion, Ala., 27, 30

Karr, C. Powell, 231
Kaufmann, Gordon, 343, 346
Keiser, Edward, 116
Keeley, Amy, 331
Kilpatrick, William Heard, 330, 331
Kimball, Mrs. David P., 244, 246
King, Bessie, 112, 113
King, Francis T., 105–07
Klauder, Charles Z., 268, 317
Koch (Carl) & Associates, 293 *n.* 29
Kuebler, Dorothy A., 348

Lady Principal:
  Barnard, 135
  Smith, 78
  Vassar, 38–39, 59
La Farge, C. Grant, 206
Lamb & Rich, architects, 251
landscape design:
  Barnard, 141, 253
  Bryn Mawr, 122, 126, 374 *n.* 24
  Mount Holyoke, 228, 230–31
  rituals and, 174, 178
  Sarah Lawrence, 328
  Smith, 309, 314
  Wellesley, 210–13, 262–64, 316–17
    faculty involvement, 204, 208, 262,
      265–69, 272, 316
Lathrop, Julia, 222, 297
Latin and Greek, *see* classical languages
Lawrence, Dudley, 324
Lawrence, William Van Duzer, 320–24 *passim*
Leach, Abby, 100, 102
Leigh, Robert Devore, 331–32, 334, 338
lesbianism:
  of faculty women, suggested, 188, 190
  openness of (post–World War II), 352
  of students, 282
  see also female friendship
liberal arts curriculum:
  Bryn Mawr, 107
  coeducational institutions, 56, 73
  for men, 28
  Smith, 73
  Vassar, 32, 40–41
  Wellesley, 83, 84

library:
  Mount Holyoke, 44–45 and *illus., illus.* 235,
    236, 303
  Radcliffe, *illus.* 103, 244–45
  Smith, 216–17
    opposed (early), 75
  Vassar, 35, 92, 219, 221
  Wellesley, 51
literary societies:
  Amherst, 22
  and study of literature, 28
  Vassar (Philaletheis), 63, 162
location of colleges:
  Bryn Mawr, 106
  Mount Holyoke, 19–20
  Smith, 70–71
  Vassar, 32–33
  for location of buildings on specific campuses, see
    buildings: site selection *under each college*
Longfellow, A. W., 246
Longfellow, Alden & Harlow, architects, 238
Lord, Frances E., 54
Lord and Hewlitt, architects, 217
Lossing, Benson J., 90, 369 *n.* 25
Low, Seth, 136, 137, 249
Lowell, A. Lawrence, 339
Lyman, Hannah, 38–39, 59, 61, 63, 66
Lynd, Helen, 320
Lyon, Mary, 4, 9
  death of (1849), 25
  early life of, 12–13
  establishes Mount Holyoke Seminary,
    18–20
  fund-raising of, 19
  and Grant, 13–14, 17, 58
  ideas on transforming women's lives, 4, 17,
    25, 58
  inattention to fashion, 20
  influence and importance of, 11–12, 27
  private quarters of, 22
  religious experience and beliefs of, 13, 15
  seminary system developed by, 14–17

MacCracken, Henry Noble:
  and Sarah Lawrence, 320–25
  at Vassar, *illus.* 220, 221, 296
    Euthenics program, 297, 298, 319
    views on femininity publicized, 322

Macleod, Annie, 298
Magoon, Elias L., 35
male attire (for college women), 162, 163,
    illus. 165
male faculty:
  Bryn Mawr, 115, 116
  Radcliffe, 95
  residences:
    Amherst, 24
    Mount Holyoke, 304
    Vassar, 36, 40, 91–92, 180
    vs. women faculty's residences, 180
  Scripps, 341–42
  Smith, 71–72
  Vassar, 4, 33, 37, 40
  see also faculty: distinction and relation
    between male and female
male students:
  college life of, 24, 71
  and female students (post–World War I),
    282–85
    chaperonage for, 288–89
    for dances, 288
    separation of genders, 292
  protecting female students from, 71, 75
Marks, Jeannette, 193, 279
  and Woolley, 191, 233, 304
marriage rates of alumnae, 280, 281, 282
  Bryn Mawr, 280
  Mount Holyoke, 27
masculinity, fears of, 58, 167, 169, 193
  male attire regulated, 163
  at Vassar, 29, 59, 60
  see also femininity, protection of
May Day festival:
  Bryn Mawr, 122, *illus.* 123, 353
  Wellesley, *illus.* 177
McCullough, Edith, 329, 330, 331
McKim, Charles Follen, 141
McKim, Mead & White, architects, 141, 244,
    260, 314
Mead, Elizabeth Storrs, 226, 230, 233
men, as benefactors:
  Barnard, 135, 137, 138, 252
  Bryn Mawr, 127
  Mount Holyoke, 19, 227, 228, 230
  Rockefeller, John D., 93, 127, 138, 218, 228,
    230

Smith, 214, 217

Vassar, 90, 92, 93, 218–19

Wellesley, 84, 87, 205

men, as faculty, *see* male faculty

men, as trustees, *see* trustees

men's colleges:

"academical village" pattern, 3, 32

buildings of, contrasted to women's, 20, 22, 24, 121, 311, 314

"Old Main" tradition of, 76

Sarah Lawrence rejects as model, 325

see also Amherst College; Harvard College

Meyer, Annie Nathan, 134–35, 136, 259, 260, 380 *n.* 38

Mills, Herbert, 222, 297

Minturn, Eliza Theodora, 98, 239

missionaries, and Mount Holyoke:

alumnae as, 27

teachers as, 19, 225

Mitchell, Maria, 38, 39, 40, 54, 60–61 and *illus.*, 65–66, 116, 180

monitoring students, *see* supervision of students

Morgan Julia, 343

Morse, Lewis Kennedy, 267

mother-daughter bond, 4, 17, 25, 58

Mount Holyoke Seminary (*later:* College), 18–27, 223–36, 302–06

alumnae:

as critical of Mount Holyoke, 224–25

at disadvantage (Seminary graduates) professionally and socially, 224

marriage and career statistics, 27

raise funds for buildings, 228, 236

and Seminary Hall fire (1896), 228

on Woolley's successor as president, 304

becomes a college, 225–26

buildings, 234, 236

cottages, 228; Brigham Hall, *illus.* 230, 231; siting of, 230–31

Dwight Memorial Art Building, 234

Gymnasium, 26, 231–32

library, 44–45 and *illus.*, *illus.* 235, 236; Williston Memorial, 303

Mary Lyon Hall, 228–30 and *illus.*

observatory, 230

recent (1960s–1980s) architectural choices for, 393 *n.* 29

Seminary Hall, 20 and *illus.*, 21–22; additions to, 26 and *illus.*; destroyed by fire (1896), 228; dining room, 21, *illus.* 23; exterior, 20 and *illus.*; inhibits autonomous student life, 24; internal plan, 20–22

site selection, 230–31, 234, 236

Torrey Hall (originally Lakeside), *illus.* 305, 306

Williston Hall, 227

Williston Memorial Library, 303

campus, *illus.* 26, *illus.* 235

lake, 230, 306

landscape planning, 228, 230–31

planning, 234, 236, 302–03, 304, 306

collegiate department, 225–26

erosion of status of, 223–24

established by Lyon, 18–20

faculty:

gender ratio shifting, 304

as missionaries, 19, 225

residences of, 21, 231

selected from graduating class, 225

upgraded, 226, 233–34

fees, 25

financial support for, 19

fire at (1896), 228, 230

influenced by:

Smith, 227, 228, 232

Wellesley, 302, 303

influence of, 3, 4, 27, 30

on Bennington, 328–29

on Smith, 57, 71, 72

on Vassar, 62

on Wellesley, 42, 44, 48, 53, 54–55, 56–57

naming of, 19

changed to College (1893), 226

president, 22, 233, 234

male *vs.* female, 304

see also Gettell, R. G.; Ham, R.; Mead, E. S.; Woolley, M. E.

rooming policy of, 24, 58, 155

site secured, 19–20

students:

admission standards for, 25, 225, 226

characteristics of, sought, 18–19, 24–25

freedoms attained by (20th century), 288–89

Mount Holyoke Seminary (*continued*)
  geographic distribution of, 25, 226–27,
    304
  homogeneity of, 62
  number of, 232
  residences of, 20 and *illus.*, 21–22;
    cottages, 228, 230–31, 232, 233
  rooms of, 21, 231
  smoking by (as 20th century issue), 292
  trustees:
    and gender of president, 304
    and Smith, 227
    and Wellesley, 45
    women as, 45–46
Munro, William Bennett, 339, 340 and *illus.*
music course:
  Smith: School of Music, 213–14
  Vassar, 35
  Wellesley, 84

Neff, Wallace, 343
Neilson, Nellie, 234
Neilson, William Allan, 284, 307, 309
  and Bennington, 329, 330
Newcomer, Mabel, 297
New Jersey College for Women (*later:*
  Douglass College), 297, 334
Newkirk, Eliza J., 187, 266
Newton, George F., 231, 234, 236, 302
Nolen, John, 309
normal school: Wellesley, 83, 84
North, Louise McCoy, 263

Oberlin College, 27
Ohio Wesleyan Female College, 29
Olmsted, Frederick Law, 93, 126
Olmsted, Frederick Law, Jr.:
  and Mount Holyoke, 234
  and Wellesley, 204
    landscape planning (1902 report), 210–11,
      263, 269, 272
    siting of Quadrangle, 212
Olmsted, John C., 126, 132
organizations:
  time devoted to, 156
  see also Philaletheis; societies; sororities
Orr, Douglas, 306

Packard, Theophilus, 19

Palmer, Alice Freeman, 85–86 and *illus.*, 87,
  182, 203, 204–05, 209
  Memorial to, *illus.* 204
Palmer, George Herbert, 203–04, 205, 262,
  384 *n.* 4
Park, Edwards A., 70, 71
Park, Marion, 292
Peabody & Stearns, architects, 76, 78, 214,
  227, 383 *n.* 35
Pearsons, D. K., 228
Pendleton, Ellen Fitz, 207, 262, 266
Philaletheis (Vassar literary society), 63, 162
philanthropy, *see* men, as benefactors; women,
  as benefactors
Phillips, Wendell, 59, 60
physical training, *see* athletics, competitive;
  exercise and physical training
playing fields, *see* athletic fields
Plimpton, George A., 135, 136, 390 *n.* 30
"point system" (Smith), 156–57
Pomona College, 339
Porter, Andrew W., 19
Pratt, Charles M., 218–19, *illus.* 220, 221, 222
  and MacCracken, 296
Pratt, Mary Seymour Morris, 218, 221
Pratt, Thomas, 77
preparatory department:
  rejected for Bryn Mawr, 107
  Vassar, 41, 62, 78
  Wellesley, 83, 86
preparatory schools, 86
president:
  faculty and, 179
  male *vs.* female, 48, 53, 71–72, 208, 304,
    331
  residence of:
    Amherst, 22, 24
    Mount Holyoke, 22, 233, 234
    Smith, 76, 310
    Vassar, 35, 91, 92
    Wellesley, 48, 52–53, 89
  role of, 38, 179
  term limited (Bennington), 332
  and trustees, 179
  see also trustees *under specific colleges*
privacy:
  for faculty, 182, 193, 194
  for students:
    Bryn Mawr, 110, 119

Mount Holyoke, 20
Vassar, 39
professional women:
  careers of (19th century), 188–90
  Lawrence's distaste for, 320–21
  Seelye's distaste for, 73
protection of female students:
  from college men, 75
  of their femininity, *see* femininity,
    protection of
  rejected by Bryn Mawr, 120–21
Putnam, Bertha Haven, 234
Putnam, Emily James Smith, 137, 239, 248–50
Putnam, Karl S., 310
Putnam & Cox, architects, 234

Quakers:
  Bryn Mawr faculty and, 184
  Bryn Mawr students as, 127
  Thomas and, 113, 121
  and women's education, 105–06
quota system for admissions, 259

racial policy, 155
racism, 279–80
Radcliffe College, 95–104, 237–47
  alumnae:
    and dormitories, 245
    and Harvard degree, 239
  as Annex (1879–93), 95–104, 237–39
  buildings:
    Agassiz House, 242, *illus.* 243, 244
    Barnard Hall, 247
    Bertram Hall, 245, 246 and *illus.*
    Briggs Hall, 247
    Carret House, Appian Way, *illus.* 101, 102
    Fay House, *illus.* 103, 104; redesign of
      (1890), 238, 244
    gymnasium, 242
    library, 244–45
    opposition to, 95, 102, 241
    Quadrangle, 244
    Whitman Hall, 247
  campus, 242, 244–47
    athletic grounds, 247
    Homestead, 246
    Radcliffe Yard, 245
    see also Radcliffe: buildings
  charter granted (1894), 239

faculty, 95, 102, 238
fees, 102
founding of, 95–104
fund-raising for, 102, 242, 245
and Harvard, 5–6, 95–104, 238–40
influenced by Bryn Mawr, 104, 237, 241–42
influence on:
  Barnard, 134
  Bryn Mawr, 115
intentions of founders, 5–6, 95–96
  circular describing, *illus.* 99, 100, 102
named College (1893), 239
president, *see* Agassiz, E. C.; Briggs, Le
  B. R.
students:
  geographic distribution of, 104
  number or, 238
  residences for, 104, 242, 245–47
  type sought, 102, 104
Ramée, Joseph Jacques, 32
Raymond, John H., 38–41 *passim*, 59, 60, 62,
  66
religious affiliation of students, 148, 155
  Barnard, 256, 258
  Bryn Mawr, 127
religious life:
  chapel, *see* chapel (services)
  Christian Association, 286
    Barnard, 258
    Wellesley, 86
  devotions, private, 15, 21, 54, 55, 201
  worship (regular): Smith, 77
Renwick, James, Jr., 31–34 *passim*
residences:
  for faculty, *see* male faculty: residences;
    women faculty: residences
  for president, *see* president: residence of
  for students, *see* student residences
residential policy, *see* rooming policy
restorations of buildings, *see* adaptations of
  buildings
Rhoads, James E., 106, 111, 113, 116, 117
Rich, Charles A., 139, 142, 217; *see also* Lamb
  & Rich, architects
Richards, Ellen Swallow, 60, 64–65, 93
  on Euthenics, 296
Rickert, Edith, 150, 166, 191
rituals, 172, *illus.* 173, 174, 175 and *illus.*, *illus.*
  176–77, 178

rituals (*continued*)
   Barnard: Greek themes, 252, *illus.* 253
   Bryn Mawr, 175–76
      Lantern Night, 172, 174–75
      May Day, 122, *illus.* 123, 353
   decline of (early 20th century), 287
   male attire worn for, 162–63
   Mount Holyoke, *illus.* 173
   Smith: Ivy Day, *illus.* 174, 175 and *illus.*
   step-singing, 172, 216, 287
   Vassar, 172
      Daisy Chain, *illus.* 176
   Wellesley, 174
      Flower Sunday, 172
      May Day, *illus.* 177
      Tree Day, *illus.* 86, 172, 175, *illus.* 176–77
Robinson, James Harvey, 137
Rockefeller, John D., as benefactor to:
   Barnard, 138
   Bryn Mawr, 127
   Mount Holyoke, 228, 230
   Vassar, 93, 218
Rogers, Julia, 113
room-and-board fees, *see* fees, for room and
      board
rooming houses, *see* student residences: off
      campus
rooming policy, 152
   Bryn Mawr, 155
   Mount Holyoke, 24, 58, 155
   Smith, 153–55
   Vassar, 66, 152, 155
   Wellesley, 152, 155, 156
roommates assigned/selected, *see* rooming
      policy
rooms, students':
   Bryn Mawr, 126–27, *illus.* 170
   college life in, 169
   Mount Holyoke, 21, 231
   Scripps, 348
   single:
      Bryn Mawr, 126–27
      Mount Holyoke, 231
      Radcliffe, 246
      Scripps, 348
      Smith, 77, 314
      Vassar, 93
      Wellesley, 83
   Smith, 77, 311, 314

Vassar, 39, 93
Wellesley, 52, 83, 318
Rotch, Arthur, 84
Routt, Mary, 340
Ruskin, John, 121

sabbatical leave for faculty, 181, 234
Salmon, Lucy:
   conflict with Taylor, 186–87, 194, 222
   home of her own, 193
   Is This Vassar College?, 353–54
   kitchen of, Poughkeepsie, *illus.* 192
   leadership of faculty (1914), 296
   study, Main building, Vassar, *illus.* 192
   and Underhill, 191, 193
   on Vassar faculty, 180, 184, 186
   and Vassar library collection, 196
Sarah Lawrence College, 319–28
   becomes 4-year college (1930s), 328
   buildings, 324–25
      Dudley Lawrence, *illus.* 323
      Westlands, *illus.* 323, 324, 328
   campus planning, 328
   faculty, 325, 328
   founder's intentions, 325
   influenced by:
      Smith, 324, 328
      Vassar, 322
   president, *see* Coats, M.; Warren, C.
   students (type sought), 321
   tutorial and seminar systems, 325, 328
schedule, imposed:
   inhibits student visiting and bonding, 24,
      58–59
   Mount Holyoke, 24, 26, 58–59, 227
   rejected by Bryn Mawr, 119
   in seminary system, 16
   Smith, 80
   Vassar, 63
   Wellesley, 54–55
Schiff, Jacob, 252, 259
Schuyler, Montgomery, 208
Schweinfurth, J. A., 212
science apparatus, courses, and buildings:
   Barnard, 138
   Smith, 214, 227
   Vassar, 35
   Wellesley, 353
Scott, Charles Angus, 116

Scripps, Ellen Browning, 338–41
Scripps College, 319–20, 339–50
    buildings: Toll House, *illus.* 344–45, 346,
        illus. 347
    campus planning, 343, 346 and *illus.*, 348
    curriculum, 341, 343
    faculty, 341, 342
    Humanities program, 343
    president, 341
    trustees, 340 and *illus.*, 341
Scudder, Horace, 204, 206, 209
Scudder, Vida, 188, 194
    Dewey House room of (Smith), *illus.* 189
    on students of 1920s, 293
Scull, David, Jr., 106, 111
Seelye, Julius, 70
Seelye, L. Clark:
    and Bryn Mawr's planning, 107, 110
    at dedication of Wellesley's Simpson
        Cottage, 88
    retirement of (1910), 308
    as Smith president, 72–73, 75, 78, 80, 213,
        217
self-governance, 149, 185
    Bennington, 338
    Bryn Mawr, 119–20, 130
    and new freedoms (20th century), 288–89
    Sarah Lawrence, 325, *illus.* 327, 328
    Wellesley, *illus.* 164
self-reporting system, 15, 24, 26, 55, 223, 225,
    227
seminary, 11
    claim of college status, 56
    vs. college, 28
    "daughters" to Mount Holyoke, 27, 224
    matriculation at (1870s), 56
    Radcliffe intends to differ from, 95–96
    Vassar attempts to differ from, 33
seminary system, 4
    and asylum planning, 14
    components of, *see* confessional, public;
        devotions, private; domestic work,
        done by students; schedule, imposed;
        self-reporting system; single building;
        supervision of students; worship,
        communal
    devised and refined by Grant and Lyon,
        13–14, 15–17
    psychic sameness of students assumed, 16

    at Vassar, 37, 40
    Wellesley's repudiation of (1899), 205
    see also Mount Holyoke Seminary
separate culture, women's:
    19th century, 16
    Thomas and, 118–19
separate education for women, 57–58, 73–74,
    280
    and founding of:
        Bennington, 334
        Radcliffe, 95–96, 97
        Smith, 71, 73, 75
    and masculine attributes of students, 163
    post–World War II rejection of, 351
    social aspects of, 283–84
servants, domestic work done by, 18, 119
Seven College Conference, 248, 260–61
sexuality:
    erotic attachments between students, 65, 66,
        166–67, 191, 193, 282
    fears of masculinity and "unsexing," 29,
        58–59, 60, 163, 167, 169, 193
    as issue in planning women's colleges, 68,
        69, 74–75, 315–16, 322, 324, 334
    post–World War I, 282–83
    see also "crush"; femininity, protection of;
        heterosexuality; "smash"
Shepley, Rutan & Coolidge, architects, 219,
    264
Shirk, Mary Kimberly, 340
Shorey, Paul, 116
Shurtleff, Arthur A., 244, 264, 302–03
Simpson, M. H., 88
single building:
    falls from favor (1860s) for institutions, 74
    inhibits autonomous student life (Mount
        Holyoke), 24
    in seminary system, 15
    Wellesley, 48
single rooms for students:
    Bryn Mawr, 126–27
    Mount Holyoke, 231
    Radcliffe, 246
    Scripps, 348
    Smith, 77, 314
    Vassar, 93
    Wellesley, 83
single-sex education *vs.* coeducation, *see*
    separate education for women

"smash," 65–68
Smith, Henry Welles, *see* Durant, Henry
    Fowle
Smith, Alys, 122
Smith, De Witt, 154
Smith, Emily James, *see* Putnam, Emily James
    Smith
Smith, Kennedy, 374 *n*. 24
Smith, Logan Pearsall, 122
Smith, Mary, 122
Smith, Sophia, 69–70
Smith College, 69–81, 213–17
    assessment of:
        by Higginson (1876), 96
        by Thomas (1883), 114
    buildings:
        College Hall, 76 and *illus.*, 77; as model
            for Mount Holyoke's Mary Lyon Hall,
            228–29
        Dewey House, 77
        endowment of, limited by Sophia Smith,
            78
        Greene Hall, 217
        gymnasium, *illus.* 160–61, 169, 216, 353
        Hatfield House, 78, *illus.* 79
        Hillyer Art Gallery, 214, 382 *n*. 34
        library, 217
        Lily Hall of Science, 214
        Music Hall (*later*: Pierce Hall), 214, 383
            n. 35
        original, 75–78, *illus.* 76, *illus.* 79
        President's House, 310
        Quadrangles, 310–11, *illus.* 312–13,
            314–15; Wilder, *illus.* 313, 314
        Seelye Hall, 214
        student residences, 76, 77–78, 307,
            308–16; off campus, 153–55, 307, 308,
            310; *see also* Smith College: cottage
            system
    campus:
        aerial view, *illus.* 312–13
        Paradise Pond, 310, *illus.* 311
        planning, 309, 314
        and town, 228
    college life at, 213, 216
    cottage system at, 71, 75, 78, *illus.* 79, 80,
        153, 214, 216
        contrasted to dormitories, 315
        impact of, 227–28

    removal recommended by Nolen, 309
    criticism of, 74–75
    dramatics at, 162
    faculty, 71–72
        residences of, 180
        women as, 72, 213
    family life simulated at, 5, 75, 80
    fees, 114, 152
    founding and planning of, 69–72
    Freshman Frolic (dance), 162
    influenced by:
        Amherst, 70, 71, 72–73
        Mount Holyoke, 57, 71, 72
        Vassar, 57, 75, 78
    influence on:
        Bennington, 329–30
        Bryn Mawr, 6, 105, 107, 114
        Mount Holyoke, 227, 228, 232
        Sarah Lawrence, 324, 328
        Vassar, 5, 94
        Wellesley, 5, 90
    Ivy Day, *illus.* 174, 175 and *illus.*
    "point system" of, 156–57
    president:
        residence of, 76, 310
        see also Burton, M. L.; Neilson, W. A.;
            Seelye, L. C.
    racial policy of, 155
    religious life, 77, 217
    School of Art, 213–14, 382 *n*. 34
    School of Music, 213–14, 383 *n*. 35
    site selected, 70–71
    students:
        admission standards for, 78, 213, 308
        femininity of, protected, 68, 69, 75, 80,
            315
        freedoms attained by (20th century), 289
        involvement in life of Northampton, 71,
            75, 80, 153, 315
        number of (1910), 213
        participation of, in extracurricular
            activites, 156–57
        religious affiliations of, 148
        residences of, 76, 77–78, 307, 308–16
        social structure of, 153–55
    trustees, 70, 71, 227, 315
smoking:
    faculty privacy allows, 194
    Thomas against, 184

as 20th century issue, 289, 292
societies:
  for debating, 152
    disbanded, 287
  as disguised sororities, 152, 227
  houses for:
    Mount Holyoke, 227
    Wellesley, 152–53, 209–10
  literary, 22, 28, 63, 162
  Smith, 155
Society of Friends, *see* Quakers
sororities, 152, 154
  Barnard, 248, 256
  Mount Holyoke, 227
South Hadley, Mass., 19, 303
sports, *see* athletic fields; athletics,
    competitive; exercise and physical
    training; gymnasium
standards for admission, *see* admission
    standards and requirements
step-singing, 172, 216, 287
Stewardson, John, 118
Stone, Valeria G., 83
Strong, Augustus H., 218
Strong, Bessie Rockefeller, 93
Stubbins, Hugh, 393 *n.* 29
student fees, *see* fees (including tuition); fees,
    for room and board
student government, *see* self-governance
student organizations, *see* organizations;
    societies; sororities
student residences:
  Barnard, 141, 248, 251, 260
  Bennington, *illus.* 333, 334
  Bryn Mawr, 110–11, 122, 124 and *illus.*,
    illus. 125, 126 and *illus.*, 127
  cottages, *see* cottage system
  invitation houses (Smith), 154
  Mount Holyoke, 20 and *illus.*, 21–22,
    232–33, 306
  off campus:
    Barnard, 260
    Mount Holyoke, 233
    (1920s–1930s), 307–18
    Radcliffe, 245
    Smith, 153–55, 307, 308, 310
  Radcliffe, 242, 245–47
  rejected in early years, 104
Sarah Lawrence, *illus.* 323, 324, 325

Scripps, *illus.* 344–45, 346, *illus.* 347, 348
Smith, 76, 77–78, 307, 308–16; *see also*
    cottage system
Vassar, 92–94, 300, 301 and *illus.*
    coeducational, 352–53
Wellesley, 83–84, 209, 210–11, 307, 314–16
  Quadrangle, 87–90
  Tower Court, 264–65
see also rooms, students'
students:
  autonomy of, *see* autonomy of students
  dominance and subordination among, 167
  "freedoms" struggled for (early 20th
    century), 287–92
  political activity of, 255, 286–87; *see also*
    self-governance
  standards of success by, 149, 150, 157, 159
  types, 150–52, 156
  see also male students
students, male, *see* male students
students' building, 170, 378 *n.* 70
  Barnard, 252
  Radcliffe, 242, *illus.* 243, 244, 378 *n.* 70
  Smith, *illus.* 171, 216, 378 *n.* 70
students' rooms, *see* rooms, students'
student-teacher relationship, *see* teacher-
    student relationship
Sturgis, Russell, 121
success, standards of (for students), 149, 150,
    157, 159
suffrage, woman's
  as issue:
    at Barnard, 255
    for students (20th century), 286
    for women faculty, 193–94
  Meyer and, 380 *n.* 38
  parade (Radcliffe), *illus.* 168
  Taylor and, 193, 194, 222
supervision of students:
  Bryn Mawr, 110, 119, 181, 185
  as imposition on faculty, 182
  male faculty excused from, 40, 180
  in men's colleges (minimal), 22, 24
  Mount Holyoke, 181,
  in seminary system, 15
  Smith: in cottages, 78, 181, 185
  Vassar:
    student resistance to, 63–64
    thwarted by private suites, 39

supervision of students (*continued*)
  by women faculty only, 40
  Wellesley, 53, 55
  see also Lady Principal; wardens
Swallow, Ellen, *see* Richards, Ellen Swallow
Swarthmore College, 105
"swell" (student type), 150–51

Talbot, Marion, 137, 281, 384 *n.* 4
Taylor, James Monroe, 91–93, 218, *illus.* 220,
    222
  conflict with Salmon, 186–87, 194
  retirement of, 295
  and suffrage issue, 193, 194, 222
Taylor, Joseph Wright, 105–07, 110, 111
teacher education:
  by and for academies, 10
  by seminaries, 11, 19, 27
  Wellesley, 83
teacher-student relationship:
  Bennington, 338
  as "dons" and independent students (Sarah
    Lawrence), 325, 328
  as intimate friendship, 17, 25, 58–59, 167,
    179, 191
  mother-daughter bond as model, 4, 17, 25,
    58
  as separate and more distant, 145, 167, 179,
    185, 196, 293
    Vassar, 64
  supervision and oversight, *see* supervision of
    students
Tefft, Thomas A., 31
Thomas, James Carey, 105, 106
Thomas, M. Carey, 6, 111–33, *illus.* 131
  anti-Semitism of, suggested, 184
  applies for Bryn Mawr presidency, 111–12,
    113
  assessment of women's colleges by (1883),
    113–15
  as dean of Bryn Mawr (1883–93), 113, 116
  early life of, 112–13
  education of, 105, 112–13
  and faculty, 115, 130, 180
  friends and associates of, 112, 113
  as fund-raiser, 127, 375 *n.* 32
  and Garrett, 112, 113, 114, 117, 122, 130,
    131 and *illus.*, 193

influence on Bryn Mawr, 111, 117
  planning of campus, 118, 373 *n.* 5
  love of pageantry and drama, 117, 121–22
  love of power, 120, 130, 133
  as president of Bryn Mawr, 117–33
  religious views of, 113, 121
  and trustees, 113, 116, 117–18, 127, 129–30
Thompson, Frederick Ferris, 92
Thompson, Mary Thaw, 219
Thompson, Mildred, 320
Tilden, George Thomas, 84
Tree Day, Wellesley, *illus.* 86, 172, *illus.*
    176–77
Trig ceremony, Vassar, *illus.* 67
trustees, *see* women, as trustees; *and* trustees
    under specific colleges
Tudor architectural style:
  Mount Holyoke library (Gothic), 236
  Smith: Students' Building, 216
  Wellesley: Simpson Cottage, 87–88
tuition fees, *see* fees (including tuition)
Tyler, William S., 70, 72

Underhill, Adelaide, 191
Union College, Schenectady, N.Y., 28, 32
University of Michigan, 56, 85
University of Virginia, 3, 32

Van Brunt & Howe, architects, 88
Van Ingen, Henry, 61, 221
Vassar, Guy, 90
Vassar, Matthew, 4, 29–38 *passim*
  decision to found women's college, 29–31
  and governance of college, 33–34
Vassar, Matthew, Jr., 90
Vassar College, 28–41, 90–94, 218–22,
    295–302
  alumnae:
    critical of college, 292, 300
    on home economics, 29
    as trustees, 46, 222, 300
  assessment of:
    by Higginson (1876), 96
    by Thomas (1883), 114–15
  buildings, 90–94, 219, *illus.* 220, 221,
    299–301 and *illus.*
    Blodgett Hall of Euthenics, 298, *illus.*
      299, 300–01
    Calisthenium, 36 and *illus.*

chapel, 35, 219, *illus.* 220
Cushing Hall, 300, 301 and *illus.*
Davison House, 94
faculty houses, 36, 40, 91–92, 180, 187
Kenyon Hall of Physical Education, 300
Lathrop, 94
library, 92, 219, 221; Memorial Hall,
    383–84 *n.* 49
Main, 34 and *illus.*, 35–36, 41, 49, 91–92;
    reconstruction of, 353
observatory, 35
Quadrangle, 94
Raymond House, 94
Rockefeller Hall, 93
site selection, 92, 93
Strong, 94, 221
Taylor Hall, *illus.* 220, 221–22
Williams and Kendrick faculty
    apartments, 187
compared to men's college, 3
criticism of, 37, 57
Euthenics program and buildings, 295–302
faculty, 4, 33, 37, 39–40
    and Euthenics program, 297, 298
    political activism of, 222
    residences, 36, 40, 91–92, 180;
        apartments, 187
    women as, 37–38, 62, 90, 180
    see also Mithell, M.; Salmon, L.
fear of masculinity and mannishness at, 29,
    59, 60
financial difficulties of, 90–91
health and exercise concerns, 32–33, 36
influenced by:
    Mount Holyoke, 62
    seminary system, 33, 39, 40
    Smith, 5, 94
influence on:
    Sarah Lawrence, 322
    Smith, 57, 75, 78
    Wellesley, 5, 46, 48, 56–57, 68
literary society (Philaletheis), 63, 162
location selected, 32–33
preparatory department, 41, 62, 78
president:
    residence of, 35, 91, 92
    see also Caldwell, S. L.; MacCracken,
      H. N.; Raymond, J. H.; Taylor, J. M.
rituals, 172, *illus.* 176

rooming policy, 66, 152, 155
students:
    admission standards for, 41
    college life of, 63–68
    dances, 162
    diversity of, 62
    dramatic productions, 162, *illus.* 165
    enrollment, level of, 91
    residences, 92–94, 300, 301 and *illus.*;
      coeducational, 352–53; internal
      planning of, 93
    rooms of, 39, 93
    "smashing," 65–68
trustees:
    alumnae as, 46, 222, 300
    and Baptist sources of funds, 218
    consider Vassar their "playground,"
      221–22
    influence of Matthew Vassar's nephews
      on, 90
    and MacCracken, 296
    Rockefeller as, 93
    as Sarah Lawrence trustees, 322
Vassar's (Matthew) decision to found, 29–31
Wimpfheimer Nursery School, 300
Vaux, Calvert, 122

wardens, 119, 185
Ware, William R., 368 *n.* 8
Ware & Van Brunt, architects, 83–84
Warren, Constance, 325
Washburn, Edward, 116
Washburn, Margaret, 297
wealthy students, 147
    Barnard, 256, 258
    Bryn Mawr, 127, 152
    Mount Holyoke, 226
    Radcliffe, 245
Weed, Ella, 135–36, 259
Weld, Angela Grimké, 31
Wellesley College, 42–55, 203–13, 262–75
    alumnae:
      and Houghton Memorial Chapel, 207
      and landscape planning, 265–69 *passim*,
        316
      marriage rate of, 280
      and Severance Hall, 318
    assessment of:

Wellesley College (*continued*)
    by Higginson (1876), 96
    by Thomas (1883), 115
    benefactors of, 83, 84, 87, 205, 263, 390
      n. 30
    buildings, 82–90, 209
      Claflin Hall, 316–17
      College Hall, 46, *illus.* 47, 48, 49–53, 82;
        Browning Room, 51, *illus.* 52; Centre,
        49–50 and *illus,* 53, 262; destroyed by
        fire (1914), 262; plan of first story,
        illus. 49
      cottage system, 85, 87–90, 210, 211
      Eliot House, 88 and *illus.*; life in, 152, 156
      Farnsworth, 84, 209, 269
      Founders Hall, 272
      Freeman, 88
      Hazard Quadrangle, 204, *illus.* 211,
        212–13
      Horton Quadrangle, 187
      Houghton Memorial Chapel, 204,
        205–08, *illus.* 207
      Music Hall, 83, 84, 209; reconstruction,
        353
      Norumbega, 88, *illus.* 89, 89–90
      Pendleton Hall, 272
      Science Center, 353
      Severance Hall, 316, 317 and *illus.,* 318
      Simpson Cottage, 88
      siting of, 204, 206–07, 262–72
      society houses, 152–53, 209
      Stone Hall, 84, 209
      Tower Court, 264–65, 316
      Waban, 88
      Wilder, 209, 210–11, 269
    campus, 262–75
      aerial view, *illus.* 211, *illus.* 270–71
      College Hill, 264, 265, 316
      expansion of, 209
      faculty attitudes toward and influence on,
        204, 208, 262, 265–69, 272, 316
      Great Meadow, 265
      Lake Waban, 48
      Norumbega Hill, 210, 263, 266, 269
      planning of, 46, 48, 210–13, 262–72,
        316–17
    college life, 68, 89
    College of Art, 84

    College of Music, 84
    faculty, 48, 53–54, 181
      conflict with administration, 82, 194, 196,
        204, 207
      friendships among, 191
      and landscape of campus, 204, 208, 262,
        265–69, 272, 316
      power and influence of, 197, 262, 293
      religious test for, 184
      residences of, 48, 53, 55; Horton Quad-
        rangle; private houses and households,
        188
      search for professional respect, 181–82
    fees, 85, 86, 152
    fire (1914), 84, 213, 262, 268
    founder's intentions for, 4–5, 54
    influenced by:
      evangelical Christianity, 43–44, 54
      Mount Holyoke, 42, 44, 48, 53, 54–55,
        56–57
      Smith, 5, 90
      Vassar, 5, 46, 48, 56–57, 68
    influence on:
      Bryn Mawr, 114, 115
      Mount Holyoke, 302, 303
    planning of, 45–46, 48
    preparatory department, 83, 86
    president, 48, 53, 208–09
      residence of, 48, 51–53, 89
      see also Freeman, A.; Hazard, C.;
        Howard, A.; Irvine, J.; Pendleton, E. F.
    racial policy, 155
    religious life, 86, 205
    rituals, 174
      Flower Sunday, 172
      May Day, *illus.* 177
      Tree Day, *illus.* 86, 172, *illus.* 176–77
    rooming policy, 152, 155, 156
    as Seminary (1870–73), 45
    societies and society houses, 152–53, 209
    students:
      admission standards for, 85
      characteristics of, sought, 53
      college life of, 68, 89
      freedoms attained by (20th century), 288
      residences of, 83–84, 209, 210–11, 307,
        314–16; Quadrangle, 87–90
      self-governance of, *illus.* 164

smoking by, 289, 292
social structure of, 152, 156
Teachers Collegiate Course, 83, 84
trustees, 45–46, 204–05
and faculty, 184, 194, 204, 207, 267–69
Freeman a member, as president, 85,
204–05
and Houghton Memorial Chapel, 206–08
ministers as, 54
and Mount Holyoke board, 45
women as, 45, 85, 204–05, 263
Wheeler, Emily, 182
Whitall, James, 106
White, Orra, 13
Willard, Emma, 11
Williston, A. Lyman, 227, 230, 236
Wilson, Woodrow, 116
Wimpfheimer Nursery School, Vassar, 300
women, as benefactors:
Barnard, 135, 137–39, 251
Bennington, 334
Bryn Mawr, 117, 130, 131
Mount Holyoke, 44
Radcliffe, 242, 244, 246
Scripps, 339–40
Vassar, 219, 297
Wellesley, 83, 87, 205, 263, 390 *n.* 30
women faculty
and academic freedom, 193–94
life of, 179–97
households of, 187–88
intimate friendships, 188, 190–91, 193
religious affiliations of, 184
and presidents, 179
privacy for, 182, 193, 194
public attitudes toward, 181–82
qualifications and status of, 62
residences of:
Bryn Mawr, 180, 185, 186 and *illus.*
Mount Holyoke: in cottages, 231; private,
off campus, 233; in Seminary Building,
21
private homes, 187–88
in separate buildings built by college,
185–87, *illus.* 186
Vassar, 40, 187
Wellesley, 48, 53, 55; Horton Quadrangle,
187

restrictions and controls on, 180
Bryn Mawr (minimized), 119
Vassar, 40
see also supervision of students
salaries of, 180, 185
college housing as supplement to, 187
Mount Holyoke, 233, 234
Smith, 308
struggle for influence and control, 179, 181,
193–94
and students, *see* teacher-student
relationship
see also faculty; *and* faculty *under specific
colleges*
women, in the professions, 73, 188–90,
320–21
women reformers, 282, 293
women's colleges:
advantages over coeducational institutions,
73–74; *see also* separate education for
women
Barnard as, 251, 253, 259, 260
contact among, 56–57, 155; *see also* Seven
College Conference
developments since World War II, 351–53
Higginson's assessment of (1876), 96
matriculation at (1870s), 56
publicity about (20th century), 279
Radcliffe, 239–47
aversion to, 95, 98, 104, 237, 239–40
contrasted to, 240–41
social structure of, 150–52
Thomas's assessment of (1883), 113–15
Wheeler's criticism of (1889), 182
women's education, *see* education, women's
women's health, concern for, 25–26, 33, 281
women's intimate friendship, *see* female
friendship
women's separate culture, *see* separate culture,
women's
women's sexuality, *see* sexuality
women, as trustees, 45–46
alumnae as, 46, 222, 263, 300
Barnard, 259
Bennington, 331
Scripps, 340
Vassar, 46, 222, 300
Wellesley, 45, 85, 204–05, 263

Woolley, Mary Emma, 223, 232–36
  bitter finale of career, 304
  impact of long tenure of, 294, 303–04
  and Marks, 191, 233, 304
  on smoking, 292
worship, communal:
  in seminary system, 15
  see also chapel (services)
Wylie, Laura, 341

Yale University, 121
York & Sawyer, architects, 298